How To
Make A Million At
The Track

How To Make A Million At The Track

Paul Ader

 Contemporary Books, Inc.
Chicago

Published by Contemporary Books, Inc.
180 North Michigan Avenue, Chicago, Illinois 60601
Manufactured in the United States of America
Library of Congress Catalog Card Number: 77-91196
International Standard Book Number: 0-8092-8093-0 (cloth)
                                                 0-8092-7531-7 (paper)

Published simultaneously in Canada by
Beaverbooks
953 Dillingham Road
Pickering, Ontario L1W 1Z7
Canada

For Cicely
Who gambled only once in her life—
when she married me

Contents

Introduction

My name is Sam Hirsch, which means nothing to you, I'm sure, unless you happen to live in my neighborhood, Miami Shores, Florida, a location I selected carefully because it lies midway between Hialeah and Gulfstream Park. If you read the entire book, you'll know me quite well, which makes me both happy and proud. After all, it's not every man who can say that he's been made the subject of a book.

I've been many things during my short lifetime, which began in 1919, the year of the famous "fix," when Arnold Rothstein (the gambler) is supposed to have bought a number of the Chicago White Sox players, enough of them to throw the World Series. Arnold also made quite a killing at the races, but not by gambling. And while we're on the subject, this book is not about gambling. It is certainly not an inducement to gamble. Its true subject is: How To Make a Nice Profit on Your Investment.

By profession I'm an investment consultant. In Dade County, Sam Hirsch is known as The Man Who Knows Money. I'm not responsible for the title of this book. I have made a million in track investments, but I'm not a millionaire. Church and state have seen to that. Although I'm not a member of the Christian church, one of my strictest precepts has to do with tithing. One-tenth of all I make goes to the church. If you happen to be in my tax bracket, you know how much goes to Uncle Sam. In order to make a million, you must gross at least a couple of million. And this will undoubtedly require some time to accomplish, even with the best system of handicapping and the best methods of money management.

I would recommend that you start with more modest intentions. And before you start along the road, you must first get over one great psychological hurdle: you must rid your mind of the idea of gambling. I do not gamble myself, at least no more than any other businessman. I make investments. For many years I have been making investments for other people, as well as for myself: in the stock market, in real estate, in mutual funds, in the commodities market, even in currency futures. All such investments are subject to risk. I have found that investing in the races is considerably less risky than most other forms of investment. This is so for me because I have done everything possible to eliminate the element of risk. Don't imagine that making investments at the track is a way of getting something for nothing. Not so. The truth is that no one ever gets something for nothing. There's always a price. Yet the gambling instinct is a powerful one. It's almost universal. Americans today spend more than fifty billion dollars each year betting on sporting events. In his *Guide To Sports Betting*,[1] Kelso Sturgeon points out that thoroughbred racing is both a fascinating and a frustrating game and "by far the most complicated betting sport facing mere man." More than twenty million Americans go to thoroughbred races every year, taking with them at least ten million different systems and philosophies for winning. Sturgeon repeats the oldest saying in the game: "You can beat a race, but you can't beat the races!" I believe just the opposite. I'm not your conventional handicapper. I'm a true revolutionary. I bet *every* race! I'm not out there *Picking Winners*. Andrew Beyer has written a horseplayer's guide under that title,

---

1.   Kelso Sturgeon, *Guide to Sports Betting* (New York: Harper & Row, 1974), p. 178.

and Tom Ainslie will give you the low-down on handicapping. The aim of the conventional handicapper is to select the one horse most likely to win a particular race. I don't do that. I'm concerned with the business of *making money* at the track. Of course I know most of the rules of handicapping. I made it a point to learn as much as I possibly could on that score. If I dealt with first and second favorites only (which win half of all races), I'd never get a payoff larger than about $8. Now and then, $9 or so. But you can't build a winning system around payoffs that low. I rarely look twice at the first three or four favorites. I handicap a race, but I start at the *top* of the odds board.

Horseracing is neither a product nor a service in the conventional sense, although it does provide entertainment to millions and a living to thousands. In his best-selling novel *The Money-changers*, Arthur Hailey has a character named Miles Eastin, a bank employee who has "gambled" heavily, involving himself with bookies and loan sharks. He bets on major sporting events but never on the horses. Sturgeon reminds us that betting on *all* sporting events in this country is a fifty-billion-dollar-a-year industry, most of it illegal. Miles Eastin turns to embezzling bank funds to get out from under the loan sharks. When asked why he never bets on horses, he says, "Everybody knows horse-racing is crooked." He implies that most races are fixed and that only a few insiders really benefit. No so. Are all banking employees embezzlers?

When you gamble, more than likely you do so on games of chance, where the outcome has no real relation to logic or reason and the results are completely arbitrary. Where gambling is concerned, there is no sure thing. Perhaps the only certainty about gambling is that the outcome is *always* uncertain. Tom Aislie, undoubtedly America's current top handicapping author, once said that whereas most forms of betting are games of chance, horse racing is not. I agree and I repeat—horse racing is *not* a game of chance. As Ainslie says, you simply cannot treat horse racing as though it were roulette. If you do develop a winning technique, no one is going to change the rules of the house on you.

That's the essence of the thing: if you develop a winning technique, you *must* win. What you hold in your hand is a book which is full of winning techniques. *The problem you face is not the problem of crooked operators or fixed finishes. It is the problem of developing your own winning technique and applying it successfully at the track.* People follow the sport of kings for many reasons, but I have observed that there are generally only two significant classes of race goers: those who come for sheer fun, and those who come expecting to profit. Many people undoubtedly belong to both classes. They enjoy the outing, but at the same time they hope they will make a hit or two and cash a ticket that will bring them a bundle.

Which class do you belong to? Maybe you go to the window and put down $2, or five or ten, in anticipation of walking away later with a fifty or a hundred or two. Maybe you simply go to the races for entertainment. You know in advance that you probably won't come home any richer, but there is always the faint and tantalizing hope that you *will* pick a good one. I was once a member of that very large group of Americans. I knew nothing about a horse's form, his readiness, his speed-rating, or what he had done in his last outing. I even did what I've seen hundreds do: I've bet the favorite to *show*, just to be able to cash a ticket. Today I realize what nonsense that is.

Let me tell you a little story that happened back in April of 1972. At that point I hadn't fully developed my two systems, and yet I had enough knowledge of the track and its operations to be of service to a woman who came to me for advice. She knew only that I was an investment consultant, and when she arrived at my office in a Miami suburb, I naturally thought that she wanted advice on the real estate market or elsewhere. I was somewhat surprised to see her in the first place because her husband was a member of the clergy, and I knew from experience that these people hadn't too much money to invest.

She seemed a little flustered when she sat down in the chair across from me and said: "I don't know how to ask you things like this. I'm not even sure you can help me."

"Let me try," I said. I could see that she was reluctant, but I could also see that she had great confidence in me.

"My husband and I don't indulge ourselves by going to the races very often," she said, "but tomorrow is our wedding anniversary. We were married April 4, just fifteen years ago. We want to do something different to celebrate, and we thought we'd start out in the afternoon at Hialeah, maybe even have dinner there. Anyway, as you can imagine, we don't know anything about horses or about racing, and what I'm really here for is to ask you how to spend our little fund."

I had to smile at her pleasant challenge. She added:

"Of course, we don't have a lot to spend. But we've saved up a hundred dollars, which should cover the afternoon and dinner."

I agreed that a hundred dollars was a nice little fund, and I told her that I would give her the best advice I could on how she and her husband should invest the money. I always use the word *invest* rather than *bet* or *wager*. Let me say again that betting is not my business; investing is. And so I told the clergyman's wife what I tell you now: If you have only a small entertainment fund and you want to make the very most of it, follow my tips.

First of all, stay strictly away from the favorites. Stay away from the selections of the public handicappers. I said:

"At Hialeah tomorrow there will be ten races. But you won't want to spend ten dollars on each race, I'm sure. You'll need something for transportation and something for dinner. Then, of course, there's the Daily Double, and there happen to be four Perfecta races."

"Oh, dear, I don't know," she said. "Doubles? Perfecta races? What are they?"

I explained these to her, and then I said:

"Since tomorrow is April 4, perhaps you should allocate four dollars for the double and four dollars for each of the Perfecta races. That means only two tickets on each, and it comes to twenty dollars. Then, four dollars on each race, and that means another forty dollars, for a total of sixty dollars. That leaves enough for dinner and a big evening, even if you lose it all."

"Which we probably will!"

"Not necessarily. Because you're going to be *with* the odds."

"We are?"

"Yes, *that's the secret of success. Always be with the odds.* The average race has nine or ten horses, so you will invest only in those horses whose odds are 9-1 or 10-1 on the board."

Of course I had to explain about the odds and the board and

the lighted numbers. The more I talked to her the more ridiculous the whole thing seemed, and yet I knew that I was giving her sound advice. You *have* to give sound advice to the wife of a clergyman. I explained to her how to watch the odds on the board before the first race and how to select those two horses that were 9-1 or 10-1, because they were going to wager on *two* horses in each race. But first I dealt with the double. Take the horse with odds nearest to 9-1 or to 10-1 and combine him with one in the second race that was listed in the probable-odds lineup at 10-1. On the program, it would be the morning-line odds. She wouldn't have to buy a *Form*. If there were *no* horses in any race with odds of exactly 9-1 or 10-1, then go up the odds scale to 11-1 and to 12-1, and so on, until you get two wagers. I beg your pardon: two investments.

That took care of the Daily Double. In the first race itself, take the two horses whose odds were 9-1 or 10-1 or the closest odds to those numbers, moving upward. In fact, do the same for every race through the tenth and last race. *By all means, stay for the last race.* Winners at 9-1 or 10-1 frequently come in the last race, or the next-to-the-last race.

"Oh, we'll stay," she said. "And we might even have dinner right at Hialeah. I've heard it's a very pleasant place."

"Very pleasant," I assured her. And then there came the problem of explaining the Perfectas and how to make their straight investments, to win, on such races, and then how to choose the two horses and how to complete the investment.

"For example," I said, "let's assume that the number-two horse has odds of 9-1 and the number-nine horse has odds of 10-1. You ask for two nine, and then you ask for nine and two. Your two tickets will carry those numbers in that sequence."

"Yes, I see," she said. "Well, thank you so much, Mr. Hirsch."

I wished them both a happy and a prosperous anniversary.

As you may imagine, I closed my office and went to Hialeah the next afternoon, April 4. I did not see either the woman or her husband at the track; I was quite involved with my own calculations. And I followed my own instructions to the letter, just to see how they would fair in the market place, which is the acid test. I was quite discouraged, I must admit, when absolutely nothing happened to the 9-1 and the 10-1 horses in the first four races. True enough, in the second race, a horse named Slippery Bill went off at 11-1 (the closest to nine or ten that you could get) and came in second. But there had been no mention of place investments. Not enough money in the little fund for that. So we continued to the fifth race, which was also a Perfecta race. And here, lightning struck. There was an entry, that is, *two* horses on one ticket, at 10-to-one on the board, and also a horse named Mahlan at 10-1. Right on the nose. (I only hoped she wouldn't be confused by the entry. And I later learned that she hadn't been. She'd played it right.) Anyway, I put down $10 to win on the Entry and $10 to win on Mahlan, and I took out a pair of $10 Perfecta tickets on the combination, which was 1-10 and 10-1. An odd coincidence, I thought, but there you were. I had $40 riding on the race, and it was one of the best investments I have ever made. Mahlan was the number-ten horse and came out of the eleven-post position first. By the quarter, he had dropped back to fifth place, but the astonishing thing is that all *five* horses were within a length of each other. This was a short race, for maiden fillies, and I was on my feet with the rest of the crowd when Mahlan came around the stretch turn leading by two lengths. It was at that point that I noticed Out of the Past, one of the horses in the entry. At the head of the stretch, Out of the Past was in second place, and that's how they finished: Mahlan was first across by half a length, and Out of the Past was second. Mahlan paid $21.80 to win, and I got back $109 for my single $10 win ticket.

The Perfecta paid an astonishing $776.40 for each $2 ticket, and I had five of these for a take-home of $3,882. I could only hope and pray that the woman and her husband had the $776.40. Of course, the remainder of the program was an anticlimax, although as a matter of fact there was a nice little surprise in the ninth race: Sub Home went off at precisely 10-1, according to the board, and brought back $21.80 for $2. (This means that the actual odds were 9.90-1.) I happened to have $20 to win and took out another $218 from the total mutuel pool of $918,635 "invested" at Hialeah that afternoon.

Later that evening, around ten o'clock, I received a telephone call from the woman, who shall remain nameless. She was bubbling over.

"Do you know," she said, "that we came home with nearly *eight hundred dollars?*"

It was indeed astonishing, I admitted. "It probably wouldn't happen again in another fifteen years."

"We just wanted to thank you," she added.

"Don't mention it," I told her. I didn't say a thing about being at the track myself or what luck I had had, following the advice I had given her.

"Don't forget," I said before I rang off, "eighty dollars goes into the general fund."

She seemed a little taken aback, but it finally hit her. "Oh," she said, "oh, yes, you mean the general fund at the church. Ten percent."

"And if you'll give me the address of the church," I said, "I'll send a check myself."

"But you don't have to do that!"

"I always do," I said. "Happy anniversary again."

I heard from them one more time. That was a letter of thanks from the pastor when he received my check for $420. It was, he wrote, more than generous. But it was ten percent of the gross. Sam Hirsch could do no less.

I had told the pastor's wife that it wouldn't happen again in fifteen years, and of course that particular series of events would *never* recur. However, out of curiosity, I followed the results at Hialeah for the next four days, and I discovered that there were six hits in those four days; that is, on six occasions, by investing in the *two* horses whose odds were nearest to 9-1, moving upward, you would catch a winner. One winner had odds of 16-1 and another was 27-1. On Saturday, too, there was a Perfecta, a 10-1 and a 13-1 pair, which paid nearly $300. But another thing astonished me when I followed the results during those four days: there were winners at 69-1, at 27-1, and at 40-1. I was spurred into action. The system, which had been just a blur in my mind, suddenly took shape. In April of 1972, I began to approach every race from the point of view of the top odds, rather than from the other end, the favorite. It occurred to me that those high-odds winners must have something in common—something more than the fact that they crossed the line *first*. Just *why* did those high-odds winners get to the wire a neck or a head or a length, or sometimes *six* lengths, ahead of the pack?

Eventually, of course, I came up with The System, which I showed to the author of this volume. Along the way, I stumbled onto the Automatic Method of Play, which the author calls *SAM*. Not really! It was simply a logical development needed to fill a gap. When I make my own track investments, I use both systems at the same time. And I have investments in every race. I invest in the Daily Double and in every Perfecta race. In short, I cover the entire waterfront, not being satisfied with two or three solid plays per day. And if there is a secret to my success, it lies in one simple principle: I make the odds work *for* me. I won't say more here. You'll get a great deal later about the odds, and about the principles upon which the system, or systems, work.

If you are skeptical about making a million at the races, I don't blame you a bit. I'm a born skeptic myself. I doubt everything until it's proven beyond a shadow. Having spent a little more than three years developing the handicapping rules revealed here, and putting together the systems for their use, I have looked at—either on paper or in person—several thousand races. So have a dozen other people. But I have looked at those races with a specially trained eye. I claim no more intelligence than my peers. I have simply directed my thinking along certain lines, I have come to some solid conclusions, and I have tested those conclusions in every way I know how. The principles are good; they are universal; they work any time at any track under any conditions. I have even stumbled onto some races that were set up. I don't say they were fixed. It is practically impossible to fix a race, so that one and *only* one horse wins, and you *know* in advance that this *one* will win. Of course, it *is* possible to influence the outcome of a race to some degree. The jockey, more than anyone else, can do this. He can't make a horse *win*, but he can make a horse do *less* than his best, even when that horse is a thoroughbred, trained to run his heart out for one purpose: to *win*. I have run onto these races where it is clear that some influences have been put into play, where the results are not *all* up to chance. But it doesn't matter, so far as my system is concerned. By its very nature, my system will generally catch the winners of these *set up* races, or it will come up with the one-two combination in a Perfecta that produces a spectacular pay-off. Therefore, you needn't worry whether or not a race is fixed or isn't fixed. You can be sure of two things: first, horseracing is just about as honest and as straight as any large sport in America. It is probably *more* honest than most. It has to be. Both as a sport and as a business, it could not continue to exist unless it were operated completely above board. And secondly, even if there are·a few shenanigans going on in certain cases, if you go along with the system you will have the satisfaction of knowing that you are just as well off as the insiders. Your investment will undoubtedly be on the right horse, and you will share in the windfall.

The one who suffers is the average fan, the chap sitting in the stands who doesn't know that there are inside operations, or, if he does know or suspect that there are, he is powerless to do anything about them. Let me repeat: 999 races out of a 1,000 are straight and uninfluenced. But in that one race in a thousand, if you use my system you will be as well off as if you were completely in the know. If this is unclear to you now, when you have read the book you will understand.

It is a common statistic, also, that only one racegoer in a thousand emerges a winner. Just one tenth of one percent. With odds like that, how can *you* expect to make a *hundred* at the races, much less a thousand or a million? This entire book is the answer to that question. There *is* a way that you can make a hundred, or a thousand, or even a million, if you have such ambitions. Personally, I'll settle for a couple of hundred thousand a year. The taxes on that I can stand. I don't even want to *think* of the taxes on a million!

Is there a way for you to make money on the races?

Most certainly there is, but you will have to know a great deal more than the pastor's wife did.[2] What happened to her and her husband was a holy accident, perhaps, or wholly accidental. On their fifteenth wedding anniversary, in the fifth race, using numbers 10-1 and 1-10, they came close to grossing $1000. I never have believed in miracles, but that April I began to see the light. My eyes were opened. I regard this event, to me, as providential. But the money I give to the church is not conscience money. I have no qualms about tapping in on the billions that pass through the mutuel machines each year. In 1973, the last year for which I have records, 47,234,843 Americans attended thoroughbred races, while 29,517,729 paid admission to the harness races, and they pushed through the machines a total of $6,889,248,822.

And all I want to do is to tap off a few hundred thousand for Sam Hirsch. That six or seven billion a year represents an opportunity and a challenge. I have met the challenge by developing the two systems outlined in this book. But why have I revealed them to you? Won't that revelation influence my own and your chances for winning in the future? If *everyone* plays the system, won't that kill the goose that laid the golden egg? The answer is *no*. It really doesn't matter *which* two or three horses end up with the highest odds on the board. You *must* catch a horse that will be in-the-money. And that's what we're after. If the fickle fans jump on a high-odds horse and make him one of the first three favorites, that simply means that one of the horses that would have been among the first three favorites is now upstairs, in the high-odds bracket, and *his* chances of winning, or of being in-the-money, are just as good as any other's. If that fact isn't clear in your mind, it will be when you've read the book. Let me assure you of one thing:

You are in for a marvelous ride in the pages that follow. Don't miss a single one of them. Even the notes are significant. And the charts and tables are gold mines. For instance, hidden in one of the charts, as a note, there is a very simple formula for discovering, by use of everyday arithmatic, *where* the inside money is going. Which horse is *most* favored by its stable to win? It's as easy as one-two-three. The odds board will tell you, if you know

---

2.   For the rules of the Pastor's Wife Play, see page 209.

how to read it. But I'm not going to give you the formula here; you'll have to find it. Meanwhile, brace yourself. You're beginning a startling adventure. You are about to discover that among the ten thousand systems floating around in this country there are only a handful that are worth a ten-spot, and a ten-spot is about the price of this book. That ten-spot will bring *you* the golden egg.

My satisfaction is that *I'm the goose that laid it!*

1

Winners, Winners, Winners

Sam Hirsch had two regrets. The first was that the profile in the ad for the well-known Scotch, the one that never varies, came out just one month after the divorce became final. It hit the news stands a few days too late to do any good, so far as his influence on the Princess was concerned. The Princess was Connie, his ex-wife, who was far far away by that time. He wondered if she would see the back cover of *Money*, the magazine which dealt with his favorite subject. Probably not. *Money* wasn't exactly the type of magazine Connie would be reading.

The profile carried his photograph and underneath it his name in black print:

SAMUEL L. HIRSCH

HOME: Miami Shores, Florida.
AGE: 54.
PROFESSION: Investment Consultant.
HOBBIES: Sailing, Thoroughbred Racing.
LAST BOOK READ: "Anyone Can Still Make a Million."
LAST ACCOMPLISHMENT: Created and refined a method of

selecting winners of thoroughbred races, applicable at all tracks in any season.

QUOTE: "Wisdom consists of one thing—to know what steers All through All."

PROFILE: Inquiring. Dynamic. Desirous of exploring the broad vistas of life. Hopeful of man's betterment. Determined to leave his mark.

The profile had come out too late. Perhaps he had been rather too dynamic for Connie. She hadn't enough tolerance for his spirit of inquiry. Sailing she did like. She and the kids had always been happy to go with him on the lake or the waterways. But the kids were all married now, and it was being alone with Sam that had finished Connie. Rather, it was being alone, *without* Sam, that had finished her. She never *had* liked horseracing.

Sam's inquiring spirit was, in Connie's eyes, an obsession. She called him a compulsive gambler and urged him to join that group which had a name somewhat like Alcoholics Anonymous. Sam had only smiled. Connie didn't *see* what he was doing. She didn't understand that an investment consultant was not and never had been a gambler. Take that last book he had read, for instance. He had first read the book when it had appeared in 1966.

The divorce was his second and greater regret. Losing Connie was like losing a close and dear friend. But he and Connie had not been able, during the past two years, to communicate on the same wavelength. She blamed his obsession with horseracing, but that was just a convenient handle. That was something visible. There must have been a hundred other fears and frustrations that were the real cause of the trouble. Since he couldn't discover what they were precisely, he couldn't solve the problem. In fact, it was his inability to solve *that* problem which had led him to intensify his efforts on the other problem: looking for good investments in the field of thoroughbred racing.

During World War II, Sam Hirsch had been a bombardier in a very fine Liberator squadron in the 8th Air Force, stationed in the English midlands. He was the Squadron Bombardier, and he'd made Captain on the first list. Before his tour was over he had been promoted again, and he was moved up to Group Bombardier. Sam Hirsch had always been on target. He had gone directly from college to bombardier school, and from bombardier school to an antisubmarine patrol squadron flying out of Charleston, South Carolina. By the time they had gone overseas, to England, the Navy had taken over the job of antisubmarine patrol. Sam had moved with his squadron into pathfinding, a good deal more challenging than antisubmarine patrol, even if it happened to be over the Bay of Biscay.

But he got out of the Air Force in 1946 and had gone back to school for a master's degree. He met Connie and married her, and they had settled in Miami, where he joined an investment house which was looking for just such a bright and upcoming lad as Sam Hirsch. Now, of course, since Connie was gone, he also had moved his base of operations. He bought a house in Miami Shores, which he regarded as an ideal spot, halfway between Hialeah Park to the south and Hallandale to the north. Gulfstream Park was at Hallandale, and Sam was on his way to begin a week of pure indulgence. April 15 had passed. This was Monday, the sixteenth, the beginning of his vacation, the beginning of his own very serious investment program.

Convinced that all other available investment programs were either too risky or too slow, and that the percentage of return was not good enough, Sam had begun to give his attention two years ago to the field of thoroughbred racing. This was sheer lunancy, so far as Connie was concerned, but to Sam it was nothing of the sort. He knew more about real-estate investments than anyone else in Dade County. He knew how to buy and sell stocks without putting up a dime. He had the best insurance protection program in the state of Florida. Connie hadn't considered that. If she had outlived him, she would be well off indeed. But Sam came from a long line of men and women who lived to ninety or more. He figured he had forty good years ahead of him, and that was almost half a lifetime. This was April 1973, and Watergate was all over the TV, but he was not concerned with Watergate. He was ready to put his system to work.

Two years ago he had seen an advertisement in one of these Sunday weeklies, and he had sent a check to a fellow up in Brooklyn, who claimed that he had the system to end all systems. Sam was no fool, but if this fellow had spent a few thousand for a full-page ad in a Sunday weekly, he must have something. Norris Strauss sent him a very simple and straight-forward system, which he called Horses for Profiit. According to Mr. Strauss, the system would bring him four to five plays per day per track, with an average of thirty percent winners (about the same winning percentage as favorites), but with an average win-mutuel of $9.55.

This, of course, was just a beginning. To test the system on paper, Sam had to order a supply of old *Racing Forms*. He got the first six months of 1972, and with these *Forms* he began his own investigations. Mr. Strauss may have been right about his system, or he may not. Sam never found out. An average win-mutuel of $9.55 did not turn Sam on at all. It would require too much capital to make the system work, and even then, with two losses out of three, it would never make a million.

Meanwhile, Sam was receiving mail from all corners of the United States. He purchased two other systems, and very shortly there were more. He got them from New Jersey and California and Louisiana and Nevada. Apparently, there were a hundred-thousand systems afloat in this country. They were very much a part of the investment climate of the U.S.

Sam should not have wondered about this. After all, racing had become the number-one spectator sport in America. Attendance at thoroughbred racing events had already topped fifty million a year, and there had been almost as many fans at harness tracks during the same year. The parimutuel turnover at thoroughbred tracks had been more than three billion in 1968, and today it had nearly doubled. And no end was in sight. Sam knew that there must be a way to tap this monumental flow of cash. He got ideas from the systems he bought. He discovered areas that were distinctly unprofitable. He filled notebook after notebook with symbols that looked like the dreams of a deranged physical scientist. The following is an entry in his notebook for April 1973, Gulfstream Park, under the heading of Exactas:

$$\text{Ap 3 } 10^{11} \text{ 684}^{40} \text{ Q2 F5 P(5-6)}$$

What this entry means is that in the tenth race on April 3 at Gulfstream Park, there were eleven starters, and the Perfecta paid $684.40. The winning horse was the second highest qualifier (based on certain criteria he had evolved), and the place horse was the fifth favorite. In the morning-line projection, these two horses were listed in the fifth and sixth position, moving up the odds scale.

Sam had page after page of such detailed entries, extracted from his stock of *Racing Forms*. In the course of his two-year investigation, which had all been manual since he had no computer available, Sam discovered a number of revealing facts. He discovered definite patterns. Daily Double patterns and Exacta or Perfecta patterns. The spectrum was quite broad. Winners came from divergent categories. If one were to hit them all, it would take a double-barreled shotgun. This was impossible, certainly, and he had to narrow his field. He began to concentrate on the high payoffs, although these were not so frequent.

Sam discovered not one pattern, but many patterns, The more data he accumulated, the more varied were the patterns. Beyond a certain point, therefore, the mere recording of data was a self-defeating process. Not even a computer could help. The key to success lay in his analysis of all the patterns, in the isolation of winning factors and losing factors. The first thing one had to do was to eliminate some of the losers. In any race with ten or more starters, there would inevitably be a couple of fairly obvious losers. There were two-year-old races, and maiden races with first-time starters, where the problem of eliminating losers was much more complex. But that was another story.

On this April 16, the sky was a bit cloudy when Sam arrived. He hadn't counted on such heavy traffic, and he was definitely late. The first race was in progress, a fact that annoyed him no end, until the conclusion of the race, when he saw the favorite, Pink Lei, hold off a drive by Stabella and win by half a length. In the second race, Sky Travels won and paid $5.40.

Sam was already well into his handicapping chores with the third race. This was a maiden race at special weights, six furlongs out of the chute. All the horses were three-year-olds, and not one of them looked particularly outstanding. Indian Ambush had been third in his last race fourteen days ago. Sam was not surprised when Indian Ambush became the favorite. Meanwhile he was looking for something better than 16-1. There were twelve starters in the field, and Sam's method called for him to select two horses, both of which he would play to win and place, or across-the-board if the odds were high enough. Two horses were already appearing on the board at 99-1: Wiltelya and Bolinas Intent. Wiltelya was a colt, a first-time starter, who had worked just two days ago and before that, on April 6. No criteria were applicable. Wiltelya was an automatic bet: qualifier number one.

Bolinas Intent had run two months ago, finishing tenth in a field of twelve, twenty-seven lengths off the winner. His only other race had been on February 2, when he ran last in a field of twelve, thirty-one lengths behind the winner. Sam disqualified Bolinas Intent. Eliminate one positive loser; there was a dramatic drop in the odds. The number-three horse was listed at 21-1 and was called System to Win. A quick look at the *Form* showed that System to Win hadn't been out this year. The colt's last race had been in June 1972 when he'd run eighth in a field of twelve. Still a maiden he had had two fairly recent works and was carrying the standard weight of 120 pounds. Not a great deal to go on, but Sam took him as qualifier number two. Actually, Sam took System to Win for the odds of 20-1, now appearing on the board. The next highest odds were 11-1 on Sleep Lonely, not good enough in a maiden race in which literally anything could happen.

The three-year-old maidens were in the gate. Keep Truckin' was out first, followed a fraction of a length later by Dancero. System to Win was out fourth, and Sam was already on his feet in anticipation of victory. Coming along the backstretch System to Win took the lead over Keep Truckin' and was a length in front as they swung around the stretch turn. Lonetree was now in second place, followed closely by Seducer, who was ridden by MacBeth and was driving for the wire. Moving along the outside, Seducer came to within three-quarters of a length, but it wasn't good enough. System to Win was across in front and paid $42.40 to win and $20.40 to place. Sam had $20 to win and $20 to place and the same on Wiltelya, who ran last all the way. Sam collected $628 and settled down to look at the fourth race.

It was a $6,500 claiming race for fillies, all three-year-olds. There was a first-time starter named Saxony Princess, and of course Sam had to think about Connie, who had always been called the Princess. Forget it. Hunches were absolutely out. Please Show Me was trailing the pack on the odds board, at 99-1, had run fourteen days ago at Gulfstream Park, and had picked up a length in the stretch run of that race; these were two definite points in her favor. But she had finished eleven in a field of twelve, and in the last four races had never run better than tenth. She showed Sam exactly nothing. DQ, for *disqualify*. Sway Baby was lighting up the board at 90-1, and Sam checked her record. Sway Baby hadn't been out since the middle of October last year, but she had a couple of recent works, and she *had* been sixth in her last race. Sam could count three points for Sway Baby, which meant she was marginal but a possibility for a minimum investment in a race for three-year-old fillies.

Saxony Princess opened at 90-1. Sam looked at her record, and there was none. A first-time starter, she was getting in at 111 pounds, a big point in her favor. She had had three fairly recent works, and that was all, except that she was being ridden by Gonzalez, who was the fourth or fifth ranking jockey at the track this season. Sam put $20 across-the-board on Saxony Princess and $10 to win and $10 to place on Miss Eggers, who was dropping a thousand dollars in class for today's race. In maiden races and races for fillies only, or fillies and mares, Sam often went for a third bet. Today he chose Manchi for his third bet with $10 to win and $10 to place. The odds were 21-1, just a bit too low for an across-the-board bet.

But this was a Perfecta race. The fourth, the seventh, and the tenth races were run under Perfecta rules, and the problem was to pick the horses which would come in first and second, in that order. Sam usually crisscrossed four horses in a Perfecta race. Today he had Saxony Princess, Miss Eggers, and Manchi, and to these three he added Granny the Grouch. Four horses meant twelve tickets to cover all the one-two combinations among them. That was $24, and Sam took two of each, which raised his investment to $48 on the Perfecta. He had $60 on Saxony Princess and $20 each on Miss Eggers and Manchi, ridden by Mac-

Beth, who had also taken Seducer to the lead over System to Win in the third race. Sam's total investment in the race was $148. Three-year-old fillies were out of this world. Still, if he really wanted to test his system, this was the very type of race on which to test it. All the factors were there.

Saxony Princess was in the number-twelve post, a disadvantage in this six-furlong race. Gonzalez was a bit slow, too, and got her out ninth. Granny the Grouch, with Bruschino in the irons, jumped out first, as though she had been stuck with a hat pin. Leading by a head at the first quarter-pole, she increased her lead to two lengths at the half. She looked like a winner, but there was room to run in that field of twelve, and Poppy Beau seemed to be doing the running. At the stretch turn it was Granny the Grouch and Poppy Beau, but Manchi was moving up. Saxony Princess had raced wide and was in dead center of the pack at the half, but she managed to get into fourth position on the stretch turn. Poppy Beau had overtaken Granny the Grouch. Since Poppy Beau was nowhere in Sam's calculations, this was a bad development. But there was still a lot of race to go. Manchi, under the urging of MacBeth, was now in second place, as the fillies were driving for the wire. All of a sudden it was Saxony Princess in the lead, and Saxony Princess opened up a length and a half by the time she had reached the wire. It was a photo for second place.

Sam spent a moment or two in prayer. The judges faced a crucial decision. Poppy Beau would spoil everything. Manchi would do fine. The photo light disappeared and the number "10" appeared. Number ten was Manchi. Poppy Beau went in at third and paid $4.40 to show. Saxony Princess paid $164.40 to win, $43.80 to place and $19.60 to show. Manchi paid nothing to win and $15 to place. Of course he should have had Manchi to show too, but he didn't. Perhaps he'd look again at his rules on show betting. The 12-10 Perfecta startled him when it appeared on the board, although it really shouldn't have, with Saxony Princess at 80-1. The Perfecta paid $1,138.40 for $2, and Sam had two tickets, which mean a return of $2,276.80.

The other payoffs were as spectacular. Sam's $20 across-the-board on Saxony Princess brought him $1,644 to win, $438 to place and $196 to show. The $10 to place on Manchi was worth $75. Total income from straight betting was $2,353. Add that to the Perfecta return, and you get $4,629.80. Deduct the $148 investment, and Sam's net on the race was $4,481.80. What about that, Princess?

The race took so much out of Sam, emotionally speaking, that he let the fifth go by without a bet. The favorite of the fans was Stockholder, and this was enough in itself to drive Sam off. He hardly glanced at the *Form*. The truth was that he was too busy stuffing money in his wallet, and he was beginning to be afraid that he might have been observed standing quite a long time at the cashier's windows. But that was foolishness. There were guards everywhere. The money in his wallet was as safe as in the bank.

Like the five races before it, the sixth had twelve starters. The highest odds on the board was a 55-1 shot called Aturnchorus, which Sam quickly disqualified. Aturnchorus had been claimed in his last race and was moving up $5000 in class. No way. Soar On at 35-to-1 was a possibility, having finished sixth in his last race, which was also a mile and a sixteenth on the turf. Soar On had just enough to gain a bet of $10 across-the-board. No Time for Games was next at 35-to-1, with a recent race, only eleven days ago, but the colt had run dead last. Still, he had gained a couple of lengths in the stretch run and had a good work just three days ago. Good enough for $10 across-the-board, but no more. Sam folded the *Form* and sat back to watch the race. The favorite, Classic King, finished first by a length, a good ride by the jockey Hole. Restless Mood took second money and No Time for Games finished third, paying $11.80. Sam collected $59 and almost broke even. Actually, he lost a dollar on the race. Forget it. He turned his attention to the seventh race, for fillies and mares, a $10,000 claiming race with a field of twelve. Since it was also another Perfecta race, it was worth a minute of study.

The first thing that shook Sam was the fact that of the twelve starters, seven had finished either first or second in their last race. This meant, in effect, that it was going to be a free-for-all, and there was only one smart thing to do. Wait until the odds developed, and then play the two highest of those seven horses. This was certainly not according to the rules of the game, in Sam's book, but there were times when one had to extemporize. At 17-1, Back in Clover was the highest odds. Next came Extensive Care at 10-1, followed by Musical Annie at 9-1. Something clicked in Sam's mind. The race was for fillies and mares, and usually it was best to take three contenders in such a race, as in a maiden race. So he bet $5 across-the-board on each of the three; he added Joan R. H. at 8-1 for his fourth horse in the Perfecta combinations. Twelve tickets again, for an investment in the Perfecta of $24. If he had had more guts, he would have doubled the bet and bought two tickets on each combination, but the odds were really not attractive enough.

Bruscino, riding Musical Annie at 105 pounds, got out of the gate a bit slowly, about the middle of the pack, but he moved her forward gradually and steadily, between horses, and beat out Extensive Care by a length and a quarter. Extensive Care was running tenth at the quarter-pole but began to move like a house afire when she came round the stretch turn, taking second place by a head over Lot of Eve. Back In Clover could do no better than ninth. Still, it was a small victory for Sam, who picked up $128 for his across-the-board tickets on Musical Annie and Extensive Care. Deducting $45, that left a net of $83 on his straight bets. The Perfecta was good for $146.80, less the $24 investment, a net of $122.80. Total net: $205.80 on the race.

LAST ACCOMPLISHMENT: Created and refined a method of selecting winners....

With nine starters, the eighth race didn't look like much of anything. There was nothing over 35-1 on the board, and Sam spent little time choosing his two horses. The winner was King of Cornish, the second favorite at 7-2. No bet for Sam. The ninth race was coming up. It was for three-year-old fillies who had not won two races. Five of them, however, had been in the money in their last race. Miss Warhoop was 90-1 at the first flash of the board, and Sam took her on because she had finished sixth in her last race and had gained a length in the stretch run. Table Topic at 50-1 had the only other decent odds, but there was nothing really to support her possibilities. Delta De looked somewhat better at 40-1, and Sam went with her. The race was won by Introspect, the third favorite, who paid $11.

The final race of the day. Like Hialeah Park, Gulfstream featured ten races on a card. Any hunch player could have told you that this was the time to play the number-ten horse, which happened to be Oxbridge at 6-1. Oxbridge was the third favorite, and the third favorite had just won the preceding race. Repeat, repeat, repeat. Sam was no hunch player. He looked around for odds again, and the early leader was Arts Village at 45-1. There was, in fact, no other horse anywhere near Arts Village, who was dropping from $5000 to $3500 in today's race, but the drop was not immediate. It came from the next-to-last race, in which Arts Village had finished eleventh. A borderline case, but the next highest odds were far down the line at 25-1, a horse called Timberlea Tune. Since the race was a mile and a sixteenth, and Arts Village was getting in at 109 pounds, Sam took him for $10 across-the-board.

A successful system for picking winners, or for picking in-the-money possibilities, must not be a purely mechanical thing. It can't be. In order to take every advantage of the situation, a system player must be adaptive. Sam had a feeling for the tenth race at Gulfstream. Under ordinary circumstances, Arts Village would not be a qualifier. But he had two powerful advantages: his odds were high and he was getting in a long race at 109 pounds, which was eight pounds less than his last race. Two definite points in his favor. He had run nineteen days ago, but that was a little long for a horse to lay off. To be in peak form, a horse should be running again within fourteen days. Nevertheless, he was running in less than three weeks, and that was something. Half a point. Arts Village had been out six times this year, and he had picked up $2,400 for his win on the first of January. An average of $400 a race for his six outs was no great shakes, but Timberlea Tune had been out eight times and hadn't pulled in more than $150 a race.

Arts Village's last race had been at a mile and an eighth, and he had never got closer to the leader than ten lengths. In the long stretch run he had actually lost nine lengths, which meant that the jockey had eased him off to let him finish tenth, twenty-two lengths off the winner. That gave him a last-race rating of thirty-two in Sam's book, and thirty-two was ordinarily a sign for disqualification. But there may have been a good reason for that twenty-two-length loss. Arts Village was dropping eight pounds off that race, and certainly it had had the effect of building the odds. The colt was now 40-1 on the board, the longest odds available. Ten across-the-board was a minimum bet, actually. Sam went back and bought another ticket at $10 across-the-board, giving him a $60 investment in the race.

For his second choice, Teuton II looked better than Timberlea Tune. They were both geldings, getting in at 116 pounds, but Teuton II was dropping $1500 in class. In the end, there was nothing with any odds that might constitute a second qualifier, and Sam was left with Arts Village alone. But this was a Perfecta race, and Sam was forced to consider at least three other horses for a series of twelve combinations. He reverted to an idea which he had developed months ago but had not used systematically. He hooked his one qualifier with the third, fourth, and fifth favorites. Exactly twelve combinations for a $24 investment. By the time he got to the window he had decided to go for broke: he doubled the investment and bought two tickets on each of the twelve combinations. That gave him a total race investment of $108, considering the $60 he had bet on Arts Village across-the-board. The number-ten horse was the third favorite, number-one horse was the fourth favorite, and the number-four horse was the fifth favorite. If either of these came in first or second, with Arts Village in the other slot, he had himself a good-sized Perfecta.

Arts Village was two pounds over, but this hardly mattered to Sam. One hundred eleven pounds was very good weight for so long a race, and only one other horse, Chief Difficulty, had it so good. Of course, weight wasn't everything in any race, but it could be the deciding factor here. It just might put Arts Village in the winner's circle.

The race went off promptly at 5:26 and the start was good. Smart Flushing was first out of the gate, then dropped back to eighth, as though the jockey, Russello, were carrying lead in his pocket. It's a Corker was out second, followed closely by Teuton

II, who promptly took the lead and stayed there as if glued until they came to the half-pole. Arts Village was running second to Teuton II as they moved along the backstretch, then suddenly It's A Corker took the lead. Neither It's A Corker nor Teuton II were in Sam's plan of action, and this development was extremely disturbing. But it lasted only a moment or two. Coming into the stretch turn, It's A Corker was leading by two lengths and Arts Village was a head in front of Oxbridge. They came driving down the stretch, amid the roar of the crowd, and it was Arts Village and Oxbridge in a photo, with It's A Corker third, a length or so back.

Sam let out his breath. He had the Perfecta, unless there was a disqualification. But the real question was *who was the winner?* It made a thousand dollars difference to Sam, and he groaned a little when the lights went down and the photo disappeared. The number "10" took the top slot, followed by number "6", for Arts Village. Too bad. But Arts Village paid $20.20 to place and, strangely enough, $22.20 to show. That meant Sam had $424 coming for his $20 across-the-board. Had it been the other way round, he would have made—

Forget it! The results were official. Arts Village had lost it by a neck. But the Perfecta price was soothing. $539.20 for $2. Sam's two tickets brought him back $1,078.40, less his investment of $48. A net of $1,030.40. Put that with his straight net of $364, and he was $1,394.40 in the black on the last race.

Total for the day: $6,630.00. Less $46 in losses. New total: $6,584.00.

And this was just the *first* day of Sam's vacation.

What would tomorrow hold? Would the Hirsch System stand up?

"Oh, Princess," said Sam as he drove himself home to Miami Shores. "Why couldn't you wait?"

On April 16, 1973, nearly a million dollars went through the mutuel machines at Gulfstream Park. Sam had managed to tap a little less than $6,600 for his afternoon's work. As an investment consultant, it would take him two months to gross that amount. Very possibly, if his vacation went well, he would find himself in a new line of business with the coming of summer.

QUOTE: "Wisdom consists of one thing—to know what steers All through All."

It was Sam's quotation all right. But Heraclitus had said it, five-hundred years before the coming of Christ.

To *know* what steers ALL through ALL. There, indeed, was the rub. In a field of ten, it is conceivable that any of the ten will be the winner of the game. This basic fact is the reason that Sam will not invest in a horse whose odds are *less* than the number of horses in a race. By following this rule strictly and consistently, he put himself in the position of being unable to lose. Then he added a positive factor to his position: he weeded out one or two of the "impossibles." In most races, he eliminated at least two of the contenders. Still demanding odds of at least 10-1 in a field of ten, he began to build an overlay. It was no longer a matter of being unable to lose. Now he *had* to win. The point was not merely to make a profit on his investment: the point was to make a large enough profit so that the investment was irresistible.

To what degree he was successful, the remainder of this volume will show.

2

Losers, Losers, Losers

Sam did a very sensible thing during the days and the weeks that he had to himself. He went back and re-read everything he could lay his hands on about handicapping. He did this not because he intended to follow any of the rules. He did it so that every one of a thousand details would be in his mind, ready for possible application, if and when needed. The human mind was far better than any computer.

Practically all the books and pamphlets he read on handicapping devoted numerous pages to the subject of losers. Up to this point, Sam had concentrated on winners. He had looked only at the record of winners, to isolate the factors which led to winners. But he realized now that he must look at losers and be able to identify them in advance.

A gentleman at Ascot, dressed as a gentleman at Ascot should be dressed, approached the lady in the broad hat.

"Good afternoon, Duchess," he said. "You seem to be uncommonly lucky today. I've noticed your constant appearance at the cashier's window."

The Duchess smiled.

"What is your secret, Duchess?"

"No secret," said the Duchess. "I simply eliminate the losers!"

Yes, very well. There were always a great many more losers than winners in any race. But everything is relative, is it not? A loser in one race might well be a winner in another. Sam found a fairly recent work on winner selection[1]. Not surprisingly, the author was strong on the elimination of losers. A three-year study of winners and losers at southern California tracks had revealed that 84.3 percent of all winners had raced within fourteen days. It was clear that a *recent* race was a good sign of a possible winner today. His first rule was to eliminate from further consideration all horses which had not raced within fourteen days.

Sam dug into his cache of statistics, and he came up with the following table.

WINNERS who were racing again within seven days:	64%
WINNERS who were racing again within fourteen days:	21
(that is, between eight and fourteen days)	
WINNERS who were racing again within fourteen days:	85% (Total of above)
WINNERS who carried same or less weight today:	78%
WINNERS who carried more weight today than last:	22
WINNERS who finished in-the-money last race:	60%
WINNERS who won their last race:	22
(Included in the 60% above)	
WINNERS who raced today in same or lower class:	90%
WINNERS who raced today in higher class:	10
WINNERS of mixed races: Males:	76%
Females:	24

But these were not to become absolute rules in Sam's System. They were only guidelines. Don't eliminate a horse simply because he hasn't had a recent race or didn't finish in-the-money last time out. A horse who worked a day or two before a race was probably in good shape and ready to go. Two workouts

---

1. Lawrence Voegele, *Professional Method of Winner Selection* (Los Angeles: Financial Publishers).

within ten or twelve days were also good. Sam began to assign points to these various categories. One point to a high-odds horse with a workout within so many days. Two points if the workout was within three or four days. Sam liked a horse who had worked the day before a race.

It was becoming apparent that in the Hirsch system of winner selection, a long-odds horse must accumulate a certain number of points (say, five points) to qualify. But these points may come from any of several categories:

CATEGORY A: RECENCY OF RACE OR WORKOUT

To a horse that has raced within twenty-eight days: ONE POINT

To a horse that has raced within fourteen days: TWO POINTS

For a workout within sixteen days: ONE POINT

For a workout within four days: TWO POINTS

For a race within twenty-eight days *and* a workout in ten days: TWO POINTS

For two races within twenty-eight days: TWO POINTS

The date of the last race is given to the left, on the top line of the past performance chart. Drop down one more line for the next-to-last race to find whether or not the horse has raced twice within the specified twenty-eight days. The dates of a horse's workouts are found at the bottom of the chart, usually in boldface type. The latest work is listed on the left, and all other works arre listed on the same line, to the right. It takes only seconds to determine how many points a horse should get for recency of race(s) and work(s).

The maximum number of points which a horse can accrue from Category A is two points.

Even if a horse receives no points for race or workout, he's not automatically eliminated. There are at least four other categories from which to garner points toward qualification.

Category B is for Last Race Finish and is perhaps the most important of all.

CATEGORY B: LAST RACE FINISH

1.   If a horse is running today at the same class, or in a lower class, as his last race, use that last race to garner points for qualification. If a horse has two races within the past twenty-eight days, use the better of the two races to garner points. For fillies, maidens, two-year-olds, and three-year-olds, use either of the last two races, regardless of when they were run. Choose the better race.

2.   If a horse is moving up in class, check the last race and also check the last race at today's distance. Select the better race to garner points, if run within past 28 days.

Point Awards

In fields of eight or less horses, for a finish of fifth or better: ONE POINT

In fields of nine or more, for a finish of sixth or better, or six or less lengths off the winner, award: ONE POINT

If you are dealing with fillies or mares, with maidens or two-year-olds, *add* one to each figure above, e.g., in fields of nine or more, for a finish of seventh or better, or seven lengths or less off the winner: ONE POINT

Compute the last-race rating by adding the finish position to the number of lengths off the winner.

For a last-race rating of ten or less, award: TWO POINTS

For a rating of twenty or less (except when a horse finished last in the race) award: ONE POINT

For maidens, fillies & mares and two-year-olds, for twenty-five or less: ONE POINT

If a horse finished fifth or better in small fields, sixth or better in larger fields, or seventh or better if a filly or maiden, and if the horse gained in the stretch run of his last race (the race used to qualify him), for every length gained in that stretch run, award: ONE POINT

If a horse finished worse than fifth (in small fields) or worse than sixth in larger fields (or worse than seventh for fillies, maidens, etc.), for every two lengths gained in the stretch run, award: ONE POINT

For every three races in the past performance when a horse

finished six-and-one-half lengths or less off the winner, award:
ONE POINT

CATEGORY C: IN-THE-MONEY

For finishing in-the-money once in entire past performance:
    ONE POINT
For a win in last three races: ONE POINT
For two wins in last five races: TWO POINTS
For five or more firsts and seconds in past performance:
    ONE POINT
For finishing in-the-money in half or more of all races in past
performance (minimum, four races), award: ONE POINT
For two fourths in fields of ten or more: ONE POINT
For fillies, mares or maids, etc., for one fourth in field of ten-
up: ONE POINT
Or, for one fifth, if less than six lengths off winner: ONE
POINT

NOTE: If a horse has *not* finished in-the-money in his listed past performance, but has
TWO POINTS from Category A, and shows one fourth in a field of ten or more, award:
ONE POINT

CATEGORY D: WEIGHT

For carrying 105 pounds or less today: TWO POINTS
For carrying 106–110 pounds today: ONE POINT
For dropping 3–6 pounds off last race: ONE POINT
For a drop of 7 or more pounds: TWO POINTS
If horse is carrying 5 or more pounds LESS than the top-
weighted horse in the race: ONE POINT
If horse drops in class AND drops 2 pounds: ONE POINT
Maidens, two-year olds, fillies & mares who are dropping 2
pounds this race: ONE POINT

Penalties:
For carrying 188–122 pounds today: Minus ONE POINT
For carrying 123 upward today: Minus TWO POINTS

NOTE: A horse who drops in class may pick up as many as four pounds without penalty.
Also, any horse may pick up four pounds without penalty if his weight today is 114 or
less. Do not exact penalties when horse's low weight last race was due to apprentice
jockey's allowance, indicated in last race by two or three asterisks.

If *all* the horses in a race (or all but one) are carrying the same weight, say 122 pounds, then it is not necessary to impose the penalty on the high-odds contenders. In fact, do *not* impose the penalty, since such an action might reduce the number of points of a contender to the level of a non-qualifier.

However, if there are two horses in the race carrying less weight than all the others, then the penalty should be imposed.

Sam was aware of the fact that high weight in a short race had a somewhat different effect upon a horse than did weight in a long race. But the difference was not one which could be measured in points, under his system. Therefore, for simplicity's sake, he did not make any distinction between weight-carrying in short and long races. All rewards and penalties were the same in his book, whether the race was a five-furlong dash or a lung-bursting mile and a quarter. Some handicappers contend that in a race of average length it is a rule of thumb that one pound of weight is equivalent to a length at the finish. A horse who lost a race by five lengths in his last race at today's class, and is getting in today's race at the same class with five pounds off, has a good chance of winning today's race, all other factors being equal, of course. Still, one length for one pound is a good enough rule for his purposes. Watch out for the horse who is dropping weight and also dropping class—unless he has some physical problem. And on this note, Sam came at last to that very important but also very tricky matter of class.

CATEGORY E: CLASS

In his examination of the results of some 5,000 races at all the major tracks in southern California, Lawrence Voegele found that during the three-year period of the test, class always told. Just over 4,500 of these winners were running in the same class or lower, whereas less than 500 winners were running in a higher class. In short, 90.7 percent of the winners were running in the same or lower class, while 9.3 percent were running in a higher class than their last race.

An upward move in class from the last race is usually fatal to a horse's possibilities, so far as winning is concerned—not always, of course, and we must therefore be fair in our awards and penalties. We are just as interested in high-odds horses finishing in-the-money. A 60-1 shot can pay $30 to place, which is the same as a win at 14-1, and it can pay $16 to show, which is as good as 7-1 to win. And our qualifier, once we find him, has two chances to reach that place position and three chances to show. If we are betting two top-odds qualifiers, we are miltiplying our chances of cashing a ticket, sometimes more than one ticket, in a race.

Sam also discovered that in maiden races and races involving fillies and mares, it was often the third qualifier who either won the race or ran in-the-money. Thus it was wise to select three qualifiers and bet all three to win and to place. If the odds were high enough, a show bet was also in order. While this increased the investment, it also greatly increased the chances of a good payoff.

The horse with a class advantage must be given priority. However, the fact that a horse is moving up in class should not be a reason for eliminating him from contention. This is a hard and fast rule in many systems, and it cuts out an occasional big winner, or a horse with high odds who ends up in-the-money. Class differences weigh heavily in the public mind, and a horse dropping dramatically in class often winds up the favorite, or the second or third favorite. If this happens, we rarely look at that horse for more than a moment. He is out of consideration so far as straight bets are concerned. However, we will look at him when we come to Daily Doubles and Perfectas or Exactas.

In the Hirsch system of winner selection, a drop in class is simply one of many considerations. But differences in class must be studied. For his purposes, Sam arranged the various classes in descending order:

Class 1:   Stakes races and name handicaps, often with added money.

Class 2:   Claiming races of $16,000 and higher.

Class 3:   Allowance races and overnight handicaps, and $15,000 claiming races.

Class 4:   Claiming races of $14,500 and lower.

Class 5:   Starter handicap races and starter allowance races.

Class 6:   Maiden races and maiden special weights races.

Class 7:   Maiden claiming races.

Class 8:   Two-year-old races and races for first-time starters.

Some handicappers would not grant that $16,000 claiming races and above are of a higher class than allowance races. However, Sam agreed with Lawrence Voegele that there must be a point at which claiming races should be divided. At most major tracks, certainly, a horse running in a $30,000 claiming race is higher in class than a horse running in an allowance race at that track. By the same evaluation, a horse running in a $15,000 claiming race would be approximately the equal of a horse running in an allowance race at the same major track.

But it takes a good close look at the past performance charts to determine the true class of a horse. The mere fact that a horse has been running in allowance company and then drops into a $10,000 claiming race does not mean that he is superior to the other horses running in that claimer. The horse must have been winning, or at least running in-the-money, in the higher class race before we can say that he is a superior choice. Nevertheless, in Sam's book, any horse dropping from allowance company into a claiming race at less than $15,000 gets a point. If the drop is more than $5,000, he gets two points. Following is a summary of Sam's statement on Class, Category E:

For a class drop of $1,000 to $5,000:   ONE POINT
For a class drop of $5,500 to the limit: TWO POINTS
An allowance race is equal to a $15,000 claiming race.
For any two-class drop: TWO POINTS

Penalties:

Moving UP in class by $1,000 to $5,000:   Minus ONE POINT
Moving UP in class by $5,500 or more: Minus TWO POINTS
Moving UP in class by two steps: Minus TWO POINTS

If you refer to Class Five, you can see that this class concerns starter handicap races and starter allowance races. In the past performance charts, if you see H5000, it means simply that this horse ran in a starter handicap at $5,000; this is the same class as a $5,000 claimer. Similarly, the reference A10000 means a starter allowance, with a value of $10,000 on the horse and is equal to a $10,000 claimer. But only in the claiming race is the horse actually for *sale* at that price.

Sam made no distinction among horses within a class. Nor did he actually evaluate any horse who was dropping or moving up in class. Therefore, a horse who had never finished better, say, than tenth in $15,000 claiming races, and who is dropping now into a $12,500 claiming race, should not necessarily receive a point. Under the system, we do give him a point, but when you do so you must always be aware of what you are doing. If you "feel" that horses of this type should not be awarded a point, of course you are free to withhold it. However, when dealing with borderline cases, when one more point will make a high-odds horse a qualifier, and the only source for that point is a drop in class, it might be well to give the horse the benefit of the doubt.

Every race is a puzzle to be solved. The puzzle is a complex one, and, given the facts available to the public, there is no simple or easy way to pinpoint the winner. In most races, there are several potential winners. There are several horses who have the capability of winning, or of running in-the-money. The final determining factor in a race may be very simply a matter of luck or fortune or circumstance. If you have chosen for your qualifiers, horses who are among the potential few, then there is always a chance that you have a winner now and then. Since you only select high-odds horses, the payoff when it comes is a big one. Sam found that either Q1 or Q2 or Q3 produced an average of one winner a day. Since he made an average of two win bets a race, and there were ten races a day at Gulfstream and Hialeah, he was making twenty win bets a day, and in order to stay ahead of the game on win bets he must have odds of better than 20-1. Indeed, he had just that. A check of results during the past year showed that the average odds on Q1 horses had been 48-1, while the average odds on Q2 horses had been 22-1. The mean was 32-1. In hard cash, this meant that he was getting back $66 for every $40 invested, for a net profit of $26 a day.

He found that place bets were coming in at the rate of two a day, that is, twice in ten races. The investment was the same, computed on the basis of two $2 place bets a race. The average odds on Q1 and Q2 place bets were such that he was getting back an average of $28 every time one of his selections placed. This occurred twice a day, for a return of $56, giving a net profit on place bets of $16 a day.

Show bets were coming in three times a day, but the return per $2 ticket was only about $10. For $40 invested (at two show bets a race each day) he was not breaking even. Show betting was therefore unprofitable on a flat-bet basis. It had to be handled, if at all, on a money-management system, in which a set progression was used and a cut-off point established to prohibit large losses due to a run of No Shows. He decided to bet Q1 or Q2 to show only if the odds were 30-1 or better. The purpose was not to make a profit on these show bets but to provide some insurance.

Before getting into a discussion of the Daily Double, it is time to do some summarizing. As he gained more experience with his own methods and after analysis of a large volume of results, Sam came to a very positive conclusion: he had the system whipped. He had nine distinct rules for qualifying a horse with high odds. And he had five categories from which a horse might garner points on its way to qualification—or to disqualification. All this has been presented already in rough form, but now we will look at it in final form. There have been some additions, some alterations, and a few deletions. Forgetting the past, we will look at the rules as they now are. We will examine the various categories in great and varied detail. Sam realized that his system or method needed variety and flexibility. Any system that is too mechanical will never work at all tracks and in all seasons. There must always be some room for human judgment and for a little adjustment here and there.

For example, if a high-odds horse comes up with just four and two-thirds points, what do you do? Strictly speaking, he wouldn't qualify unless he were one of those who need only four points. But remember that if today's race is at the same distance and on the same surface as a horse's last race, there's half a point available, which might bring the horse up to qualification. But even without that assistance, there are other ways of making a decision. Use your own best judgment!

RULES FOR SELECTING Q1, Q2, Q3

1. To qualify for Q1, Q2, or Q3, a horse generally needs FIVE POINTS. Race should have eight starters.
2. However, horse *may* qualify with only FOUR POINTS if:
   a) He or she has only one race in their past performance chart *and* two of the points come from Category A, Race Recency.
   b) Horse shows *both* a race *and* a workout within fourteen days.
   c) Horse is a two-yr-old or a three-yr-old maiden, or is a filly. In a filly/mare race, the fillies need FOUR POINTS, the mares FIVE POINTS.
   d) Horse is carrying *less* than 109 pounds today *and* has TWO POINTS from Category A.
   e) Horse is a three-yr-old Maiden running against winners for the *first* time.
3. A horse needs SEVEN POINTS to qualify *if:*
   a) His last-race odds were 102 or more. (Exception: Maiden Races and races for three-yr-olds.)
   b) Fillies or mares running against males this race. (Exception: same as above.)
   c) Maidens running against winners this race. (Except: Maiden's *first* try vs. winners.)
   d) Any horse (except a maiden) who finished twenty lengths or more off the winner in *both* of his last two races.
4. A horse is an Automatic Bet (needs no points) *if:*
   a) He is dropping $10,000 or more in class, or moving down two steps or more in class. His odds today must be in the top four—top five in 10-12 field.
   b) If his odds today are in the top four *and* he finished fourth or better in 60 percent or more of his past races, with a minimum of eight races shown.

    c)   He or she is a first-time starter in a Maiden Race, a two-yr-old race, or a race for three-yr-old fillies, *and* has at least one recent workout shown.

    d)   A two-yr-old with one race shown, and that race was within fourteen days, or one recent race *and* a workout within ten days.

5.   A horse claimed last race is disqualified, unless:
    a)   he is running again within fourteen days; and
    b)   he is carrying less than 118 pounds today; and
    c)   he has a last-race rating of less than SIXTEEN POINTS; *or*
    d)   he can produce at least EIGHT clear POINTS.

6.   A horse claimed last race *and* moving up in class for today's race is disqualified, unless he can produce TEN clear POINTS.

7.   In maiden races with special weights, if there are two distinct age and weight groups, take the lower-weight group first and examine the contenders with the top odds and go down the odds scale to find your qualifiers. If you do not find three qualifiers in the lower-weight group, go to the top odds of the higher-weight group.

8.   In pursuing qualifiers, go down the odds scale from the top, but do not go below those odds which equal the number of horses in the race. For instance, in a twelve-horse race, do not go below 12-1. (Except: when you definitely disqualify two or more horses, drop the odds requirement TWO POINTS.)

9.   Disqualify any horse who ran dead last in his last race if he was fifteen or more lengths off the winner, unless:
    a)   the horse is dropping in class, *and*
    b)   he has two points from Category A.

CATEGORY A: RACE RECENCY

For a race within twenty-eight days: ONE POINT

For maidens, fillies, and mares, for a race within thirty days: ONE POINT

For a race within fourteen days: TWO POINTS

For maidens, fillies, and mares, for a race within fifteen days: TWO POINTS

For a workout within fourteen days: ONE POINT

For maidens, fillies, and mares, for a workout within fifteen days: ONE POINT

For a workout within four days: TWO POINTS

For maidens, fillies, and mares, for a workout within five days: TWO POINTS

For *two* races within twenty-eight days: TWO POINTS

Maidens, fillies, and mares, *two* races within thirty days: TWO POINTS

For *two* workouts within fourteen days: TWO POINTS

Maidens, fillies, and mares, *two* workouts within fifteen days: TWO POINTS

For a race within twenty-eight days *and* a workout within ten days: TWO POINTS

NOTE: If any horse has received one or two points in Category A, *and* if his or her last race was at the same distance and on the same surface as today's race, award: ONE-HALF POINT

CATEGORY B: LAST RACE FINISH

1.   Check the last race at today's class *or* at today's distance, whichever is the better race.

2.   If the horse has two races within twenty-eight days at today's class, check them both and choose the better race. Use last two races for maidens, fillies, and mares.

3.   If a horse is moving up in class, check the race at today's distance, or as close to today's distance as possible.

Point Awards

For a finish of fifth or better in a field of eight horses, last race used: ONE POINT

For a finish of sixth or better (or six lengths or less off the winner) in a field of nine or more horses: ONE POINT

For maidens, fillies, and mares, add ONE to above figures. For instance, for a finish of seventh or better (or seven lengths or less off the winner) in a field of nine or more horses: ONE POINT

Compute last-race rating by adding the finish position to the number of lengths off the winner. For a rating of ten or less: TWO POINTS

For a last-race rating of twenty or less (except when horse finished *last* in the race), award: ONE POINT

For maidens, fillies, and mares, allow a last-race rating of twenty-five or less: ONE POINT

If a horse received a point for finishing sixth or better (fifth or better in small fields, or seventh or better for fillies, mares, and maidens), *and* if the horse gained in the stretch run of that last race checked, award for every length gained in that stretch run: ONE POINT

If horse finished worse than sixth (or worse than fifth in small fields, or worse than seventh for maidens, fillies, or mares) *but* gained in the stretch run of the last race checked, for every two lengths gained, award: ONE POINT

If a horse won his last race, is in top-five odds (in large fields) or in top-four odds in smaller fields, and is not moving up more than $1,000 in class, award: ONE POINT

If a horse has run in four or more races at a class higher than today's class, and has gained in the stretch run in *more* than half of those races: ONE POINT

If a horse improves his position in the field as he goes from the head of the stretch to the finish wire (e.g., fifth at head of stretch, fourth at wire) in 75 percent of the races listed in his past performance (minimum: four races):   ONE POINT

For every three races in his listed past performance, when a horse finishes 6½ lengths or less off the winner: ONE POINT

In maiden races and races for three-yr-olds and for fillies, if a horse has gained a point from Category A, *and* if he gained just one length in the stretch run of his last race (regardless of finish position):   ONE POINT

CATEGORY C: IN-THE-MONEY

For finishing once in-the-money in past performance: ONE POINT

For one win in last three races: ONE POINT

For two wins in last five races: TWO POINTS

For five or more firsts or seconds in past performance: ONE POINT

For finishing in-the-money in half or more of all races in the past performance (minimum: four races):   ONE POINT

For TWO fourths in a field of ten or more:*   ONE POINT

For maidens, fillies, and mares, for ONE fourth in a field of ten or up: ONE POINT

Or, for one fifth, *if* less than six lengths off the winner: ONE POINT

NOTE: These last two awards are for horses who have *not* finished in-the-money in any of their races listed. Horses who have finished in-the-money in any of their listed races are not eligible for these awards.

*If a horse has TWO POINTS from Category A, Race Recency, but has not finished in-the-money in his listed past performance, but has ONE fourth in a field of ten or more: ONE POINT

CATEGORY D: WEIGHT

For carrying 105 pounds or less today: TWO POINTS

For carrying 106–110 pounds today: ONE POINT

For dropping 3 to 6 pounds from last race: ONE POINT

For dropping 7 or more pounds today: TWO POINTS

Horses dropping in class, maidens, 2-yr-olds, fillies and mares dropping two pounds from last race: ONE POINT

Any horse carrying 5 or more pounds LESS than the top-weighted horse in the race: ONE POINT

Penalties

For carrying 118-122 pounds today: Minus ONE POINT

For carrying 123 pounds or more today: Minus TWO POINTS

For picking up 3 to 6 pounds over last race: Minus ONE POINT

For picking up 7 or more pounds today: Minus TWO POINTS

NOTE 1:   Do *not* exact penalty if *all* the horses in a race are carrying the same high weight, e.g., 122 pounds. OR: All horses but one.

NOTE 2:   Do *not* exact penalty if horse carried exceptionally low weight last race due to apprentice jockey allowance, shown by two or three asterisks: ** **

NOTE 3:   If horse is dropping in class, he or she may pick up as much as four pounds without penalty.

NOTE 4:   Any horse may pick up as much as four pounds without penalty *if* he is carrying a total weight of no more than 114 today.

NOTE 5:   Before exacting penalty for carrying 118 or more today, examine last few races and see whether or not horse has carried this high weight successfully before today. If so, no penalty today. For instance, if horse was in-the-money at 122 last race and is carrying 122 pounds today, no penalty.

CATEGORY E: CLASS

For a drop in class, either from last race or from next-to-last race: ONE POINT   (Class drop must be $1,000 to $5,000.)

For a drop in class of $6,000 or more: TWO POINTS

For a one-step drop in class: ONE POINT

For a two-step drop in class: TWO POINTS

Penalties

For moving UP in class $1,000 to $5,000:   Minus ONE POINT

For moving UP in class $6,000 or more: Minus TWO POINTS

For a one-step move UP in class: Minus ONE POINT

For a two-step move UP in class: Minus TWO POINTS

CLASS RANKINGS

Class One: Stakes races and named handicaps (often with money added).

Class Two: Claiming races for $16,000 and up.

Class Three: Allowance races and overnight handicaps; claiming races at $15,000 and up to $16,000.

Class Four: Claiming races for $14,500 and less.

Class Five: Starter handicap and starter allowance races.*

Class Six: Maiden races and maiden special weight races.

Class Seven: Maiden claiming races.

---

*A Starter Handicap with a number following, e.g., H5000, is the equivalent of a $5,000 claiming race. Similarly, a Starter Allowance Race with a number following, e.g., A10000, is the same as a $10,000 Claiming Race.

NOTE 1:   If today's race is the second step UP in a row, i.e., two step ups in three races (including today's), then double the penalties.

NOTE 2:   If all of a horse's races (except the last race) have been run at a higher class than today's class, consider the horse to be DROPPING in class and award the appropriate points.

NOTE 3:   If a horse shows FOUR or more races at a class higher than today's class, consider that horse to be dropping in class.

DAILY DOUBLES

In all his days at the track and in all his reading on the subject, Sam had never come across a sensible method of play on the Daily Double. Innumerable proposals had been made, but when he checked them out, they invariably led to disaster. Yet he knew that Daily Double payoffs were often above $100 and occasionally were above $500. A few rare ones paid better than a thousand dollars for a $2 investment.

It was a difficult problem. Sam knew that high odds on at least one of the two winning horses was a guarantee of a good payoff. In the daily double, the problem was to pick the winner of the first race *and* the winner of the second race, getting their numbers on a single ticket purchased before the running of the first race. So far as odds were concerned, you could read them off the board for the horses in the first race. But you had only one clue as to the possible odds in the second race; the morning-line odds given in the *Form* or on the day's program.

Checking over his results from past races, Sam came to a preliminary conclusion: the really big payoffs frequently involved Q1 or Q2 horses (Q3 in maiden or filly/mare races). He could find the two or three qualifiers in the first race in his usual manner. Guided by the odds on the tote board, he found his Q1 and Q2 in less than three minutes. But which horses should he combine them with in the second race?

Back he went to his charts and notebooks. He found that Q1 or Q2 in the first race rarely combined with Q1 or Q2 in the second race. This happened at a particular track perhaps once in a month, a frequency not great enough to make it profitable as a day-by-day investment. (If, however, he noticed that these two high-odds horses in the first two races had not combined for a daily-double win in fifteen or twenty days, he would start playing the four combinations in the hope of a hit soon.) As a general rule, when the big payoffs came, and when they involved Q1 or Q2 (and Q3 if it were a maiden or a filly race, and even Q4 if they were maiden fillies), the winner in the second race came from the first five favorites.

The problem was how to spot these winners in advance of the first race. He had to make-do with the morning-line odds, or with the selections of a public handicapper, such as Hermis at Gulfstream Park. Hermis graded the card in advance, and these predictions were published. Sam took the predictions in the second race, and by studying his notebooks he found that F2 through F5 were most frequently involved. That is, those horses listed on the first five or so lines with probable odds ranging from 7-5 to 8-1. The horse with the lowest probable odds he called F1 and this horse he ignored because almost everyone at the track used it. When this top horse won the second race, the payoffs were low. But the next four, F2 through F5, were generally good in terms of probability of win and in terms of high payoffs, when combined with Q1 or Q2 (and Q3 when appropriate) in the first race.

Assuming that the first two races on the card were regular claiming races, then Sam's daily double combinations were:

First Race		Second Race
Q1	with	F2, F3, F4, F5
Q2	with	F2, F3, F4, F5

This meant four tickets with Q1 and four with Q2, or an investment of $16.

More frequently than not, however, the winner of the first race fell within the first five favorites. Once again, the favorite in the first race, when combined with most of the horses in the second race, produced a low payoff. Therefore, ignore F1 in the first race. Take F2, F3, F4, and F5 and combine with Q1 and Q2 in the second race. But how to determine these two qualifiers when the actual odds were not available? Sam went back to the predicted or probable odds in the second race, as given by Hermis or the morning line. He noted that often Hermis did not list the horses in morning-line-odds order. A 20-1 or even a 30-1 horse would fall somewhere up the table and not on the bottom two or three lines. Sam rearranged the horses so that the highest probable-odds horse was on the bottom, usually at 30-1. If there were two or three of these, he listed them in the order that Hermis had them on the chart, that is, the lowest 30-1 at the bottom, the next 30-1 on the second-line up, and so forth.

To find his two or three qualifiers, he started with the bottom horse and checked his past performance. In order to qualify, the horse needed a total of five points from Categories A through E. After he had found Q1 and Q2, he proceeded upward and found Q3 and often Q4. If Q3, for example, had seven or eight or more points, Q3 was an outstanding horse and might very well replace Q2. Or, as sometimes happened, if Q2 and Q3 were both at the same odds on the board, then Sam had to decide between the two, or else play them both. If he decided not to play them both, he would have to break the tie, and this he usually did by selecting the horse that had raced or worked most recently. Or had the higher five-race rating.

Sam now had his Q1 and Q2 in the second race. Checking the odds board, he would take the second through the fifth favorites and combine with Q1 and Q2 for his second group of tickets. This was eight more tickets, or another $16 investment. Of course he would not hit every day, but when he did hit, it would be for more than $100. Frequently, it would be for $300 or even $500. If he were shooting for the really big payoffs, a thousand or over, he would combine Q1 and Q2 in the first race with Q1 and Q2 in the second race.

Why not combine F2 through F5 in the first race with F2 through F5 (as projected by the public handicapper or the morning-line odds) in the second race?

As a matter of fact, records showed that this system would produce quite frequent hits, and the payoffs were moderate to good.

Sam had a feeling of dissatisfaction when he went back over his method of play on the daily double. He couldn't immediately put his finger on the source of his feeling, but it was there all the time, particularly when he went to Gulfstream one afternoon in April, trying out his doubles play.

When he returned home that evening, Sam settled in for some work on the notebooks and the charts in the *Form*. He went back over the past performances of a dozen or two horses in Daily

Double and Perfecta races, those horses selected in the second race by using the probable odds, and those horses which the public favored in the first race and in Perfecta races. He was looking in particular for signs that pointed to losers, and of course he found a great many such signs. But he had to start somewhere, and he set down the following conditions and specifications for selecting *three* horses in a race which he labeled F2, F3 and F4. It would be these three that he would combine with Q1 and Q2 to get his box in a Perfecta. That is, to get *five* horses which he would crisscross to cover all possibilities among them. If any one of the five won the race *and* any one of the other four came in second, Sam had the Perfecta. This would cost him twenty tickets at $2 each, which meant an investment of $40 a race.

RULES FOR SELECTING F2–F4

A. Race Recency.   Horse must have raced within twenty days or worked within ten days.

Exceptions: 1) Horse is dropping $3,000 or more in class, or is dropping two full steps in class.

2) Horse is dropping $1,000 to $2,500 in class *and* gained in the stretch run of his last race.

3) Horse has a last-race rating of twelve or less.

4) Horse finished in-the-money in two of his last three races.

B. Finish Position: DISQUALIFY any horse who was beaten by fifteen or more lengths in both of his last two races.

C. In-The-Money. DISQUALIFY any horse who was *not* in-the-money at least once in the last four races.

Exceptions: 1) Same as 1 in "A" above.

2) Same as 2 in "A" above.

3) Horse shows one fourth in the last four races *and* in that race he has a

rating of twelve or less.

4) Horse finished three lengths or less off the winner in one of his last four races.

D. Weight Factors. DISQUALIFY any horse who is picking up four or more pounds.

Exceptions:
1) Same as 1 in "A" above.
2) Same as 2 in "A" above.
3) Same as 3 in "A" above.
4) Same as 4 in "A" above.
5) Horse *won* his last race carrying 119 or more pounds.
6) He's getting in today at 117 or less.

E. Class Factors.
a. Horses running today in the same general class or dropping generally in class must have a last-race finish of three or more places lower than the number of horses in that race.

Exceptions:
1) He finished his last race eight lengths or less off the winner.
2) His next-to-last race was very impressive and was run at a class considerably higher than today's class.
3) He is dropping five or more pounds off his last race *and* is getting in today at 112 pounds or less.

b. Horses moving up in class generally speaking must have a last-race finish of four or more places lower than the number of horses in that race and should show the following:
1) Won his last race.
2) Or was in the money in both of his last two races.
3) Gained two or more lengths in

the stretch run of his last race.
c.   Horse moving up in class by $3,000 or more must:
1)   Be running again within fourteen days, *or*
2)   Have had a workout within the past two days.

F.   Odds Factor.   DISQUALIFY any horse whose last-race odds were 90-1 or higher.

Exceptions: 1)–4)   Same as 1–4 in "A" above.

G.   Male/Female.   a.   When fillies or mares are running against males (or when maidens are running against winners), DISQUALIFY any horse moving up in class.

Exceptions:
1)   Horse won the last race very impressively. Or, meets three out of the following requirements:
2)   Is running again within ten days or worked out in two days.
3)   Finished five or more places lower than the number of runners in that race.
4)   Gained two or more lengths in the stretch run of last race.
5)   Is dropping more than six pounds off the last race.

b.   DISQUALIFY fillies or mares running against males, or maidens against winners, even when running in the same class.

Exceptions:
1)   Horse is running again within ten days *and* finished in-the-money in two of the last three races.

H.   Claimed.   DISQUALIFY any horse who was claimed in his last race and is generally moving up in class.

Exceptions: 1)   Same as 1 in "G" above.

After you have selected F2 through F4, look at F1 if his odds are 4-1 or higher and include him if he looks outstanding. Also, look at F5, and check him against the following criteria:

1) Is racing again within fourteen days or had a work within two or three days.
2) Is definitely dropping in class.
3) Gained two or more lengths in the stretch run of his last race.
4) Finished his last race five or more places lower than the number of runners in that race.
5) Is dropping six or more pounds off the last race, or is getting in today at 112 or less.
6) Has been in-the-money in two or three of the last five races.

If the F5 horse meets several of these qualifications, add him to your list or use him in place of one of the ho-hum qualifiers between F2 and F4. It is often valuable to compare F5 with F4 and then compare the better choice with F3 and take the better of either of those two comparisons. If *both* horses competing against one another in your analysis look impressive, include them both.

When Sam reviewed his rules for qualifying F2 thru F4, he discovered that they were really quite simple. If a horse qualified, it was generally apparent at a glance or two. If he did *not* qualify, that, too, was apparent. Admittedly there were borderline cases when a bit of study was necessary to say Yes or No Sam regarded his system basically as a simple system, not an easy one He had to wrinkle his brow now and then to come up with the right answer.

Throwing out F1 was always something of a risk. Everybody used the favorite in his combinations, in Daily Doubles, in Perfecta races, and there was the trouble. The payoff when it came was abominably low. So don't worry about the favorite—*unless* his odds are about 4-1. Then take a second look at him.

But now Sam was committed to playing only three horses with his double qualifiers, the combinations were:

First Race		Second Race
Q1	with	#2, #3, #4*
Q2	with	#2, #3, #4
F2, F3, F4	with	Q1 Po*
F2, F3, F4	with	Q2 Po

*Derived from the probable-odds list, after eliminating non-qualifiers.

These combinations required twelve tickets, for an invest-ment of $24. By adding Q1 and Q2 in the first race with Q1Po and Q2Po in the second race, he needed four additional tickets, for a total investment in the daily double of $32. Many a race goer wheels one horse with all other horses in the opposite race, in the Daily-Double play, for an investment of $24 when there are twelve horses in the field. Sam never did this since he knew in advance that two or three horses in each of the first two races could easily be eliminated by a process of logic and the applica-tion of intelligence to their past performance charts.

But there was another angle which he did consider and fre-quently used. In his research on the second race, you will recall that he used the morning-line or probable-odds chart to get his Q1 and Q2 qualifiers. He found that these morning-line charts were useful also in the double. (Incidentally, before leaving those Q1Po and Q2Po selections, he used them not only in the double combinations but in his selections for the actual second race. For some reason, they were often more successful than using the real odds on the tote board in the second race.) In his double selections, he found that the morning-line odds selections in the first two races often produced a winning combination if you car-ried out the following process:

Line up the horses in morning-line-odds order, the lowest odds at the top of the chart. (You have to do this for the second race anyway, so do it for the first race, too.) Then take those horses who fall in the second, third, and fourth positions from the top down the chart in the first race, align them with the second, third and fourth horses in the second race chart, from top down. That is, combine number-two choice in the first race with number-two, number-three, and number-four in the second race, for three tickets. When you complete this process, you have nine additional tickets, for another $18 investment. An example follows:

PIMLICO RACE COURSE, Graded by Handicap
1st Race: 1 1-16 Miles

Post Psn.	Horse	Prob. Jockey	Wt	Prob. Odds
7	Quillo G	J. Canessa	120	3-1
8	Bold King	G. Cusimano	120	5-1
10	Flaming Ace	A. Garramone	120	6-1
3	Artist's Pride	R. Howard	120	6-1
5	Brandy Bout	G. McCarron	120	6-1

2nd Race: 6 Furlongs

3	Frosty Roman	R. L. Turcotte	114	3-1
5	Valiant Nurse	H. Hinojosa	112	5-1
1	First Rabbit	T. Lee	114	6-1
6	Pau Hana	C. Jimenez	114	8-1
16	Hundred Honors	N. Shuk	113	8-1

This arrangement is not in the order listed by Handicap but in order of the probable odds given by the morning-line. Your selections for the double would then be:

Bold King combined with Valiant Nurse, First Rabbit, and Pau Hana. Flaming Ace combined with the same three in the second race. Artist's Pride combined with the same three.

And the winning combination is:

Bold King and Pau Hana paid $157.40.

While five horses are listed from each race, only three are used. The low-odds horse is eliminated automatically, but why list the fifth horse? The answer is that two horses are often at the same odds, which indicates that either of them could be the Number-four selection. Take the second race for instance: both Pau Hana and Hundred Honors are listed at 8-1; the handicapper regarded both of them as equal possibilities. But we have to make a selection between them. We apply the broadest criteria. First, which of the two is the better class?

A: Both Pau Hana and Hundred Honors are moving up in class.

NEXT QUESTION: Which horse has the most recent race or workout?

A: Pau Hana raced on April 25; Hundred Honors on April 20.

Q: Which horse is a filly and which a male?
A: Both are fillies.
Q: Which horse has more than a one-pound weight advantage?
A: Pau Hana is racing at 114; Hundred Honors at 113. No real difference.
Q: Which horse has more firsts and seconds in his or her past performance?
A: Pau Hana has two to Hundred Honors' one.
Q: Which horse won the last race?
A: Both did.

It's a close contest, but Pau Hana gets the nod for the most recent race *and* for the greater number of firsts and seconds in the past performance charts.

Perhaps it should be pointed out that all these horses must qualify under the rules for selecting F2 through F4, as given on page 34. What we are doing here is breaking a tie between two horses, both of whom would qualify for F2 through F4 status. But look at a somewhat more dramatic example, which occurred at Pimlico, this time on May 12, 1972.

In the 1st Race, Number-four and Number-five appeared thus.

| 10 | Croodle | A. Garramone | 120 | 8-1 |
| 12 | Fast Man | H. Hinojosa | 120 | 8-1 |

Since both Croodle and Fast Man are listed at 8-1, we have to decide between them. Croodle is dropping $1,000 in class. Fast Man is dropping $2,000. Both are colts carrying 120 pounds. Croodle has raced more recently, which about balances the class drop difference. Croodle has a third, but was eight lengths off the winner. Fast Man finished ninth in his last race but was only five and one-quarter lengths off the winner. It's still nip and tuck between them. Look again. In his last race Fast Man *gained* four lengths in the stretch run. Croodle *lost* four lengths in his stretch run. This tips the scales in favor of Fast Man, and we take him over Croodle in the first race.

In the second race:

| 3 | Elegant Ed | R. Fitzgerald | 119 | 6-1 |
| 7 | Tudor King | J. Kurtz | 114 | 6-1 |

Both horses meet the basic F2-F4 rules for qualification. Note that Elegant Ed was claimed last race and is moving up in class, which means that he must be racing again within fourteen days. He won his last race and has a rating of less than fifteen. He fails on the score that he is carrying *more* than 118 pounds this race, but we overlook that momentarily to compare him with Tudor King, who is dropping $1,000 in class and is carrying five pounds *less* than Elegant Ed. Therefore, we have to disqualify Elegant Ed and select Tudor King as Number-four in our line-up.

The results? In the first race, Hinojosa pulled a Bill Daley. Fast Man was out of the gate first and was never headed on his way to the wire. Finishing three lengths in front of Ski Slope, he paid $19 to win. Croodle went off at 11-1 and paid $9.60 to show.

In the second race, Tudor King was 8-1. He was off rather badly, and at the half pole he was running eighth in a field of twelve. He improved rapidly, however, and at the head of the stretch he was fifth. The stretch run was what horse racing is all about: it was neck-and-neck to the wire with the favorite, Frosty Roman, for a photo finish. The picture showed Tudor King the winner by a neck, and he paid a nice $18.40. But everybody was waiting for that double payoff, and that, too, was nice: $268 for the 12-7 combination of Fast Man and Tudor King.

On Saturday, May 13, the first race had a fine group of thoroughbreds, with Row Boat as the probable favorite at 3-1. Mincing Lane and Bull of the Woods were both 6-1, and there were two at 8-1: Longpasdu and Smooth Stone. At 10-1 was Enforcer. For F4 we looked at Smooth Stone, rejecting the gelding and staying with Longpasdu, even though he was carrying 119 pounds. In the race, Longpasdu came in second.

But out of curiosity we looked also at the next horse in line, the 10-1 Enforcer and noticed one thing: the horse had raced seven days ago, on May 6, and had a good workout at Laurel on Thursday, May 11, *two days ago*. A horse who has raced in the past week and has a workout within a couple of days is some sort of ready horse. He was dropping three pounds from his last race and was getting in at 116, which was three pounds better than Longpasdu.

You have guessed it, of course. Enforcer won the race with

ease and teamed up with the number-four horse in the second race (who had also worked out on Thursday, an animal named Kith) for a double payoff of $171.80. But you can't win them all. Just for the record, it is wise always to go one more step, to look at the next horse in line (even though your list is full) and see whether or not you find an outstanding thoroughbred with a race in a week or so and a workout in two or three days. If you do, and the animal is also dropping weight for this race, or dropping in class, or has a 1-2-2-1 record that looks like a computer tape, with probable odds of 6-1 to 10-1, then don't hesitate. Substitute this animal for one of the other ho-hum qualifiers in your series, and just wait to cash a ticket. The track handicapper was asleep when he should have been awake. But you have to be alert and awake all the time.

Sam discovered that *if* the first horse listed was at 3-1, it was wise to include that horse in the group to be played. Thus, you will notice in the charts an entry such as this: First race, #1 3-1 (Boyd County) with #2 (Good Lad) $70.20

This shows the results of the daily double at Gulfstream Park on April 20, 1973. In order to limit the number of tickets to nine, you may select numbers one, two, and three in one race and combine with numbers two, three, and four in the second race. Or you may simply add the number one to the series, and by so doing you will add three more tickets to the double requirement, which now stands at twenty-five tickets, for a $50 daily invest-ment. By adding the number-one selection, you increase your daily investment by $6. But, of course, this will not occur every day. Most frequently the number-one selection is at 5-2 or lower.

Another point: if the first or second race involves maidens or fillies or fillies and mares (or a combination, such as in the first race at Gulfstream Park on April 13, 1973, an event for maiden fillies), you may wish to include F5 in your calculations. On that day, April 13, which was also a Friday, the double was won by F5 (Ride the High Wind) and Q1Po (Andalian) for a payoff of $604.60. Ordinarily, your double combinations include F2, F3 and F4 with Q1Po and Q2Po (or also Q3Po if a maiden race). In the final analysis, this is a matter of judgment.

PERFECTAS AND EXACTAS

It is now a relatively simple matter to get the proper combinations for races known as Perfectas or Exactas. In such races it is necessary to pick the winner *and* the place horse in the precise order of finish. Let us say you select the number-four horse and the number-two horse. A 4-2 ticket costs you $2, and you are betting that they finish in that order. If you wish to bet the reverse combination, number-two and number-four, it is necessary naturally to buy another $2 ticket with the numbers two and four on it in that order. If you wish to select three horses so that if they finish one-two in any combination, it requires six tickets for a complete crisscross of possibilities. Four horses require twelve tickets (four times three), and so on up the line to ten horses in a field of ten. To cover all the combinations possible, and to have a lock on the Perfecta outcome, you would have to buy ninety tickets for a total of $180. This isn't often done, of course, since the Perfecta doesn't pay that much that often.

Sam first found his Q1 and Q2 horses. If it were a maiden race, or a race involving fillies only, or fillies and mares together, he would frequently go for Q3. Then he would determine the other three horses needed to fill out his box or combination-group: F2, F3, and F4. Throwing out F1 for the moment, he looked at the charts on the next few favorites, disqualifying those that did not live up to the rules, and adding the others to his list. He came up with five horses (Q1, Q2, F2, F3, and F4) which he bet as a unit. That is, each of the five was paired with the other four in a 1-2 combination and, in reverse, in such a manner that if any one of the five won and any one of the remaining four came second, he had a winning combination. Twenty tickets were needed to get this full crisscross, at a cost of $40 in the East and Midwest and $100 in California.

Further, Sam found that the favorite (F1) was occasionally involved in the Perfecta combination, either as the winner or as the second horse. So, to catch the bigger payoffs, Sam bought two more tickets: Q1 and F1 and F1 with Q1; then two more with Q2 and F1. This insurance investment added $8 to the cost of the Perfecta tickets.

One more point: in some Perfecta races, there was only one high-odds qualifier: Q1. In his search for qualifiers, Sam always went down to a certain odds-level, then quit. In a field of twelve horses, he would generally stop at 12-1. In a field of eleven, he would stop at 11-1, and so on down the line to 6-1 in a field of six horses. For example, let us assume he was working with a field of twelve horses and he found his Q1 at odds of 40-1 but he could not get a Q2 unless he went down to 10-1. This he did not do unless the 10-1 horse was truly outstanding. In that particular race he stopped with Q1. If it were a Perfecta race, however, he would still need five horses for his "box," and he extended the F2-F4 series to include F5. He then had: Q1, F2, F3, F4, and F5 in his crisscross. Of course, F5 had to qualify under the rules for F2 through F4. Finally, he would combine his Q1 with F1, for two more tickets, for a total of twenty-two tickets, or an investment of $44. In California, be prepared for heavy investments! But if you're investing track money, don't worry. You'll come out in the end.

But it's time to summarize the wagers to be made in Perfecta or Exacta races.

After Q1 and Q2 have been determined, you need to select your F2, F3, and F4 horses to go into the "box" with Q1 and Q2. You do this, of course, using the rules outlined on page 34. But one word of caution: in dealing with maiden races and races involving fillies or fillies and mares, you should not be too strict in your application of the rules of elimination. In short, you liberalize your rules. These horses are so undependable that almost anything can happen. As an example, let's take a look at the past performance of Miss C.P.O. in the fourth race at Gulfstream Park on April 18, 1973.

Miss C. P. O.   **115**   Ch. f (1970), by Jim J.—Forgiveness, by Gun Shot.
Breeder, J.G. Lockwood (Ky.).   1973 3 M 0 0   (—)

Owner, Mrs. D. Dodson and S. Polikoff. Trainer, D.Dodson. $7,500

Mar23-73⁴GP	6 f 1:11 ft 48 119	8⁷¾ 7¹² 8¹² 7¹² Br'mf'dD¹⁰	Mdn 77	⑤Laraka119	BeachPicnic	PolarCap 11
Feb12-73¹Hia	6 f 1:11¹/₅ft 11 121	6⁵¾ 7⁸ 9¹⁵ 12¹⁶M'cB'hD¹²	Mdn 72	⑥Princ'sD're121	Gl'm'r'sM's	Bl'kT'lip 12
Jan18-73⁴Hia	7 f 1:24⁴/₅sy 16 121	4⁹½ 5¹⁵ 9²¹ 9¹⁸ Br'mf'dD¹⁰	Mdn 65	⑥R'y'IS'pic'n121	G'meH'me	S'syCy'ne 11

April 16 GP 4f ft :49¹/₅sb   March GP 6f ft 1:14¹/₅sh   March 19 GP 6f ft 1:18b

Miss C.P.O. is the third favorite in the race. She worked out two days ago and looks fit and ready for today's race. She's dropping four pounds for this race, which is a Maiden Claiming race with a field of twelve. She finished seventh in a field of twelve in her last race less than a month ago. In her last three races this year (the total of her racing experience) she has never been in-the-money once and for that reason she might be disqualified. But this is a maiden race and Miss C.P.O. is a filly, and we will have to allow her some leeway. We let her stay in as F3 for that workout two days ago and for that drop of four pounds from her last race, in which she finished four places lower than the number of horses in the race, that is, seventh in a field of eleven.

Having selected Q1 and Q2, followed by the selection of F2, F3, and F4, we have five horses and we bet them as a unit, which requires the purchase of the equivalent of twenty tickets. If the race is a maiden race or one involving fillies or fillies and mares, we add the Q3, for a total of six horses, and that requires an outlay of $60 for thirty tickets. When Sam could drop one of the three, he did so, however.[2]

But Sam was not quite through with the Perfecta picture. He had discovered that F4, F5, and F6 are occasionally involved in these races, and that when this happens, the payoffs are usually large. Even if one horse has already been thrown out (disqualified under the rules for F2 through F4), we still have to be concerned with F4, F5, and F6, which is reaching up into that middle ground just below the high-odds qualifiers and just above the first three favorites. The returns showed Sam that he had to cover this area with the purchase of six more tickets: F4, F5, and F6 as a box or unit, crisscrossing them for every one-two possibility. Six more tickets adds $12 to the Perfecta race investment, making a total now of $52 per race for twenty-six tickets. Make that $130 in California, and be sure you've got it covered before you get to the track. If there are three Perfecta races on a card for one day, that's about $390 you'll need on the West Coast. Or else, you can skip the Perfecta races altogether. But that might not be wise, in view of the high rate of return, as shown in the charts in Chapter 5.

And by the way, don't forget what Sam says about F1, the favorite who is now and then involved in these Perfecta races, either as the winner or as the place horse. We don't put F1 in

---

2. For example, when one of the three had a five-race rating 50 percent lower than one of the other two.

the "box" with all the others involved. But we do buy two tickets on F1 and Q1 (F1 with Q1 and Q1 with F1) and two more tickets with F1 and Q2, for a total of four additional tickets, costing us $8 more. And now we are up to $60 on a regular Perfecta race. If you have a maiden or filly/mare race on your hands, you must also consider Q3, which runs your investment up to $84, and that is becoming dangerously high. You are going to have to average better than $84 return on every Perfecta race where maidens and fillies and mares are concerned. (If at all possible, select the two best out of three.)

In our study of the results of several seasons of racing at different tracks (given in Chapter 5), we will break out the races where F1 is concerned and determine whether or not such an investment is profitable. We will do the same for the F4, F5, and F6 winning races, to see how profitable that investment is. Of course, it's going to vary from track to track and from season to season. All we can do here is to cover as many representative tracks as possible in the limited space we have. As in all statistical studies, the value of the results lie in the fact that they are representative. We can only hope that the factors which these results show are universal factors and hold true for the future as well as the past.

Here is a summary of the Daily Double ticket selections:

SUMMARY

First Race		Second Race	Remarks
Q1	with	#2, #3, #4	If #1 has odds of 3-1, include in list. Add #5 also, if the 2nd race is for fillies, maids, etc.
Q2	with	#2, #3, #4	Same as above.
F2, F3, F4	with	Q2Po	Also use F5 if the 1st race is for fillies, maids, etc.
F2, F3, F4	with	Q1Po	Same as above.
Q1 and Q2	with	Q1Po and Q2Po	Optional. This combination occurs quite rarely. When it does occur, it is a big one.
#2, #3, #4 Po	with	#2, #3, #4 Po	Another refinement of Sam's. Accept #1 if odds given are 3-1.

NOTE: There is one last refinement which may prove helpful, although its use is not really necessary. Sam looks at the list for the first race of morning-line odds. He checks #2, #3, and #4 in succession, moving upward in odds from a base of 3-1. If one of these three horses is *not* one of the first four favorites in the first race, Sam checks his past performance against the rules for selecting F2-F4. If this horse passes the test, although he is *not* in the actual F2 thru F4 group, Sam adds him to his double combinations; or, he uses this horse to replace one of the F2-F4 group, the one whose past performance looks weakest. He tries to eliminate, for example, a horse moving up in class, unless that horse shows great strength in other categories. He prefers horses with a recent race or a recent workout to those who have laid off for a spell. He prefers horses carrying 114 pounds or less. And so forth.

No doubt, the average race goer is not prepared for this scale of investments, but Sam was no average race goer. If his records were correct (and he kept very accurate records), an investment on Perfectas or Exactas, following all Sam's requirements, brought back a minimum return of about two dollars for every one dollar put in. At some tracks during certain meets, he would find a return of three to one and occasionally, four to one. Where else in the country could he get a return on investment that equaled this? Sam Hirsch could give you the figures on interest-return on your dollars when invested in Mexico City or Copenhagen, not to mention New York City and Los Angeles. Common stocks and no-load mutual funds were as familiar to him as caterpillars on a mulberry tree.

Nowhere in America or abroad could you get an investment return like the one he could get at the track. But it all took time. It took work. And it took capital. It also took a degree of personal and professional discipline. The old TWCD rule again. Time, Work, Capital, Discipline. Any good business required those things. Racing, too, was a big and complicated business. It was impossible to make a fortune gambling, but it was possible to make a fortune in business. Always, Sam Hirsch was in *business:* the business of handicapping a race, but not really handicapping in the conventional sense of the word. He was primarily eliminating the losers at the start, and then depending upon statistical averages to bring a reasonable number of long-shot plays into the winner's circle, or in-the-money.

Before you start a new investment career, it would be well to gather a little more information and some experience. The remainder of this book is devoted to giving you considerable information, some experience in doing your own "eliminating" and "selecting qualifiers," as well as to presenting data on past results. The purpose of these charts and summaries of results is simply to convince you of the efficacy of the system. Even if you accept in your mind the possiblity that you can make a million at the races, there is still a big hurdle: your natural feeling that this simply cannot be done.

Your emotions rule most of the decisions in your life, and these decisions come almost automatically, as though you yourself have no real control over them. They seem to be predetermined by your personality, your character, your private and innermost convictions. Most people have the conviction (rightly or wrongly) that there is something shady, sinister or evil about horse racing. It's a sport, yes. And it's a business, yes. But it is surrounded by an aura of fakery and falsehood. It's somehow *tainted,* and no amount of convincing will take away the stigma of gambling. For gambling is immoral, no matter how you cut it. Perhaps it is not illegal or unethical, but it surely is immoral. And that sticks in your craw.

As commonly understood, gambling means playing with and *losing* money you cannot afford to lose. Gambling goes on and on and on until it becomes an obsession. The gambler cannot stop gambling, until his clothes become rags and his face is unshaven and lined, and his eyes are like the eyes of an addict. There are clubs called Gamblers Anonymous, whose purpose is to try to rescue the addict from his addiction. Not a pretty picture, and it feeds the imagination. Gambling is the devil's tool, and by means of it he gets hold of you and drags you down to the very circles of hell.

If no amount of argument or convincing can rid you of this idea, then forget the whole thing. You are not a good candidate for Sam Hirsch's investment school. Sam himself does not gamble. He's much too shrewd a man for that. On the other hand, Sam would not throw out horse racing (or any other kind of racing) as a potential field of endeavor. Six billion dollars going through the mutuel machines every year means to Sam that the possibilities of investment and profit are practically unlimited.

Investment is the key word. Before you start, you will need some capital—much less than most small businesses require.

You will need enough to survive for one week, or six racing days, without counting on a single hit. Five-hundred dollars a day. Three-thousand dollars a week. But just for one week. In that short time, the system will prove itself.

There is risk in all of life. There is great risk in everyday business. Sam's aim is to reduce to an absolute *minimum* the risk in horse racing. Since there's no way to build a successful money-making system on short-priced favorites, Sam goes to the TOP of the odds board and tries to catch the high-odds winners. He knows in advance that 17% of all races are won by longshots. A longshot will win three races out of 20 and will place in six races out of 20 and will show in nine out of 20. Those are the hard and unbending facts. Twenty races would be two days' Programs at Hialeah or Gulfstream Park. Assuming that there are nine or more starters in all 20 races and that the favorites go off at higher than even-money, we bet all 20. There will be in each race an average of five longshots, or 100 in all. Sam looks for three wins, six places and nine shows out of those 100 horses. He invests in at least two, sometimes three horses in each race, covering about 50 of the longshots. By pure chance, he will catch his winners 50% of the time. Not good enough. He eliminates one, two, or three losing longshots in each race by requiring the horses to meet certain criteria. Most of the *dogs* are pretty obvious and go out quickly. Sam's chances of winning have risen to 80% or to 90% if he invests consistently in all 20 races. With high odds, the payoffs are good enough to overcome that inevitable 10% to 20% loss. If you are a serious investor, you can see the merits of Sam's approach. If you are a poor student, seeking funds for furthering your education, stay strictly away. That 20% will destroy you. In any event, before you invest, *know* exactly *what* you are doing!

3

Gamblers Move In

The year 1919 was indeed memorable. It was the year Sam
Hirsch was born. It was the year Babe Ruth, with the Red Sox
in Cincinnati, hit twenty-nine runs. The Cincinnati Reds, who
had never before won a pennant, led the National League and
went to the World Series against the Chicago White Sox. Under
the new rules, a club needed five games out of nine to win the
Series. It was also the year the Gamblers decided to move in.
Rumor has it that Arnold Rothstein was behind the move. The
same Arnold Rothstein who, two years later on Independence
Day, 1921, at Aqueduct, managed to pull off racing's biggest
coup, according to Tom Flanagan.[1] One of Arnold's two-year-
olds named Sidereal, who had shown nothing in three earlier
starts, came home in the third race against thirteen colts. Arnold hit the bookmakers for three-quarters of a million dollars.
Arnold's accomplishment proves that you *can* make a million at
the races. Remember, though, that this occurred before the in-
troduction of the parimutuel system.

---

1. Tom Flanagan, *Beat the Races* (New York: Arco, 1973).

Back in 1919, the year the Black Sox sold out, baseball players were bound by the reserve rule. The average wage was pitiful indeed. Money flowed like champagne in 1919, but there was only a trickle for the men who swung the bat. Some of them were sorely tempted, and some gave in. They were dazzled by the prospect of sudden wealth. (In 1919 a star player pulled down $7,000 or maybe $8,000 in a year.) Only 140 games had been played in the season just passed. A few of the players, we don't know how many, had been approached by the big money boys— the Gamblers, like Arnold Rothstein. (You will note as time progresses that the Gamblers are not really gamblers. They are proponents of the Sure Thing. They want a "lock" on the outcome. That's why they fixed the Series in 1919. But don't forget that it always takes two to tango. The insiders dance the jig, but the outsiders call the tune.)[2]

From the beginning of the Series, which opened in Cincinnati, there was an aura of suspicion over the games. The Cincinnati Reds were made the favorites by the Gamblers—the favorites over the best team in baseball, the Chicago White Sox. The park was jammed on that first afternoon. The Reds proceeded to knock out Chicago's Eddie Cicotte, a twenty-nine-game winner. By the fourth inning the slugging White Sox had collected exactly six hits, while the Reds had fourteen, and seven of these had been off Cicotte. Clearly, the Gamblers had Cicotte in their hip pocket.

Cincinnati took the first game 9 to 1. They took the second game 4 to 2. They did it in Cincinnati on the first and the second of October, 1919. Whiskey Face Moran insisted that the Reds won the two games on their merits. Dutch Ruether was no slouch as a pitcher, and he took the first game like a veteran. Slim Sallee allowed ten hits in the second game, but he won it fair and square, said Whiskey Face. In that second game, the White Sox put in Lefty Williams, and he gave up exactly four hits. Of course he walked six, but that could happen in any game. (The fans said Lefty got $10,000 for the game.) Chick Gandil stole one base. To a lot of people it *looked* as though the Sox were out to win. Later, after the investigation, Chick was suspended.

---

2.   Robert Smith, *World Series* (New York: Doubleday, 1967).

Chicago took the third game three to nothing. Dickie Kerr pitched for the Whites and shut out Cincinnati. A perfect game for Chicago. Scandal had never touched Dickie Kerr. Dickie went out to win, and win he did. An admirable feat. Fans and players alike gave him credit.

Game number four went to Cincinnati. A clean game, said Whiskey Face. Eddie Cicotte pitched the game and allowed only five hits. Chicago got three hits, each of them by a "suspect". Was it a put-up game? It was hard to tell. Cicotte didn't yield a base on balls.

Cincinnati pitched Hod Eller in the fifth game. Hod had won nineteen games during the regular season. He held the White Sox to three hits, and it was Buck Weaver, a "suspect", who got two of the three. Chicago's pitcher was Lefty Williams (was it Lefty who engineered the Fix?), and he gave up four hits in game number five, when Cincinnati shut out the White Sox. Lefty worked hard in the fifth game. Lefty looked good. It was Weaver on third who made a couple of costly errors, and Felsch in center field.

Dickie Kerr was back in the sixth game, and Chicago took it 5 to 4. But it was a close one. Felsch and Risberg made errors you wouldn't believe. Dickie prevailed. At the plate, Weaver and Jackson and Felsch all did well. Weaver got two doubles and a single.

In the seventh game, Cincinnati fumbled the ball. Four errors to one for the White Sox. Chicago picked up four runs in the first five innings, and Cincinnati never got close. Four errors and one run for the Reds. Four runs and one error for the White Sox. After seven games, the Series stood at four to three. Cincinnati needed five out of nine to take it all.

In the final game, played at Cincinnati, they clobbered the White Sox 10 to 5. Was it a fix? Or were the White Sox out-played and demoralized?

The investigation that followed was smelly. Chick Gandil never even showed up to play in the spring. But the other seven "suspects" showed up and played a fine season before they were tried and found guilty by the new high commissioner, Kenesaw Mountain Landis. Eight Black Sox were suspended for life.

In any business or sport, where the money is big, it sometimes happens. In any barrel of a thousand apples, five or six or eight may be bad. But don't let that blind you to the fact that the other 992 are good.

IN THE TRACES

They say that Gamblers love harness racing, and they said it in a particularly loud voice at Roosevelt Raceway in 1973.

Each race is a puzzle just as it is, but if you add any one of a dozen variations, you get a very complicated puzzle indeed. In the Daily Double, as you know, it is necessary to pick the winners of two consecutive races and combine them on one ticket before the first of the two races is run. In the Perfecta, you must pick the first two horses as they come in, first and second, in that order, and combine them in a single ticket before the race goes off. In Doubles and Perfectas, the payoffs can be tremendous when two long shots are in the combination.

But there is something called the Trifecta, where you must pick number one, number two, *and* number three, in the correct order as they cross the finish line. In a field of ten horses, if you wish to pick the first and second horses only, in correct order of finish, there are ten times nine (or ninety) possible combinations. To pick the third horse also, multiply ninety by eight, and you have 720 possibilities. The payoffs on winning tickets (which are always few) is always high.

Now suppose you try to pick the first four horses that cross the line, in correct order of finish. The possible combinations reach 5,040 in a ten-horse field. But we are speaking of harness racing, and there are generally a maximum of eight horses in the field. Very well. In an eight-horse field, what are the possible combinations for the Perfecta or Exacta? Simple: there are seven times eight or fifty-six possibilities. For a Trifecta, there are fifty-six times six or 336 possible combinations. To pick four out of the eight in that order, one-two-three-four, we need 336 times five or 1,680 combinations.

Let us say that you must pick the winner and the second or place horse in both of two races. For example, you pick number-one and number-two horse in race eight and number-one and number-two horse in race nine, and you have a total of sixteen horses (eight in each field) to choose from. Further, you must do this *before* the beginning of the eighth race and have the numbers on one ticket—two horses picked in the right order in each of the two races. You have fifty-six possible combinations in the eighth race and fifty-six possible combinations in the ninth race. And now you must get the two together on one ticket. Obviously, the payoffs on this sort of selection-combination are astronomical.

Suppose, however, that you know in advance that four of the horses in a particular race are really not in contention. They are being deliberately held back, so that only four horses in the race are candidates for the first and second finish positions. The odds drop spectacularly. That is, the odds *against* picking the right combination. If you try to pick the four horses in *one* race that will cross the line in the correct order, one-two-three-four, and you only have four contenders, then your combinations are four times three times two times one, or 24. This is down considerably from the 1680 combinations in a field of eight. If you are dealing with the first two positions of finish in two races, then of course the combination possibilities in each race are twelve. To get the Double Perfecta, you must have the correct order of finish of the first two horses in each of two races, all the correct numbers on one ticket before the first of the two races is run. With eight horses in each race, the number of possible combinations is twelve times twelve or 144—*provided* only four of the eight horses in each race are in contention, the other four having been paid off.

At Roosevelt Raceway in 1973, it was the Superfecta which the big money boys went after. This is the race where you must pick the first four finishers in the correct order of finish. When all eight horses are in contention, the number of possible combinations is 1680. But when four horses are being held back and only four are really in contention, the number of possible combinations becomes twenty-four. Given horses A, B, C, and D, there are exactly six combinations with A as the winner or first horse: ABCD, ABDC, ACDB, ACBD, ADBC, and ADCB. Of course, there are also six combinations with B as the winner, and so forth, until you end up with twenty-four. Buy twenty-four tickets on the Superfecta race, and you have a lock on the results *if* only four horses are in contention.

The big money boys were not gamblers, you see. They wanted a sure thing, and for awhile they got it. They bought heavily and on each Superfecta race they made a bundle. But they hadn't counted on the computer. A routine check revealed that only a few people were collecting heavily on each Superfecta race. This was more than coincidence. An investigation followed, and in New York the Superfecta has been suspended for the time being. Thirteen harness drivers and at least eight "gamblers" have gone to trial. Greed undid the greedy.

SCANDAL ABROAD

The Grand National, run each year at Aintree, England, is the greatest and most prestigious race in the world. It's a race for lords and ladies, but most important, it's Everyman's race. It is a stupendous spectacle watched by millions, for there is nothing more English than the Grand National. Organized in 1837, the race has had a tumultous history. It is, of course, a steeplechase over a four-mile run, across thirty of the stiffest fences in the world. Aintree is near Liverpool, in what Vian Smith calls "Sefton country," since the earls of Sefton were the original landlords. "The grass is long and pale. It weeps down the embankments, mourning the mugs who will lose today."[1]

The Grand National has always been associated with disasters of one sort of another. And the breath of scandal could not be kept away. In 1849, at the thirteenth running of the Grand National, there were twenty-three entries. T. Cunningham, at eleven stone, was riding Peter Simple, the horse destined to win the race.

The obstacles were not the clean fences known today but low banks of dark earth, apparently insignificant. Horses fell at these low banks because they were really not severe enough to challenge their jumper's instincts. The race began badly. The signal from Lord Sefton was misunderstood, and half a dozen of the horses were left at the starting line. The front-runners set a fast

---

1. Vian Smith, *The Grand National* (Cranburg, N. J., A. S. Barnes, 1970).

pace. Accidents came quickly, one upon another. Kilfane went down and was killed. Curate, who had run second in 1848, stumbled and broke his back. Equinox also went down with a broken back. The crowd looked with horror on the field which was littered with the dying and the dead.

Peter Simple moved free of the debacle and went past The Knight of Gwynne and Prince George. It was obvious to all that Cunningham had the winner and would take it all. And then it happened, as the story is told. A rider on another horse shouted to Cunningham and made him an offer: one thousand pounds to pull the horse, Peter Simple. But Cunningham was drawing away.

"Two thousand pounds!" said the voice. "Three thousand pounds!"

Cunningham heard, but the shout became fainter as he drove for the finish line.

"Four thousand pounds!"

But Cunningham was deaf to the offer, "and rode his horse into history."

A TOUCH OF SCANDAL

While modern thoroughbred racing has generally been honest and above board, there has always been, and probably always will be, a touch of scandal. Those Perfecta payoffs are too juicy to resist, and now and again some group gets together and pulls a coup. It happened not too long ago, in March, 1974, at Narragansett Park, Rhode Island. In the seventh race on March 15, C. Hubberman Jr. rode a horse called Yarak, who went off at the respectable odds of 9 1. At the wire, Yarak came in ahead of Royal Buff, whose odds were 7-2 and whose jockey was C. Gambardella. The favorite, at 13-to-10, ridden by N. Mercier, was dead last.

Now there is nothing really unusual about this order of finish. Nine-to-one horses often nose out 7-2 animals, while the favorite finishes up the track. But look again at the odds. The winner was 9-1. The place horse was 7-2. It was a Perfecta race, and ordinarily a Perfecta payoff at such odds would be better than $100. In this seventh race, the Perfecta pool was unusually high, however, running to $41,000. It was, in fact, the highest or largest pool of the night, for these were evening races under the lights.

The Perfecta payoff was $33.20.

Clearly, there was something rotten in Rhode Island. The investigation that followed lasted more than a month. It was obvious that the race had been set up, for a remarkable number of tickets had been purchased on the correct combination. Was it all done legally? Were the jockeys in on the deal? The answers to these questions may never be known, but one thing was certain: the payoff on the Perfecta was only a third of what it should have been. The Perfecta pool was higher than normal. Per-capita wagering that night at Narragansett was an astonishing $124, which comes close to the per-capita wagering of such tracks as Aqueduct or Hollywood Park. By comparison, the per-capita wagering at Boston's Suffolk Downs on that same night, March 15, 1974, was $87.

So the money boys were working on the night of March 15 at Narragansett. The uproar that followed could be heard all the way to Florida and California. The most serious repercussions were in Rhode Island itself, where Senator Ambrose Campbell (Democrat) submitted a bill to the Rhode Island legislature aimed at banning all multiple betting, including the Daily Double. The senator is quoted as saying: "Something has to be done to protect the integrity of racing.

"It is an important source of revenue for Rhode Island, about $9 million annually in taxes alone, not to mention all the people it employs. If racing isn't cleaned up, then we are going to wake up one day to find someone filing a bill to abolish racing altogether."

Senator Campbell is himself one of the best known horsemen in the state of Rhode Island. He has owned horses for more than forty years and had seven thoroughbreds in his stable at the time of the scandal. The Senator put his finger, rightly or wrongly, on the jockey as the possible offender. Jockeys were conspiring to "fix" a race now and then, because they were able to do it most easily. But the jockeys were not in it alone. For any coup to succeed, the jockey must work with someone else, with the big money boys out front. At Narragansett they managed to pull one off, but they did it much too well: they put themselves out of business. Once again, greed was their undoing, and it certainly won't happen in a long, long time in Rhode Island. The state government is watching.

Irregular riding had been noted in other Perfecta-type races during 1974, especially in Florida. But when this is spotted, and inevitably it is, the stewards crack down. It happened, for example, at Gulfstream Park on January 24, 1974, in the fourth race, which was a Perfecta Race. It was a six-furlong dash for three-year-old maidens, and the chart showing the results of the race is given below:

FOURTH RACE
GP
January 24, 1974

6 FURLONGS (chute). (1:07⁴/s). MAIDENS. CLAIMING. Purse $5,000. 3-year-olds. Weight, 120 lbs. Claiming price, $30,000; if for $25,000, allowed 3 lbs. (Preference to horses that have not started for a claiming price of $10,000 or less.)
Value to winner $3,000; second, $1,000; third, $500; fourth, $350; fifth, $150.
Mutuel Pool, $72,991. Perfecta Pool, $73,127.

Last Raced		Horse	EqtAWt PP	St	¼	½	Str	Fin	Jockeys	Owners	Odds to $1
1-12-74³	Crc⁸	Royal Poet	3 120 3	4	1²	1²	1⁶	1¹⁴	DMacBeth	Mrs A Lowenthal	1.40
1- 5-74³	Crc⁹	Waist Band	b3 117 4	5	7¹½	7²	5²	2ʰ	GGallitano	G S Krauss	23.80
1-12-74³	Crc⁹	Speedy Smith	3 120 7	8	6²	5³	2¹	3ⁿᵒ	Flannelli	Heardsdale	6.20
1- 4-74²	Crc¹⁰	Tudor Duke	b3 120 6	1	4½	4²	4¹½	4¹²	WBlum	Mrs M Zimmerman	3.70
1-14-74²	Crc³	Rens Prince	3 117 1	6	3ʰ	2½	3ʰ	5ⁿᵏ	SMaple	I F Register	10.70
		Bold n Brash	3 120 5	3	5½	6²	6¹½	6²½	JCombest	R L T Stable	2.10
		Our Zelda	3 115		2²	3¹½	7²	7³½	CBtone	Dar D Otable	23.80
1-11-74⁵	Crc³	Wise Scot	3 120 8	2	8	8	8	8	DBrumfield	K Vangeloff	4.50

OFF AT 2:42½ EDT. Start good. Won easily. Time, :22⁵/s, :46²/s, 1:11¹/s. Track fast.

$2 Mutuel Prices:

4-ROYAL POET	4.80	4.00	3.00
5-WAIST BAND		12.60	6.80
8-SPEEDY SMITH			4.80

$2 PERFECTA (4-5) PAID $96.60.

Dk. b. or br. c, by Pretense—Double Laureate, by Double Jay. Trainer, J. Bowes Bond. Bred by E. V. Benjamin, Jr. and S. Rooth and G. Levy (Ky.).

ROYAL POET, sent to a clear lead at once, saved ground to draw off at will and won with something left. WAIST BAND passed only tired horses. SPEEDY SMITH, taken under snug restraint at once, was not persevered with through the drive. TUDOR DUKE failed to menace. OUR ZELDA was through early. WISE SCOT was without speed. BIG REACH UNSEATED HIS RIDER DURING THE POST PARADE, RAN OFF INTO THE STABLE AREA AND WAS EXCUSED BY THE STEWARDS. ALL WAGERS STRAIGHT, PLACE, SHOW AND IN THE PERFECTA POOLS, WERE ORDERED REFUNDED.

Claiming Prices (in order to finish)—$30000, 25000, 30000, 30000, 25000, 30000, 30000, 30000.
Scratched—The Fuzz, Hilo, Briar Jumper, Tudor Red, Wine Sack, Big Reach.

As you see, the race was won by the favorite, Royal Poet, whose odds were 1.40-1. A $2 bet on Royal Poet got you back $4.80. It was really no contest, since Royal Poet went wire to wire and finished fourteen lengths ahead of the second horse, Waist Band, whose odds, along with those of Our Zelda, were 23.80-1, the highest on the board. The third horse was Speedy Smith, at 6.20-1, and he was ridden by jockey Frank Iannelli. It was a photo for second, third, and fourth positions, as you will note from the chart. Waist Band came in just a head in front of Speedy Smith, who was a mere nose in front of Tudor Duke. But the judges placed Waist Band second, and the Perfecta payoff was a nice $96.60. The payoff does not look abnormal, and it isn't. But there were $73,000 in the Perfecta Pool, and there were a lot of unhappy people: those who had the favorite, Royal Poet, with either Tudor Duke or Speedy Smith, especially those who had him with Speedy Smith.

None of this is unusual until you read the account of the race and note that: "Speedy Smith, taken under snug restraint at once, was not persevered with through the drive." The stewards had noticed Frank Iannelli's ride on Speedy Smith, and after the race they promptly grounded him for thirty days. There was very little doubt that Speedy Smith should have finished second, and the entire Perfecta payoff would have been different, would have been considerably lower.

As it happened, Sam saw the race, and of course he had Waist Band with the favorite in his Perfecta combinations. Not that he was in on the fix. He knew nothing of it until the next day. He had picked Waist Band from his past performance chart and from the fact that he was nearly 24-1. See the charts below of Waist Band and Royal Poet.

Royal Poet   120   Dk. b. or br. c (1971), by Pretense—Double Laureate, by Double Jay.
Br., E.V. Benjamin, Jr., S. Rooth &   1974 1 M 0 0   (—)
G. Levy (Ky.).

Owner, Mrs. A. Lowenthal.   Trainer, J. Bowes Bond. $30,000
Jan12-74³Crc   6 f 1:14²/sft 3¼ 120   3½ 3² 5⁵ 8⁶½ HoleM⁶   Mdn 74 FarM'reN'ble120   St'ffsSt'ff   Advis'dly 10
Jan 20 GP 5f ft :59³/sh   Jan 11 GP 3f ft :37b   Jan 7 GP 6f ft 1:14⁴/sh

Waist Band   117   Dk. b. or br. g (1971), by Irish Ruler—Elinol's Randi, by Royal Serenade.
Breeder, Royal Way Farm (Fla.).   1974 1 M 0 0   (—)

Owner, G. S. Krauss.   Trainer, M. Moncrief. $25,000   1973 2 M 0 0 $126
Jan 5-74³Crc   6 f 1:13⁴/sft 12 116   3½ 2½ 9⁹³ 9¹¹ M'pleS⁹   M20000 73 GT'tExch'nge109   St'fsSt'fGr'tR's'n'g 9
Dec29-73²Crc   6 f 1:14 ft 62 116   2¹ 2¹ 2³ 5⁵½ M'pleS⁸   M20000 77 UngaUnga120   Gal'tExc'ge   Tom'sNoF'l 11
Oct15-73³Crc   6 f 1:14³/sft 22 118   4⁸½ 4⁸ 4⁷½ 6¹¹ RogersC⁸   c5000 69 Bluewood 111   Red Fur   Not My Bid 11
Jan 22 Crc 5f ft 1:02²/sh   Jan 16 Crc 5f ft 1:03b   Dec 28 Crc 3f ft :39bg

It is something of a mystery why Royal Poet became such a heavy favorite, if you look only at the colt's past performance, a single race on January 12. But we are concerned with Our Zelda and Waist Band, the two horses with odds of almost 24-1. Our Zelda is a first-time starter, with three workouts in January, and is an automatic bet. Sam listed Our Zelda as Q2 on his notebook and gave the Q1 position to Waist Band, who has a net of four points from his record of three races, two of which were run last year. Here's how Sam got the four points:

Two points for the gelding's workout on January 22, two days earlier. Since Waist Band is running in a maiden race, it is permissible to take either of the last two races to garner points. Sam took the better race on December 29, 1973, in which Waist Band finished fifth, just five and one-half lengths off the winner.

For finishing fifth, ONE POINT.

For a race-rating of eleven, ONE POINT.

Waist Band has never been in-the-money, but he does have a fifth finish which was less than six lengths off the winner, for one more point. See the rules under Category C. Total: five points.

Deduct one point for moving up $5,000 in class, and you have the net requirement of four points for three-year-old maidens.

In the Perfecta, Sam played both Waist Band and Our Zelda with the favorite, as two of his several combinations. In fact, when he saw Royal Poet sink to something close to even money, and on no apparent basis, he bought two tickets on the favorite and Waist Band and Our Zelda. Of course he was not in on the fix. But he had a feeling that something was "up" in this race. Sam plays the odds, and regardless of what happens, he catches the big payoffs. Speedy Smith could have finished last. Six-to-one horses often do. The point is that Sam picked Waist Band because Waist Band was a qualifier under the system. He was one of at least two horses who might finish in-the-money, and in this race he did. He finished second and completed the payoff of $96.60. Whether there was any real hanky-panky going on in the fourth race will probably never be known for sure. But the stewards felt that one jockey had significantly affected the outcome of the race. In fact, if Frank Iannelli was guilty, he got off remarkably lightly. There must not be the slightest tampering with the results of a race. The public wagers its money on *faith* and in *good* faith. That faith has to be respected, or else.

It happened again at Gulfstream Park on March 2. On that bright day in Florida, a jockey named Gerland Gallitano rode Joan R. H. in a six-furlong Perfecta race. Joan R. H. was the 2-1 favorite of the fans. But she went nowhere. The winner was Ociosa, the second favorite at just under 5-2. In the second spot was a long shot, Pilar Elena, at 16-1. The Perfecta payoff was not spectacular, just $62.20, but that's 30-to-1 on your investment. A lot of fans tore up a lot of tickets on Joan R. H. The stewards observed the race closely and concluded that Gallitano had not made "a proper effort" on Joan R. H. He, too, was grounded for thirty days.

The stewards must always be vigilant. Where there is even the shadow of a suspicion, the jockey will suffer. And rightly so. The jockey is the key member of the team. He *can* influence the outcome of a race. Nicholas Brady, current chairman of the Jockey Club, said it all: "The integrity of racing is foremost. Something has to be done to guarantee that integrity."

4

Your First Day at the Track

If you have stuck with us to this point, you probably have the stamina to go the course. Undoubtedly you don't yet understand all the rules. But please do not be overwhelmed by the multitudes of conditions. The whole thing is basically quite simple, as we shall see in this chapter. You must first grasp the unorthodox principle that in order to succeed, you must begin with the top of the odds, with the longest shot on the board. You must learn to ignore the favorites, the choices of the tipsters, and (above all) the advice of friends and cohorts. You must wager *only* on the horses you yourself select, and you must make those selections quietly and logically, in accordance (for the most part) with the rules. Although they look complex, the rules are really quite simple. Don't be fooled, however. It is not easy to make a million at the races. It will take a little study, a little concentration, a little capital, and a great deal of self-discipline. You must be able to follow the system through to the end. And certainly, if you are serious, you must set up and use some form of money management, which is discussed in a later chapter.

You want to *make* money on your investment. You want to do this with a minimum capital outlay and with a maximum of security. While you are testing the system and acquiring experience in the field of handicapping, you can work your way from the two-dollar windows to the $20 windows and on up, possibly, to the $100 windows.

The way to learn is to get in there and perform. Therefore, let's go to Gulfstream Park on April 21, 1973, a day when the Florida skies are as blue as Wedgwood, and the air is warm and trembling; the temperature hovers in the low 80's as the horses parade before the first race. You've read the rules at least twice, and you still don't know them. You won't know them for several weeks or even months. In the meantime, get the basics well in mind. Learn how to read and interpret the *Form*. The key to success is: first, the odds; and second, the past-performance charts. A horse with long odds needs *five* points to qualify. If it's a maiden race, a two-year-old race, or a race with fillies, the horse needs only *four* points to qualify. Those are the basic facts. There are refinements, of course, but don't worry about the refinements at first. You will learn them with experience. For example, you will gradually learn that a horse who shows both a race and a workout within fourteen days needs only four points. You will learn that a horse carrying less than 109 pounds today and who has two points from Category A (race recency) can get by with only four points. You will learn that a horse with only one race in his past-performance charts, who has two points from Category A, also gets by with only four points. There are several types of horses who need seven points to qualify, such as fillies running against males, or maidens running against winners (except when that maiden is running his or her first race against winners).

Also, there are certain long-shots which get in automatically, with no points at all—for instance, a horse dropping $10,000 in class, or two full steps down in class. Horses with no past-performance (that is, first-time starters) who have one work-out shown, are automatic bets. A first-time starter must have that one workout in order to qualify. A two-year-old with only one race may get in automatically *if* that race was within fourteen days—or has a race within a month and a workout within ten days. A horse who was claimed last race can't get in at all, unless certain qualifications are met, and those are outlined in the Rules for Q1, Q2, and Q3. But don't worry about all these items at once. Simply remember that most horses require five points and go on from there. If any doubt occurs, consult the rules. You will be doing most of the work before the day of the race.

We don't know the odds the night before the race, but we have the public handicappers, such as Hermis. We have a copy of the *Form* for April 21 (Saturday) on this Friday night, and we check the first race, a mile and a sixteenth on the turf for four-year-olds and upward, a tough race to handicap.

Page 10 of the *Form:* we find that Hermis has placed Etonian Golfer at the bottom of his list, at 12-1. We look for the longer shots, however. We go to Questionable at 20-1. Questionable, we note, is a filly running against male horses, and she needs seven points to qualify. Here is her chart of past performances:

Questionable   111   B. f (1969), by Third Martini—Nice Question, by Beau Gar.
                                                          Breeder, Hobeau Farm (Fla.).   1973 5   M   0   1 $350

Owner, Al-Kabeck Farm.	Trainer, E. P. Jenks.							$5,000		1972	1	M	0	0	(—)
Apr 5-73¹GP	6 f 1·12¹/₅ft	33 116	8³¼	8³¾	7⁶¼	3³	McK'r'W¹⁰	3500 81	⑦Mahlan116	LadyPride	Questionable 12
Mar22-73¹GP	6 f1:12¹/₅gd	39 116	7²⁹	8⁹	9¹³	9¹²	McK'v'rW¹	5000 71	⑥C'ntryG'rb116	QuickCat	SquareHat 11
Mar 3-73²Hia	6 f 1:11¹/₅ft	20 113	7⁷¼	7¹³	8¹⁴	8¹⁴	TurcotteR²	7500 74	D'bleRiddle117	Sterl'gQ'n	ArrowCanas 8·
Feb 2-73⁸Hia	7 f 1:24⁴/₅ft	92 109¼	9¹⁷	9¹⁵	10¹⁸	10¹⁵	SicklesE⁷	Alw 68	⑪Tellystar112	SalesWeek	L'dySlipp'r 10
Jan25-73²Hia	7 f 1:27 sl	7⁷ 117	5³¼	3⁵¼	10²⁰	11¹⁶	RuaneJ¹⁰	7500 56	⑪LaserGirl 113	G'ntleMollie	RubyDay 12
Dec14-72⁴Aqu	6 f1:11³/₅gd	4²¾ 109♣	6¹³	6¹¹	5¹³	5¹³	AnnonioA⁶	Mdn 72	WholeTruth112	Magnifico	BigRascal 6

Feb 21 Hia 3f gd :36³/₅b

Questionable is not only a filly, she is a sprint runner and has never gone a mile and a sixteenth. Her last race was at $3,500, although she has raced in higher company. Our first check is for race-recency; she ran on April 5, finishing third, three lengths off the winner. Not bad. But it was in a $3,500 claiming race. At $5,000 and $7,500, she invariably finishes last or next to last. She gets one point for a race within twenty-eight days, then loses it for moving up in class. She gets a point for finishing third in a field of twelve and for having a last-race rating of three plus three or six. (That's worth two points.) She gets another point for finishing once in-the-money in her entire past performance. She gets one point for the five-pound drop in weight. She gets two more points for gaining two and a fraction lengths in the stretch run of her last race. Well, well! She *does* have seven points. But note that six of those seven points were gained from a race at a lower class than today's race. That's a very weak seven for Questionable, and remember that she has never run on the turf and has never gone the distance. She's going against male horses, so we put a question mark in the margin and look for a stronger qualifier as we move along the odds scale. We go to My Yah Yah, also at 20-1 in the probable-odds list. My Yah Yah is a gelding, and his chart is shown below. The first thing that strikes us is that My Yah Yah has run his last two races at $3500 and is moving up in class, and further, he was claimed in his last race! Do you recall that a horse who was claimed in his last race and is moving up in class is automatically disqualified *unless* he can show ten clear points? It takes a super-horse to get ten points, and we can see at a glance that My Yah Yah will never make it:

My Yah Yah   116   Ch. g (1969), by Don Poggio—Celtic Blue, by Celtic Ash.
Breeder, M. J. Hawley (Fla.).   1973 2 0 0 0 $532
Owner, G. Kyle.   Trainer, D. Butler. $5,000   1972 20 4 1 5 $9,946

Apr10-73¹⁰GP	1 1-8 1:52³/₅ft	4½	116	9⁶³₄	5³	6⁸¹₂	4⁴	Ced'oM¹¹	c3500	67	Haw'nV'y'ge116	Mix'dEm't'ns	SkyT'Is 12
Mar26-73²GP	1¹₁₆ 1:45³/₅ssy	7½	116	8⁸¹₂	8⁹³₄	5⁶¹₄	4⁹¹₄	CedenoM⁶	3500	65	K'ghtEr't116	H'w'nVoy'e	F'v'redP'nce 12
Dec25-72¹⁰Crc	1-70 1:46³/₅ft	11	113	9⁵¹₂	11⁸¹₂	11¹³	10¹³	ShafferJ⁹	5000	69	ReyDeChile116	Alicaido	BrandtBrat 11
Dec18-72¹⁰Crc	1 1-8 1:55³/₅ft	13	116	3¹₂	2³	3³¹₂	4⁴	ShafferJ⁷	5000	85	MinniesMiddie119	Slip'yBill	Sup'rSl'k 12
Nov29-72⁴Crc	1 1:41 ft	8¼	114	4⁷	5⁷	4⁷¹₂	2⁵	ShafferJ⁶	5000	85	AlbertsFolley104	MyY'hY'h	G'd'naD'c'r 10
Nov18-72¹CRC	1¹₁₆ 1:50²/₅ft	14	116	9⁸³₄	7⁹¹₄	8⁵	5¹³₄†	WeilerD¹¹	5000	72	RunforD'n'r116	N'twithst'd'g	E'tp'k't 12
†Dead heat.													
Nov11-72⁵Crc	1 1-8 1:58¹/₅ft	2¼	*119	6⁶³₄	1²	1¹₂	1ⁿᵏ	PernaR⁴	c3500	77	My Yah Yah119	Antigono	Sm'rtFl'shing 12
April 17 GP 3f ft :38²/sb					Apr 5 CRC 5f ft 1:06b					March 16 Crc 1m ft 1:47²/sb			

By using the last two races, both at a lower class, My Yah Yah could scrape together about seven points, but once again we are working on the weak side, and we have to disqualify him. Go next to Goodpus and average out his rating. He's at 20-1, but tomorrow he'll be about 11-1. Move on to Cultivator at 20-1, and rate him next. He's a colt, getting attractive billing at 109 pounds, worth one point. He raced last on April 17, for two points. It would appear that he's dropping from $8,000 to $5,000, but note that five of his last six races were at $3,500. In reality, the horse is moving up in class for today's $5,000 race, and we must deduct a point for this move up. A net of two points. He picks up one point for gaining two lengths in the stretch run of his last race and one more point for his win on April 6. Only once has he run a mile and a sixteenth on the turf (his last race) and then he finished tenth in a field of twelve, seventeen lengths off the winner. With a last-race rating of 27 (10 plus 17), Cultivator looks bad, and we must disqualify him. We next consider the horses at 12-1 in the projected odds. Start with Etonian Golfer, who is getting in today's race at 111 pounds.

Etonian Golfer * 111 B. g (1965), by Etonian—Star Golfer, by Sagittarius.
Breeder, F. Gilpin (Can.).

													1973	8	0	1	0		$1,105	
Owner, H. V. Howley. Trainer, G. J. Jacupke.									$5,000		1972	33	5	9	5		$29,321	4
Apr13-73²GP	1¹⁄₁₆	1:44³/sft	49	114	9⁸	8¹⁰	7⁷½	8⁵¼	McKe'rW⁵	6250	75	Andalein J16		His Cookin		Tenace 12	5
Apr 7-73²GP	⑦a1¹⁄₁₆	1:46¹/sfm	18	114	8¹¹	8⁹³	7⁸½	7¹⁵	McK'v'rW¹	7000	68	S'ndRidge111		K'yL'go II.		Malch'm'vis 12	1
Mar24-73²GP	1¹⁄₁₆	1:43¹/sft	37	114	12¹³	12¹⁶	12¹⁵	11¹⁵	McK'rW⁸	10500	72	Sinu 116		Shining Sword		Asher 12	4
Mar19-73⁷GP	⑦a1½	2:34³/sfm	5¾₄109*	11¹⁸	10¹⁰	8¹⁴	8¹⁵	Gon'zAJr⁵	8500	68	FightingWar118		C'cle ofLove		B'nchill. 12	6
Feb28-73¹⁰Hia	1⅜	1:57⁴/sft	2¾	117	9¹²	7¹¹	4⁵¼	4⁴¾	BarreraC¹c6500	86	Friendsville115		HisCookin		JuneMagic 10	20
Feb22-73⁴Hia	1¹⁄₁₆	1:58	ft	8¹⁄₄e113	9¹⁶	8¹¹	5³¼	2²¾	BarreraC⁹	7000	89	ChioiniSp'c 117		Et'nianG'lf r		Fl'p'roo 10
Feb13-73⁴Hia	⑦a1½	2:32¹/sfm	24	113	8¹⁴	8¹³	7¹⁴	6¹¹	BarreraC⁸	9000	91	Wint'rWar117		BestCharg'r		Fight'gW'r 12

Two points for racing just eight days ago on April 13.

One point for an actual drop in class. $5,000 is the *lowest* class in which he has ever run.

One point for a last-race rating of 13 (8 plus 5).

Although he finished eighth in his last race, he gets ONE POINT for finishing less than six lengths off the winner.

One point for dropping three pounds off his last race.

One point for being in-the-money on February 22.

One point for gaining two lengths in the stretch run of his last race.

With eight points already, Etonian Golfer becomes a sure qualifier, if his odds tomorrow are high enough. You're going to back this horse with cold cash tomorrow, if all goes well. But since you have your first qualifier, before you leave his chart, perform one more function. Get his five-race rating and put that, too, in the margin. Here's how you do it: you note that on April 13 he finished eighth in a field of twelve. Subtract eight from twelve and put the figure four in the margin opposite. On April 7, the finish was seventh in a field of twelve. Put a small five in the margin. And so on for five races down the line. You get the following: 4, 5, 1, 4, 6, for a total five-race rating of 20. Since these five races were at a class higher than today's class, you have a very realistic figure for Etonian Golfer. Later, you will compare or contrast that total of twenty with the five-race rating of your other qualifiers in the race. Now, go to Native Rings. His chart and the point-assessment are given below:

Native Rings   **116**   Dk. b. or br. g (1969), by Native Charger—Katalinchu, by Gun Shot.
Breeder, A. M. Liftig (Fla.).   1973   6   0   1   1 $1,290

Owner, Thelma P. Becker.	Trainer, X. Becker.				$5,000		1972	15	1	2	2	$6,330
Mar31-73¹GP	1¹⁄₁₆ 1:44²/sft	50	112	12¹⁹ 12³⁰	P'l'd up.	IannelliF¹² 7000	JuneMagic114	Ramses III.			SpiceRack 12
Mar19-73⁷GP	⑦a1½2:34³/sfm	32	112	1ʰ 4½	7¹¹ 7¹³ MacB'thD⁶ 8000	70 FightingWar118	C'cle ofLove			B'nchill. 12
Mar14-73⁸GP	1¹⁄₁₆ 1:44 ft	48	112	8¹⁶ 8¹³	5¹³ 3⁶²⁄₄ M'BethD¹¹ 7000	76 Foiled inFlight107	Joy'sT'n			N'tiveR'gs 12
Mar 7-73⁷GP	⑤a1¹⁄₁₆1:44³/sfm	40	109⧧	8¹² 10¹⁴	7¹⁴ 7¹¹ ClarkWC¹² Alw	80 AshleighII.122	GayGaucho			JuacHollow 12
Feb22-73¹⁰Hia	1 1-8 1:52⁴/sft	2½	▲117	3³ 1ʰ	2ʰ .2² Turc'teR⁶ c3500	69 Careto 117	Native Rings			Betatron 12
Jan31-73²Hia	1 1-8 1:52³/sft	8	112*	11¹² 8⁷½	9⁷ 10⁸²⁄₄ MallanoJ⁷ 5000	63 Onawa 117	Our Richard			Patrie 12
Dec 7-72⁸Aqu	1 1-8 1:51¹/sft	4½	113	7⁶ 8¹²	8¹⁷ 8¹³ VeneziaM⁶ 7500	67 N'v'r orN'w116	F'nt'sticV'y'ge			T'myP. 8
April 12 CRC 3f ft :39b					March 5 Crc 4f ft :52b						

One point for a race about twenty-one days ago.

One point for a $2,000 drop in class.

His last race was a disaster, and he was pulled up. Go down to his last race at $5,000, on January 31. One point for a race-rating of nineteen.

One point for finishing in-the-money on March 14.

Deduct a point for his picking up four pounds off his last race. His net is three points, and you must disqualify Native Rings. Consider Alfor at 12-1 in the projected odds.

Alfor *   **116**   Dk. b. or br. g (1967). by Landing—Galfor. by Fairy Manhurst.
Breeder, A. Muckler (Ky.).   1973   3   0   1   0 $800

Owner, Sunny Boy Stable.	Trainer, M. Giardelli.				$5,000	1972	18	1	3	3	$8,963	0
Apr14-73¹GP	1¹⁄₁₆ 1:45 ft	9-5 *116	2½ 9¹¹	Eased. CedenoM⁹ 5000	Pitia111	Underachiever		MixedEmot'ns 9	10
Apr 7-73¹GP	1¹⁄₁₆ 1:45³/sft	9 116	3½ 1² 1¹	2¹ CedenoM¹²5000	74 Pitia111	Alfor		Bobs B Bees 12	3
Apr 2-73⁷GP	6 f 1:09⁴/sft	18 116	11⁶½11⁹²⁄₄10¹³	9¹⁵ CedenoM¹ 6500	80 Quarterb'kSn'k116	M'sicKing		J'y'sT'n 12	5
Oct30-72⁶Crc	6 f 1:13⁴/sft	4½ 116	6⁵ 6⁶ 6³	3¹ PernaR¹ 6500	83 Semicolon 116	Vive Le Ruler		Alfor 8	6
Oct19-72⁷Crc	6 f 1:13³/sft	11 116	7¹½ 6⁴½ 7⁴¼	5² PernaR⁸ 7500	83 ReallyGrec'n109	Aguer'sll.		GeorgeC't 11	3
Oct11-72⁶Crc	6½ f 1:20 ft	5½ 116	4⁴½ 5⁷ 5⁶½	5⁸ PernaR⁷ 7500	89 Call Me Darlin 113	Smiley		Careto 8.	27
Sep25-72⁷Crc	6 f 1:12⁴/sft	14 109*	5⁴½ 5⁹ 6⁶²⁄₄	2⁴½ G'ciaJO⁵ c6000	84 Cabriel 112	Alfor		George Candoit 9	
March 14 Crc 6f ft 1:20b									

Alfor is a gelding getting in this race at 116. His last race was on April 14, seven days ago, but something went wrong and the jockey eased him up. His previous race was on April 7, and that gives him two outs within fourteen days, for two points in race recency, Category A. Look again at the race on April 7. He finished second, just one length off the winner. One point for the finish position and another point for the second (in-the-money). Another two points for the race-rating of three. Look at his class. All but one race prior to today's race have been at a higher class. He gets a point for dropping in class. And here we will learn one more thing: for every three times he finished less than six lengths off the winner, he gets one point. Only once in his career (as shown) did he finish more than five lengths off the winner.

Alfor has garnered a total of eight points thus far, and he becomes Qualifier number two, or Q2. Ignore his last race and figure his five-race rating down the line: 10, 3, 5, 6, and 3, for a total of 27. This is seven points higher than Etonian Golfer, and if you are the kind who likes to play only one horse in a race, this five-race rating gives you a clue as to which one to choose.

Remember that you have disqualified both Native Rings and Cultivator. The horse named Questionable is still questionable, and since she is a filly running against such horses as Etonian Golfer and Alfor it would be the better part of wisdom to disqualify her too. With those three out of contention, the race lies among nine horses. Alfor is your second qualifier, and when you go to the track tomorrow you will discover that Alfor gets some nice backing from the crowd and goes off at 10-1.

Strictly speaking, if you go by the rigid rules, you would bet Etonian Golfer at 23-1, the only qualifier with odds above twelve. But Sam would say, Alfor looks good for several reasons, and since we have only nine contenders, give Alfor a chance at 10-1. Don't forget that five-race rating of twenty-seven. Use both Etonian Golfer and Alfor in your doubles combinations. Stretch the rules a little especially when you are dealing with the Daily Double and with Exactas or Perfectas. By all means, therefore, keep in Alfor, and you will be perfectly right. Alfor wins the first race on this warm Saturday afternoon at Gulfstream Park. He pays $21.20 to win and $10.40 to place. Better still, he leads off a doubles combination that will pay well over $200. But we haven't arrived at the track as yet. This is Friday night, and we're looking at the second race in the *Form*. Hermis has Uncle Chris and First Score near the bottom of the list at 30-1 each.

Uncle Chris **112** B. h (1968), by Sir Gallant—Lucky Lorna, by Blue Choir.
Breeder, S. A. Alexander (Ill.). 1973 3 0 0 0 $288
Owner, F. G. Walder & S. L. Goldstein. Trainer, E. E. Thomas. $7,000 1972 6 0 0 2 $938

Apr11-73^{6}GP	Ⓣa$1\frac{1}{2}$	2:35^{2}/sfm	48	115	$9^{7\frac{1}{4}}$	$8^{7\frac{3}{4}}$	8^{11}	$7^{7\frac{1}{4}}$	VieraH^{4}	9000	72	RioC'daloso116	Fight'gW'r	Z'roPic'ro 11	4
Apr 6-73^{2}GP	$1\frac{1}{16}$	1:45^{4}/sft	16	116	11^{18}	10^{12}	$9^{8\frac{1}{2}}$	$5^{7\frac{3}{4}}$	MarquezC^{9}	3500	66	Cultivator 109	HansGrey	Montiego II. 12	7
Mar19-73^{10}GP	1 1-8	1:52^{4}/sft	19	109⁑	11^{26}	10^{13}	8^{11}	5^{8}	Wil'msLR^{1}	3500	62	Acquitted 116	Curtsey Now	Royal L. 11	6
Nov25-72^{5}Crc	1 1-8	1:56^{4}/sft	14	114	11^{24}	10^{19}	9^{17}	7^{11}	GomezS^{10}	3500	72	Conflict 114	Sir Hot	Coventry II. 12	5
Nov11-72^{5}Crc	1 1-8	1:58^{1}/sft	13	109⁑	11^{13}	4^{5}	4^{5}	$4^{5\frac{1}{4}}$	Wil'msLR^{8}	3500	72	MyYahYah119	Antigono	Sm'rtFl'shing 12	8
Nov 1-72^{9}Crc	$1\frac{1}{16}$	1:51^{3}/sft	$4\frac{1}{4}$	109⁑	10^{17}	$9^{5\frac{3}{4}}$	$6^{4\frac{3}{4}}$	$3^{2\frac{3}{4}}$	Will'sLD^{4}	2500	65	WouksWalk 122	Antigono	UncleChris 11	30
Oct27-72^{5}Crc	$1\frac{1}{16}$	1:50^{3}/sft	9-5	▲112⁑	9^{14}	9^{10}	7^{12}	7^{11}	Wil'msLR^{6}	2500	62	Sp'c'lJ'y116	L'rdCh'nc'l'r	MaH'wAp'le 12	

March 16 TrP 5f ft 1:05^{1}/sb March 10 TrP 7f ft 1:34b March 5 TrP 4f ft :51b

Uncle Chris gets one point for dropping three pounds off his last race (115 to 112).

Two points for his race just ten days ago, which was at $9,000. His race today is at $7,000, and it would appear that he is dropping in class. But look down the line of races. Today's race is only the second time he has appeared in company higher than $3,500, and two of his races are at $2,500. He's really moving up in class today, and we must deduct one point for that upward move. He has a net of two points.

His last-race rating of fifteen gives him one more point, and his third on November 1 rates one point, for a total of four points.

He gained a little more than three lengths in the stretch run of his last race, and since his finish position was seventh in a field of eleven, that nets him just one point. He now has five points and becomes a qualifier. Please note that he is garnering all but one of his qualifying points from a single race, the last one. The other point comes from his in-the-money race back in November. Any horse getting four out of five of his points from one race must be looked at very closely, especially if (as in this case) he is moving up in class. Recall that the filly named Questionable garnered most of her points from one race, and in the end we had to disqualify her. Uncle Chris will remain then as a tentative qualifier, as we move on down the odds list in the second race. We should note in passing that his five-race rating is 4, 7, 6, 5, 8, for a total of 30, which sounds and looks good, except that four of the races were at a lower class than today's race.

We look next at First Score, whose chart is just below:

First Score 109 B c (1969), by But First—Dolly's Score, by Stymie.
Breeder, R. G. Thomasson (Fla.). 1973 7 0 0 0 $165

Owner, Judith Cabrera. Trainer, E. Cabrera.								$7,500				1972	23 2 1 1		$7,639
Apr11-73⁷GP	7 f 1:22	ft 117	116	76¾	9¹²	8¹²	11¹⁸	B'v'leEM⁵	10000	76 Amasport116	SpunSilver	Friendsville 12
Mar28-73¹⁰GP	①1⅝ 1:43²/₅fm	73	112	5⁸½	8¹²	8¹⁵	8¹³	V'zanF¹¹	13000	74 B'k'gSt'ple116	HighP'k'ts	Sw'tM'nh'n 12
Mar22-73⁷GP	①a1⅛ 1:46	fm 166	116	8¹⁴	9¹³	6⁷¼	5⁵½	Val'zanF⁸	10000	78 Impres'veTime116	HeraldSq'e	BarJ'st 12
Mar 9-73⁷GP	6 f 1:09⁴/₅ft	121	116	11¹²	10²⁰	11¹⁷	11¹³	Ruj'oM¹⁰	10000	82 He'sG'tlt114	NobleD'l	Q'rt'rb'kSneak 12
Mar 1-73⁷Hia	6 f 1:10⁴/₅ft	59	114	8¹⁰	8¹²	8¹½	8¹¹	RujanoM¹	14000	79 Major Art 119	Iron Line	Great Spirit 9
Feb 8-73⁴Hia	6 f 1:11¹/₅ft	78	115	8⁷¾	9¹¹	8¹⁰	107½	PinedaR⁷	13000	80 Smartnick 117	Adoric	Famous Gun 12
Jan15-73⁷Crc	6 f 1:13³/₅ft	11	116	10⁹½	9¹¹	8⁷¾	8⁴	AstorgaC⁷	12500	81 Br'kM'rk116	Mly'gAhead	J'staDr'm'r 12
	March 21 TrP 5f sy 1:02³/₅b					March 17 TrP 7f ft 1:31b					Feb 24 TrP 6f ft 1:15bg	

First Score is a colt who raced ten days ago and gets two points. The weight of 109 gains him another point, and the drop-off of eight pounds from his last race gets him another two points. That's five points, all from one race. His last race was at $10,000 and today's race is at $7,500, so add another point for the class drop, which is genuine since this race today is at the lowest class of his career. Six points. You think you have another qualifier until you note an important fact: in his last race his odds were 117-1. Now you have to check the rules, which say that when a horse's last race was at odds above 102, he needs seven clear points. (See "Rules for Selecting Q1, Q2, Q3, page) First Score lost six lengths in the stretch run of his last race, and he has never been in-the-money. You know now that you have to check the last-race odds always as you read the top line of the charts. Disqualify First Score.

Our next candidate is Grandpa Dom, who is getting in today's race at 112 pounds. No points.

Grandpa Dom		112	Ch. c (1969), by Lurullah—Emerald Tease, by Ace Admiral.									
			Breeder, R. Grouzalis (Ky.).			1973	5	0	0	0		(—)
Owner, Mr. & Mrs. D. McKay. Trainer, C. P. Sanborn.				$7,000		1972	20	2	3	2		$9,946
Apr14-73⁴GP	1¹⁄₁₆	1:44²/sft 15	113	8⁸¹⁄₄	10¹⁹ 10¹⁷ 10¹⁶ Ast'rgaC¹⁰ 7000 65	Spice Rack 120	Floperoo	Walk Sam 11
Mar22 73¹⁰GP	7 f	1:24³/sft 11	116	10⁶	8⁶³⁄₄ 7⁶ 6⁷ Ast'rgaC¹⁰ 6500 74	RamsesIII. 112	Sar'hsT'ga	Tr'lyAmb'r 10
Mar 16-10⁷GP	7 f	1.00⁴/fl			Ast'rgaC¹⁰ 7000 79	D'lleItAldle110	BarJoint	CrossQuest'n 12
Mar 5-73⁶GP	1 1-8	1:50¹/sft 11	116	10¹⁷	12²⁰ 12²⁰ 12¹⁶ Thorn'gB⁵ 7500 67	DonSimon 116	WouksWalk.	BarJoint 12
Jan 5-73¹⁰Crc	1-70	1:46 ft 3¹⁄₄	116	6⁹¹⁄₂	6⁵¹⁄₂ 7⁶²⁄ 7⁶¹⁄₂ CedenoM³ 7500 78	Rey deChile111	Capt'nPuff	FoolishLad 8
Dec22-72¹⁰Crc	1	1:42¹/sft 8³⁄₄	114	11¹⁷	4³ 3 ¹⁄₂ 2ʰ Ast'gaC¹⁰ 7000 84	RayDavis116	GrandpaDom	D'bleR'dle 12
Dec13-72⁵Crc	7 f	1:26³/sft 7	116	12⁸¹⁄₂	11¹⁵ 9⁷¹⁄₂ 4⁶³⁄₄ Ast'rgaC¹¹ 6500 74	TwoHopes116	G'rd'naD'nc'r	VictorBay 12
April 20 GP 3f ft :37b					April 9 GP 7f ft 1:28b		April 5 GP 4f ft :48h	

The colt raced seven days ago, for two points. (His odds in his last race were 15-1. He needs just five points.)

No change in class. No points. His performance in his last race looks dismal. He finished tenth in a field of eleven. The only other point we can find is his finish in-the-money (second) on December 22. Disqualify him and move on to the next 20-1 candidate, Dragonwick. See below:

* **Dragonwick**		112	Dk. b. or br. g (1967), by Tapula—Dakma, by Uranio.									
			Breeder, Haras Uruguay (Uruguay).			1973	6	0	0	2		$1,564
Owner, Fort Royal, Inc. Trainer, L. Azpurua.				$7,000		1972	19	1	1	2		$7,636	6
Apr14-73²GP	1¹⁄₁₆	1:45 ft 17	116	9⁷	8⁶¹⁄₂ 8⁷¹⁄₄ 6⁴¹⁄₄ SalinasJ⁹ 5000 74	W'deJr.116	Notwithstand'g	QueNinf'lo 12	6
Mar 4-73⁷Rin	a 6¹⁄₂ f	1:19⁴/sft 27	108	Free Series 7a 11¹²	Salc'doJ Hcp	Donoso 115	Romanza	Yesbonin 14	3
Feb24-73⁹Rin	a 1¹⁄₄	2:09¹/shy 19	115	Free Series 7a 3⁷¹⁄₄	Guz'nRD Hcp	Joyful 108	Parce Que	Dragonwick 13	10
Feb17-73⁹Rin	a 1	1:42³/sft 8³⁄₄	112	Free Series 7a 3⁷	Guz'nRD Hcp	Grotto 117	Legendaire	Dragonwick 12	9
Jan28-73⁷Rin	a 1¹⁄₈	1:50 ft 5¹⁄₂	115	Free Series 7a 6⁴²⁄	ParraAF Hcp	TimmyBoy115	Vigitano	Elena de Troya 14	8
Jan13-73⁷Rin	a 7 f	1:25⁴/shy 16	112	Free Series 7a 9¹⁴	Gutie'zR Hcp	Jaen 115	Sirikit	Gatopardo 14	36
April 18 Crc 3f ft :38bg					April 13 GP 3f ft :36¹/sb		April 7 Crc 4f ft :53b	

Dragonwick is a gelding, getting in at the good weight of 112, off four pounds from his last race. One point.

He raced a week ago, good for two points.

His last-race rating is ten (that is, he finished sixth and he was four lengths off the winner). He picked up three lengths in the stretch run of his last race, and gains three more points. Don't forget a point for that sixth in a field of nine or more (in this case, twelve). That's about nine points already. He loses a point for the move up in class from $5,000 to $7,000, although this is not too firm a loss. Actually, prior to the last race, he has been running in handicaps, and you could build a case for a drop in class. His five-race rating is 6, 3, 10, 9, 8, for a total of 36. Very impressive. Now you have Uncle Chris as Q1 and Dragonwick as Q2. If you must choose between them and wish to play only one, certainly you will choose Dragonwick. Also, when you select your Daily Double combinations, you will be sure to include Dragonwick as your top choice in the second race. You already have Etonian Golfer and Alfor in the first race, whom you will certainly combine with Uncle Chris and with Dragonwick. When you get to the track, you will watch the odds in the first race, and you will hook up the second, third, and fourth favorites (F2, F3, and F4) with Uncle Chris and Dragonwick. If you are smart, you will also take the second, third and fourth choice of Hermis in the second race (Candy Key, Winnie's Choice, and Floperoo) and combine them with Etonian Golfer and Alfor. This may sound like a lot of combinations, but you have to use a shotgun if you're going to hit that Daily Double frequently. Right now, summing up the combinations above, you have twenty combinations, for an investment of $40 in the Daily Double.

In these first two races on April 21, 1973, you have seen enough past-performance charts to understand the method of reading them to acquire your high-odds qualifiers. You proceed through the ten races, on Friday night, placing the number of points in the margin. Get also the five-race ratings of your Qualifiers, and tomorrow at the track you are ready to X-out the scratches and watch the odds board to discover the real top-odds horses.

In the second race tomorrow you will run into a puzzling problem. We'll discuss that when we get to it. It is now Saturday at Gulfstream Park. You are watching the odds board before the first race, and you discover that the horse called Native Rings is the high-odds horse, hovering between seventy and sixty. But you have disqualified him, so you look for the next highest, which is My Yah Yah at 35-1. Also disqualified. Questionable has the next highest odds, and you throw her out too. At 25-1, Etonian Golfer becomes your first selection. Put $10 to win and $10 to place on Etonian Golfer. While you are at the window, put $10 to win and $10 to place on Alfor, who was your Q2 from last night. The odds are 10-1 (and strictly speaking you should stay above 11-1), but you have disqualified several horses, and you know there are really less than ten serious contenders in this difficult race. There are several other horses with odds of from 11-1 to 17-1, and very possibly you can find another qualifier therein. If so, add him to your wagers on the first race. Three horses (bet to win and to place) are not too many for the first race of the double. The lowest odds you are taking are 10-1, and your chances of getting one or more hits from those three win and three place bets are very good.

Alfor takes the first race and pays $21.20 to win and $10.40 to place. Multiply each by five and you have your gross. That's $158. Deduct your investment for your net. The question is, in a race such as this, what would Sam do? He would take last night's Q1 and Q2, and he would find Q1 and Q2 from among the top odds today. That could result in as many as four horses. Then he would look at the five-race ratings of each of those four. He would note which horses gained their points from a variety of races, rather than from one race. He would check the class of those five races giving him the ratings. Twenty-five from higher class races would be better in his eyes than thirty from lower class races. In the end, he would discriminate among those four horses and he would pick two to play. If one of those has odds of 30-1 or higher, he would bet across-the-board, to win, place and to show. In general, that would be Sam's approach.

Now, you have purchased your twenty doubles tickets before the first race, so you have Alfor hooked up with Uncle Chris and Dragonwick, as well as with Candy Key, Winnie's Choice and Floperoo. Those three were Hermis's second, third, and fourth choices in the projection. (You would have taken F1 also, *if* it had been 3-1 or higher. F1 was Asher at 5-2, and no bet.)

As the second race approaches, you watch the odds and find that Uncle Chris is moving between sixty and fifty. He goes off at about 58-1 finally. You put $10 across-the-board, for a $30 investment. Dragonwick is a class horse (remember those handicap races), and the odds on him are dropping. He goes off finally at 4-1, whereas the projection last night was 20-1. (Hermis was working too fast to see his mistake.) But your problem is to find a Q2, unless you are satisfied to go along with Uncle Chris as your only straight bet in the race. Grandpa Dom is 50-1, but you have disqualified him. You have disqualified First Score, who is 17-1. You will find your Q2 somewhere between the odds of 12-1 and 50-1. The next problem is: what to do about Dragonwick, your original Q2, who is now lighting up the board at 4-1? Dragonwick is obviously a horse appealing to many of the fans. His record is impressive. Most of his races have been handicaps, and here he is in a $7000 claiming race. If you really like his chances, you will bet him to win only. But you will also play your other Q1 and Q2, one or both, as you judge.

Of course, you have guessed it: the winner is Dragonwick in the second race, paying exactly $10.60. If you had $10 on him, you collect $53. But the kicker is the double payoff: $224.80 for the ticket on Alfor and Dragonwick. The double is high simply because most of the fans didn't study the second race too carefully before making their doubles choices. During the time *between* the first and second races, they did study the *Form*, and the revelation came: Dragonwick wasn't the 20-1 horse Hermis said he was. Dragonwick was very nearly the co-favorite!

Candy Key was second in the race, missing by two lengths. However, if Candy Key had won, you would have had that double too, since Candy Key was F2 at 3-1 in the projected or probable odds.

You are ready (almost) for the third race. It is a mile and a sixteenth on the turf (the same as the second race) for four-year-olds and upward, and the claiming price is $7,000. Last night you disqualified Disisdick, Fawn Art, and Conque. Paleface was a qualifier, and you take him today as your Q1 at 30-1. Here's the chart on Paleface, to give you some more practice looking for points:

Paleface 112 Ch. g (1969), by Royal Levee—Maraude II., by Vandale.

Breeder, R. R. Guest (Fla.).									1973 7 0 0 1				$755		
Owner, Sarah E. Humes. Trainer, G. W. Semlar.						$7,000			1972 19 2 0 2				$7,013		
Apr13-73²GP	1¹⁄₁₆ 1:44³/sft	24 116	11¹¹	9¹²	9⁷²⁄₄	6³¹⁄₂	ScoccaD¹⁰	6500	76	Andalein 116	His Cookin	Tenace 12	6
Mar31-73¹GP	1¹⁄₁₆ 1:44²/sft	18 112	9⁸¹⁄₄	8⁷¹⁄₄	7⁷¹⁄₄	7⁷	ScoccaD⁶	7000	74	JuneMagic114	Ramses III.	SpiceRack 12	5
Mar24-73¹GP	1¹⁄₁₆ 1:44¹/sft	125 112	11⁹	9⁷¹⁄₂	6⁵	4⁴¹⁄₄	ScoccaD⁸	7000	78	FlemishPrince112	B.B.M'tin	Mr.Sp'ts 12	8
Feb24-73⁴Hia	1³⁄₁₆ 1:57¹/sft	80 113	10¹⁷	10²⁵	11²³	11²²	ScoccaD⁶	9000	72	Mr. Fox 113	Purchaser	Tayacan 11	0
Feb14-73¹⁰Hia	1³⁄₁₆ 2:00 ft	6¹⁄₂ 117	8¹⁰	5⁴	4⁶¹⁄₂	5⁵	HoleM¹¹	c6500	75	D'bleMessage117	Purchaser	KingsHeir 12	7
Jan29-73⁴Hia	1 1-8 1:51¹/sft	25 117	9¹³	8¹¹	5¹³	3¹¹	HoleM¹¹	6500	68	Tayacan 119	Admiral's Tiz	Paleface 12	26
Jan22-73¹Hia	1 1-81:51²/ssy	20 119	8¹⁵	9¹⁹	9¹⁷	9¹⁸	MiceliM⁹	6500	57	Best Charger 117	King Ponda	Es Bey 11	

April 7 Crc 4f ft :51b   March 11 Crc 4f ft :51b

A race eight days ago gives the gelding two points.

In today at 112, he's dropping four pounds off his last race, for another point.

No class change and no points.

His finish of sixth in his last race gives him one point, and the rating of 6 plus 4 (10) is worth another two points. That's six points already. He was in-the-money on January 29, for another point, and there you have your first qualifier. Now look at Alicaido, also at 30 1 on the board:

*Alicaido 112 Dk. b. or br. h (1968), by Alyjink—Falencia, by Madison.

Breeder, Haras El Colorado (Argentina).									1973 5 0 1 0				$1,138		
Owner, D. D. Oliver, Jr. Trainer, R. S. MacFarlane.						$7,000			1972 22 1 2 4				$5,091		
Apr13-73²GP	1¹⁄₁₆ 1:44³/sft	23 111*	10⁹¹⁄₂	10¹⁴	10⁹²⁄₄	7⁴¹⁄₄	WingoR¹¹	6500	76	Andalein 116	His Cookin	Tenace 12	5
Mar 2-73¹⁰Hia	1 1-8 1:52³/sft	33 117	7⁹	5⁸	2³	2ʰ	BarreraC⁵	5000	72	Truly Amber 117	Alicaido	AwareWolf 10	8
Feb23-73¹⁰Hia	1 1-8 1:51³/sft	32 117	11¹⁶	10¹⁴	9¹²	6¹¹	StLeonG¹¹	6000	66	Blaz'gTr'pies117	AllenC.	Haw'nV'y'ge 12	6
Jan29-73⁴Hia	1 1-8 1:51¹/sft	31 117	7⁸	6⁹¹⁄₂	7¹⁷	6¹⁷	SalinasJ²	6500	62	Tayacan 119	Admiral's Tiz	Paleface 12	7
Jan16-73⁵Crc	1 1-4 2:11³/sft	5¹⁄₄ 109¾	3²	4³	4²¹⁄₂	4²¹⁄₂	G'n'zAJr⁸	c5000	84	SuperSlick116	MixedEmot'ns	Conflict 11	32
Dec29-72¹⁰Crc	1¹⁄₁₆ 1:49²/sft	15 111*	6⁸¹⁄₂	7⁶¹⁄₂	7⁶¹⁄₄	5²	WingoR³	5000	77	Great Gran'son 106	Mollecito	Z Ron 12	
Dec25-72¹⁰Crc	1-70 1:46²/sft	5¹⁄₂ 111* 3ⁿᵏ	2¹⁄₂	3¹⁄₂	2¹¹⁄₄	WingoR⁴		5000	80	ReyDeChile116	Alicaido	BrandtBrat 11	

He's moving up in class, and his point rating comes to ten, when you figure it correctly; he's a definite qualifier: Q2. His five-race rating is 5, 8, 6, 6, 7, for a total of 32, as against the following for Paleface: 6, 5, 8, 0, 7, for a total of 26. Since their odds are 30-1, bet them both $10 across-the-board, for an investment in the race of $60. (Last night, these two were Q1 and Q2 on your list, from page 10 of the *Form*.)

Copper Miner, at 4-1, won the race. He was nowhere in your calculations, since he was F3 on Hermis's selections. But cheer up! Alicaido comes in second, five lengths behind Copper Miner, and he pays $19.60 to place, as well as $10.60 to show, for a gross of $133, giving you a net on the race of $73 if you went with both of them, Q1 and Q2. Not bad. You are picking up more and more investment capital as you go along. The fourth race is a Perfecta race, one in which you are to choose the winner and the place-horse, in that order.

Last night you selected Cuzin Leslie as Q1 and Tarora as Q2, although the latter was only 10-1 on the probable odds chart given by Hermis. Music King was also at 10-1 on the chart and looked good for a possible third choice. You disqualified Kings Companion, Que Ninfulo, Anatole, and George Candoit. Your straight bets were for Cuzin Leslie at 40-1 and Tarora at 21-1. The big problem is: what to select for the Perfecta? You look again, and you disqualify Wouks Walk and Onawa. Since you wish to put four horses in a box for the Perfecta (crisscross them all possible ways), you take Cuzin Leslie, Tarora, Music King, and Acco King, one of the lower-odds horses at 6-1. This box costs $24 for twelve tickets.

The winner is Music King at 17-1, with a good second by Cuzin Leslie at 41-1, the Perfecta paying $644 for each $2 ticket. You had one ticket. You also had $10 across-the-board on Cuzin Leslie, who paid $25.40 to place and $12 to show. Incidentally, let's take a look at the chart on Cuzin Leslie to see if you can find the qualifying points. The fifth point is a little tricky, but it's there if you know what to look for:

Cuzin Leslie   **116**

Ch. c (1969), by Sensitivo—Predate, by Nashua.
Breeder, L. Combs II. (Ky.).

											1973	3	0	0	0	$120	
Owner, J. Palumbo.	Trainer, J. J. Kelly, Jr.							$6,500			1972	16	3	5	2	$9,989	1
Mar26-73⁵GP	1¹⁄₁₆1:44⁴/ssy	26	116	6⁷	10¹⁴	9¹⁹	9²¹	HoleM⁷	6500	58 Jive 111	Paradoxical	Fondest Touch 10					2
Mar10-73²GP	1¹⁄₁₆ 1:43¹/sft	31	112*11¹⁵	12¹⁷	10²⁴	10²²	G'lezAJr⁶	9000	65 SpiceRack115	ChioiniSpecial	L'tleL'rd 12						4
Jan 1-73⁶Suf	6-f1:16	sy	7-5 ▲119	7⁵	3⁶	3⁸	4¹¹	CaseyR¹	4000	50 Fr'pt'nSeal120	LympiaSea	Alw'ysSt'y'n 8					8
Nov25-72⁸LD	7-f 1:28⁴/sft	9-5 ▲115	5⁴	4³⁄₂	2²	1ʰ	MercierN⁷	4500	71 CuzinLeslie115	BobbyMore	Warr'rCr'k 9						7
Nov 8-72⁶Suf	6 f 1:12⁴/sm	7-5 ▲115	4⁴⁄₂	5⁴⁄₂	3 ½	1¹⁄₂	Car'z'laM⁵	4000	77 CuzinLeslie115	Mr.PhilipM.	TrueP'ple 8						22
Oct30-72⁶Suf	6 f 1:11¹/sm	9-5e 112	6⁶	6⁷	5⁹	4⁶⁄₂	CaseyR⁴	5000	78 KnockA Homa113	WithR'son	TwnR'te 8						
	March 2 GP 5f ft 1:03³/sb					Feb 24 GP 5f ft 1:02¹/sb											

The colt's last race was on March 26, about twenty-five days ago, for one point.

No points for weight, weight change, or for class or class move.

One point for being in-the-money at least once in his past performance.

Two points for those two wins within five races.

That's four points. Where is the fifth? It's in the finish positions of those bottom three races: all of them are within 6½ lengths of the winner (two of them being the winner, of course). That's five points for Cuzin Leslie. Today's race is seven furlongs, and it is always wise to look back to a race of the same distance, which happens to be on the 25 of November. Cuzin Leslie won that one. His last two races at a mile and a sixteenth each were clearly "bad", but perhaps those were "conditioning" races and served as odds-builders for today's race.

Thus far it has been more than a good day! In four races, you've hit a $224 double and $644 Perfecta. You've had a 10-1 winner in the first race and (maybe) you had that 4-1 winner in the second. Then there were two high-odds horses who caught second-money, at odds of 30-1 and 40-1. And the day's not half over. You could hardly expect this pattern to continue for ten races! Don't forget that the favorites and the second-favorites have to get in there sometime. So be it. The winner of the fifth race pays $7.60 and in the sixth it's $7.40. The winner of the seventh takes down $6.80. The second horse goes off at 18-1, and the Perfecta pays $96.20, in combination with the winning favorite. In the feature race, Snurb comes in for $9, and in the ninth Malwak gets $9.40, whereas Acquitted can get only $8 for winning the last race. Acquitted is the favorite again, and with Cherry Sun running second, at 8-1, the Perfecta pays exactly $101.

Now and then it happens just that way: the money comes rolling in during two or three races bunched together. On some days (though rarely) there is only one good hit in a day. And there will be one of those very rare days, once in a month, maybe, when nothing hits. But when that happens, it is usually preceded, or followed, by some sensational wins. That's why you must play them all; you must be both consistent and persistent. You will need enough capital to ride out those occasional losing streaks, which do come, but which are punctuated by comfortable hits day after day. The charts which follow will show the results of following Sam's high-odds horses for a month at a time at any one track. The charts should give you confidence in the system. After you've become convinced that the system works, the next thing you have to do is to train yourself to recognize a qualifying horse as you start at the top of the odds scale and move downward until you have two or three or even four selections. You can then weed out one or two or three of those four.

Of course, the Daily Double poses a problem. We have gone through one day's double above, but at a later period we will summarize the ways and means of getting your doubles selections. The same is true of the Perfecta-Exacta races, when you must pick the winner and the second horse in the correct order of finish. We have simplified this latter problem thus far by saying that you should pick four horses and put them in a box, which requires twelve tickets, or $24. Later we will expand the scheme somewhat and pick five horses, which will require twenty tickets, or $40. That may seem a little high for an investment in one race, but the rewards are generous and fairly frequent. Naturally, the more you invest, as you spread your wagers, the more likely you will hit a winner.

If you have a little time this Saturday evening, after your successful first day at the races, using Sam's revolutionary approach of starting at the top of the odds board, you might check over the *Form* for today's program and look at yesterday's results. You will discover that those four good races on Saturday followed a Friday when there was only one winning wager! That is, only one high-odds horse won a race or was in-the-money in ten races. It occurred in the third race of the day, which happened to be a maiden claiming race, one of the most difficult of all races to figure. And Sam has a special approach to maiden races, which we might as well explain to you now. Look at the results of the third race on Friday, April 20, at Gulfstream Park:

THIRD RACE GP April 20, 1973		5 FURLONGS (:57^{1}/s). MAIDENS. CLAIMING. Purse $3,500. 2-year-olds. Weight, 118 lbs. Claiming price, $10,000. Value to winner $2,100; second, $700; third, $350; fourth, $245; fifth, $105. Mutuel Pool, $60,389.									
Last Raced		Horse	EqtAWt PP	St	$\frac{3}{16}$	⅜	Str	Fin	Jockeys	Owners	Odds to $1
		Love Hit	2 118 11	4	3½	2²	2½	1²½	GStLeon	Casey-Mullin	49.50
		Beau Classic	2 118 7	6	2½	1½	1ʰ	2⁴	DMacBeth	Larkabit Farm	4.80
3- 6-73³	GP⁴	Ohmylove	b2 118 4	5	6⁶	5¹½	3⁴	3½	CPerret	Mrs I Cowan	1.40
		Joy Quibu	2 118 2	9	11⁴	8²	4ʰ	4¹½	RPerna	A Moore	40.70
		Ancient Times	2 118 `5	1	4ʰ	4ʰ	6ʰ	5ⁿᵒ	MARivera	W J Resseguet Jr	9.50
3-23-73³	GP⁹	Dunlovin	b2 118 1	8	7ʰ	7¹½	8⁴	6½	EMBelville	T Tanner	21.10
4- 3-73³	GP⁹	Hell's Extra	2 118 10	3	1½	3¹½	5½	7ⁿᵒ	FValdizan	C Bryant	8.50
4-12-73³	GP⁵	Famous Winner	2 115 9	2	5ʰ	6⁵	7¹½	8³½	GWalker	G W McCall	6.10
2-20-73³	Hia¹²	Flying Legend	2 118 6	7	8½	9³	9⁵	9⁴	Jimparato	D Shaer	20.40
		Little Whisper	2 115 3	10	9½	10²	10³	10²½	JHarrison	W Krauss	19.90
		Chance Orphan	2 108 12	12	10¹	11⁴	11⁶	11⁷	DBruscino⁷	H R Caple	24.40
		Marengo Pride	2 118 8	11	12	12	12	12	Flannelli	Dogwood Stable	13.90

Time, :22⁴/s, :46³/s, :58⁴/s. Track fast.

$2 **Mutuel Prices:**	11-LOVE HIT	1.01.00	31.00	11.00
	7-BEAU CLASSIC		6.00	3.40
	4-OHMYLOVE			2.80

B. g, by Hitting Away—Yes Love, by Double Jay. Trainer. W. Mullin. Bred by Fairview Farms, Inc. (Ky.).
IN GATE—2:10. OFF AT 2:10 EASTERN STANDARD TIME. Start good. Won driving.
LOVE HIT, away alertly, raced wide on the turn, engaged BEAU CLASSIC in midstretch, put him away a sixteenth out and drew clear. BEAU CLASSIC gained command on the turn, continued on well to the final sixteenth, then weakened. OHMYLOVE raced along the inside and outfinished the others. JOY QUIBU steadily improved his position. ANCIENT TIMES flashed brief speed. HELL'S EXTRA gave way when outrun to the head of the stretch. FAMOUS WINNER was outrun.
Ohmylove claimed by R. Berrie, trainer A. Monterio.
Claiming Prices—All $1000.
Scratched—A Bit Mean, Marvelous Mix, Southern Legend, Southside Story, Tender Moment, Speedy Rick.

The winner was Love Hit, a first-time starter, at the respectable odds of 49.50-1. That is, Love Hit paid $101 for every $2 on the nose. (The favorite, Ohmylove, came in third and paid $2.80.) Love Hit is a gelding running for the first time and carrying 118 pounds. Since he has no record at all, his odds are naturally quite high. In fact, his are the highest odds on the board. Love Hit paid $31 to place and $11 to show. Since the odds are over 30-1, you would have bet him across-the-board. But how do you approach a maiden race, under Sam's system?

You approach it just as you would any other race, from the top of the odds board. Love Hit is the first horse you consider, and when you check the entries for the third race at Gulfstream Park, you note that he is a first-time starter. See the next page for all the charts on the entries for this remarkable but very nearly typical maiden race. (All, that is, except one or two horses who were scratched from the race.) Love Hit, like all the other entries, is a two-year-old, and the claiming price is $10,000. The rules state that if the high-odds first-time starter has at least one workout to his credit, then he is an automatic qualifier. Love Hit worked out on April 2, and before that, on March 19 and on March 7. He qualifies. In such maiden races, Sam plays three horses, moving down from the top of the odds board. His selections were: (1) Love Hit; (2) Joy Quibu, at just over 40-1, another first-time starter with a recent workout; and (3) Chance Orphan, also a first-time starter with a recent workout. If you had just $10 across-the-board on Love Hit (for a $30 investment), the same on Joy Quibu, and $10 to win and $10 to place on Chance Orphan, whose odds were only 24-1, your total investment in the race would have been $80. The return would have been $505 from the win, $155 from the place, and $55 from the show. You're probably asking, how do I know how much to wager on these races?

3rd Gulfstream Park

Start

5 FURLONGS
GULFSTREAM

Finish

5 FURLONGS. (:57¹/s). MAIDENS. CLAIMING. Purse $3,500. 2-year-olds. Weight, 118 lbs. Claiming price, $10,000.

Dunlovin　118
B. c (1971), by Dunfee—Love Link, by Beau Gem.
Breeder, Ivy Knoll Stable (Fla.)　　　　1973　2　M　0　0　　(—)
Owner, T. Tanner.　Trainer, H. J. Rose.　　　　$10,000
Mar23-73³GP　　5 f　:58³/sft 113 118　12¹³ 10¹⁴　9²² 9¹⁹ Belv'leEM⁵Mdn 74 L'c'nBr'ze118　Ch'lieC'llins　Sm'thO'N'l 12
Mar13-73³GP　　3 f　:33²/sft 65 118　12　　13¹⁷ 13¹⁴ HerronP⁹ Mdn 81 S'ma'sP'de118　Dr.Arn'dT.　L'nh't'dR'h 14
　　April 14 Crc 5f ft 1:03b　　　　April 4 Crc 3F ft :36¹/shg　　　　March 21 Crc 2f ft :25²/sbg

Joy Quibu　118
Dk. b. br br. g (1971), by Our Joy—Miss Quibu, by Quibu.
Breeder, Mrs. S. Jones (Ky.).　　　　1973　0　M　0　0　　(—)
Owner, A. Moore.　Trainer, W. F. Caple.　　　　$10,000
　　April 14 Crc 3f ft :37²/sb　　　　April 10 Crc 4f ft :50b　　　　April 3 Crc 4f ft :52b

Little Whisper　115
Dk. b. or br. f (1971), by Ampose—Mardan Rose, by Persian Sea.
Breeder, Whispering Pines Farm (Fla.).　　1973　0　M　0　0　　(—)
Owner, W. Krauss.　Trainer, M. Moncrief.　　　　$10,000
　　April 17 Crc 4f ft :52b　　　　April 12 Crc 3f ft :37b　　　　April 7 Crc 4f ft :51b

Ohmylove　118
Dk. b. or br. c (1971), by Your Alibhai—Mel Sands, by Mel Hash.
Breeder, R. M. Marks (Fla.).　　　　1973　4　M　0　1　　$845
Owner, A. N. Winick.　Trainer, A. N. Winick.　　　$10,000
Mar 6-73³GP　　3 f　:33³/sft　6 118　5　　4⁴　4³ Log'rcioA⁸ Mdn 91 Pr'celyPl's're118　H'y'sS't'n　W'kAtMe 14
Feb27-73³Hia　3 f　:33²/sft　4¼ 120　5　　5⁶　4³ Tur'tteR¹² Mdn 92 LeClub120　NiceToHave　CheChe'sPride 14
Feb13-73³Hia　3 f　:33³/sft　9¼ 120　1　　1¹　3½ TurcotteR⁹Mdn 93 VillaFire120　DeterminedK'g　Ohmyl've 14
Jan30-73³Hia　3 f　:33　ft 30 120　3　　2³　7⁷ TurcotteR¹Mdn 90 NearGale120　H'ds'nC'ty　Am'c'nMys'y 14
　　April 19 GP 3f ft :38³/sb　　　　March 24 Hia 3f ft :35⁴/sh　　　　Feb 22 Hia 2f ft :23³/sh

A Bit Mean　118
B. g (1971), by Blushing Bull—A Bit Sweet, by Swedak.
Breeder, J. F. Dunn (Fla.).　　　　1973　3　M　0　0　　$105
Owner, Mrs. Harriet Robinso...　Trainer, V. J. Cincotta.　　$10,000
Apr13-73³GP　　5 f 1:00¹/sft　4¼ 118　5⁴½ 6⁷¾ 8⁹ 10⁷½ Ce'oM⁷ M10000 77 No Mount 118　Aurora Gray　Unction 12
Apr10-73³GP　　5 f　:59¹/sft 55 118　8⁷¼ 8¹⁰ 6¹² 5⁹½ CedenoM¹¹ Mdn 80 CheChe'sPride118　PlayHouse　Ekwanok 12
Mar27-73³GP　　5 f　:59⁴/sft 66 118　4²½ 9⁷¾ 10¹² 10¹⁴ LesterW⁷ Mdn 73 Im'd'te118　P'ncet'nTig'r　L'nh'rt'dR'ph 12
　　April 7 Crc 3f ft :37³/sb　　　　April 4 Crc 3 ft :38b　　　　March 24 Crc 3f ft :38b

Ancient Times　118
Ch. c (1971), by Olden Times—Topping Idea, by Vertex.
Breeder, Asbury, Mainons & Price (Ky.).　1973　0　M　0　0　　(—)
Owner, W. J. Resseguet, Jr.　Trainer, W. J. Resseguet, Jr.　$10,000
　　April 6 GP 4f ft :50bg　　　　March 30 GP 3f ft :36³/sbg　　　　March 23 GP 3f ft :37bg

Flying Legend　118
Ch. c (1971), by Bold Legend—Bring Back, by Carry Back.
Breeder, David Shaer (Md.).　　　　1973　1　M　0　0　　(—)
Owner, D. Shaer.　Trainer, J. H. Pierce, Jr.　　　$10,000
Feb20-73³Hia　3 f　:33³/ssl 41 120　13　　13¹⁸ 12¹⁶ V'squezJ¹² Mdn 78 Gr'ndstar120　UngaUnga　Gold'nG'inea 13
　　April 14 Hia 5f ft 1:01b　　　　April 6 Hia 4f ft :49hg　　　　March 24 Hia 5f ft 1:01³/sb

Beau Classic　118
B. g (1971), by Classic Work—Helio Beau, by Sunhelio.
Breeder, Larkabit Farm (Ga.).　　　　1973　0　M　0　0　　(—)
Owner, Larkabit Farm　Trainer, S. Branham.　　　$10,000

Marengo Pride　118
Dk. b. or br. c (1971), by Better Bee—Caledon Pride, by Requested.
Breeder, Timberlawn Farm, Inc. (Ky.).　　1973　0　M　0　0　　(—)
Owner, Dogwood Stable.　Trainer, H. Shillick.　　　$10,000
　　April 19 Crc 3f ft :39b　　　　April 10 Crc 4f ft :51b　　　　April 7 Crc 4f ft :52b

Famous Winner　115
Ch. f (1971), by Bolinas Boy—Win Willow, by Winonly.
Breeder, Farnsworth Farms (Fla.).　　　1973　2　M　0　0　　$105
Owner, G. W. McCall.　Trainer, E. Plesa, Sr.　　　$10,000
Apr12-73³GP　　5 f　:59　ft 11 117　7³² 6⁶½ 4⁶½ 5⁸² Ro'zCJr¹⁰ Mdn 82 ⓕCornB'll 117　Sp'k ofF'me　OldW'sT'e 12
Mar15-73³GP　　3 f　:33³/sft 11 117　5　　5⁵　6²¾ Rodr'zCJr⁹Mdn 90 ⓕNice toHave112　AmVoy　ScholarLea 14
　　April 19 Crc 3f ft :38³/sb　　　　March 30 Crc 4f ft :51³/sb　　　　March 23 Crc 4f ft :52²/sb

Hell's Extra　118
Ch. c (1971), by News Again—Hell Halberd, by Wilton Road.
Breeder, C. E. Bryant (N.C.).　　　　1973　1　M　0　0　　(—)
Owner, C. Bryant.　Trainer, R. A. Felix.　　　　$10,000
Apr 3-73³GP　　5 f　:59　ft 142 118　4³ 6⁶½ 9¹¹ 9¹¹ Val'zanF¹² Mdn 80 Mr.A.Z. 118　Jimmy'sBow　Be aNative 12
　　April 12 GP 5f ft 1:03bg　　　　March 30 GP 5f ft 1:01bg　　　　March 24 GP 4f ft :49b

Love Hit   **118**   B. g (1971), by Hitting Away—Yes Love, by Double Jay.
                                             Breeder, Fairview Farms, Inc. (Ky.).   1973 0 M 0 0   (—)
Owner, H. Casey & W. Mullins. Trainer, W. Mullins $10,000
        April 2 Crc 3f ft :38bg   March 19 Crc 3f ft :38bg   March 7 Crc 2f ft :24³/shg

Horses Shown Below on 'Also Eligible' List and Not in Order of Post Positions.

Marvelous Mix   **118**   B. g (1971), by Mr. Right—Brawl, by Rough'n Tumble.
                                             Breeder, Tartan Farm Corp. (Fla.).   1973 0 M 0 0   (—)
Owner, Tartan Farm. Trainer, F. Gomez. $10,000
        April 16 Crc 4f ft :50b   April 7 Crc 4f ft :51b   March 31 Crc 4f ft :51b

Southern Legend   **118**   Ch. c (1971), by Ways and Means—Vera, by Kesrullah.
                                             Breeder, Sunshine Stud (Fla.).   1973 0 M 0 0   (—)
Owner, G. Browles. Trainer, R. Andersen. $10,000

Southside Story   **115**   Dk. b. or br. f (1971), by Roi Dagobert—Southside Miss, by First Cabin.
                                             Breeder, B. Levkoff (Fla.).   1973 1 M 0 0   (—)
Owner, I. Lippert. Trainer, R. Merritt. $10,000
Apr12-73³GP   5 f :59 ft 52 117   8⁴⅔ 8¹⁰ 8¹² 7¹³ Russ'lloA¹ Mdn 78 ℗CornB'll 117   Sp'k ofF'me   OldW'sT'e 12
        April 18 Crc 4f ft :52b   April 11 Crc 3f ft :38bg   April 4 Crc 5f ft 1:05²/sb

Chance Orphan   **108**   Ro. f (1971), by Chancero—Litany, by Primate.
                                             Breeder, H. R. Caple (Fla.).   1973 0 M 0 0   (—)
Owner, H. R. Caple. Trainer, H. R. Caple. $10,000
        April 13 Crc 4f ft :49¹/shg   April 2 Crc 3f ft :38bg   March 28 Crc 3f ft :38²/sbg

The answer is forthcoming in the section on money management. You play enough to win not only this race but something
for every previous race which missed. It's not too complex a
subject, but it does require some explanation. At the moment,
let's take a general look at Sam's system of winner (or in-the-
money) selection. Sam's approach is broad enough to take into
account many factors, and it takes them into account automatically, with no real consideration for "emotional" factors which
often sway a stable or a trainer when he decides whether or not
to back a horse. Of course, the owner, the trainer, and the jockey
do have certain information which Sam does not have. For instance, Sam can never be absolutely certain that a horse is being
sent out to win. Today's race may simply be a conditioner for
some future race. Once in a long while, a horse will win a race in
spite of the trainer and the jockey. He will win when the stable
doesn't have a dollar on him, and the odds are high. In this case,
Sam *will* have a dollar or two on him, if he qualifies. The point
is, of course, that Sam uses the odds to work *for* him in any race.
It really doesn't matter too much why a horse is going off at
these high odds. When the high-odds horse does win, and it happens often enough as we have seen, the reason often is that the
public has overlooked the merits of the horse.

When you confine your bets to the high-odds horses, you insure a good payoff. This is a basic truth and the one on which Sam's system essentially rests. When he wins, Sam is going to get paid well. Given that fact, we proceed to the next principle in Sam's system: that of eliminating the losers. Of course, all the fans at the track consider that they are eliminating the losers when they look at the *Form* and evaluate the horse's past performance. But remember, they are looking primarily at the first four favorites. They figure simply that they will cash more tickets if they look only at the first four or five favorites in a race with a large field. And they are right to the extent that they do cash more tickets than Sam will ever cash. But the tickets are not worth very much in dollar-terms, and they certainly do not represent a good return-on-investment percentage.

By eliminating the losers, Sam means the *high-odds* losers first and foremost. In the case of second races in a double, it is the morning line which gives him the probable odds, and he proceeds from that point. In most other races, it is the tote board which gives him the odds. But he must not throw away those horses which last night were listed at high odds and which today, on the board, have dropped dramatically. He must balance good judgment with the requirement for high odds in order to gain a high return.

One great advantage of Sam's system is that it permits us to play almost every race. The exception is that race with few runners and low odds. It's hardly worthwhile to play a race with four or five horses, the highest odds being six-to-one. We would do better to sit out a race now and then, investing our capital when and where it can really work for us.

We go to the races for two reasons. We go for enjoyment, as well as to make money. Somehow, the pleasure is lessened when we have nothing going in the race. A race without a wager is completely academic. Nine hundred and ninety-nine fans out of a thousand want to have something hanging on the outcome of the race. That may be called gambling. But we are not there to gamble. We are not lured by the prospect of failure. Quite the opposite. We are serious investors. We want a good return on our money. We enjoy it even more when the return is a fast return. In no other investment can we get such a fast turn-over of capital as in racing. Actually, we can use the same capital over and over again, during a day. This amplifies the return on investment. Furthermore, we can use that rapid turn-over to our advantage. Not without risk, however. There will always be an element of risk in racing, as there is an element of risk in any type of investment. We live in the very midst of chance, but we know, fundamentally, that the *whole* of life is not a matter of chance.

Life is a problem-solving struggle for existence, and perhaps the best we can do is to reduce to a minimum the amount, or the degree, of chance in our lives. Sam found a way to reduce the degree of chance involved in a race. Eliminate the losers! Get rid of the dogs! When at last you do invest, make sure in so far as possible that the odds are working for you. What you must have is an overlay. That is, the horse may have an actual chance of one in ten of winning, but you must get, if he does win, a return of 20-1 on your investment. Sam's specialty was invest ing in overlays. His System was designed to pick those horses which would almost automatically *become* overlays.

But Sam also knew that if you make a hundred thousand dollars a year, it will take ten years to make a million. And Sam didn't have ten years. Therefore he needed something more than a winning system: He needed a method of managing his money.

In the next few pages, you will find the charts that reveal the degree of success of Sam's selection system. You may want to read them line by line. Or you may prefer to skim the charts quickly and go on to the meat of the matter, which is: what do they mean? To some degree, at least, the meaning of the charts is given in the notes that follow them. The charts, then, have two good reasons for being. First of all, they show, in terms of hard cash, what happens when you consistently follow the Hirsch System of Winner Selection.

Secondly, they furnish an emotional underpinning for your activities in the future. If the charts have any validity at all, they will convince you that Sam has the right way. This conviction is necessary if you wish to follow the path yourself. Two reasons for the charts. And surely, two reasons are enough.

5

The Charts and What They Mean

SYMBOLS USED AND THEIR MEANING

Q1, Q2, Q3—indicate the first, second, and third qualifying horses.

$Q1^1$—indicates that qualifier number one is also the highest odds on board.

$Q1^2$—indicates that qualifier number one is the second highest odds on board.

$Q2^3$—indicates that qualifier number two is third highest odds on board; etc.

2_f^{11}—indicates the second race, with a field of eleven horses, all fillies.

$5_{f/m}^{12}$—indicates fifth race, a field of twelve, fillies and mares
‣Fillies are up to four-years old. Mares are five and up.

1_M^9—indicates first race, a field of nine, and a maiden race.

3_{Msw}^{10}—indicates third race, a field of ten, a maiden race with special weights.

(5)—indicates the horse has accrued five (5) points; etc.

Po—indicates probable odds; as in Q1ₚₒ—which means, the

number one qualifier in a second race, at the highest probable odds (usually 30-1).

Lionized^{115}—indicates that the horse Lionized is carrying 115 pounds in the race.

DQ—indicates disqualified.

E—indicates entry, where two horses are coupled together on one ticket, for wagering purposes.

Fco—indicates co-favorite; horses that are favorites at the same odds.

F1—indicates the first favorite. F2 indicates the second favorite; etc.

F2$_q$—indicates the second favorite in our system, not the actual second favorite, who has been disqualified. F2$_q$ may be the actual third or fourth favorite.

Ao—indicates actual odds, as opposed to Po for probable odds.

(A)—indicates automatic bet, a horse who has not accrued any points.

CHART I   Hialeah Park, Straight Bets: April 1972

Apr. 1: Sat.	2^{11}_1	$Q1^1_{Po}$	Dear Little Devil^{116} (7) 14–1	$ 29.60	$13.00	$11.20
		$Q2_{Po}$	Our Port^{116} (9) 38–1	——	——	——
		$Q3_{Po}$	Pot Peeker^{111} (8) 11–1	——	——	——
	6^8	$Q1^1$	Dancers Gift^{115} (7) 59–1	120.00	28.20	7.40
		$Q2^2$	Belmont Brook^{115} (11) 45–1	——	——	——
	8^6	$Q1^1$	Lionized^{115} (5) 11–1	23.80	8.80	4.40
		$Q2^2$	Salvo^{115} (5) 9–1	——	——	——
	9^6	$Q1^1$	Victors Verse^{114} (7) 61–1	——	——	——
		$Q2^2$	Head of the River^{112} (10) 19–1	41.00	8.40	8.40
Apr. 3: Mon.	$7^8_{f/m}$	$Q1^1$	Day and Age^{113} (6) 24–1	——	——	——
		$Q2^2$	Quick Cat^{116} (6) 21–1	——	14.60	8.80
		$Q3^3$	Girl Returns^{116} (6) 14–1	——	——	——
Apr. 4: Tues.	2^{12}	$Q1_{Po}$	Sub's Bay^{114} (5)	——	——	——
		$Q2_{Po}$	Mesmer^{113} (5) 52–1	——	——	15.60
	9^9	$Q1^4$	Sub Home^{114} (6) 10–1	21.80	8.40	4.40
Apr. 5: Wed.	$2^{12}_{f/m}$	$Q1_{Po}$	Be Seeing You^{114} (7) 39–1	79.80	28.80	14.40
		$Q2_{Po}$	Bally Bolero^{114} (5) 20–1	——	——	——
		$Q3_{Po}$	Blue Nalanda^{114} (5) 17–1	——	16.60	10.00
	3^{12}_{Msw}	$Q1^2$	Lucky Amoureaux^{118} 51–1 (A)	——	——	——
		$Q2^5$	Allervale^{118} (5) 42–1	——	35.80	12.00
		$Q3^6$	Picoco^{118} (5) 13–1	——	——	——
	7^{12}	$Q1^4$	Majestic Isle^{117} (7) 19–1	——	——	——

CHART I (continued)

	$Q2^5$	Rio Caudaloso^{117} (9) 18–1	38.80	16.60	8.80
8^9	$Q1^2$	Fota^{110} (9) 43–1	———	———	———
	$Q2^5$	Coupon Cutter^{115} (7) 16–1	34.40	11.00	4.80
9^{10}	$Q1^2$	Best Level^{115} (8) 33–1	———	———	———
	$Q2^3$	Seminole Joe^{115} (8) 27–1	56.20	13.00	5.20
10_f^{10}	$Q1^1$	Back In Clover^{112} (6) 56–1	———	35.60	12.40
	$Q2^2$	Grey's Lea Tank^{112} (5) 28–1	———	———	———
	$Q3^3$	Demerits^{114} (5) 23–1	———	———	———
Apr. 6: 2^{11}	$Q1_{Po}$	Barkhouse^{114} (5) 69–1	140.40	52.80	16.40
Thurs.	$Q2_{Po}$	Lebanese Doctor^{114} (7) 38–1	———	———	———
4^{11}	$Q1^1$	Bill Jack^{115} (7) 38–1	78.20	28.00	12.00
	$Q2^2$	Bug Spray^{107} (9) 36–1	———	———	———
5^{12}	$Q1^1$	Wise Lark^{109} (7) 80–1	———	———	———
	$Q2^4$	Immortal Life^{114} (4) 50–1	———	28.80	14.80
6^{12}	$Q1^2$	Fleet Bolina^{108} (5) 42–1	———	———	———
	$Q2^3$	Good Balance^{117} (5) 40–1	82.00	29.80	15.80
Apr. 7: 6^{11}	$Q1^3$	Bamboo^{114} (5) 16–1	———	17.60	9.20
Fri.	$Q2^4$	Saidir Sue^{116} (6) 15–1	31.80	15.80	9.20
7^5	$Q1^3$	My Pal Kurt^{110} (9) 19–1	———	———	———
	$Q2^2$	E(Getajetholme^{115} (3) 19–1	40.00	12.20	6.20
		(Holme Early (6)			
8^7	$Q1^1$	Clover Over (7) 19–1	———	———	———
		(No system horses in-the-money this race.)			
$9^9_{f/m}$	$Q1^1$	Carol Song^{115} (5) 18–1	———	———	———
	$Q2^2$	Jolly Fox^{115} (5) 15–1	———	———	———
	$Q3^3$	Big Swinger^{115} (6) 14–1	29.80	7.00	4.40
Apr. 8: 4^{10}	$Q1^3$	Boxhaul^{117} (6) 19–1	———	17.00	7.60
Sat.	$Q2^4$	Rock II^{117} (6) 14–1	———	———	———
Apr. 10: 3^{11}_{MSW}	$Q1^3$	Sweeping Prince^{120} (A) 31–1	———	———	———
Mon.	$Q2^4$	Shoe Size^{120} (A) 24–1	———	———	———
	$Q3^5$	Bold Umber^{120} (A) 15–1	32.00	11.20	5.40
6^{10}	$Q1^2$	Sing Out Roma^{115} (7) 21–1	———	———	———
	$Q2^4_q$	Fisherman's Wake^{117} (7) 10–1	22.60	10.80	5.60
Apr. 11: 2^{11}	$Q1_{Po}$	Consanguineous^{113} (9) 14–1	29.20	14.80	4.60
Tue.	$Q2_{Po}$	Ponderosa Dee^{117} (5) 20–1	———	———	———
5^{12}	$Q1^2$	Bud n Kelley^{112} (5) 66–1	———	56.00	20.60
	$Q2^3$	Early Eagle^{114} (5) 32–1	———	———	———
Apr. 12: 1^{12}	$Q1^5$	Lost Horizon^{116} (5) 29–1	60.20	24.80	13.00
Wed.	$Q2^7$	Sunset Sweetie^{116} (5)	———	———	———
4^9	$Q1^1$	Big Riddle^{117} (5) 31–1	———	———	———
	$Q2^4$	Papa Requested^{117} (5) 11–1	———	8.80	6.60

NOTE: Blink Prince was 11–1, with six points, but gave way to Fisherman's Wake who had a more recent race and also had seven points.

CHART I (continued)

5^{12}	$Q1^1$	Jowildor[117] (5) 45–1	———	———	———
	$Q2^2$	Margin of Victory[117] (6) 24–1	———	20.80	12.40
Apr. 13: $3^{10}_{MSW/f}$	$Q1^2$	Sheila's Chick[117] (A) 96–1	———	———	———
Thurs.	$Q2^4$	Goodby Juanita[117] (5) 26–1	53.40	11.00	5.80
9^8	$Q1^1$	Classy Breeze[114] (5) 23–1	———	18.80	7.40
	$Q2^3$	Logistical[118] (5) 20–1	———	———	———
10^{12}	$Q1^3$	King Ray[115] (7) 12–1	———	———	———
	$Q2^4$	Mid Rascal[117] (5) 12–1	25.20	9.40	6.20
Apr. 14: 10^{11}_f	$Q1^1$	Pot Peeker[109] (5) 38–1	———	———	———
Fri.	$Q2^4$	Dally Not[113] (8) 20–1	———	14.20	9.00
	$Q3^3$	Dear Little Devil (6) 27–1	———	———	10.40
Apr. 15: 2^{12}_{MSW}	$Q1_{PO}$	Commander Fayette[117] (5) 42–1	———	———	12.20
Sat.	$Q2_{PO}$	Native Shoes[122] (5) 20–1	———	12.20	6.00
	$Q3_{PO}$	On Loan[122] (5) 13–1	———	———	———
7^{12}	$Q1^1$	E(Maui King[113] (6) 39–1	———	———	———
		(Dun Hayen			
	$Q2^2$	Best Level[117] (5) 27–1	———	26.20	8.20
Apr. 17: 2^{12}	$Q1_{PO}$	Linlar[116] (5) 20–1	———	23.60	9.20
Mon.	$Q1^*_{o}$	Think Twice[116] (5) 230–1	———	———	———
$4^{12}_{f/m}$	$Q1^2$	Andrea's Star[113] (6) 123–1	———	———	———
	$Q2^4$	Secret Advisor[116] (6) 20–1	———	12.60	9.40
	$Q3^{6†}$	Be Seeing You[116] (6) 19–1	39.40	18.00	9.40
7^8	$Q1^4$	Cades Cove[115] (5) 11–1	24.20	8.00	7.40
10^9	$Q1^1$	Careto[110] (5) 40-1	———	———	11.80
Apr. 18: 2^{12}	$Q1_{PO}$	Ponderosa Dee[112] (6) 20–1	———	———	———
Tues.	$Q2_{PO}$	Secured Note[110] (7) 32–1	———	———	14.00
6^7	$Q1^1$	R Js Star[113] (5) 10–1	21.40	6.20	4.20
7^{10}	$Q1^3$	Dust Emission[115] (5) 27–1	———	27.00	13.80
	$Q2^5$	Glenjour[116] (5) 17–1	———	———	———
$8^7_{f/m}$	$Q1^2$	Exciting Divorcee[112] (8) 14–1	29.60	10.00	4.80
Apr. 19: 8^{11}	$Q1^3$	High Hearted[106] (8) 37–1	———	———	———
Wed.	$Q2^4$	Oconee[113] (6) 24–1	49.40	19.80	9.80
9^7	$Q1^1$	In Camera[117] (6) 14–1	———	———	———
	$Q2^2$	Country Friend[113] (7) 10–1	22.80	7.60	4.00
Apr. 20: 1^{12}_f	$Q1^6$	Ellie Belle[114] (5) 23–1	49.20	11.40	7.60
Thurs.	$Q2^7$	Lost Star[104] (8) 16–1	———	———	———
$2^{11}_{M(f)}$	$Q1_{PO}$	Civdad[110] (7) 20–1	27.20	9.20	6.20
	$Q2_{PO}$	Cotton Miss[105] (A) 52–1$_{AO}$	———	———	———
7^{10}	$Q1^1$	Caught In The Rain[113] (6) 55–1	———	———	———

*Instead of Q2 Possible Odds, we have substituted Q1 Actual Odds, due to the fact that a horse at 230–1 has five points and COULD do it.

†Be Seeing You was a co-favorite at 19–1 with Roses Day. Selection went to Be Seeing You who had WON her last race and has raced more recently than Roses Day.

CHART I (continued)

	$Q2^2$	Bird of Thoria^{117} (5) 19–1	———	———	———
	$Q3^3$‡	Automatic Harvey^{113} (5) 14–1	———	12.20	6.80
10^7	$Q1^1$	Count For More^{113} (6) 32–1	———	19.80	8.60
	$Q2^2$	Foreign Actor^{115} (6) 29–1	———	———	———
Apr. 21:3^8_M	$Q1^2$	Regal Bloom^{113} (8) 21–1	———	14.00	6.20
Fri.	$Q2^1$§	Needalift^{108} (5) 21–1	———	———	———
4^8	$Q1^1$	Jowildor^{115} (5) 52–1	———	———	9.60
	$Q2$	(None, for lack of odds.)			
5^9_M	$Q1^1$	Swoon's Pinto^{120} (A) 76–1	———	———	———
	$Q2^3$	Malicious Music^{120} (4) 47–1	———	———	5.80
Apr. 22:$1^{11}_{M(0)}$	$Q1^1$	Tepacaro^{114} (4) 63–1	———	28.60	11.60
Sat.	$Q2^2$	T. V. Miss^{114} (4) 46–1	———	———	———
	$Q3^3$	Lindaria^{114} (4) 33–1	———	———	———
6^7	$Q1^2$	Master In Chancery^{114} (6) 14–1	———	8.40	4.40
8^7	$Q1^1$	King Ray^{115} (5) 39–1	———	———	6.20
	$Q2^2$	Pagan King^{115} (5) 17–1	———	———	———
Apr. 24:$2^{11}_{f/m}$	$Q1_{PO}$	Lesville^{115} (5) 20–1	———	15.80	7.60
Mon.	$Q2_{PO}$	Nartan^{112} (5) 27–1$_{AO}$	57.00	22.00	9.20
8^6		No Hits. $Q1^1$ was Belmont Brook with 0 points, at 28–1. $Q2$ was Li'lbit O.K. with 9 points at 9–1. At 8–1 was Sir Holme with 7 points, the winner. You can't win 'em all.			
10^{12}	$Q1^2$	Blink Prince^{117} (5) 86–1	———	———	10.40
	$Q2^3$	Subterfuge^{115} (5) 24–1	———	———	———
Apr. 25:1^{12}_M	$Q1^2$	First Snow^{114} (4) 64–1	———	———	23.20
Tues.	$Q2^5$	Paddy's a Corker^{109} (6) 53–1	———	———	———
	$Q3^7$	Solid Port^{109} (6) 15–1	———	———	———
2^{12}	$Q1_{PO}$	Sub's Bay^{117} (6) 30–1	———	———	———
	$Q1_{AO}$	Gentle Times^{117} (6) 43–1	———	———	15.20
$7f^1$	$Q1^2$	Carlin B^{116} (4) 24–1	———	17.60	10.80
	$Q2^3$	Greys Lea Tank^{114} (5) 22–1	———	———	———
10^{11}	$Q1^1$	Zorzala^{110} (8) 170–1	———	———	———
	$Q2^2$	Chang^{117} (A) 32–1	65.20	18.60	15.20
Apr. 26:8^{12}	$Q1^3$	Challenging^{115} (5) 19–1	———	———	———
Wed.	$Q2^4$	Yakityak^{115} (4) 18–1	38.60	16.80	7.80
9^7	$Q1^1$	Anatole^{115} (6) 26–1	53.80	19.00	10.00
	$Q2$	(None, for lack of odds.)			
$10^{12}_{f/m}$	$Q1^1$	Iron Tonette^{109} (6) 67–1	———	———	———
	$Q2^3$	Georgia Grey^{112} (7) 56–1	———	———	13.40
Apr. 27:1^{12}_M	$Q1^5$	Indeput^{114} (4) 35–1	72.60	28.40	13.00
Thur.		(No Q2 for lack of odds.)			

‡In a Perfecta race, always check Q3, which came in second in this race and was part of the Perfecta payoff.
§Needalift and Regal Bloom were co-favorites at 21–1 each.

CHART I (continued)

2^{10}_{MO}	Q1po	Alcinative[117] (4) 30–1	30.40	13.20	12.00
	Q2po	Amber Wink[109] (A) 10–1	———	———	———
4^{8}_{m}	Q1[1]	Fidlers Lane[112] (5) 21–1	———	———	———
	Q2[2]	Brewster Belle[112] (5) 19–1	———	13.20	5.40
10^{12}	Q1[5]	Mehuin[114] (6) 20–1	42.60	16.40	7.60
		(No Q2 for lack of odds.)			

Apr. 28:   No records.

Apr. 29: 5^{10}	Q1[3]	Goodpus[113] (7) 15–1	32.00	11.80	6.00
Sat.	Q2[4]	Table Conquest[117] (5) 11–1	———	———	———
7^{9}	Q1[4]	Second Passage[117] (6) 25–1	———	13.60	4.80
	Q2[5]	Our Scene[115] (6) 11–1	———	———	———
$9^{9}_{f/m}$	Q1[1]	Western Idol[115] (8) 51–1	———	26.00	9.60
	Q2[2]	Desert Sense[115] (7) 26–1	———	———	———

Hialeah Park, April, 1972—Straight

SUMMARY:

Number of Racing Days: 24

Number of Races: 240   (10 races per day at Hialeah Park)

Unit of Investment: $2 $2 to Win, $2 to Place. Also, $2 to Show if odds are 30–1 or higher.

	Q1		Q2		Q3	
	Win	Place	Win	Place	Win	Place
Return	966.00	680.60	658.40	410.00	386.00	249.40
Invested	480.00	480.00	480.00	480.00	———	———
Net Profit	486.00	200.60	178.40	–70.00	———	———
Percentage	101%	41%	35%			
TOTALS:	*Q1, Q2 Win*		*Q1, Q2 Place*		*Combined Total*	
Return	1624.40		1090.60		2715.00	
Invested	960.00		960.00		1920.00	
Net Profit	664.40		130.60		795.00	
Percentage	69%		13%		41%	

		Total return	Average	
Number of Q1 hits:	18	$ 966.00	$53.65	WIN
Number of Q2 hits:	14	658.40	47.00	WIN
Number of Q1 hits:	34	680.60	20.20	PLACE
Number of Q2 hits:	25	410.00	16.40	PLACE
Q1, Q2 Win Hits:	32	1624.40	50.75	
Q1, Q2 Place Hits:	59	1090.60	18.30	

CHART II   Hialeah Park, Daily Doubles: April 1972

Apr. 1:	F2 (Bobs B Bees) with Q1$_{Po}$ (Dear Little Devil)	$ 202.20
Apr. 6:	F4 (Road Fathom) with Q1$_{Po}$ (Barkhouse)	478.60
Apr. 7:	#2Po (Elkwood Flash) with #4Po (J.P. McCarthy)	36.20
Apr. 8:	#3Po (Maw Nipper) with #3Po (Prince Needles)	61.00
Apr. 11:	F4 (Naptown Nabob) with Q1$_{Po}$ (Consanguineous)	263.80
Apr. 12:	Q1 (Lost Horizon) with #3Po (Ben Hur Brad)	438.00
Apr. 17:	#3Po (Sail Ahoy) with #2Po (Royal Care)	128.40
Apr. 20:	Q1 (Ellie Belle) with Q1$_{Po}$ (Civdad)	532.00
Apr. 22:	#2Po (Kathy Flys) with #4Po (First Score)	61.20
Apr. 24:	#2Po (Come October) with Q2$_{Po}$ (Nartan)	346.60
Apr. 27:	Q1 (Indeput) with Q1$_{Po}$ (Alcinative)	781.60

Gross Return: $3329.60

There were twenty-four racing days in April, 1972. The investment in daily doubles during this period was twenty-five tickets (or $50) a day, for a total of $1,200. The following is a breakdown of the twenty-five tickets:

1st Race	2nd Race	Totals
Q1	#2, #3, #4Po	3 Tickets
Q2	#2, #3, #4Po	3
F2, F3, F4	Q1$_{Po}$	3
F2, F3, F4	Q2$_{Po}$	3
Q1, Q2	Q1, Q2	4
#2, #3, #4Po	#2, #3, #4Po	9

Total cost per day: $50.00   25 Tickets

Gross Return: $3329.60   Return on Investment: 177%
Investment: 1200.00

Net Profit: $2129.60

CHART III   Hialeah Park, Perfectas: April 1972

Apr. 1:	5^{12}	F3$_q$	(Topi) with F2 (Successfully)	$ 55.80
Sat.	7^9	F2	(Buffare) with F4 (Landing More)	51.60
	10^7	F2$_q$	(Bookish) with F3$_q$ (Classic Hit)	50.00
Apr. 3:	5$^{12}_{f\,m}$	F6$_q$	(Nana Blanch) with F5 (Mrs. Barbara M)	318.00
Mon.	10$^8_{f\,m}$	F3	(Miss Tracer) with F4$_q$ (Pisis)	89.00
Apr. 4:	3$^{11}_M$	F2	(Lamp) with F4 (Penruss)	33.80
Tues.	5^{12}	F4	(Mahlan) with F5 (Out of the Past)	776.40
Apr. 5:	3$^{12}_M$	F2	(Big Spruce) with Q2 (Allervale)	633.80
Wed.	5^{12}	F2	(Ajedrez) with F3 (Road Mail)	69.20

CHART III (continued)

	7^{12}	Q2	(Rio Caudaloso) with F3 (Whitsun)	341.50
	10^{10}	F1	(Farm for Cash) with Q1 (Back In Clover)	271.60
Apr. 6:	3^{12}_M	F3	(Ladies Agreement) with F4 (Hard Pocket)	70.80
Thurs.	5^{12}	F4$_q$*	(Naturally Tops) with Q2 (Immortal Life)	1,417.00
Apr. 7:	7^9	Q2	(E: Getajetholme with F4$_q$ (Gay Gaucho)	177.40
Fri.			Holme Early)	
	10^8	F2$_q$	(Shadowman) with F3$_q$ (Count For More)	56.40
Apr. 8:	3^{10}_M	F3	(Rastaferian) with F2 (Looms Great)	81.20
Sat.	5^{10}	F4	(County Judge) with F5 (Sui Generis)	294.00
	10^8	F2	(Flying Brick) with F4 (Palmer's Son)	59.00
Apr. 10:	3^{11}_M	Q3	(Bold Umber) with F1 (Scotch Mark)	116.20
Mon.	10^{10}	F2	(Sir R) with F4 (Whoa Gus)	75.80
Apr. 11:	3^{12}_M	F3	(Luv Nancy) with F2 (Speed Personified)	56.20
Tues.	5^{12}	F4	(Picadilly Red) with Q1 (Bud n Kelley)	785.80
Apr. 12:	5^{12}†	Q4	(Cellophane) with Q2 (Margin of Victory)	(513.20)†
Apr. 12:	7^9	F2	(Tellystar) with F4 (Behaving Honey)	85.60
Wed.				
Apr. 13:	$3^{10}_{Msw_f}$	Q2	(Goodby Juanita) with F1 (Hard Pocket)	116.40
Thurs.	5^{10}	F3	(Eleven Cuidado) with F4 (Wayward Lad)	134.40
	7^{11}	F2	(Wintex) with F3$_q$ (First Passion)	122.80
	10^{12}	Q2	(Mid Rascal) with F2 (Hardy Hugh)	217.60
Apr. 14:	5^9	F2	(Daddy's Here) with F3 (Pride of Kentucky)	52.60
Fri.	7^{12}	F2	(Gabriel) with F3 (Inside Tackle)	50.20
	10^{11}_f	F2	(Born To Behave) with Q3 (Dally Not)	162.20
Apr. 15:	5^9	F4	(Dr. C. Salk) with F2$_q$ (Boxhaul)‡	62.80
Sat.				
Apr. 15:	7^{12}	F4	(Better Sea) with Q2 (Best Level)	206.40
Apr. 17:	3^{12}	F4	(Mangoright) with F2 (Chieftan's Glory)	121.40
Mon.	5^{11}	F3	(Welsh Miner) with F4 (Shepherd's Song)	50.20
	7^{10}	Q1	(Cades Cove) with F2 (Fanny Farkel)	117.40
Apr. 18:	3^{12}_M	F3	(Joy to Behold) with F4$_q$ (Reverend Rose)§	210.00
Tues.	$5^{11}_{f/m}$	F4	(Piggyback) with F5 (Day and Age)	296.60
	7^{10}	F4	(Trader Tim) with Q1 (Dust Emission)	297.00
	10^8	F3	(Alvar Fanez) with F4 (Hans Grey)	46.80
Apr. 19:	10^{12}	F3$_q$	(Margin of Victory) with	
Wed.			F4$_q$ (Table's Conquest)	173.40

*Naturally Tops was F5 but replaces the real F4, I'm In Favor. Naturally Tops is dropping $2,000 in class, while I'm In Favor is running in same class. Naturally Tops is also running again after a more recent race. I'm In Favor has a three-pound weight advantage, but that is overbalanced by the class drop and the more recent race.

†This one falls outside the system and is included here to show that you can't win 'em all. We don't go down as far as Q3 in a race of this type, much less to Q4, which is also F7. Cellophane has odds of 12–1, despite the fact that he is dropping $1,500 in class and raced just four days ago. This is some sort of ready horse with good odds, but we simply had too many other qualifiers.

‡Boxhaul and Rock II were co-favorites and one had to be disqualified. Boxhaul had the better record all around, and Rock II went out.

§The regular F4 (La Crosse) was DQ'd for not having raced in past month. Reverend Rose and Interlude, both at 8–1, were next in line, and Reverend Rose got the nod for being an automatic bet.

CHART III (continued)

Apr. 20: 7^{10}	F3	(Mi Rebano) with Q3 (Automatic Harvey)‖	(259.60)
Thurs. 10^9	F1	(Dashing Prince) with Q1 (Count For More)	115.60
Apr. 21: 3^8_M	F2	(Top Duel) with Q1 (Regal Bloom)	108.20
Fri. 7^8	F2	(Nequal) with $F4_q$ (Naturally Tops)#	62.20
Apr. 22: 5^9	F4	(Break Or Make) with F2 (Moon Eagle)	77.60
Sat. 7^{10}	F3	(New Alibhai) with F2 (Flying Brick)	46.20
10^8	F4	(Papa Requested) with F2 (Cherry Sun)	86.00
Apr. 24: 5^7_M	F4	(Wooglin) with F3 (Armed Control)	77.60
Mon.			
Apr. 25: 7^{11}	F3	(Antifreeze) with Q1 (Carlin B)	236.60
Tues. 10^{11}	Q2	(Chang) with $F4_q$ (Empeltre)	487.60
Apr. 26: 5^8_{f2}	F5	(Natural Sound) with F2 (Straight Trip)**	(71.40)
Wed. $10^{12}_{f/m}$	F4	(Royal Platza) with F2 (Piggyback)	65.00
Apr. 27: 7^9	F2	(Mi Rebano) with F4 (Ray's Rebel)	44.00
Thurs. 10^{12}	Q1	(Mehuin II) with F4 (Luengo)	275.80
Apr. 28:		No Racing.	
Fri.			
Apr. 29: 5^{10}	Q1	(Goodpus) with F3 (Manny L)	287.80
Sat. 7^9	F1	(Country Friend) with Q1 (Second Passage)	58.60

‖Here is another miss, since we do not bet Q3 in a regular race. As good handicappers we might have substituted Q3 for Q2, but both horses did qualify under the rules. This payoff is not included in the computations that follow.

#Naturally Tops has more recent race than actual F4; gained in stretch run, last race, *and* is dropping in class.

**This is a race for two-year-old fillies, and it is difficult to know which horses to keep in and which to disqualify. F3 and F4 are both moving up sharply in class and probably should be disqualified, making Natural Sound $F3_q$. Natural Sound has run in an Allowance race before and recently and really should be the F3 selection.

SUMMARY:

Number of racing days: 24

Number of Perfecta races: 96

Investment per race: $60, for a total investment of: $5,760.00

Gross Return on all Perfecta investments: $9,945.50

Total invested:	5,760.00
Net Profit:	4,185.50

Percentage of Net Profit: 72%.

Breakdown of F4, F5, and F6:	Return:	1,685.00
	Investmt:	1,152.00
	Net Profit:	433.00

Breakdown of F1 with Q1, Q2:	Return:	678.40
	Investment:	768.00
	Net Loss:	$ 89.60

NOTE 1: As you will see in the calculations for other charts, that is, at other tracks, the F1 net return is most often a profit. For that reason, we keep it in the system. The total or net percent-profit for all flat-bets on Perfectas remains at 72 percent, which is very good in anybody's book. With a little careful progressive investing, the profits on Perfectas and Exactas can become out of this world. Of course, the same is true of Daily Doubles, that other source of high monetary return on your investment.

CHART III (continued)

NOTE 2:   It is perhaps a bit misleading to say that we have a total investment in Perfectas of $5,760 for these twenty-four racing days. From an overall point of view, this statement is true. In reality, we are investing and getting returns almost every day. At no time do we have more than a few hundred dollars invested, and after the first week practically all of our investment money is track money, as the saying goes. We've already pocketed our original "investment".

Hialeah, April 1972

	Straight	Doubles	Perfectas	Totals
Return	2,715.00	3,329.60	9,945.50	15,999.10
Invested	1,920.00	1,200.00	5,760.00	8,880.00
Net Profit	795.00	2,129.60	4,185.50	7,110.10
Percentage	41%	177%	72%	81%

CHART IV   Pimlico, Straight Bets: May 1972

May 1: Mon.	4^7	Q1^1	Go Bet^{114} (6) 12–1	$25.00	12.60	6.60
		Q2^2	Double A^{112} (7)—12–1	——	——	——
	5^{12}	Q1^3	Ducksummer^{114} (7) 51–1	——	15.60	8.60
		Q2^5	Beau Sock^{114} (6) 21–1	43.40	16.60	11.20
	9^{12}	Q1^2	Typo Roman^{114} (6) 24–1	——	——	——
		Q2^3	Fiendish Lad^{112} (5) 20–1	41.60	15.60	9.40
May 2: Tues.	4^9_M	Q1^1	Amelem^{115} (A) 42–1	86.00	23.00	9.00
		Q2^2	Gambler's Blues^{115} (A) 20–1	——	——	——
	$6^8_{f/m}$	Q1^2	Bona Dea^{114} (6) 13–1	——	——	——
		Q2^3	Boogaloo Dancer^{112} (5) 11–1	24.60	8.00	6.00
	7^{12}	Q1^2	Carry My Hope^{112} (7) 47–1	——	——	10.00
		Q2^3	Bellwood^{112} (6) 35–1	——	——	——
	8^6	Q1^3	Little Seth^{117} (10) 6–1	14.00	4.80	3.20
May 3: Wed	1^2_M	Q1^2	Marvin's Windy^{112} (5) 73–1	——	57.00	20.00
		Q2^3*	Little Nasrulla^{112} (A) 45–1	——	——	——
		Q3^6	Dawning Sun^{110} (4) 24–1	——	——	——
	3^{12}_M	Q1^2	Kiss Me Kacy^{107} (8) 46–1	——	——	15.00
		Q2^5	Black Watch^{102} (5) 25–1	——	18.80	9.60
		Q3^6	Tribon^{107} (A) 23–1	——	——	——
May 4: Thurs.	$2^{12}_{f/m}$	Q1$_{Po}$	Snake Bit^{114} (7) 20–1Po	——	22.00	8.80
May 5: Fri.	3^8	Q1^2	Branee^{114} (6) 18–1	——	——	——
		Q2^3	Lady Jester^{109} (8) 11–1	25.20	8.40	5.20
	8^6	Q1^1	Native Wave^{117} (6) 16–1	——	——	——

*In this maiden race there were two distinct age groups and weight groups. Take the lower weight group first and go through the odds scale from top down, before going to the higher weight group. Both qualifiers came from the lower weight group.

CHART IV (continued)

	Q2^2	Last Triumph^{117} (6) 15–1	——	——	——
	(Q3^3	Gentleman Conn^{119} (6) 9–1	20.60	6.00	3.80)†
May 6: 7^9	Q1^1	Lemon Mist^{117} (6) 24–1	——	——	——
Sat.	Q2^2	Crooked Answer^{107} (6) 23–1	——	——	——
	Q3^3	Profundity^{107} (5) 11–1	——	11.00	5.80
May 8: 1^{11}	Q1^3	Yorktown Class^{109} (10) 67–1	——	32.20	15.40
Mon.	Q2^5	Aureole Boy^{113} (5) 48–1	——	——	——
2$^{12}_{Msw}$	Q1$_{Po}$	Morning Star^{107} (5) 20–1Po	——	——	——
	Q2$_{Po}$	Mongo Bongo^{112} (6) 20–1Po	——	——	——
	Q3$_{Po}$	Rounder's Choice^{115} (A) 13–1	28.40	12.60	7.00
5^9	Q1^1	Mongo's Image (5) 24–1	50.20	16.40	9.80
	Q2^2	Verace^{117} (4⅔) 21–1‡	——	17.40	13.80
6^7	Q1^1	Res Gestae^{115} (5) 13–1	——	——	——
	Q2^2	Hostynsky^{112} (7) 12–1	26.20	10.00	5.40
9^8	Q1^1	Social Curtsey^{112} (6) 12–1	26.20	10.60	4.80
	Q2^2	Flight Ruler^{115} (8) 12–1	——	——	——
May 9: 1$^{12}_M$	Q1^1	Tor's Riddle^{107} (4) 102–1	——	——	23.80
Tues.	Q2^3	Isshecute^{112} (A) 48–1	——	——	——
2^{10}	Q1$_{Po}$	Open Draft^{107} (5) 34–1Ao	——	——	9.80
	Q2^4	Timber Tavern^{107} (6) 16–1Ao	34.20	14.00	7.40
3^8	Q1^2	Hong Kong Lady^{107} (4) 13–1	28.80	8.00	5.80
4^5	Q1^1	Winnie Roe^{112} (7) 12–1	——	——	——
	Q2^2	Brave Maid^{112} (5) 6–1	13.00	4.60	3.40
9^8	Q1^1	Luengo^{114} (5) 17–1	——	——	——
	Q2^2	Typo Roman^{113} (8) 10–1	——	——	——
	(Q3^3	Karenadee^{108} (8) 9–1	——	10.40	4.20)§
May 10: 7^8	Q1^3	Doverland^{119} (5) 22–1	45.40	8.40	5.00
Wed.	Q2^5	Toure Sur^{115} (5) 11–1	——	——	——
May 11: 2^{11}	Q1$_{Po}$	Cherry Red^{108} (12) 42–1	85.40	40.00	17.60
Thurs.	Q2^4	Hap's Pepe^{113} (6) 27–1	——	——	——
May 12: 5^{10}	Q1^1	No Brag Just Fast^{115} (6) 49–1	——	37.60	17.00
Fri.	Q2^2	Dilimar^{117} (5) 28–1	——	——	——
May 13: 3^9	Q1^2	Kiddie O^{114} (3) 43–1	——	——	14.40
Sat.	Q2^3	Seditious^{112} (5) 12–1	——	——	——
	Q3^4	Fellas Little Lady^{115} (5) 12–1	——	——	——
5^{10}	Q1^1	I'm Irving^{103} (22) 46–1	——	31.00	11.60

†Not a hit, strictly speaking, and is not included in the money totals at the end of the chart. All three horses had six points, but Gentleman Conn worked two days ago and is dropping three pounds off last race.

‡Verace has only 4⅔ points, but Hartack is riding and the odds are good. ⅔ of a point comes from the fact that twice Verace finished 6½ lengths or less off the winner.

§Not a hit in the system since Karenadee is Q3 in a regular race. But we often look at the number-three qualifier to see if there is anything really outstanding. Karenadee is dropping in class, raced just eight days ago, is getting in at 108 pounds, and gained nearly two lengths in the stretch run of her last race. She ran second to Light Airs and was part of a $142 Perfecta. Light Airs was F5 and Karenadee was F6. She is covered in the Perfecta betting by the F4, F5, F6 combination of tickets, which Sam recommends as insurance in Perfecta-Exacta wagering. Money is not counted in the straight-bet calculations at the end of this chart.

CHART IV (continued)

		(No Q2 for lack of qualifiers with high enough odds.)‖			
8^9	Q1[1]	Magoni[103] (7) 48–1	——	——	——
	Q2[2]	Onandaga[110] (8) 33–1	68.20	17.20	5.80
9^9	Q1[1]	Transformer[112] (4) 27–1	——	——	——
	Q2[2]	Carderock[114] (6) 16–1	34.20	10.00	5.80
May 15: 5^8	Q1[3]	Full of Fight[119] (7) 12–1	——	10.80	7.00
Mon.	Q2[4]	Lipp Mann[112] (6) 10–1	22.00	10.00	6.20
8^9	Q1[2]	Rockem Back[115] (5) 17–1	——	15.00	8.40
	Q2[3]	Amber Hawk[113] (7) 12–1	25.40	14.40	8.80
May 16: 1^{11}_M	Q1[1]	Back Issue[112] (4) 36–1	——	23.60	11.60
Tues.	Q2[2]	Lena Carla[107] (A) 34–1	——	——	——
	Q3[3]	Iron Bound[105] (4) 29–1	——	——	——
2^{12}_M	Q1[1]$_{Po}$	Battle Image[107] (5) 30–1	——	——	——
	Q2[5]$_{Ao}$	Secret Rule[107] (6) 31–1	——	19.80	9.40
	Q3[6]	Homebrew[107] (A) 18–1	——	——	——
3^{10}_{MSW}	Q1[1]	Forgene[120] (3) 53–1	——	——	——
	Q2[2]	National Password[120] (A) 52–1	——	22.60	10.00
	Q3[4]	Norther Park[120] (4) 20–1	——	——	——
8^8	Q1[2]	Tiger Wood[113] (6) 17–1	——	——	——
	Q2[3]	Boogaloo Dancer[112] (9) 10–1	22.80	6.60	4.40
May 17: 8^6	Q1[3]	Prairie Sailor[112] (5) 10–1	——	5.20	3.20
Wed.					
May 18: 1^{11}_{rm}	Q1[1]	Blessed Rhythm[116] (5) 68–1	——	——	——
Thurs.	Q2[3]	Sarabon[119] (A) 34–1	——	20.20	11.00
	Q3[5]	Late Copy[114] (6) 12–1	——	——	——
5^{12}	Q1[1]	Ronny Z114 (8) 43–1	——	——	——
	Q2[4]	HowSweetheeis[114] (5) 21–1#	43.60	18.40	8.80
7^7	Q1[1]	Fiendish Lad[113] (5) 13–1	——	——	——
	Q2[3]	Bold David[114] (5) 9–1	——	8.00	5.20
May 19: 1^{10}	Q1[3]	Premediate[114] (4) 31–1	——	14.20	5.80
Fri. 5^{12}_{MSW}	Q1[2]	Nymph's Son[120] (5) 55–1	——	33.60	15.60
	Q2[3]	Crown Coinage[110] (6) 30–1	——	——	——
	Q3[4]	Mister Gunn[120] (6) 21–1	——	——	——
	(Q4[5]**	Ambi Hula[120] (5) 17–1	36.00	21.60	11.80)

‖When no Q2 is available for lack of odds, it is permissible to drop down to a four-point requirement. If none available, then there is no Q2 wager. In the Exacta, use Q1 and F2, F3, F4 and F5 for the five-horse box or crisscross combination.

#A recheck of this race reveals that Cogitate (114) at 28–1 should be Q2[3], with five points. Cogitate ran out of the money. Since this is an Exacta race, we always look carefully at Q3, which is HowSweetheeis at 21–1, with five points. Both horses finished sixth last race; both gained in the stretch run, last race. Both are at 114 pounds; and both are moving up slightly in class. Cogitate is a gelding; HowSweet is a colt. Their odds are within seven points of each other, and it would be a difficult choice. Since it is an Exacta race, Sam would play them both, in straight bets. As for the Exacta, HowSweetheeis becomes F6 when Immediacy and Am Brer Fox are disqualified for not having a race within 18 days. Be Certain, the Place horse, is F6, and the Exacta of $708.60 would be captured by the combination of F4, F5 and F6.

**Not a hit, strictly speaking. Here again, the next horse outside the regular qualifiers is the winner. Since this is a maiden race for three-yr-olds, it is well to consider the top four qualifiers. It is also an important Exacta race. Q4 and Q1 are the correct combination, paying $1134.00.

CHART IV (continued)

7^{10}	Q1³	Tip O Flag^{114} (8) 17–1	37.00	12.00	8.40
	Q2⁴	Herald Square^{117} (6) 16–1	——	——	——
May 20: 1^{12}	Q1⁴	Empire Knight^{113} (6) 27–1	——	——	——
Sat.	Q2⁵	Smooth Stone^{113} (6) 19–1	——	——	——
	(Q3⁶††	Island Chant^{113} (13) 17–1	35.40	17.20	9.40)
2^{10}	Q1ᴘₒ	Rhythm^{107} (7) 20–1Po	24.40	9.60	6.20
	Q2ᴘₒ	Count Porter^{114} (5) 15–1Po	——	——	10.20
May 22: 3^{8}	Q1³	Bow Shannon^{116} (5) 9–1	19.20	9.20	6.20
Mon.					
May 23: 4^{8}	Q1¹	Lady Ara^{117} (3) 30–1	——	19.40	10.20
Tues.	Q2²	Royal Carle^{117} (A) 27–1	——	——	6.60
	Q3³	Solitary Tune^{117} (3) 13–1	——	——	——
	(Q4⁴‡‡	Strong Side^{120} (A) 10–1	22.40	10.20	6.40)
May 24: 2^{10}	Q1ᴘₒ	Forward Star^{113} (5) 30–1Po	——	——	——
Wed.	Q2ᴘₒ	Aureole Boy^{119} (5) 30–1Po	——	20.60	10.00
4^{7}	Q1²	Run Jackie Run^{109} (8) 20–1	——	——	——
	Q2³	Lively Nip^{106} (7) 12–1	——	6.60	4.00
7^{6}	Q1¹	Irish Tenor^{114} (5) 14–1	30.40	13.00	7.60
	Q2²	Don George^{119} (7) 10–1	——	——	——
May 25: 5^{9}_{M}	Q1¹	Jungle Journal^{117} (A) 25–1	——	14.80	10.20
Thurs.	Q2²	My Boy Joe^{120} (A) 22–1	——	——	——
	Q3³	Jane Lacy^{117} (A) 17–1	——	——	8.20
7^{7}	Q1²	Question the Devil^{114} (7) 12–1	——	——	——
	Q2³	Bargain Price^{112} (5) 9–1	——	9.00	4.80
May 26: 4^{6}_{M}	Q1¹	Mister Gunn^{120} (4⅔) 13–1	28.80	8.60	3.60
Fri.	Q2²	Free At Last^{120} (4) 8–1	——	——	——
May 27: 1^{7}	Q1²	Empire Knight^{106} (8) 14–1	——	7.20	3.80
Sat.	Q2³	Forest Tax^{113} (4⅔) 9–1	——	——	——
5^{7}	Q1²	Floperoo^{116} (4⅔) 9–1§§	20.00	10.00	5.20
May 29: 5^{8}	Q1¹	Try n See^{114} (8) 18–1	——	——	——
Mon.	Q2²	Duke David^{120} (8) 9–1	19.80	7.20	5.60
$8^{8}_{f/m}$	Q1¹	Kwiatuczek^{118} (8) 39–1	——	——	——
	Q2²	Evasive Lady^{120} (4⅔) 14–1	——	11.40	6.60
	Q3³	Riding Teddy^{120} (5) 10–1	——	——	6.80
$9^{9}_{f/m}$	Q1²	Olney Miss^{115} (5) 54–1	——	——	——
	Q2³	Miss Goose Valley^{113} (5) 19–1	——	——	——
	Q3⁴	Gaorach^{113} (6) 12–5	25.80	12.20	8.20
May 30: $4^{7}_{Msw_f}$	Q1³	Plucky Star^{112} (4) 27–1	——	——	——

††Not a hit, since Q3 is the next qualifier in this claiming race for four-yr-olds. When considering the next horse in line, we note that Island Chant has thirteen points, almost a record, and that Willie Hartack is up, always a consideration, although not incorporated in Sam's system. Also, this is the first race in the daily double that paid $715, with the system horse Rhythm in the second race. See below.

‡‡This is a maiden race for two-year-olds, and you will note that all three of the horses in-the-money came from the top four odds. The winner happened to be Q4, an automatic bet, just as Royal Carle was an automatic bet. These winners in parentheses have not been included in the final computations at the end of the chart.

§§Only 4⅔ points, but a nice drop in class. Odds of 9–1 are good in such a small field.

CHART IV (continued)

Tues.	Q2⁴	Ramekin[112] (5) 8–1	17.80	6.40	3.00
6⁷	Q1²	Valerie's Dunce[109] (8) 8–1	———	———	———
	Q2³	Apiculture[117] (5) 7–1	15.80	5.40	3.80
9¹¹	Q1⁴	Rolling Ridge[114] (6) 25–1	———	———	———
	Q2⁵	Wizardry[116] (6) 11–1	———	9.00	5.20

Pimlico, May 1972—Straight

SUMMARY:
Number of racing days: 24
Number of races: 216
Unit of investment: $2

	Q1		Q2		Q3	
	Win	*Place*	*Win*	*Place*	*Win*	*Place*
Return	520.80	487.00	478.00	336.20	54.20	35.80
Invested	432.00	432.00	432.00	432.00	———	———
Net Profit	88.80	55.00	46.00	−95.80		
Percentage	20%	12%	10%	———		
TOTALS:	*Q1, Q2 Win*		*Q1, Q2 Place*		*Combined Totals*	
Return	998.80		823.20		1,822.00	
Invested	864.00		864.00		1,728.00	
Net Profit	134.80		−40.80		94.00	
Percentage	15%		———		5%	

		Total return	*Average*
Number of Q1 Win hits:	13	$520.80	$40.00
Number of Q2 Win hits:	16	478.00	30.00
Number of Q1 Place hits:	29	487.00	16.80
Number of Q2 Place hits:	26	336.20	13.00
Q1, Q2 Win hits:	29	998.80	34.40
Q1, Q2 Place hits:	55	823.20	14.95

CHART V   Pimlico, Daily Doubles: May 1972

May 2:   #4/5 (Bargain Price)* with #1 (Nashvee) 3–1 $ 99.40

*In the first race, both Pierre the Greek and Bargain Price are listed at 8–1. A comparison of their charts shows that they both ran in the same race on April 4, nearly a month ago. Bargain Price, however, worked out on May 1, the day before this race. In terms of race recency, they are the same, but Bargain Price has a very recent workout and is clearly the more ready animal. Pierre the Greek finished fourth in that race together on April 4, but lost two lengths in the stretch run, an indication of tiring. Bargain Price finished ninth (that looks bad) but the colt gained two lengths in the stretch run and obviously had a good workout in that race. Some may favor the gelding, but Sam would take the ready colt, despite the finish positions of the last race. In the second race, Nashvee is listed at 3–1 and is the first choice. As noted elsewhere, when the first choice has odds of 3–1 or up, he or she is usually included in the series.

CHART V (continued)

May 4:	#4 (First Flag) with #2 (All the Luck)	37.60
May 5:	#2 (Bold King) with #4 (Pau Hana)	157.40
May 6:	#1 (Prince's Way) 3–1 with Q2Po (Donlands)	69.40
May 9:	#3 (Cutie's Uncle) with #3 (Timber Tavern)	280.40
May 11:	F3 (Lightard Knot) with Q1Po (Cherry Red)	536.00
May 12:	#4q (Fast Man) with #4q (Tudor King)	268.00
(May 13:	#5q (Enforcer) 10–1 with #4 (Kith)	171.80)†
May 15:	#3 (Artist's Pride) with #2 (Song From the Mountain)	143.40
May 16:	#2 (Maintow) with #1 (Restless Jib) 3–1	28.20
May 19:	#2 (Nashvee) with #3 (Frosty Roman)	32.60
May 20:	Q3 (Island Chant) with Q1 (Rhythm)	715.00
	Hartack up!!	
May 23:	#4 (Sindhi Chief) with #4 (Verulam Miss)	187.40
May 24:	#2 (Cowabunga) with #3 (Aunt Polly)	96.20
May 27:	#2 (Classy Guy) with #2 (Bundle of Twigs)	25.40

Gross Return: 2,676.40

†This double is not included in the computations at the end of this chart. The incident is discussed, however, in this book to illustrate the fact that the next horse in line may be really ready to win. Check his record to see whether he has raced within a week or so and has worked within a couple of days, is dropping in class and weight, etc. to see whether or not he should replace some ho-hum horse in your series.

SUMMARY:
Number of racing days: 24
Number of investments: 24
Amount of each investment: $50, for a total investment of: $1,200.00
Gross Return: $2,676.40
Total Invested: 1,200.00

Net Profit: 1,476.40

Net percentage of profit: 123%

CHART VI   Pimlico, Exactas: May 1972

May 1:	3¹²ᴴ	F3	(Paddy J) and F4 (Didn't Show)	61.00
	5¹²	Q2	(Beau Sock) with Q1 (Ducksummer)	440.00
	7⁸	F3	(Crafty Landing) with F4 (Two Hasty Guys)	47.60
	9¹²	Q2	(Fiendish Lad) with F1 (Probability)	259.00
May 3:	9⁸	F3	(Ground Mist) with F4 (Carderock)	111.80
May 4:	5¹⁰ₘ	F5	(Sway Me) with F6 (Pretty Proud)	190.00
	7⁸	F3	(Private Times) with F2 (Smoky Johnny)	30.00
May 5:	3⁸	Q2	(Lady Jester) with F2 (Thunderhorn)	69.00
	5⁹	F2	(Black Lighting) with F4 (Jamie C)	69.60
May 6:	7⁹ᴴ	F1	(Interstellar) with Q3 (Profundity)	110.80
	9⁸	F3	(Native Heir) with F4 (Onandaga)	106.40

CHART VI (continued)

May 8:	5^9	Q1	(Mongo's Image) with Q2 (Verace)	921.40
	9^8	Q1	(Social Curtsey) with F1/2* (Zadig)	210.60
May 9:	3^8	Q1	(Hong Kong Lady) with F1 (Parthian King)	103.20
	7^{10}	F3	(The Great Ethel C) with F2 (The Whole Bunch)	29.40
	9^8	F5	(Light Airs) with F6 (Karenadee)	142.00
May 10:	7^8	Q1	(Doverland) with F1 (Sonny Says Quick)	103.60
	9^9_M	F2	(Treacherous Turn) with F3 (Path O' Ray)	44.40
May 11:	5^{11}_M	F3	(Off to Cuba) with F2 (Cowabunga)	48.00
	9^{10}	F4	(Foolhearted) with F5 (Nativette)	178.40
May 12:	5^{12}	F1	(Proud Mary) with Q1 (No Brag Just Fast)	263.40
	7^{10}	F4	(Curling Iron) with F3 (Brooks Best)	190.00
May 13:	3^9	F3	(Triple Royal) with F2 (Pau Hana)	50.00
	$5^{10}†$	F5	(Power Peddler) with Q1 (I'm Irving)	1,083.00
	7^7	F3	(Lucky Lord) with F2 (Northern Jove)	41.60
	9^9	Q2	(Carderock) with F1 (Probability)	163.80
May 15:	5^8	Q2	(Lipp Mann) with Q1 (Full of Fight)	202.80
May 16:	3^{12}_{Msw}	F1	(I Can't Talk) with Q2 (National Password)	230.00
	5^{12}	F3	(Mr. L.B.G.) with F4 (Tygart)‡	525.40
	$7^{10}_{f/m}$	F2	(Sway Me) with F5 (Jamie C)	67.20)§
May 17:	3^{12}_M	F6	(With Pluck) with F5 (Stewart Little)	298.60
	5^8	F2	(Get Aboard) with F3 (Monroe's Hobo)	25.80
May 18:	3^9	F2	(Middle Date) with F3q (Mountain Greenery)	89.80
	5^{12}	Q3	(HowSweetheeis)‖ with F4q (Be Certain)	708.60
		F6	(HowSweetheeis)‖ with F4q (Be Certain)	708.60
	7^7	F2	(Honey Taylor) with Q2 (Bold David)	68.00
May 19:	5^{12}_{Msw}	Q4	(Ambi Hula)# with Q1 (Nymph's Son)	1,134.00
	7^{10}	Q1	(Tip O Flag) with F1/2 (Spanish Storm)**	115.80
	$9^{11}_{f/m}$	F3	(Inda Muffin) with F2 (Run Columbia)	52.20
May 22:	3^8	Q1	(Bow Shannon) with F4 (Accordingly)	86.20
	5^{11}_{Msw}	F3	(Ocala Milisa) with F4q (Day of Magic)	106.80
	9^8	F2	(Rosaryville) with F4 (Triangle Miss)	45.80
May 23:	9^9	F3	(Etonian Golfer) with F2 (Jim's Hat)	24.80
May 24:	7^6	Q2	(Irish Tenor) with F4 (Little Nassau)	163.00

*Zadig and Stellar Shot were co-favorites, and one had to be eliminated. Zadig had the better record on past performance.

†Since there was no Q2, we combined Q1 with F2, F3, F4 AND F5, to get our five-horse box-combination.

‡These were actually the fifth and sixth favorites. However, Lisa's All and Slic Grik were disqualified. Lisa's All is a filly racing vs. males this time and moving up in class from her next-to-last race. Slic Grik's last race was a disaster, at a mile and a sixteenth. He finished tenth in a field of twelve and lost six lengths in the stretch run. Far outclassed today. Mr. L.B.G. is a first-time starter, with one workout on April 28. This is a low-class claiming race for three-year-olds, and first-time starters are accepted automatically. Tygart is a colt who finished third in his last race just fourteen days ago.

§Not a hit. At 11–1, Jamie C. is a bit too far out for this series. Between F2 and F4, only Spin A Wheel was disqualified. Jamie C. was next in line. She was second in her last race, at today's class, just eleven days ago. Eleven to one are good odds for such a ready mare. But this one is not included in the computations at the end of the chart.

‖HowSweetheeis is F6q and teams with F4q for the payoff. See discussion in Chart IV.

#See discussion in Chart IV. In a maiden race or a race with three-year-olds, the top four qualifiers should always be looked at closely. Ambi Hula raced just nine days ago, vs. seventeen days for Mister Gunn. The gelding also finished second in a race at M10500, which is $1,000 higher than Mister Gunn has ever raced. When it is very difficult to choose between two such horses, play them both.

**The co-favorite was Smart Fellow, who has not raced in nearly a month, and has no recent workout. Spanish Storm almost won his last race and is dropping two pounds in weight.

CHART VI (continued)

9^8	F2	(Tomevy) with F4 (Adaptive)	50.40
May 25: 3^7	F3	(Tudor King) with F2 (Rose Colored Glasses)	34.60
5^9_M	F2	(Flag Salute) with Q1 (Jungle Journal)	193.20
7^7	F3	(Pagan Pagan) with Q2 (Bargain Price)	96.00
$9^7_{/m}$	F3	(Snake Bit) with F2 (Colorcast)	42.60
May 26: 9^6	F2	(Nativette) with F4 (Rash Maid)	31.80
May 27: 5^7	Q2	(Floperoo) with F3 (Lili Panche)	179.60
7^6	F4	(Parchment) with F3 (Tom Be Wise)	44.20
May 29: 5^8	Q2	(Duke David) with F3 (Going Away)	97.40
7^8	F3	(Black Lighting) with F2 (Jaipur's Jet)	51.40
$9^9_{/m}$	Q3	(Gaorach) with F3 (No Matter What)	191.60
May 30: 9^{11}	F1	(Row Boat) with Q2 (Wizardry)	59.20

SUMMARY:

Number of racing days: 24

Number of Exacta races: 96

Investment per race: $60, for a total investment of: $5,760.00

Gross Return: $10,726.40

Total invested: 5,760.00

Net profit: 4,966.40

Percentage of net profit: 86%

Breakdown of F4, F5, F6:   Return: $1,517.60

                                  Invested: 1,152.00

                                  Net profit: 365.60

Breakdown of F1 with Q1, Q2:   Return: 1,822.20

                               Invested: 768.00

                               Net profit: $1,054.20

Pimlico, May 1972

	Straight	*Doubles*	*Exactas*	*Totals*
Return	1,822.00	2,676.00	10,726.40	15,224.80
Invested	1,728.00	1,200.00	5,760.00	8,688.00
Net Profit	94.00	1,476.40	4,966.40	6,536.80
Percentage	5%	123%	86%	75%

CHART VII   Gulfstream Park, Straight Bets: April 1973

Mar.31: 2^{12}*	Q1$_{Po}$	Merister[112] (5) 49–1	100.40	31.80	15.00
Sat.					

*This race on Saturday, March 31, 1973 is shown because a 49-to-1 long shot completed an interesting daily double, for $492.20, with F2 in the first race. This was a Sam Hirsch System winner on both counts.

CHART VII (continued)

Apr. 2:	$2^{12}_{f/m}$	Q1Po	Dispute[116] (6) 12–1Po	40.80	13.80	8.00
Mon.		Q2Po	Gentle Widow[116] (5) 12–1	———	———	———
	$3^{12}_{Msw_f}$	Q1³	Hastie Cutie[119] (A) 21–1	43.80	13.00	10.80
		Q2⁵	Sheba Sham[119] (5) 17–1	———	———	———
	4^{11}_{Msw}	Q1¹	Star True[120] (A) 100–1	———	———	———
		Q2²	Indian Ambush[120] (A) 67–1	———	———	8.60
		Q3³	The Conck[120] (A) 54–1	———	———	———
	5¹¹	Q1⁴	Native Flight[113] (5) 21–1	———	17.40	8.00
		Q2⁵	Acco King[116] (5) 11–1	———	———	———
	6⁹	Q1¹	Pagan King[116] (8) 71–1	———	———	———
		Q2³	Action Potential[114] (8) 34–1	———	20.40	10.80
	$9^{9}_{f/m}$	Q1¹	Double Dancer[113] (5) 36–1	———	———	———
		Q2²	Native Goddess[113] (5) 21–1	43.20	17.20	9.40
		Q3³	Smiling Jacqueline[112] (9) 19–1	———	———	7.00
Apr. 3:	2^{12}	Q1Po	Peaceful Ruler[116] (6) 20–1Po	———	———	———
Tues.		Q2Po	Cabbage Looper[116] (5) 56–1Ao	———	———	12.00
	3^{12}_{Msw}	Q1¹	Hell's Extra[118] (A) 142–1	———	———	———
		Q2³	A Good Turn[118] (A) 68–1	———	———	———
		Q3⁴	Jimmy's Bow[118] (3) 36–1	———	19.80	9.60
	$7^{12}_{f/m}$	Q1¹	More Family[116] (6) 96–1	———	———	———
		Q2²	Musical Annie[105] (10) 42–1	———	21.00	6.40
		Q3⁴	Ribbon Red[112] (6) 22–1	———	———	———
	$8^{8}_{f/m}$	Q1²	Dutch Clover[111] (6) 13–1	———	———	———
		Q2³	Dream Date[116] (7) 11–1	23.20	9.00	4.40
	10¹¹	Q1⁴	Dabit[116] (5) 66–1	———	30.80	11.20
		Q2⁵	Hikahill[116] (6) 29–1	———	———	———
Apr. 4:			No record.			
Apr. 5:	$1^{12}_{f/m}$	Q1⁵	Questionable[116] (5) 33–1	———	———	8.80
Thurs.			No other qualifiers.			
	2¹²	Q1Po	Gentle Upset[116] (5) 20–1Po	———	———	———
		Q2Ao4†	Mannello[116] (5) 13–1	28.60	11.60	8.20
	6¹²	Q1³	Bon Joujou[116] (6) 55–1	———	———	———
		Q2⁴	Satin Stitch[113] (6) 55–1	———	———	12.40
	7¹²	Q1³	Natural Artist[116] (4⅔) 35–1	———	———	10.20
		Q2⁴	Gary Longlegs[116] (5) 23–1	———	———	———
	9¹²	Q1¹	Tootieboy[112] (6) 40–1	———	———	———
		Q2²	Chocolate Donut[113] (7) 39–1	———	19.20	8.00
Apr. 6:	2¹²	Q1Po	Rigid[111] (5) 20–1Po	———	———	———
Fri.		Q2Po	Cultivator[109] (6) 110–1	222.60	58.00	16.60
	3^{11}_{Msw}	Q1²	Stop Watch[120] (5) 104–1	———	50.00	22.60
		Q2³	Applicable[120] (6) 61–1	———	———	———

†The next qualifier in the Po series was Never the Least at 15–1Po, but his actual odds were a border-line 12–1. Mannello, whose Po were 8–1, had gone up to 13–1, and this became the bet.

CHART VII (continued)

	Q3^4	Procam^{120} (5) 17–1	—	—	—
6^{10}	Q1^1	Mr. Swinger^{116} (6) 25–1	52.00	18.60	11.00
	Q2^2	Jolly Husky^{114} (6) 13–1	—	—	—
8^{10}	Q1^1	Freeze^{114} (7) 26–1	—	—	—
	Q2^2	Congressional^{113} (8) 22–1	—	—	—
	(Q3^3	Haveago^{112} (6) 13–1‡	—	11.80	7.00)
Apr. 7: 3^9	Q1^3	The Keeper^{116} (5) 10–1	—	7.00	4.60
Sat.	Q2^4	Amber Prey^{116} (6) 10–1	—	—	—
4^{12}	Q1^1	Hurtado^{116} (5) 69–1	—	—	—
	Q2^3	Ready Now^{116} (5) 43–1	—	—	13.60
5^{10}	Q1^2	Panicum Repens^{115} (5) 14–1	—	12.00	6.20
	Q2^3	King Duck^{112} (7) 13–1	—	—	—
10^{12}	Q1^5	Screen Pass^{114} (6) 36–1	—	—	—
	Q2^6	Rejucilo^{116} (6) 13–1§	29.00	12.40	7.20
Apr. 9: 2^{12}	Q1$_{Po}$	Representative^{116} (4) 20–1Po	—	—	—
Mon.	Q2$_{Po}$‖	Proud As Punch^{116} (4) 20–1Po	—	25.80	11.80
4$^{12}_{Mf}$	Q1^4	Miss Tim^{116} (5) 71–1	—	—	—
	Q2^5	Blushing Miss^{116} (5) 33–1	—	—	—
	Q3^6	Lady Dor^{116} (4) 22–1	—	—	—
	Q4^7	Kilpedder Lady^{107}#	41.80	14.60	4.00
7^{12}	Q1^2	Fond Reward^{116} (4) 61–1	—	—	17.80
	Q2^4	Goodbye Juanita^{116} (6) 43–1	—	—	—
	Q3^6	Rocky Tip^{111} (4) 21–1	—	17.40	7.60
	Q4^{7**}	Kilpedder Lady^{107} (6) 16–1	34.60	15.80	7.60
10$^{12}_{f/m}$	Q1^4	Mutual Benefit^{111} (5) 21–1	—	—	—
	Q2^5	Fair and Warmer^{116} (5) 16–1	—	—	—

‡Not a hit in the system. The first two qualifiers ran out. Haveago was Q3 with six points, at 13–1, and ran second. Nothing in the three past performance charts suggested that today was Haveago's turn to run in-the-money. Not included in the calculations at the end of this chart.

§Rejucilo and Little Lord were both at 13–1 and are competitors for Q2. Both raced ten days ago, but Rejucilo had a workout just four days ago. Rejucilo's last race (at $8,500) was the lowest class he has ever run in, and he finished third, gaining two lengths in the stretch run. The $1,500 move-up in class is "true" only in the factual sense; he is actually dropping in class from his third and other races back. Little Lord is running basically in his class, although it appears that he is dropping $1,000. This is a $10,000 claiming race, and Little Lord is going in at $9,000 to get a four-pound weight advantage. Rejucilo was second out of the gate and was leading by two lengths at the half of the mile-and-a-sixteenth on the turf. He won by a nose over Roji, the second favorite.

‖Here is an example of a straight claiming race for four-yr-olds and upward, in which none of the high-odds horses accrued five points to qualify. You can either pass the race, or you can take the two four-point qualifiers and play them. The latter is the case here, since Q4 is seventh down from the top in odds. Also, this is a Perfecta Race, and it is wise to look at Q4 in the maiden and filly races. Q4 teamed up with the F2 horse Chili Bowl at 5–1 and paid $190.80. Ken's Gal Chris is moving up rather a lot in class, but she raced fifteen days ago and was third in that race.

**A race for three-yr-old fillies! All the money-horses were in the top-four qualifiers, and this is an excellent example of the Perfecta Race where Q4 and Q3 combine for the payoff: $342.00. To combine Q1 thru Q4 would cost you twelve tickets, and well worth it. Kilpedder Lady raced nineteen days ago, but worked two days ago; is getting in at 107 pounds; was second in her last race. With that record, a move-up in class doesn't hurt too much.

CHART VII (continued)

	Q3^6	Sleepless Rule^{116} (5) 14–1	30.20	7.00	4.20
Apr. 10: 2$^{12}_{M}$	Q1$_{Po}$	Gentle Upset^{116} (4) 20–1Po	88.60	29.60	15.40
Tues.	Q2$_{Po}$††	Duel's Destiny^{104} (5) 10–1Po	——	10.00	7.20
8^8	Q1^1	Le Moqueur^{112} (5) 81–1	——	——	——
	Q2^2	Minneapolis Phil^{112} (6) 17–1	36.00	11.20	6.00
Apr. 11: 3$^{12}_{MSW}$	Q1^3	Sky Kingdom^{120} (A) 34–1	——	——	——
Wed.	Q2^4	Procam^{120} (5) 30–1	——	14.00	7.20
	Q3^5	Vasa Lopp^{120} (4) 21–1	——	——	——
7^{12}	Q1^5	Spun Silver^{116} (6) 34–1	——	13.00	9.20
	Q2^6	Phantom Leader^{115} (6) 29–1	——	——	——
8^9	Q1^2	Commander Fayette^{113} (5) 32–1	65.20	21.20	9.40
		(No Q2 here.)			
9$^8_{f/m}$	Q1^2	Student Skipper^{112} (6) 31–1	——	——	——
	Q2^4	Smiling Jacqueline^{112} (6) 9–1	19.20	7.20	3.40
Apr. 12: 2^{12}	Q1$_{Po}$	Arctic Bullet^{112} (6) 30–1Po	——	——	——
Thurs.	Q2$_{Po}$	Roanesian^{114} (5) 20–1Po	94.20	26.80	10.80
5^{12}	Q1^2	Marquee Idol^{112} (A) 67–1	——	——	——
	Q2^3	Polar Dance^{116} (6) 37–1	——	——	14.00
9^9_f	Q1^1	Madam Moody^{112} (5) 45–1	——	——	——
	Q2^2	Vally Holme^{107} (7) 16–1	——	——	——
	Q3^3	Our World^{112} (8) 11–1	24.00	9.00	4.80
10$^{10}_{M}$	Q1^4	Moonrush^{120} (5) 20–1	——	13.60	4.00
	Q2^6	Walther F^{120} (5) 15–1	——	——	——
Apr. 13: 2^{12}	Q1$_{Po}$	Andalien^{116} (5) 20–1Po	44.60	19.80	10.80
Fri.	Q2$_{Po}$	Water Gun^{111} (5) 12–1Po	——	——	——
3$^{12}_{M}$	Q1^3	Tropic Mood^{118} (5) 44–1	——	——	——
	Q2^4‡‡	Aurora Gray^{115} (5) 22–1	——	19.80	10.20
	Q3^5	Twice the Fun^{118} (A) 17–1	——	——	——
4$^{11}_{f/m}$	Q1^3	Turn Turtle^{109} (6) 26–1	——	——	——
	Q2^4	Las Tropas^{116} (5) 26–1	——	——	——
	Q3^5	Rolla Bowla Ball^{112} (7) 17–1	——	12.00	7.00
6^{12}	Q1^2	Jokers Wild^{105} (9) 50–1	——	——	10.40
	Q2^3	Mr. War Man^{112} (A) 48–1	——	——	——
7$^{12}_f$	Q1^1	Rose Lilly^{116} (6) 132–1	——	——	——
	Q2^2	Iron Poker^{116} (3) 84–1	——	——	14.80
	Q3^3	Dolls and Dreams^{116} (5) 42–1	——	——	——
8^{10}	Q1^2	Autumn's End^{112} (7⅔) 18–1	38.60	15.60	7.00
	Q2^3	Putt Putt^{112} (9) 17–1	——	——	——
Apr. 14: 1^9	Q1^3	Pitia^{111} (8) 11–1	24.80	11.60	8.00

††There was no second qualifier at odds above 12–1. Ordinarily, we would stop with one qualifier, but this is a maiden race. and Duel's Destiny looks good at 9–1 or 10–1. An optional play. Since we are concerned here with the second half of the daily double, we take it.

‡‡Aurora Gray is a filly running against males this race, but remember that these fillies require only five points when they run in Maiden Races, as opposed to seven points minimum when running in regular races against males.

CHART VII (continued)

Sat.		Q2[4]	Mixed Emotions[116] (A) 10–1	——	——	6.20
	2[12]	Q1Po	Notwithstanding[111] (5) 20–1Po	——	11.20	6.00
		Q2Po	Goodpus[116] (5) 12–1Po	——	——	——
	6[10]	Q1[2]	Proper Escort[113] (5⅔) 18–1	——	14.60	7.40
		Q2[3]	Delicate John[112] (6) 17–1	——	——	6.00
	10[9]	Q1[2]	Scout[113] (7) 51–1	——	——	14.00
		Q2[3]	King Duck[115] (5) 35–1	——	20.80	10.00
Apr. 16:	3[12]Msw	Q1[1]	Wiltelya[120] (A) 135–1	——	——	——
Mon.		Q2[3]	System to Win[120] (4) 20–1	42.40	20.40	7.60
	4[12]	Q1[2]	Sway Baby[116] (4) 89–1	——	——	——
		Q2[3]	Saxony Princess[111] (A) 81–1	164.60	43.80	19.60
		Q3[5]§§	Manchi[112] (4) 21–1	——	15.00	8.00
	6[12]	Q1[2]	Soar On[116] (5) 37–1	——	——	——
		Q2[3]	No Time for Games[114] (6) 37–1	——	——	11.80
	10[12]	Q1[1]	Arts Village[109] (7) 41–1	——	20.20	22.20‖‖
		Q2[2]	Timberlea Tune[116] (5) 25–1	——	——	——

§§Miss Eggers at 23–1 was high-odds qualifier for this position. But Manchi also had four points, and although she was going up $1000 in class, she had two seconds in her recent past performance. Since this is a race for three-yr-old fillies and is a Perfecta Race, too, we should really include Miss Eggers as Q3 and add Manchi as Q4. Q2 ran first and Q3q (Manchi) was second, for a payoff of $1138.40.

‖‖Arts Village, at 41–1, paid more to show than to place, which means that there was some heavy betting, probably by the stable itself, to win and to place. Stables usually bet to win and place, whereas the public is inclined to spread their bets to show also. If you wish to find out where the heavy stable money is going in a race, the best method is to add the win and place pools on a particular horse, then divide the total by the show pool. Do this for each horse in the race, and you will get a series of constants. Naturally, the highest constant in the series is the horse getting the most stable money, or smart money, as the phrase goes. This horse doesn't always win, of course, but that's the horse which is being backed most heavily by the owner, trainer, jockey, and stable hands. Arts Village, at 41–1, was a very good thing, losing out for the win by a neck to Oxbridge, the second favorite. Arts Village was scheduled to race at 109 pounds, but actually two pounds were added, probably due to the weight of the jockey, and those two pounds cost the stable a win. Arts Village would have paid $84.80 for $2. But do not feel badly; this was also a Perfecta Race, and the payoff was $539.20. The stable made a bundle of hay in the tenth race on Monday, April 16.

This tenth race at Gulfstream Park on April 16, 1973 is almost a classic example of legal, behind-the-scenes race manipulation. In fact, it merits a little study here, and we show below the two charts that tell the story, if you know how to read between the lines. The first chart is the one published the day after the race and shows exactly how the race was run. Arts Village was in the sixth post position, got out of the gate fourth, and at the quarter-pole DeStefano had him running second, just a length behind the leader, Teuton II. At this point, the eventual winner, Oxbridge, was running in seventh position. At the head of the stretch, Arts Village was second by a head, fighting for the lead with It's A Corker, who had come up to set the pace at the ¾ pole. Oxbridge was now running third, three lengths behind the leader. In the stretch drive, it was a duel between Arts Village and Oxbridge, and undoubtedly Arts Village would have been the winner if he had been carrying his scheduled weight of 109 pounds. At this distance, it is said, one pound costs a horse one length. Carrying 109 pounds, Arts Village probably would have won by about two lengths. Note that the standard weight for the horses in this race was set at 122 pounds. Arts Village was due six pounds off for being non-winner of three races in 1973. The jockey DeStefano has a small [7] after his name, indicating that he is allowed a seven-pound weight advantage for apprentice status. But DeStefano was two pounds overweight, and instead of getting thirteen pounds off the 122 total, Arts Village only had eleven pounds off. Here's the chart:

TENTH RACE GP April 16, 1973	1¹⁄₁₆ MILES. (1:40¹/₅). CLAIMING. Purse $3,800. 4-year-olds and upward. Weight, 122 lbs. Non-winners of three races in 1973 allowed 2 lbs.; two races, 4 lbs.; a race, 6 lbs. Claiming price, $3,500. Value to winner $2,280; second, $760; third, $380; fourth, $260; fifth, $114. Mutuel Pool, $33,941.											

Last Raced		Horse	EqtAWt	PP	St	¼	½	¾	Str	Fin	Jockeys	Owners	Odds to $1
3-28-73[1]	GP[7]	Oxbridge	7 116	10	6	7½	7½	4½	3[3]	1[nk]	JImparato	C Kimlin	5.50
3-28-73[1]	GP[10]	Arts Village	b4 111	6	4	2[1]	2[2]	2½	2[h]	2[1½]	WDeStefano[7]	S Schieder	41.40
3-28-73[2]	GP[12]	It's A Corker	b5 118	2	2	3[1½]	3½	1[h]	1[2]	3[1]	MHole	Martino-Neal	5.20
3-19-73[10]	GP[8]	Smart Flushing	b5 116	1	1	8[3]	8½	9[3]	5[h]	4[no]	ARussello	G S Smith	8.10
4- 1-73[10]	GP[4]	Sir Jester	b7 118	5	10	10[3]	9[1½]	8[h]	7½	5[no]	CPerret	Saturn Stable	1.90

CHART VII (continued)

3-21-73[10]	GP3	Poe II.	b6 116	11	11		9[1]	11[7]	10[2]	6[1]	6[1¼]	HViera	P Marti	11.30
4- 3-73[5]	GP9	Khanhai Warrior	b6 116	12	7		5[h]	6[½]	7[½]	9[4]	7[½]	WMcKeever	D H Nord	19.10
3-30-73[1]	GP5	Chief Difficulty	b4 111	7	8		6[½]	5[1]	6[2]	8[h]	8[2½]	AGonzalezJr5	Judith Bartlett	15.10
3-21-73[10]	GP7	Timberlea Tune	7 116	8	9		11[4]	10[h]	11[14]	10[4]	9[h]	MCedeno	Engle-DeAngelo	25.20
3-21-73[1]	GP10	Teuton II.	5 116	3	3		1[½]	1[h]	3[4]	4[h]	10[7]	GStLeon	J Wall	23.20
3-20-73[10]	GP11	Thunder Hunder	4 116	9	5		4[4]	4[4]	5[½]	11	11	MMiceli	T E Hays	20.80
3- 8-73[J]	GP12	Usk	7 116	4	12		12	12	12	Eased.		CAstorga	Maria E Coto	8.90

Time, :24, :47⁴/s, 1:13¹/s, 1:40, 1:47. Track fast.

$2 Mutuel Prices:

10-OXBRIDGE	13.00	9.60	5.80
6-ARTS VILLAGE		20.20	22.20
2-IT'S A CORKER			6.40

B. g, by Hornbeam—Canadair II., by Vimy. Trainer, R. Bohn. Bred by Estate of Lord Astor (Eng.).

IN GATE—5:26. OFF AT 5:26 EASTERN STANDARD TIME. Start good. Won driving.

OXBRIDGE, unhurried early, rallied from between horses in the stretch run and edged ARTS VILLAGE. The latter raced with the pace from the outset, rallied with the winner in the final eighth, but was outfinished. IT'S A CORKER raced forwardly, gained command from the inside at the head of the stretch, opened a clear, but could not stay. SMART FLUSHING finished with good energy. SIR JESTER was never a serious threat. TIMBAELEA TUNE came back sore. TEUTON II. set the early pace. USK showed nothing and was eased in the stretch.

Corrected weight—Arts Village, 111.

Sir Jester claimed by S.G. Babbitz, trainer R.E. Jacobs.

Claiming Prices—All $3500.

Scratched—Rolling Along, Dougie's Lark, Retired, Our Richard, Princess Alice, Ridgid.

Perfecta (10-6) Paid $539.20; Perfecta Pool, $68,546.

Attendance, 8,336; Total Mutuel Pool,$942,810.

The past performance chart on Arts Village is shown below. Arts Village is a four-yr-old colt, whose record as a three-yr-old is not impressive. He was out ten times and was second twice, bringing in $1,570, which means that he did not earn his keep, since it costs six to eight thousand dollars just to stable and work a horse. He's been out six times this year, 1973, and has one win to his credit, on January 1. He picked up $2,400 for that win, which came in a $3,500 claiming race, the same class as today's race. In his next race, on January 16, Arts Village was moved up by his trainer and raced in a $5,000 claiming race. He finished seventh in a field of eleven, ten lengths off the winner, SuperSlick. On February 8, he had another race at that price and wound up tenth in a field of twelve, eleven lengths off the winner. He was obviously out of his class, so he was dropped in the next race to $3,500 again, a race at a mile and ³/₁₆. He did very well in this long race, finishing fifth, after running second for half the race. He lost 5½ lengths in the stretch run of that race, which means that the race was a bit too long for him. But the trainer, S. Branham, saw the light in that race. Arts Village was coming to form. He probably needed a little shorter distance, however. But Branham couldn't show his hand too clearly at this stage of the game. He moved his horse up to the $5,000 class on March 13, in a seven-furlong dash. His jockey Rotz had a ten-pound apprentice allowance, but he couldn't take full advantage of that, and Arts Village went into the race carrying 116 pounds. Either accidentally or deliberately, Rotz got him out of the gate last in a field of twelve horses, and he never got closer than fifteen lengths from the winner. His odds in that race were 14–1. He finished eleventh in the field, nineteen lengths off the winner, and in his next race, on March 28, his odds moved up nicely to 45–1. His new jockey, Scocca, got him out of the gate fourth in this race at a mile and ⅛, but kept him well back in the pack. He was ninth at the stretch turn and he coasted in to the wire, finishing tenth, a full twenty-two lengths off the winner. This race, when he carried 118 pounds, was the conditioner for the race on April 16. Branham rested the horse for eighteen days, looking for a chance at a mile and a sixteenth, which appeared on the Monday we know about. It was the tenth race on that day, and the conditions were just what Branham wanted, six pounds off for not winning the past three races in 1973. He needed a jockey with a weight-allowance, and he got DeStefano at seven pounds. Unfortunately, DeStefano had steak for dinner the night before the race, with potato salad, and he could only use five of his seven-pound allowance. But the distance was right. The odds were right, at 41.40 to 1. Arts Village was in his class, was rested, and ready. A workout three or four days before the race might have been in order, but Branham let it go. Anything could happen during a workout, and Branham didn't want to spoil his chances. He put a year's wages on Arts Village to win and place, and he combined him with everything that moved in the race for second position. He (and his cohorts) bet Arts Village for both first and second positions; they were rewarded with a handsome payoff.

Of course, Sam Hirsch had Arts Village crisscrossed many ways in the race, due to his system of play. Arts Village was the number-one Qualifier, with the highest odds in the race. He received one point for racing within twenty-eight days, one point for getting in at 109 pounds (a point he later lost when Sam discovered the fact that he had to race at 111). Still, he received two points for dropping down from 118 in the last race, and he got one point for his win on January 1, that is, for being in-the-money at least once in his past performance. That's a net of four points. Looking more closely, Sam found that he had finished three races less than 6½ lengths off the winner, for another point, a total of five points. He was Qualifier Number One. With odds of 41–1, he was bet across the board, and Sam was surprised to get that extra two dollars on the show tickets. In the Perfecta, Sam had Arts Village with F1 through F4. It's A Corker and Oxbridge were both at 5–1 for second favorite, and Sam had them both with Arts Village. As you see from the chart, Oxbridge wound up as the actual third favorite, since It's A Corker got more of the loose change and had odds of 5.20 to 1, for Oxbridge's 5.50 to 1. Here's the chart of Arts Village's past performance:

Arts Village   109   B. c (1969), by Pure Village—Sky Ramp, by Skytracer.
Breeder, F.D. Fancher (Ky.).

1973	6 1 0 0		$2,400

Owner, S. Scieder.   Trainer, S.E. Branham. $3,500   1972 10 0 2 0 $1,570

Mar28-73[1]	1 1-8 1:51[1]/sft	45 118	4[3]	8[10]	9[13]	10[22]	ScoccaD[12]	3500 56	Wade Jr. 116	Wooglin	Acquitted 12
Mar13-73[1]GP	7 f 1:24 ft	14 116	12[15]	12[17]	11[19]	11[19]	RotzJL[10]	5000 65	S'c'sfully116	MistyM'gic	Winnie'sCh'e 12
Feb23-73[1]Hia	1[3/16] 1:58[4]/sft	20 117	2[1/2]	2[1]	3[4]	5[9 1/2]	RotzJL[9]	3500 76	TrulyAmber117	Royal L.	OnlySunny 12
Feb 8-73[2]Hia	1 1-8 1:51[4]/sft	13 117	4[3/4]	4[6]	9[16]	10[19]	RotzJL[7]	5000 57	Fl'tl'der112	Mix'dEmot'ns	Ch'fF"fyf w 12
Jan16-73[5] Crc	1 1-4 2:11[3]/sft	7[1/4] 116	1[1]	6[5 1/2]	6[9]	7[10]	Gaffg'eR[11]	5000 77	SuperSlick116	MixedEmot'ns	Conflict 11
Jan 1-73[5]Crc	1 1-4 2:11[4]/sft	11 116	1[h]	1[h]	1[h]	1[1/2]	Gaffgl'eR[5]	3500 86	ArtsVillage 116	Betatron	Coventry II. 12
Dec19-72[5]Crc	1[1/16] 1:50[2]/sft	5[1/2] 116	8[8]	5[4 3/4]	3[1 1/2]	4[2 3/4]	Cesp'esR[12]	3500 71	She's aG'kl13	L'nd'nT'v'n	Prin'yCh'm 12
Dec13-72[10]Crc	1 1-8 1:56[4]/sft	50 113	1[1/2]	1[h]	1[1/2]	2[h]	Gaffg'neR[2]	3500 83	Princ'lyCh'rm112	ArtsVil'ge	S'p'rSlick 11
Dec 2-72[5]Crc	1 1-8 1:57 ft	25 105[3/4]	7[8 1/2]	4[2 1/2]	7[13]	7[10]	DeSt'oW[10]	3500 72	Super Slick 114	KwikGeorge	BillJack 11

Apr. 17: 2[12]f/m	Q1[Po]	Executrix[116] (6) 30–1Po	——	——	——
Tues.	Q2[3][Ao]	Rambler Gambler[107] (4⅔)	——	21.80	8.00
	Q3[4][Ao]	Royal Care[116] (5) 22–1	——	——	——
4[12]	Q1[3]##	No More Sir[116] (5) 40–1	——	20.00	12.80
		(No Q2 for lack of odds.)			
5[12]Mf	Q1[2]	Ah So Proud[116] (4) 54–1	——	——	11.80
	Q2[4]	Petite Bonnie[120] (4) 37–1	——	——	——
	Q3[5]	Foggy Lady[120] (4) 29–1	——	——	——
8[11]	Q1[2]	Don Simon[114] (7) 83 1***	——	107.00	84.00
	Q2[5]	Princess Shirley[113] (8) 15–1	31.40	14.00	7.00
10[10]Mf	Q1[3]	Pondering Jon[120] (7) 18–1	——	——	6.80
	Q2[4]	Federal Empress[120] (4) 14–1	30.20	10.40	6.80
Apr. 18: 2[11]	Q1[Po]	Nota Bad Girl[104] (11) 15–1Po	29.00	12.80	6.00
Wed.	Q2[7][Ao]	Mighty Size[116] (5) 12–1	——	——	——
3[12]Msw	Q1[3]	Fast Acquittal[120] (4) 42–1	——	——	——
	Q2[4]	Bob Twinkletoes[120] (5) 24–1	——	——	——
	Q3[5]	Gems and Roses[115] (A) 22–1	——	——	——
7[12]	Q1[2]	Speedy Lark[116] (5) 79–1	——	——	——
	Q2[3]	King Cross II[113] (6) 47–1	95.60	24.60	13.80
10[10]f/m	Q1[3]	Fair and Warmer[116] (5) 16–1	——	——	——
	Q2[4]	Bokamy[116] (5) 13–1	29.00	8.80	6.20
Apr. 19: 5[10]	Q1[2]	K.G. Roman[116] (6) 22–1	——	15.00	11.80
Thurs.	Q2[3]	Spiritis[118] (5) 10–1	——	——	——
6[7]	Q1[1]	Spear Carrier[113] (6) 14–1	——	10.40	6.00
	Q2[2]	Somewhat Striking[112] (10) 10–1	——	——	——
7[12]Msw	Q1[1]	Crimson Twins[120] (4) 65–1	131.20	45.20	16.60
	Q2[2]	Black Diplomat[113] (6) 56–1	——	——	——
	Q3[3]	Violation[120] (4) 39–1	——	——	13.00
8[9]f/m	Q1[1]	Western Idol[114] (5) 28–1	——	14.00	8.00

##No More Sir gets a fifth point for dropping in class from his race at $7,000 on February 14. We have to ignore his actual last race, since the horse did not finish. Everything slides back one race. Actually, we would have played him at four points, since no other horse in the race could muster that number. That is, no other horse with high odds.

***Don Simon's own stable was probably caught by surprise in this race. The $107 for $2 to place indicates that practically everybody, except Sam, was napping. A filly at 15–1 won the race. Had this also been a Perfecta race, imagine what the payoff would have been! Astronomical!!

CHART VII (continued)

	$Q2^2$	Ninety Day Wonder^{112} (9) 28–1	——	——	11.40
	$Q3^4$	Hot Buttons^{116} (6) 16–1	——	——	——
10^8_f	$Q1^1$	Solo Voyage^{116} (4) 21–1	——	——	——
	$Q2^2$	Kilpedder Lady^{116} (5) 15–1	32.80	8.00	4.60
	$Q3^3$	Cabinetcat^{112} (8) 10–1	——	——	——
Apr. 20: 1^{12} Fri.	$Q1^1$	Jame of Eloise^{109} (5) 85–1	——	——	——
	$Q2^3$	Sure True^{114} (5) 38–1	——	——	15.00
3^{12}_M	$Q1^1$	Love Hit^{118} (A) 49–1	101.00	31.00	11.00
	$Q2^2$	Joy Quibu^{118} (A) 41–1	——	——	——
	$Q3^3$	Chance Orphan^{108} (A) 24–1	——	——	——
Apr. 21: 2^{12} Sat.	$Q1_{Po}$	Uncle Chris^{112} (6) 30–1Po	——	——	——
	$Q2_{Po}$	Dragonwick^{113} (5) 20–1Po	10.60	5.40	4.60
3^{12}	$Q1^4$	Paleface^{112} (6) 32–1	——	——	——
	$Q2^5$	Alicaido^{112} (11) 30–1	——	19.00	10.60
4^{12}	$Q1^3$	Cuzin Leslie^{116} (7) 41–1	——	25.40	12.00
	$Q2^4$	Tarora^{113} (9) 21–1	——	——	——
7^{12}	$Q1^4$	Andalien^{116} (5) 29–1	——	——	——
	$Q2^5$	Key Largo II^{116} (6) 19–1	——	10.40	5.80
Apr. 23: 1^{12} Mon.	$Q1^2$	Bo's Gig^{109} (4) 38–1	——	——	——
	$Q2^3$	Please Show Me^{116} (5) 31–1	64.00	25.80	12.20
3^{12}_{Mf}	$Q1^2$	Southside Story^{117} (4) 41–1	——	——	——
	$Q2^3$	Bit o' Spice^{117} (A) 30–1	——	24.00	14.60
	$Q3^4$	Good Humor Girl^{117} (A) 20–1	——	——	——
10^{12}	$Q1^4$	Chief Difficulty^{111} (4⅔) 37–1	——	——	——
	$Q2^5$	Teuton II^{116} (5) 35–1	——	25.20	7.80
Apr. 24: 1^{12} Tues.	$Q1^5$	Hikahill^{118} (6) 14–1	——	——	——
	$Q2^6$	Lotta Esteem^{116} (8) 13–1	28.60	10.00	6.20
$2^{11}_{f/m}$	$Q1_{Po}$	Royal Care^{116} (6) 20–1Po	——	——	——
	$Q2_{Po}$	Suyin^{116} (5) 15–1Po	——	12.00	7.40
3^{12}_{Msw}	$Q1^1$	Indian Cup^{118} (3) 55–1	——	——	——
	$Q2^2$	E(Handsome Whirl^{118} (A) 23–1 (Rhonda's Tex)	——	——	——
	$Q3^3$	Feudal King^{118} (A) 19–1	41.00	12.00	10.60
Apr. 25: 1^{12}_{Msw} Wed.	$Q1^2$	Amquillo^{120} (7) 53–1	——	——	——
	$Q2^3$	Foster Son^{120} (6) 52–1	——	——	——
	$Q3^4$	Sky Kingdom^{120} (4) 24–1	——	24.40	12.20
2^{11}	$Q1_{Po}$	Miss Dolly Martin^{113} (7) 30–1Po	——	31.00	8.60
	$Q2_{Ao}$	Mighty Size^{116} (7) 31–1	——	——	——
4^{12}_{Mf}	$Q1^4$	Gay Hornet^{116} (6) 37–1	——	——	——
	$Q2^5$	Git Up and Fly^{109} (6) 34–1	69.80	34.20	10.00
$5^9_{f/m}$	$Q1^1$	Zippy Do^{116} (6) 38–1	——	——	——
	$Q2^2$	One Free Shot^{114} (5) 25–1	——	——	——

CHART VII (continued)

	Q3^3	Ponderosa Jane^{116} (5) 15–1	32.80	11.00	6.60
6$^9_?$	Q1^1	Suasion^{122} (6) 17–1	———	12.20	6.80
	Q2^2	Crazy Kilts^{106} (6) 17–1	———	———	———
	Q3^3	Martha Faye^{116} (6) 12–1	27.60	13.60	6.80
7^{12}	Q1^3	Phantom Leader^{112} (7) 23–1	———	———	———
	Q2^5	Rush A Bet^{112} (6) 18–1	———	23.60	11.40
Apr. 26: 1$^{12}_M$	Q1^3	Amazing Business^{116} (A) 22–1	———	———	———
Thurs.	Q2^6	Bearcat Turn^{113} (6) 18–1	———	———	———
	Q3^7	Grossecat^{120} (5) 18–1	38.20	12.60	8.80
2^{10}	Q1^3	Nay Not So^{106} (6) 21–1	———	———	8.80
	Q2^4	LaMorale^{106} (A) 12–1	———	12.20	10.00
Apr. 27: 1^{12}	Q1^3	Prince Cliney^{116} (5) 24–1	———	———	———
Fri.	Q2^4	Manner of Speaking^{116} (7) 20–1	41.60	12.60	7.80
3$^{12}_M$	Q1^1	Southside Story^{115} (4) 52–1	———	31.20	14.40
	Q2^2	All Dusty^{118} (A) 30–1	———	———	———
	Q3^4	Tropic Mood^{118} (4) 12–1	———	———	6.20
6^7	Q1^1	Montiego II^{112} (5) 22–1	———	———	———
	Q2^2	Prohibido^{114} (5) 16–1	34.40	8.00	4.00
8$^9_?$	Q1^1	Goodbye Juanita^{119} (5) 27–1	56.40	11.80	4.60
		(None for lack of odds.)			
Apr. 28: 1^{12}	Q1^1	Lin-Walvis^{116} (5) 69–1	———	52.60	22.00
Sat.	Q2^3†††	Mesmer^{116} (4) 43–1	———	———	13.60
2^{12}	Q1$_{Po}$	Court Page^{116} (6) 15–1	———	———	6.40
	Q2$_{Po}$	Whichway Didhego^{116}			
		(4⅔) 15–1Po	———	10.60	7.60
3$^7_{/m}$	Q1^1	Glider Girl^{114} (5) 13–1	———	———	———
	Q2^2	Turn Turtle^{109} (5) 10–1	———	———	———
	Q3^3	Alhoa Miss^{116} (5) 8–1	18.00	5.80	3.80
4^{12}	Q1^1	Brandt Brat^{113} (5) 63–1	———	37.20	12.60
	Q2^2	Native Flight^{112} (10) 38–1	———	———	———
5^{11}	Q1^1	Proud As Punch^{112} (4⅔) 50–1	———	———	15.40
	Q2^2	Little Lord^{109} (6) 29–1	———	———	———
7^{11}	Q1^2	Brilliant Charger^{113} (6) 32–1	———	———	———
	Q2^3	Real Image^{119} (6) 26–1	———	30.80	11.60

†††Mesmer had only four points, but the odds were good, and he had raced just five days ago.

Gulfstream Park, April 1973—Straight

SUMMARY:

Number of racing days: 23

Number of races: 230

Unit of investment: $2

	Q1		Q2		Q3	
	Win	*Place*	*Win*	*Place*	*Win*	*Place*
Return	716.00	789.80	1,171.00	720.00	288.20	172.60
Invested	460.00	460.00	460.00	460.00	———	———
Net Profit	256.00	329.80	711.00	260.00	———	———
Percentage	55%	71%	154%	56%		
TOTALS:	*Q1, Q2 Win*		*Q1, Q2, Place*		*Combined Totals*	
Return	1,887.00		1,509.00		3,396.00	
Invested	920.00		920.00		1,840.00	
Net Profit	967.00		589.80		1,556.00	
Percentage	105%		64%		84%	

		Total returns	*Average*
Number of Q1 Win hits:	12	$ 716.00	$59.90
Number of Q2 Win hits:	21	1,171.00	56.00
Number of Q1 Place hits:	33	789.80	23.95
Number of Q2 Place hits:	39	720.00	18.45
Q1, Q2 Win hits:	33	1,887.00	57.00
Q1, Q2 Place hits:	72	1,509.00	20.95

CHART VIII   Gulfstream Park, Daily Doubles: April 1973

Mar. 31:	F2 (June Magic) with Q1$_{Po}$ (Merister)	$492.20
Apr. 2:	F2 (Coinmat) with Q1$_{Po}$ (Dispute)	286.20
Apr. 5:	#2 (Mahlan) with #4$_q$ (Mannello)	92.80
Apr. 6:	F2 (Swinging Duel) with Q2$_{Po}$ (Cultivator)	685.00
Apr. 7:	#3 (Aware Wolf) with #1$^{3-1}$ (Sandy Ridge)	62.60
Apr. 10:	F3$_q$ (Granny the Grouch) with Q1$_{Po}$ (Gentle Upset)	475.60
Apr. 12:	F4$_q$ (Arabian Voyage) with Q2$_{Po}$ (Roanesian)	779.60
Apr. 13:	F4$_q$* (Ride the High Wind) with Q1$_{Po}$ (Andalien)	604.60
Apr. 14:	Q1 (Pitia) with #4Po (Wade Jr.)	165.40
Apr. 17:	#1$^{3-1}$ (Mahlan) with #3 (Clearance Sail)	58.20
Apr. 18:	F3 (Dabit) with Q1$_{Po}$ (Nota Bad Girl)	268.40
Apr. 19:	#4 (Sterling Mint) with #2 (Jolly Knave)	36.60

*Beach Picnic was disqualified for two bad races in her last three outings. F4 was Trifle Fluffy and F5 was Ride the High Wind, both of whom should be considered in this Maiden Race for three-yr-old fillies. Trifle Fluffy has a more recent race, but she finished seventh in that race and lost nearly five lengths in the stretch run. Ride the High Wind finished third in her last race at today's distance, and she moved up from fifth to third place in the stretch run. It's a difficult choice, but Sam would probably have picked Ride the High Wind, or he would have played it safe and bet them both.

CHART VIII (continued)

Apr. 20:	#1$^{3\text{-}1}$ (Boyd County) with #2 (Good Lad)	70.20
Apr. 21:	F4 (Alfor) with Q2$_{Po}$ (Dragonwick)	224.80
Apr. 23:	Q2 (Please Show Me) with #4$_q$ (Kampur)	557.00
Apr. 24:	Q2 (Lotta Esteem) with #2Po (Social Trim)	100.80
Apr. 26:	Q3 (Grossecat) with #3Po (Father Bill H.)	263.20
Apr. 27:	Q2 (Manner of Speaking) with #4/5 (Z Ron)†	160.40
Apr. 28:	#4 (Bonze) with #4 (Ambitious Cesere)	47.20

Gross Return: $4938.60

†In the second race, the number-four selection is Gimmick, a qualifying horse. However, we automatically take a look at the record of the number-five selection, Z Ron, and we note that Z Ron has a very recent workout and is dropping $1,500 in class. In fact, Z Ron has never before run in so low a class as today's $3,500. Also, Z Ron had a very impressive win at $5,000 a few weeks ago. Sam would probably pick Z Ron at 10-1Po over Gimmick, the number-4 selection. By the time the second race came up, the fans had "got the word" or for some reason jumped on Z Ron, for he was made the favorite. Z Ron won the race and completed the payoff combination, for $160.40. The size of this payoff can be attributed not to Z Ron but to the general *lack* of favor shown to Manner of Speaking in the first race.

SUMMARY:

Number of racing days: 23

Number of investments: 23

Total investments, at $50 per day: $1,150.00

Gross Return: $4,938.60

Total invested: 1,150.00

Net profit: $3,788.60

Percentage of net profit: 328%

CHART IX   Gulfstream Park, Perfectas: April 1973

Apr. 3:	7^{12}	F3	(Carry Nancy) with Q2 (Musical Annie)	$310.80
	10^{11}	F3$_q$	(Calculated Gambler) with Q1 (Dahit)	684.40
Apr. 5:	7^{12}	F4	(Just Curious) with F3 (Wise Solomon)	178.60
	10^{10}	F2	(June Magic) with F4$_q$ (Red and Ready)	73.00
Apr. 6:	4^{12}	F2	(Hand Signal) with F3 (Bronze Gem)	63.40
	10^{12}	F5	(Bonze) with F4 (Our Richard)	256.40
Apr. 7:	4^{12}	F5	(He's A Card)* with F2 (Major Art)	126.00
	10^{12}	Q2	(Rejucilo) with F2 (Roji)	129.80
Apr. 9:	4$^{12}_{Mf}$	Q4	(Ken's Gal Chris)† with F3 (Chili Bowl)	190.80

*Not a hit, strictly speaking, because He's A Card is F5, and F2, F3 and F4 were qualified. However, it is advisable always to look at F5 to see whether or not he or she is outstanding, as this F5 turned out to be. E.g, he's dropping $3,000 in class; he worked out yesterday; he gained three lengths in the stretch run of his last race; and his odds are 11-1! With qualifications like that, Sam would say, he's an automatic additional bet. Or, you could take him over the other qualified horse, F4, Channel Tide, in this race. We count this one in as a bet, so far as our calculations at the end of the chart are concerned.

†Since this is a race for maiden fillies, we include Q4 (Ken's Gal Chris) in spite of a sharp move-up in class. She finished third in her last race, only six lengths off the winner. It is wise to go to Q4 in maiden races or races with three-year-old fillies. Especially if it is a Perfecta Race, as the seventh race also turned out to be. See below.

CHART IX (continued)

	7_f^{12}	Q4	(Kilpedder Lady) with Q3 (Rocky Tip)	342.00
	$10_{f/m}^{12}$	Q3	(Sleepless Ruler) with F1 (Princess Alice)	232.60
Apr. 12:	10^{12}	F2	(Hawaiian Voyage) with F4 (Mixed Emotions)	102.80
Apr. 11:	7^{12}	F1	(Amasport) with Q1 (Spun Silver)	94.20
	10^{12}	F2	(Dr. Belcher) with F4 (Leonard R. Lee)	94.60
Apr. 12:	4^{12}	F4$_q$	(Major Appointment) with F2 (Ever Ready John)	75.20
	10^{10}	F1	(Sir Ribot's Jet) with Q1 (Moonruch)	76.80
Apr. 13:	$4_{f/m}^{11}$	F1	(Moon Stitch) with Q3 (Rolla Bowla Ball)	184.40
	7_f^{12}	F4$_q$/5	(Miss Tom Cat)‡ with F3 (Black Tulip)	188.80
Apr. 14:	10^9	F1	(Don Quixote II) with Q2 (King Duck)	110.40
Apr. 16:	4_f^{12}	Q2	(Saxony Princess) with Q3 (Manchi)	1138.40
	$7_{f/m}^{12}$	F4$_q$	(Musical Annie) with F5$_q$ (Extensive Care)	146.80
	10^{12}	F3	(Oxbridge) with Q1 (Arts Village)	539.20
Apr. 17:	4^{12}	F1	(Adam's Jet) with Q1 (No More Sir)	183.40
	10^{10}	Q2	(Federal Empress) with F2 (Candy Chief)	361.80
Apr. 18:	4_M^{12}	(F3	(Miss C.P.O.) with F5 (Changing Wind)§	121.60)
	7^{12}	Q2	(King Cross II) with DH F3 (Jolly Husky)‖	312.80
			(King Cross II) with DH F4$_q$ (Dreki)	564.40
	10^{10}	Q2	(Bokamy) with F2 (Last End)	143.40
Apr. 19:	7^{12}	Q1	(Crimson Twins) with F3 (Barclay Jet)	394.80
	10^8	Q2	(Kilpedder Lady) with F1 (Ken's Gal Chris)	78.60
Apr. 20:	10^{10}	F3	(T. Attack) with F2 (Landing Gear)	63.00
Apr. 21:	4^{12}	F4$_q$	(Music King) with Q1 (Cuzin Leslie)	644.00
	7^{12}	F1	(Rio Caudaloso) with Q2 (Key Largo II)	96.20
Apr. 23:	4^{10}	F4$_q$	(Pseudo Nurse) with F3 (Irish Kamikaze)	122.80
	7^{12}	F5	(Big Whippendeal) with F6 (Beach Picnic)	142.20
	10^{12}	F3	(Wooglin) with Q2 (Teuton II)	355.60
Apr. 24:	7^{12}	F2	(Tombros) with F4 (Whirling Sword)	100.60
Apr. 25:	4^{12}	Q1	(Git Up and Fly) with F4 (Miss Eggers)	1064.00
	7^{12}	F4$_q$	(Like the Dickens) with Q2 (Rush A Bet)	418.60
Apr. 26:	10^{11}	F4	(Freedom's Fling) with F2 (Candy Chief)	78.60
Apr. 27:	4_M^{12}	F3	(Jennie Bearcat) with F5 (Banner Waves)#	138.00
	10^9	F3	(Yaba) with F4 (Turnip)	101.00
Apr. 28:	4^{12}	F2	(Aware Wolf) with Q1 (Brandt Brat)	430.40

‡F4 is Effective, but Miss Tom Cat F5 looks better on Form in this race for three-yr-old fillies. Take Miss Tom Cat over Effective, or play them both.

§Not a hit. Changing Wind is F5 and is questionable on the basis of her record. The only point in her favor is that she is a maiden running for the first time in a claiming race. Unpredictable. This one is not included in the calculations that follow the chart.

‖Jolly Husky is F3 but is actually F2$_q$, because of the disqualification of T.V. Doubletalk. Although dropping in class, T.V. Doubletalk finished ninth in a field of ten, and in his last race at this class he finished dead last, thirty lengths off the winner.

#In this race for three-yr-old maiden fillies, F4 is Quadrilateral, a qualified horse. We add F5, a first-time starter, who is an automatic bet. Since there is no way to choose between them, play the two of them.

CHART IX (continued)

7^{11} $F4_q$ (Harry Sayd)** with Q2 (Real Image)   442.00

**Three of the horses in the first five favorites were in one race on April 13: F2, F3, and F5. The F5 horse (Harry Sayd) finished third; the F2 horse (Billy Come Lately) finished sixth; and F3 (Stretch Turn) finished fifth. Harry Sayd was 3¾ lengths off the winner, whereas Billy Come Lately was 9¼ lengths off the winner. The race was fifteen days ago, and all three horses are ready. Stretch Turn had a workout four days ago, and is carrying 113 pounds today. Billy has no recent workout and is carrying 119. Harry worked out YESTERDAY, but is carrying high weight of 122. Despite the higher weight, Harry gets the nod over the other two. His finish position last race and that recent workout put him far ahead of Billy and a bit ahead of Stretch Turn. Disqualify Billy, but keep Stretch Turn and Harry in. During the race, Harry Sayd was third at the quarter-pole, second at the half and first at the head of the stretch. He won by half a length over Real Image, who was just a nose ahead of the Favorite, Strike or Spare. That nose produced a nice payoff in the Perfecta: $442.00.

Finally, in the April 13 race, when Harry Sayd finished third, he was disqualified and placed last. This threw a lot of people off him when they considered this race today. Rivera is riding again, and it's a cinch that Rivera isn't going to make the same mistake twice in a row. Harry's odds are better than 8-to-1, when they probably should be no more than 4- or 5-1.

SUMMARY:
Number of racing days: 23
Number of Perfecta races: 92
Total investment, at $60 per race: $5,520.00
Gross return: $11,575.60
Total invested: 5,520.00
_____
Net profit: 6,055.60

Percentage of net profit: 109%

Breakdown of F4, F5, F6.   Return: $ 515.40
                             Invested: 1,104.00
                             _____
                             Net loss: 558.60

Breakdown of F1 with Q1 and Q2:   Return: $1,056.60
                                  Invested: 736.00
                                  _____
                                  Net profit: $ 320.60

Gulfstream Park, April 1973

	Straight	Doubles	Perfectas	Totals
Return	3,346.00	4,938.60	11,575.60	19,860.20
Invested	1,840.00	1,150.00	5,520.00	8,510.00
Net Profit	1,506.00	3,788.60	6,055.60	11,350.20
Percentage	81%	328%	109%	133%

CHART X   Aqueduct, Straight Bets: April 1972

Apr. 1: 2^8 $Q1_{Po}$ Black Mamba^{106} (6) 12–1Po   ——— ———   5.60

CHART X (continued)

Sat.	Q2$_{Po}$	Morrosen^{114} (5) 10–1	———	12.60	6.20
4^{10}	Q1^2	Cab Calloway^{116} (6) 36–1	———	———	———
	Q2^4	Folsom Blues^{116} (6) 17–1	———	14.00	6.00
6^8	Q1^2	Vested Power^{112} (5) 18–1	———	———	———
	Q2^3	Imasuper^{112} (7) 11–1	———	6.20	3.60
Apr. 3: 5^8	Q1^1	Ocalamine^{106} (7) 24–1	———	———	———
Mon.	Q2^3	Messmate^{116} (6) 9–1	19.80	8.00	5.60
6^{10}	Q1^2	Class Medal^{121} (6) 25–1	———	———	———
	Q2^5	Ruritania^{121} (5) 16–1	———	12.80	5.60
8^{10}	Q1^2	Social Spree^{105} (7) 33–1	———	———	———
	Q2^3	Tinsel Time^{116} (6) 23–1	———	———	———
	(Q3^4*	Dodeys Sky High^{116} (5) 19–1	39.60	13.20	6.60)
Apr. 4: 1$^{12}_{f3}$	Q1^1	Bonny Starlet^{112} (A) 81–1	———	———	———
Tues.	Q2^3	Dandy Smile^{112} (A) 51–1	———	———	———
	Q3^5	Alcibalita^{115} (4) 15–1	32.60	13.40	11.20
2$^{12}_{M3}$	Q1^1	Jolly Swagman^{117} (A) 68–1	———	———	———
	Q2^2	Wearin O the Green^{121} (A) 35–1	———	———	———
	Q3^5†	Cut Back^{111} (7) 19–1	39.20	10.40	5.40
4^9	Q1^1	First Cut^{116} (5) 43–1	———	———	10.40
	Q2^2	Nationalist^{107} (5) 38–1	———	———	———
5^7	Q1^2	She's Staunchness^{115} (4) 14–1	———	———	———
	Q2^4	Leslie Flag^{108} (4) 8–1	18.40	6.00	3.00
Apr. 5: 3$^{10}_{Mf}$	Q1^3	Lip Talk^{120} (4) 35–1	———	———	———
Wed.	Q2^5	I'll Be Here^{110} (8) 14–1	———	11.20	4.20
6$^{10}_{f}$	Q1^2	Countess Georgia^{114} (6) 25–1	———	———	10.20
	Q2^3	Bolinas Favor^{114} (5) 19–1	———	———	———
	Q3^4	Just A Duchess^{116} (5) 18–1	———	———	———
	(Q4^5‡	Overlay^{116} (4) 12–1	———	11.60	9.00)

*Dodeys Sky High is the third qualifier in this ordinary race. Strictly speaking, this is not a play under the system. But Sam says, especially when dealing with an Exacta Race (as this one is), look at the next horse in line. Dodeys Sky High is at 19-1 and Tinsel Time is at 23-1. Both are carrying the same weight this race. Both were in the same race seven days ago, which means that both are ready for today's contest. Tinsel Time finished seventh in that race, and Dodeys Sky High finished sixth. That doesn't always mean that history repeats itself, but Dodeys Sky High won the race and started an Exacta combination that paid $229.80. Looking closely at the past performance of both horses, we note that Tinsel Time has never been in-the-money; Dodeys Sky High has been in twice in six races. Dodeys must be the pick, of course.

†Strictly speaking, Q3 in this race is Benissimo at 25-1. However, since this is a race for three-yr-old maidens, we look also at Q4, Cut Back, at 19-1. Cut Back is dropping 10 pounds from his last race and has a ten-pound weight advantage over Benissimo this race. Benissimo has 4⅔ points, and Cut Back has seven points. Both have had a workout within three days, but Cut Back must be given the nod for that big weight advantage.

‡In this race for three-yr-old fillies, again it was Q4, the next in line, that provided the place horse in the race. Q1 accounted for the show position. The winner was Wondrous Sky, who was F4q. The Exacta was covered in the system betting by F4q and F5q. You will recall that F4, F5 and F6 (qualifiers, of course) are a separate crisscross in Exacta betting. Comparing the records of the two, we find that Just A Duchess, who is dropping in class, finished last in her last two races. She worked a few days ago but hasn't had a race in over two-and-a-half months. Overlay, on the other hand, raced fifteen days ago. She appears to be moving up in class by $3,500, but actually her move up is only about $1,000. She finished second and sixth in her last two races. She's had four races since Just A Duchess was in a race. The comparison of two horses, in this manner, is very revealing and is a much easier business than comparing or contrasting all the horses in a race. Take just two horses and look closely at those two only, and as a general rule you can come up with the one which is the better. Essentially, that is the way Sam works when he is handicapping a race.

CHART X (continued)

Apr. 6: Thurs.	2^{14}_{M3}	$Q1_{Po}$	Bold Rule^{122} (5) 20–1Po	——	——	——
		$Q2_{Po}$	Plum Good^{122} (5) 20–1Po	——	——	——
		$Q3_{Po}$	E(Sharp Glance^{122} (5) 15–1Po	——	21.40	9.60
			(Idealistic			
	6^9	$Q1^1$	Linstock^{102} (5) 62–1	——	——	——
		$Q2^2$	Movie Man^{114} (5) 17–1	——	——	10.00
	$8^5_{f/m}$	$Q1^1$	Gay West^{116} (5) 13–1	——	——	——
		$Q2^2$	La Bertha^{116} (6) 7–1	16.60§	5.00	5.60
Apr. 7: Fri.	2^{14}_M	$Q1_{Po}$	Gentle Spring^{112} (5) 20–1Po	201.80	86.60	25.60
		$Q2_{Po}$	Taconic^{117} (5) 20–1Po	——	——	——
		$Q3_{Po}$	Cocky Beth^{106} (4) 20–1	——	——	——
	5^{13}_{Mswf}	$Q1^1$	Foreign Strand^{117} (4) 60–1	——	——	——
		$Q2^2$	Pago Queen^{117} (A) 30–1	——	26.80	13.60
		$Q3^3$	Shiraza^{117} (A) 30–1	——	——	——
	6^7	$Q1^1$	Merry Score^{116} (4) 12–1	——	12.00	4.40
		$Q2^2$	Cable Royale^{108} (5) 11–1	——	——	——
		$Q3^3$	Ring of Steel^{108} (6) 8–1	——	——	——
Apr. 8: Sat.	2^{11}	$Q1_{Po}$	Unto Heaven^{116} (5) 20–1Po	——	19.00	10.00
		$Q2_{Po}$	Eye on the Sky^{116} (5) 15–1Po	31.00	12.80	6.20
	4^{10}_{Msw}	$Q1^1$	Barbiswoon^{122} (4) 87–1	——	——	——
		$Q2^2$	Cupid's Comet^{122} (A) 48–1	——	——	——
		$Q3^3$	Ship Gunn^{122} (4) 33–1	——	——	9.00
	7^{13}	$Q1^1$	Dundas Prince^{114} (6) 62–1	——	——	——
		$Q2^2$	E(Freetex^{126} (6) 32–1	65.40	26.40	14.40
			(Festive Mood^{114}			
	9^9	$Q1^2$	Interwood^{114} (5) 26–1	——	21.40	12.80
		$Q2^4$	Moonreindeer^{116} (5) 11–1	——	——	——
Apr. 10: Mon.	2^{12}_m	$Q1_{Po}$	Angel Cake^{107} (6) 12–1Po	53.40	22.40	12.00
		$Q2_{Po}$	Cute Little Devil^{117} (4) 12–1	——	——	——
		$Q3_{Po}$	T. Bag Annie^{117} (4) 10–1Po	——	——	7.00
	7^6	$Q1^1$	Mindy Malone^{112} (6) 23–1	48.40	9.20	3.60
		$Q2^2$	Stacey d'Ette^{112} 8–1	——	——	3.00
	8^{10}	$Q1^1$	The Continent^{116} (5) 33–1	68.20	21.00	10.20
		$Q2^3$	Army Hitch^{116} (5) 25–1	——	——	——

§The fact that this horse paid more to show than to place indicates that a large amount of "inside" money was bet on La Bertha to win and to place. The stable and owners rarely bet to show. La Bertha went off at a good 7-1 in a field of only five horses. At the quarter, the jockey Vasquez had her in the lead by four lengths and she was never headed, beating out Cute n' Crafty, the co-favorite at almost even money, by three good lengths. The favorite, Entrap, ran dead last. She dwelt at the start and trailed the field throughout the race. The Exacta paid a very respectable $52.80. In her last race, by the way, La Bertha ran at a claiming price of $15,000 and was eighth in a field of nine horses. This no doubt accounts for the odds of 7-1 in today's race. While this maneuvering is all quite legal and above board, the stewards might have missed an opportunity by not penalizing St. Leon for his ride on Entrap. Sam's method of high-odds qualification caught the winner of this race, with no knowledge of the fact that a "set up" was, or might have been, planned. Sam's system also "caught" the winner of the second race the next day, April 7, when Gentle Spring probably surprised everybody by winning at 100-1 odds, paying $201.80 to win and completing a daily double that paid $2041.00. It really matters not whether a race is or is not setup, if such is actually possible. Sam's system catches the big ones willy-nilly.

CHART X (continued)

Apr. 11:4^{11}	Q1^1	Talking Leaves^{116} (6) 25–1	——	——	——
Tues.	Q2^2‖	Cosmic Price^{112} (5) 23–1	48.40	18.00	12.00
$7^8_{f/m}$	Q1^1	Breach of Promise^{115} (5) 26–1	——	——	——
	Q2^2	Miss Monette^{112} (5) 21–1	——	17.40	7.60
	Q3^3	Spit and Polish^{118} (5) 15–1	——	——	——
8^{12}	Q1^1#	My Guiding Light^{116} (4⅔) 50–1	——	——	——
	Q2^4	Billy Silver II^{112} (6) 21–1	——	18.60	12.60
Apr. 12:2^{10}	Q1$_{Po}$	Spear^{116} (5) 20–1Po	——	——	——
Wed.	Q2$^3_{Ao}$**	Tudor Tune^{103} (7) 34–1	69.20	26.20	11.20
$5^8_{f/m}$	Q1^1	Sister Sky^{112} (6) 14–1	31.00	9.40	5.80
	Q2^2	Seeds of War^{116} (5) 10–1	——	——	——
	Q3^3	Out of School^{112} (5) 9–1	——	——	5.00
6^7	Q1^1	Lady Brava^{112} (5) 32–1	——	——	7.80
	Q2^2	Lover's Walk^{111} (5) 12–1	——	——	——
8^8_f	Q1^1	Dacquare^{109} (5) 37–1	——	——	——
	Q2^2	Hong Kong Spree^{113} (5) 15–1	31.60	11.00	7.20
	Q3^3	Bonspiel Dixie^{112} (4) 11–1	——	——	——
Apr. 13:1^9	Q1^2	Scottish Blend^{112} (5) 13–1	——	11.40	5.00
Thurs.	Q2^3	Steeple Jack^{102} (6) 12–1	——	——	——
3^{12}_M	Q1^2	Pour Le Sport^{115} (5) 38–1	——	——	——
	Q2^3	Feminist^{112} (8) 17–1	35.60	13.80	8.60
	Q3^4	With Heart^{113} (9) 14–1	——	——	8.60
4^9	Q1^1	Tabi's Turn^{118} (5) 20–1			

‖Cosmic Price had not raced since February 16, almost two months ago. However, the five-yr-old gelding had worked out twice since March 30, that is, within the past twelve days, and was clearly "ready" for today's race. His last two finishes were tenth in fields of twelve each, and that fact helps to account for the fact that he was the second highest odds in the race, at 23-1. The 4-1 co-favorite, Gottogo, led all the way to the stretch turn, where he was leading Cosmic Price by a head, but in the stretch drive Cosmic Price won the race going away, a length in front of Gottogo. This race illustrates the reason for Sam's awarding of two points for two workouts within fourteen days. Cosmic Price's other three points are as follows: one point for dropping four pounds for this race; one point for a finish of second in October 1970; and one final point for finishing 6½ lengths off the winner (or less) in three races. Cosmic Price, like Eye On the Sky in the second race on April 8 (and many others, of course), garnered exactly five points under Sam's method of selection, was second in line going down the odds-scale from the top, and became a winner paying a nice price. Notice in this fourth race on April 11 that Q1, the first qualifier, Talking Leaves, had six points and his odds were 25-1. Talking Leaves ran out this race. This is the reason Sam selects two horses in each race. When dealing with horses in these upper-odds range, you cannot compare the top two closely and pick the better horse. As often as not, the horse with the lower number of points is the winner. Comparative handicapping, between two contenders, works better in the middle and lower odds ranges, and there is exactly where Sam uses it; for example, to choose between F4 and F5, if he must make a choice there. For the next example of this principle, see the eighth race on April 12, just below. Hong Kong Spree is Q2^2 with five points, is 15-1 and wins the race. Q1^1 is Dacquare, at 37-1, also with five points, but he ran out of the money.

#My Guiding Light has only 4⅔ points. The two-thirds comes from two races with a finish of less than 6¾ lengths off the winners. My Guiding Light had one finish of 1½ lengths off the winner, one finish of 2½ lengths off, and one at 6¾. This latter is just ¼ too high; Sam let My Guiding Light in anyway, due to the other points accrued and to the good odds of 50-1. Nothing came of it this time, since My Guiding Light finished tenth in a field of twelve. My Guiding Light garnered two points from Category A, and he might have got half-a-point more IF today's race had been at the same distance and on the same surface as his last race. But today's race is one mile, and his last race was seven furlongs. Also, the colt is dropping $5,000 in class, gaining one point. Another $1,000 in the drop, and he would have had two points. Such an obvious borderline case has to get in.

**Jim's Finance was the next in line in probable odds, at 15-1. However, when it came down to betting the race itself, Tudor Tune, with odds of 34-1, had seven points and looked much better than Jim's Finance at 6-1. This is also a race for three-yr-olds, including males, and in all three-yr-old races Sam watches the odds closely in making selections. Tudor Tune was actually Q3$_{Po}$, or the third qualifier in probable odds, which is the reason Sam had him in the Daily Double combinations. The wisdom of this becomes clear when you discover that the double paid $450.80.

CHART X (continued)

Date	Dist	Qual	Horse	Win	Place	Show
		Q2$^{2/3}$††	Broken Penny^{106} (9) 16–1	———	13.20	8.00
	6$^{12}_{r3}$	Q1^1	She's Staunchness^{114} (4) 51–1	———	———	———
		Q2^2‡‡	Soft and Silky^{121} (4) 43–1	———	28.20	15.40
		Q3^3	Instinctively^{121} (4) 27–1	———	———	———
	8$^8_{f/m}$	Q1^1	Road Way Miss^{112} (6) 14–1	———	———	———
		Q2^2§§	Sky Cache^{112} (5) 14–1	———	———	6.00
Apr. 14: 1$^{14}_{f/m}$		Q1^1	Seven Pac^{106} (6) 35–1	71.80	24.40	14.20
Fri.		Q2^2	Mere Trifle^{114} (4⅔) 31–1	———	———	———
		Q3^3	Helens Restless^{106} (5) 28–1	———	———	———
	6$^6_{f/m}$	Q1^1	Our Nesta^{113} (5) 16–1	———	———	———
		Q2^2	Vikeena^{115} (6) 11–1	———	5.20	2.80
	8$^7_{f/m}$	Q1^1	Quilt^{112} (7) 23–1	———	———	5.80
		Q2^2	Miniture Pieces^{116} (7) 16–1	34.60	8.00	4.40
		Q3^3	Crystal Dawn^{114} (4⅔) 16–1	———	———	———
	9^9	Q1^1	Busy Singing^{113} (5) 14–1	———	———	7.00
		Q2^2	Oh Jak Kyo^{115} (6) 12–1	———	———	———
		(Q3^3‖‖	Sky Dandy^{113} (9) 9–1	21.00	9.80	6.20)
Apr. 15: 2$^{13}_M$		Q1ₚₒ	Idealic^{122} (5) 15–1Po	———	———	———
Sat.		Q2ₚₒ	Gay Pierre^{122} (5) 15–1Po	———	———	———
		Q3ₚₒ	Commoner^{122} (5) 10–1Po	22.20	9.20	5.60
	8^7	Q1^1	Dam Buster^{114} (9) 26–1	———	———	———

††Broken Penny and Your Lordship both had odds of exactly 16-1. Sam had to choose between the two, since this is a race for four-yr-olds and he could not very well bet them both. (If it had been a three-yr-old race, he might indeed have bet them both.) Both horses have raced recently. Your Lordship raced twelve days ago; Broken Penny raced five days ago. Both are going up in class, and about the same amount. Broken Penny was claimed last race, which means he is subject to disqualification unless he has eight clear points, or meets the stiff criteria for such horses. He does both, and in so doing gets the nod over Your Lordship, who, incidentally, finished last in the race. Broken Penny with nine points and getting in at 106 pounds, with odds of 16-1, is a stand-out. He ran second to the favorite, Shining Sword, who paid $5.40 to win. As you see, Broken Penny paid $13.20 to place and $8.00 to show. Thousands of fans cashed $5.40 tickets, while a few of Sam's followers took home $13.20 for every two they put through the windows. We should say, all of Sam's followers!

‡‡In this race for three-yr-old fillies, all horses (except maidens) ran at the same high weight of 121. Therefore, none of them were penalized for carrying this weight. Any time one factor is true of all horses in a race, then ignore that factor since it will tell you nothing. A one point penalty for carrying 121 pounds would have disqualified Soft and Silky and Instinctively. It would have knocked out all the high-odds horses, and you would have had no bet. As it was, with four points (and ignoring the weight factor), Soft and Silky got the nod and came in second at 43-1; $28.20 is a nice payoff in anybody's book, including Sam's.

§§There is no other qualifier with odds high enough to play. The next highest odds are 7-1, and since there are eight horses in the race, we can't go down that low.

While we are on the subject, let us explain the reason for not playing horses whose odds are lower than the number of horses in the race. In a ten-horse race, for example, only one of the ten is going to win, barring a dead-heat. If the horse you are playing has odds of 10-1 or higher, you have a realistic chance of getting a good return on your investment. If you play a 10-1 horse and he wins, you get back $12, which is your two plus ten more. Statistically speaking, you are right on the button. Any odds above 10-1 are really an overlay, which means that the payoff will be better than the real chances of winning that payoff. All of Sam's wagers are in this overlay area, and that ignores completely the merits of the animals. Now, when you add quality to statistics, you get a genuine overlay. A horse earning four or five points is actually in contention and has the capability of getting in-the-money. Of course, if you play two horses in a ten-horse race, as Sam does, your average return on the winner has to be 20-1 or better. That is exactly what Sam expects and is what he gets.

‖‖This is not a hit since it is a race for four-yr-olds and up, and we do not go to the third qualifier. However, we do look at the third qualifier, and we can compare him with the second qualifier. Oh Jak Kyo is dropping in class, while Sky Dandy is running in his class again. But Sky Dandy has the more recent race and was in the money in both of his past two races. Oh Jak Kyo was fourth in each of his last two. It's a close one, but Sky Dandy does have nine points, three more than Oh Jak Kyo. Of course, his odds are three points lower, too. They are still 9-1, which are qualifying odds in this race of nine horses. Sky Dandy wins.

CHART X (continued)

Date		Q	Horse			
		Q2²	Odie Bob^{124} (10) 14–1	29.80	5.80	4.00
Apr. 17:1^{14}		Q1¹	Slightly Misty^{112} (9) 35–1	——	——	16.20
Mon.		Q2²	Bear the Cup^{112} (5) 32–1	——	——	——
Apr. 18:2^{13}		Q1ₚₒ	Smidge Boy^{113} (5) 30–1Po	——	17.60	9.20
Tues.		Q2ₚₒ	Reely Good^{118} (6) 15–1Po	——	——	——
		(Q3ₚₒ##Halfway Home^{115} (6) 12–1Po	31.00	15.40	8.00)
	3^{7}_{f3}	Q1¹	Vain Beauty^{112} (4) 32–1	——	22.40	5.60
		Q2²	Huge Joke^{105} (5) 22–1	46.40	19.20	7.00
	8^{11}	Q1¹	Royal Quester^{116} (6) 33–1	——	——	——
		Q2²	Spiritual Leader^{116} (5) 27–1	——	——	——
		(Q4*** Scungagad^{114} (8) 14–1	29.20	13.20	10.20)
Apr. 19:4⁹		Q1¹	Talking Leaves^{116} (5) 21–1	——	——	9.00
Wed.		Q2²	Good Voyage^{116} (5) 19–1	——	——	——
	8⁹	Q1²	Unbendable^{109} (7) 14–1	——	——	7.60
		Q2³	Tabi's Turn^{115} (6) 13–1	——	13.20	9.60
	9⁸	Q1¹	Swiss Bounce^{105} (4⅔) 27–1	——	——	——
		Q2²	Sharp Doer^{112} (5) 17–1	——	——	6.00
Apr. 20:2^{10}		Q1ₚₒ	Bet Jay Be^{116} (5) 20–1Po	——	——	——
Thurs.		Q2ₚₒ	Borgia's Brew^{116} (6) 15–1Po	——	——	8.00
	4^{9}_{Mf}	Q1²	Sweet n Costly^{117} (8) 22–1	46.80	15.80	9.60
		Q2³	Jovial Josie^{117} (4) 14–1	——	——	7.60
	6⁷	Q1¹	Your Lordship^{112} (5) 13–1	——	——	——
		Q2²	Harkville^{112} (7) 10–1	22.20	8.40	3.80
	$8^{10}_{f/m}$	Q1²	Es Cabalistica^{116} (6) 18–1	——	——	——
		Q2³	Jill the Queen^{113} (6) 14–1	——	10.40	5.40
	$9^{8}_{f/m}$	Q1¹	Tud Knowz^{115} (6) 21–1	44.40	13.20	6.00
		Q2²	Hasty Tibaldo^{113} (4⅔) 21–1	——	——	——
		Q3³	Libbet Cloud^{106} (6) 13–1	——	——	——
Apr. 21:4^{8}_{M}		Q1²	Belfry^{105} (5) 15–1	——	——	——
Fri.		Q2³	Grandpa Dom^{114} (7) 14–1	——	12.60	7.60
	5^{8}_{f3}	Q1¹	National Dancer^{109} (5) 37–1	——	——	——
		Q2³	Wee Dee Dee^{113} (4) 12–1	25.60	10.00	5.00
		Q3⁴	Orthosurg^{108} (4) 12–1	——	——	——
	7⁷	Q1¹	Supper Show^{121} (5) 11–1	——	8.20	3.80
		Q2³	Commercial Break^{112} (5) 9–1	——	——	——

##This is not a hit, strictly speaking. The third qualifier comes through again. However, since it is a second race and is involved in the daily double, Sam would seriously consider playing three qualifiers. Or, he would compare Reely Good with Halfway Home and play the one he considered the better. In this case, both horses raced in the same race eight days ago. Reely Good finished seventh, while Halfway Home lost his rider, and you can't prove anything by that. However, Halfway Home won his race on April 4, and Reely Good has won only one race in two years of trying. Halfway Home has run five past races at higher classes than today's race. Reely Good is moving up in class from three races back. In short, Halfway Home looks better on the *Form*. If you have to choose between them, the choice is clear. Halfway Home actually finished second in the race, but the winner, Tenth Round, was disqualified and placed last. Halfway Home went into the winner's circle, and holders of his win tickets collected $31 each.

***Not a hit. Scungagad is Q4, too far down the line to catch. Shown here, once more, to prove that you can't win 'em all. However, Scungadad was F6q and with Duplicate Bridge (F5) was a system winner in the Exacta, which paid $373.20. Win mutuel shown here is not included in the calculations at the end of this chart.

CHART X (continued)

8[10]	Q1[1]	Queens Jester[112] (6) 28–1	——	——	——
	Q2[3]	Shadyside[116] (7) 13–1	——	12.80	6.60
Apr. 22:2[8]	Q1po	Mt. Kenya[112] (5) 15–1Po	——	——	9.00
Sat.	Q2Ao	Little Mahoney[113] (5) 9–1	19.80	8.60	5.80
5[9]	Q1[1]	Sun Festival[115] (6) 28–1	——	——	8.00
	Q2[2]	Wondrous Sky[113] (6) 16–1	——	——	——
	Q3[3]	Potato Salad[108] (8) 13–1	——	——	——
6[7]	Q1[1]	Lonesome River[107] (8) 13–1	——	8.80	4.20
	Q2[2]	Wildcat Country[121] (7) 13–1	——	——	——
8[9]	Q1[1]	Handy Admiral[114] (8) 22–1	——	——	8.40
	Q2[4]	Trupan[116] (5) 14–1	——	——	——
Apr. 24:1[13]M3	Q1[2]	Charlie Mist[117] (4) 33–1	——	24.80	17.60
Mon.	Q2[3]	Simply Staunch[117] (4) 22–1	——	——	——
	Q3[4]	Come Collect[110] (4) 21–1	——	——	——
6[6]	Q1[1]	Liberal Emperor[116] (8) 10–1	——	7.80	3.40
	Q2[2]	Gay Greeter[116] (6) 9–1	——	——	——
9[7]	Q1[1]	Money Destroyer[116] (5) 23–1	——	——	3.60
	Q2[2]	Agueros II[116] (5) 9–1	——	——	——
Apr. 25:5[8]	Q1[1]	Sea Rider[110] (5) 33–1	——	14.20	6.40
Tues.	Q2[2]	Twin Angle[116] (5) 15–1	——	——	——
8[10]f/m	Q1[1]	Crafty Action[114] (4) 44–1†††	——	30.40	10.60
	Q2[2]	Quilt[114] (5) 41–1	——	——	——
	Q3[3]	Nectar Queen[116] (5) 25–1	——	——	——
Apr. 26:1[14]Mf/m	Q1[1]	Pams Darlin[116] (5) 46–1	——	——	——
Wed.	Q2[2]	Pagan Moon[121] (5) 40–1	——	——	——

†††This is a filly/mare race, and we recall that a filly needs only four points to qualify, whereas a mare needs five points. Shown below is the past performance chart of Crafty Action, to illustrate the important point that you do have a choice of races by which to qualify a contender. Crafty Action's last race was at today's class, and we may use that race to try for qualification. See chart.

Crafty Action*   114

Dk. b. or br. f (1968), by Crafty Admiral—Comet Action, by Jet Action.
Breeder, J.H. Hartigan (Fla.).   1972   4   0   0   0 $480
Owner, Halm Stable.   Trainer, R.J. Sanseverino. $12,000   1971 32   3   3   3 $22,030

Apr 7-72[4]Aqu	7 f 1:25³/₅ft	13 114	5⁹½	8⁰½	8¹⁰	8¹⁸ Velas'zJ³	12000 55 ⓕImpasse116	Sense ofR'son	Dispute 8
Feb 3-72[8]Lib	1 1:40²/₅gd	16 114	6⁶½	9¹⁷	8²¹	9³⁰ Rodrig'zD⁴	Alw 42 ⓢSc'r'sW'ys112	O'tinTheC'd	C'ceMiss 10
Jan25-72[8]Lib	6 f 1:15²/₅gd	20 114	6⁹½	6⁷½	4⁵½	4⁷½ Rodrig'zD³	Alw 61 ⓒC't'sG'r'ld'e105	WeeL'd'g	Sch'sW's 7
Jan15-72[7]Lib	6 f 1:14³/₅shy	32 112	6⁶	7¹¹	7⁹	7⁸½ Gua'lupeJ²	Alw 63 ⓒCol'be122	Wh'eTh'esS'ke	C'p'eMiss 7
Dec30-71[8]Lib	1-70 1:45 gd	7½ 113	5⁷½	6⁹	6¹³	5²⁰ DittfachH²	Alw 55 ⓡR'y'lKn't're113	Y'uC'tT'l	S'wOfK'gs 7

April 22 Bel 5f ft 1:02¹/₅sh   April 15 Bel 4f tf :49¹/₅b   April 5 Bel 4f ft :49¹/₅bg

We see by that last race, which was on April 7, that Crafty Action ran seven furlongs and finished dead last, eighteen lengths off the winner. The filly looks bad, and our impression is not enhanced by a glance at her next-to-last race, at a mile, when she finished ninth, thirty lengths off the winner. But today's race is at the strange (to some) distance of 6½ furlongs. Crafty Action has no race at that distance, but she does have a race at six furlongs on January 25, when she finished fourth, just 7¼ lengths off the winner. This clearly is her best race, and this is the race we use for qualification purposes. She already has two points for a workout on April 22 (three days ago). The finish of fourth gives her one point and her race-rating is eleven, for another point. That gives her a total of four points, which she needs to qualify. But the filly has been running largely in Allowance company, which means, when we note the claiming price of today's race ($12,000), that essentially she is dropping in class. Four of her past five participations have been in Allowance Races, and technically we could give her one more point for class drop, since Allowance races are rated at $15,000–$15,500 on the class scale. At any rate, she gets in, and she finished second, at odds of 44-1, paying $30.40 to place and $10.60 to show. More importantly, she completes the combination for an Exacta (with F4, Miss Huntress) that paid a handsome $726.80.

CHART X (continued)

	$Q3^4$‡‡‡ f—Sheshall Reward^{117} (4) 20–1		———	12.40	6.80
2^8	$Q1^1_{Ao}$ Bold Lord^{114} (6) 19–1		———	———	———
	($Q2_{Po}$§§§Edna's Sultan^{116} (6) 15–1Po 6–1Ao		13.60	7.20	4.40)
6^7	$Q1^1$ Little Dix Bay^{112} (6) 20–1		———	———	———
	$Q2^3$ Sullivan Road^{112} (9) 11–1		———	8.00	6.00
7^6	$Q1^1$ Will Hays^{114} (6) 13–1		———	———	———
	$Q2^2$ Rule By Reason^{112} (6) 9–1		19.00	5.20	2.20
Apr. 27: 1^8_{Mf}	$Q1^1$ Smoke Screen^{117} (4) 22–1		46.60	21.60	11.80
Thurs.	$Q2^2$ Barbilada^{115} (4) 21–1		———	———	
2^9	$Q1_{Po}$ Aerolithe^{116} (6) 15–1Po				
	$Q2_{Ao}{}^3$ Little Red Rocket^{112} (6) 14–1		———	14.60	6.60
4^7	$Q1^2$ Angel Cake^{108} (4) 8–1		18.40	8.00	3.60
	$Q2^3$ Recency^{116} (5) 8–1		———	———	
5^6	$Q1^1$ King Swoon^{118} (6) 13–1		———	———	
	$Q2^2$ Little On^{108} (9) 7–1		16.40	5.20	2.40
9^7	$Q1^1$ Spear^{105} (7) 19–1		———	———	5.60
	$Q2^2$ Belfry^{105} (5) 10–1		———	———	
Apr. 28: $2^{12}_{f/m}$	$Q1_{Po}$ Wonderful Time^{106} (8) 20–1Po				
Fri.	$Q2_{Po}$ Helens Restless^{113} (5) 15–1				
	$Q3_{Po}$‖‖‖In the Pink^{109} (5) 12–1Po		9.20	6.60	5.60
5^{14}_{Mf}	$Q1^1$ Foreign Strand^{117} (4) 78–1		———	———	———
	$Q2^2$ Dear Native^{121} (A) 53–1		———	———	———
	$Q3^3$ Royal Taster^{107} (A) 41-1		———	———	———
	$Q4^4$###Swing^{117} (4) 22–1		46.60	20.60	11.60
9^8	$Q1^1$ Delver^{116} (4) 18–1		38.80	15.60	7.60
	$Q2^2$ Nederboy^{114} (8) 10–1		———	———	7.40

‡‡‡Sheshall Reward is one of a mutuel field of two horses. The other horse, Keynas Way, did not qualify, but Sheshall Reward had four points, which was enough to get the "field" in as an entry-bet. That is, one bet covers both horses. When a race shows fourteen horses running, there are still only twelve different tickets sold on the race. There were two groups of two horses coupled together on one ticket each. It should be made clear that when such entries are checked, If one horse qualifies, bet the entry.

§§§Not a hit, strictly speaking. Edna's Sultan would have been bet in the daily double combinations, since he is listed at potential odds of 15-1. However, when race time arrived, he was bet down to 6-1. This has happened before, and you can take your choice: either go along with the lower odds and bet the horse straight, or select one of the higher-odds qualifiers in the race. Or, you could bet them both, of course. The fans often take a long-odds horse and bet him down (for any of a hundred different reasons). Now and then they are right and the horse wins, as he did in this second race on April 26 at Aqueduct. Horses shown in parentheses, as above, are not counted in the compilations at the end of the charts.

‖‖‖Here is another case of a horse with probable odds given as 15-1, but when race time came around the fans jumped on her and made her 7-2. As second favorite, In the Pink went wire to wire for what seemed an easy win. This time the fans were right. But of course they are right three times out of ten, where favorites are concerned.

###Here again, in a race for maiden fillies, the number-four qualifier proves to be the winner. Sam would bet the number-four qualifier in a race like this, especially since two of the qualifiers are first-time starters and got in automatically. But you *must* keep the first-time starters in. Both of them had three workouts in April, and their odds are too good to neglect. And one of them does come in often enough to make it a profitable investment.

Aqueduct, April 1972—Straight

SUMMARY:

Number of racing days: 24

CHART X (continued)

Number of races: 216
Unit of investment: $2

	Q1		Q2		Q3	
	Win	*Place*	*Win*	*Place*	*Win*	*Place*
Return	625.20	445.20	550.40	427.40	165.60	112.80
Invested	432.00	432.00	432.00	432.00	———	———
Net Profit	193.20	13.20	118.40	−4.60	———	———
Percentage	44%	3%	27%			

TOTALS:	*Q1, Q2 Win*		*Q1, Q2 Place*		*Combined Totals*	
Return	1175.60		872.60		2,048.20	
Invested	864.00		864.00		1,728.00	
Net Profit	311.60		8.60		320.20	
Percentage	36%		1%		18%	

		Total return	*Average*
Number of Q1 Win hits:	9	$ 625.20	$69.50
Number of Q2 Win hits:	17	550.40	32.50
Number of Q1 Place hits:	21	445.20	21.20
Number of Q2 Place hits:	33	427.40	13.00
Number of Q1, Q2 Wins:	30	1,175.60	39.15
Number of Q1, Q2 Places:	50	872.60	17.45

CHART XI   Aqueduct, Daily Doubles: April 1972

Apr. 1:	#1$^{3-1}$ (Solar Nail) with #1$^{3-1}$ (Predator)	$ 21.40
Apr. 3:	#3 (Kurlash Kid) with #2 (Belle Decoy)	147.20
Apr. 4:	Q3 (Alcibalita) with #4$_q$ (Cut Back)	718.20
Apr. 7:	F5$_q$ (Marite)* with Q1$_{Po}$ (Gentle Spring)	2041.00
Apr. 10:	F2 (Big Imposter) with Q1$_{Po}$ (Angel Cake)	407.20
Apr. 11:	#4 (That's Done) with #3 (Debbeereb)	118.80
Apr. 12:	F4 (Double Velvet) with Q3$_{Po}$ (Tudor Tune)†	450.80
Apr. 14:	Q1 (Seven Pac) with #4$_q$ (Cunning Stunt)‡	809.20
Apr. 15:	#1$^{3-1}$ (I'm Glad) with Q3$_{Po}$ (Commoner)	278.60

*Marite was #4$_q$ selection in the probable-odds lineup of the first race. It is always well to check these three horses (#2, #3 and #4 in the probable-odds lineup) with the actual F2, F3 and F4 in the race. Since this is a race involving fillies and mares, we also check #5 and F5, to see whether or not they should be included, or should replace the #4 or the F4. If you find that #2, #3 and #4 are not the same as F2, F3 and F4, and many times this will be so, then look carefully at the #2 #4 horse which falls outside the F2-F4 range. Either add him to your series or substitute him for one of those you already have.

†See Chart X for an explanation of Q3$_{Po}$, Tudor Tune. Incidentally, while Tudor Tune was Q3 in the probable-odds line up, when the race came around, he was Q1$_{Ao}$. Two reasons for an investment.

‡Flora Neff was #4, while Cunning Stunt was #5. But, on form, Cunning Stunt looked much better. Dropping $1,500 in class, he was also getting in at the low weight of 105 pounds, dropping four pounds off his last race.

CHART XI (continued)

Apr. 18:	F2 (Channeling) with Q3$_{Po}$ (Halfway Home)	214.40
Apr. 19:	#1$^{3-1}$ (Rare Adventure) with #1$^{3-1}$(Solar Nail)	24.20
Apr. 20:	#2 (Poly Joy) with #4 (Tourist Hitch)	56.80
Apr. 22:	#1$^{3-1}$ (Le Taquin) with #4 (Little Mahoney)	108.60
Apr. 25:	#3 (Cute Little Devil) with #4 (Sprinkler)	48.40
Apr. 27:	Q1 (Smoke Screen) with #4 (Smidge Boy)	452.40

Gross Return: $5,682.80

SUMMARY:

Number of racing days: 24

Number of investments: 24

Total investment, at $50 per day: $1200.00

Gross Return: $5,682.80

Total invested: 1,200.00

Net Profit: $4,482.80

Percentage of net profit: 373%

CHART XII   Aqueduct, Exactas: April 1972

Apr. 1:	4^{10}	F4$_q$	(Brumidi) with Q2 (Folsom Blues)	$619.60
	6^8	F1	(Feathered Ruler) with Q2 (Imasuper)	28.00
Apr. 3:	4^{11}	F5	(Rock Sun) with F6 (Ring Star)	378.80
	8^{10}	Q3	(Dodeys Sky High) with F3 (Domineer III)	229.80
Apr. 4:	4^9	F3	(Halfway Home) with F2 (Marquis de Sade)	71.60
	6^7	F3	(Delta Lady) with F2 (I Move)	43.80
Apr. 5:	6^{10}	F4$_q$	(Wondrous Sky) with F5$_q$ (Overlay)	282.20
	8^{10}	F3	(New Tune) with F2 (Return to Paradise)	70.60
Apr. 6:	4^8	F2	(Dealer) with F3 (Village Rebel)	40.00
	6^9	F2	(Plucky Lady) with F3 (Wicked Man)	65.40
	8^5	Q2	(La Bertha) with F2 (Cute n Crafty)	52.80
Apr. 7:	6^7	Q1	(Merry Score) with F3 (Supper Show)	170.60
Apr. 10:	6^8	F2	(Harbor Prince) with F3 (Candyville)	45.00
	8^{10}	Q1	(Continent) with F1 (Major Strike)	415.80
Apr. 11:	4^{11}	Q2	(Cosmic Price) with F1/2 (Gottogo)	419.40
	8^{12}	F4	(Fondest Touch) with Q2 (Billy Silver II)	603.40
Apr. 12:	4^9	F2	(High Timber) with F3 (Blue Summer)	61.80
	6^7	F2	(Fearless Gal) with F4 (Ninfa Squaw)	48.80
	8^8	Q2	(Hong Kong Spree) with F2 (Countess Georgia)	148.20
Apr. 13:	4^9	F1	(Shining Sword) with Q2 (Broken Penny)	122.20
	6^{12}	F1	(Table Flirt) with Q2 (Soft and Silky)	289.60
Apr. 14:	4^8	F4	(Lord's Lady) with F2 (Irish Manor)	65.80
	6^6	F1	(Noble Splash) with Q2 (Vikeena)	20.00
	8^7	Q2	(Miniture Pieces) with F1 (Fun Filled)	127.20
Apr. 15:	8^7	Q2	(Odie Bob) with F1 (Pass Catcher)	78.00

CHART XII (continued)

Apr. 17: 6^6	F3	(Country Belle) with F4 (Merry Score)	49.60
Apr. 18: 4^7	F2	(Wind River Lad) with F3 (Lucky Pants)	36.60
6^9	F2	(Tartar Chief) with F3 (North Sea)	96.60
8^{11}	F6_q	(Scungagad) with F5_q (Duplicate Bridge)	373.20
Apr. 19: 8^9	F3	(Spread the Word) with Q2 (Tabi's Turn)	128.20
Apr. 20: 4^9	Q1	(Sweet n Costly) with F1 (Pago Queen)	203.60
6^7	Q2	(Harkville) with F1 (Astronomer)	92.00
8^{10}	F1	(Return to Paradise) with Q2 (Jill the Queen)	105.20
Apr. 21: 4^8	F4	(Grape Jelly) with Q2 (Grandpa Dom)	173.20
8^{10}	F4	(Mister Do Bee) with Q2 (Shadyside)	207.40
Apr. 22: 6^7	F1	(Invested Power) with Q1 (Lonesome River)	62.00
Apr. 24: 6^6	F1	(King Elinol) with Q1 (Liberal Emperor)	54.00
Apr. 25: 8^{10}	F4	(Miss Huntress) with Q1 (Crafty Action)	726.80
Apr. 26: 6^7	F2	(Irish Mate) with Q2 (Sullivan Road)	65.00
8^8	F4	(Straight and Level) with F2 (Trade Tails)	108.00
Apr. 27: 4^7	Q1	(Angel Cake) with F3 (Exchange Place)	95.60
Apr. 28: 4^{11}	F2	(Ripple Mark) with F3_q (Tranquility)	116.20
6^{10}	F4	(Prime Prince) with F2 (Straight to Paris)	68.40
8^6	F3	(That's Done) with F4_q (Preying Mantis)	65.80

SUMMARY:

Number of racing days: 24

Number of Exacta races: 72

Total investment in Exacta races, at $60 each: $4,320.00

Gross return: $7,325.80
Total invested: 4,320.00

Net profit: $3,005.80

Percentage of net profit: 70%

Breakdown of F4, F5, F6:	Return:	$1,034.20
	Invested:	864.00
	Net profit:	$ 170.20
Breakdown of F1 with Q1 and Q2:	Return:	$1597.60
	Invested:	576.00
	Net profit:	$1,021.60

Aqueduct, April 1972

	Straight	*Doubles*	*Exactas*	*Totals*
Return	2048.40	5682.80	7325.80	15059.00
Invested	1728.00	1200.00	4320.00	7248.00
Net Profit	320.40	4482.80	3005.80	7811.00
Percentage	18%	373%	70%	107%

CHART XIII   Gulfstream Park, Straight Bets: Jan. 21–Feb. 20, 1974

Jan. 21: $6^{10}_{f/m}$	Q1[1]	Flor De Naranjo^{116} (5) 27–1	——	——	——
Mon.	Q2[2]	Following Wind^{112} (5) 23–1	——	18.40	9.20
	Q3[3]	Show Girl^{114} (7) 12–1	——	——	7.20
8^{10}	Q1[2]	Mad Prince^{116} (5) 31–1	——	23.40	8.80
	Q2[3]	Cocoa Lane^{116} (7) 25–1	——	——	——
$9^{11}_{f/m}$	Q1[1]	Courtsey Princess^{119} (5) 58–1	——	——	——
	Q2[2]	Bend An Ear^{113} (6) 37–1	75.60	23.40	9.00
	Q3[3]	Fair Skies^{114} (8) 21–1	——	——	——
10^{12}	Q1[3]	Arms and Armor^{114} (5) 44–1	90.80	36.40	21.60
	Q2[4]	Talk Less^{109} (6) 28–1	——	——	——
Jan. 22: 2^{12}	Q1Po	Desoto Belle^{114} (7) 30–1Po	37.20	13.60	9.00
Tues.	Q2Po	Magnifico II^{113} (5) 15–1Po	——	——	——
$4^{12}_{Msw f3}$	Q1[2]	Speedy Lois^{119} (4½) 43–1	——	29.60	15.20
	Q2[3]	Laudable^{119} (4) 36–1	——	——	——
	Q3[4]	Bayou Bend^{119} (5) 28–1	——	——	——
7^{10}	Q1[1]	Covered Hoop^{113} (6) 61–1	——	——	——
	Q2[2]	Selma's Pride^{111} (4) 35–1	——	——	9.80
	Q3[5]*	Never Never Stop^{116} (A) 17–1	36.00	9.20	6.20
$8^{12}_{f/m}$	Q1[1]	Missionary Voyage^{116} (7) 41–1	——	——	——
	Q2[3]	Miss Tom Cat^{116} (4) 22–1	——	——	——
	Q3[4]	Divine Light^{116} (6) 18–1	——	15.20	9.00
Jan. 23: 3^{12}_{Msw3}	Q1[1]	Sandy Hill^{120} (A) 81–1	——	61.80	26.20
Wed.	Q2[3]	Prompt Cash^{115} (7) 66–1	——	——	——
	Q3[5]	Finest Hope^{120} (5) 26–1	——	——	——
$8^{9}_{f/m}$	Q1[1]	Jenny Song^{112} (7) 104–1	——	——	——
	Q2[2]	Smiling Jacqueline^{112} (6) 31–1	——	——	6.80
	Q3[3]	Cornish Princess^{107} (8) 23–1	——	——	——
9^{12}_{3}	Q1[1]	High Wycombe^{110} (9) 115–1	——	——	——
	Q2[2]	Stanley the Great^{111} (5) 90–1	——	——	——
	Q3[3]†	Totheend^{114} (7) 34–1	70.20	29.40	9.40
10^{12}	Q1[1]	Vasa Lopp^{116} (5) 57–1	——	——	——
	Q2[3]	The General^{116} (5) 37–1	77.00	32.00	14.60
Jan. 24: 1^{12}_{3}	Q1[1] ·	Miss Tony Linn^{106} (7) 34–1	——	——	——
Thurs.	Q2[2]	Gemini Jack^{116} (5) 30–1	——	25.80	11.00
	Q3[3]‡	Miss Mud Pack^{111} (6) 30–1	——	——	——
3^{11}_{M3}	Q1[1]	Sherwood Point^{120} (A) 112–1	——	——	——
	Q2[2]	Born Back Stage^{120} (A) 32–1	——	25.00	12.80

*As you know by now, even in a regular race which gets only two qualifiers, you always check for Q3 and see whether or not the horse is outstanding for some reason. Never Never Stop is indeed outstanding for the fact that he is dropping $12,000 in class, making him an automatic bet. Since he is also the fifth horse down from the top, in odds, he is a bet in the SAM system which is described in a later chapter. In short, Never Never Stop would be a double bet, if you are playing both systems at the same time.

†Since this is a race for three-year-olds, Sam would go for Q3, even though it is not a maiden race and not for fillies or mares.

‡Gemini Jack and Miss Mud Pack were both 30-1. Since we are dealing with a race for three-year-olds, take them both.

CHART XIII (continued)

		$Q3^3$	Thirty Love^{120} (A) 29–1	——	——	——
	4^8_{M3}	$Q1^1$§	Waist Band^{117} (4) 24–1	——	12.60	6.80
		$Q2^2$	Our Zelda^{115} (A) 24–1	——	——	——
		$Q3^3$	Rens Prince^{117} (4) 10–1	——	——	——
	6^8	$Q1^1$	Charollius^{116} (6) 15–1	32.40	10.60	6.20
		$Q2^2$	Gallant Exchange^{111} (6) 14–1	——	——	——
	7^{12}	$Q1^2$	Fall Rush^{112} (7) 35–1	——	22.20	10.20
		$Q2^4$	Marine Flyer^{116} (5) 26–1	——	——	——
Jan. 25: 1^{12}		$Q1^1$	Indian Note^{107} (9) 46–1	——	——	——
Fri.		$Q2^2$	Slick Slade^{116} (7) 21–1	——	——	——
		$Q3^3\|$	Pari A. Docs^{114} (7) 20–1	41.00	16.80	9.80
	3^8_p	$Q1^2$	Funny Landing^{116} (9) 13–1	——	9.60	5.00
			(No more due to lack of odds.)			
	7^{11}_3	$Q1^1$	Iron and Steel^{116} (7) 23–1	——	——	——
		$Q2^2$	Aroyoport^{116} (4) 25–1	——	——	16.60
		$Q3^4$	Roman Decade^{116} (7) 16–1	——	14.80	7.80
Jan. 26: 3^{12}_3		$Q1^1$	Call Me Jackey^{114} (9) 25–1	——	——	9.80
Sat.		$Q2^2$	Soho^{111} (6) 23–1	——	——	——
	6^{11}	$Q1^2$	Our Traveller^{107} (5) 40–1	——	——	11.40
		$Q2^3$	Strand of Gold^{112} (6) 15–1	——	——	——
	10^9	$Q1^1$	ConvoyII^{107} (5) 30–1	——	——	——
		$Q2^2$	King's Reel^{116} (A) 25–1	——	——	——
		$Q3^3$#	Shark Boat^{114} (5) 16–1	35.00	10.60	3.20
Jan. 28:** 3^{10}		$Q1^2$	Neroville^{112} (6) 23–1	——	15.80	6.20
Mon.		$Q2^3$	Live Free^{114} (5) 15–1	——	——	——
Jan. 29: 3^{10}		$Q1^2$	Repville^{116} (5) 38–1	——	20.60	11.60
Tues.		$Q2^4$	Added Splendor^{109} (5) 21–1	——	——	——
	10^{10}_3	$Q1^1$	Hello Sweetie^{112} (7) 25–1	——	——	——
		$Q2^2$	Market Forge^{112} (6) 20–1	——	——	——
		$Q3^3$††	Clear Echo^{107} (8) 16–1	34.20	13.60	7.20
Jan. 30: 2^{11}		$Q1^4_{Ao}$	Snow Hovel^{112} (8) 13–1	——	14.40	6.40
Wed.		$Q2^5_{Ao}$	Only Sunny^{113} (7) 11–1	24.60	10.60	5.60

§Since all horses are going up in class, penalize none. This is the race which resulted in the stewards setting jockey Frank Iannelli down for thirty days for holding the horse Speedy Smith under "snug restraint". See description of the race in "A Touch of Scandal."

‖Q2 and Q3 are at almost equal odds, and both are dropping in class. Both were in-the-money five times in past performances. Pari A. Docs had a race seventeen days ago and has a two-pound weight advantage. Since this is the first race and is involved in the Daily Double, bet them both. If you want to limit yourself to two horses in this race, you would have to prefer the horse that has raced most recently and has the weight advantage.

#In a Perfecta race we always consider Q3 as well as the first two qualifiers. We include Q3 especially when one of the qualifiers is rated an automatic bet, meaning that he is a completely unknown quantity if he is a first-time starter. If he is an automatic bet due to dropping $10,000 or more in class, there must be a reason for such a big drop, but of course we are not in the know. The trainer may just be looking for a good "spot" for the horse, or there may be something wrong. You'll probably be able to supply the answer *after* the race is over.

**There were no good "hits" on this date, but it is interesting to note that there were three #5-Down hits under the SAM system, described later. The two systems compliment one another and should be played simultaneously. When the Big System falls short, the Little System comes through.

††In three-year-old races, we almost automatically go to Q3, unless Q3 has too low odds or does not, for some reason, look good.

CHART XIII (continued)

Date	Race	Q	Horse	Win	Place	Show
	$3^{12}_{f/m}$	$Q1^{1}$	Ociosa^{112} (5) 101–1	——	——	23.60
		$Q2^{2}$	Reneged's Degree^{112} (5) 79–1	——	——	——
		$Q3^{3}$	Zulu^{106} (6) 31–1	——	——	——
		$Q4^{4}$‡‡	Goodbye Juanita^{113} (7) 29–1	60.40	23.20	12.40
	4^{12}_{Msw3}	$Q1^{2}$	Arctic Normal^{120} (A) 53–1	——	——	——
		$Q2^{3}$	Maharajo^{120} (4) 46–1	94.40	33.40	11.80
		$Q3^{4}$	Tudor Duke^{120} (5) 33–1	——	——	——
	6^{11}	$Q1^{1}$	Loyal Friend^{114} (5) 83–1	——	——	19.00
		$Q2^{2}$	Paris Ruler^{116} (5) 61–1	——	——	——
	8^{9}_{f3}	$Q1^{1}$	Chica Linda^{110} (9) 24–1	——	——	——
		$Q2^{2}$	Maud Muller^{112} (8) 22–1	——	17.80	6.80
		$Q3^{3}$	Superstitious^{112} (8) 10–1	——	——	——
Jan. 31: Thurs.	4^{9}	$Q1^{2}$	Gatoprado^{105} (7) 25–1	——	——	——
		$Q2^{3}$	Guy Lee^{116} (7) 15–1	——	9.20	5.80
	6^{10}	$Q1^{4}$	Challenging^{112} (7) 13–1	27.20	10.20	5.40
		$Q2$	(none)			
	7^{12}	$Q1^{1}$	Ala Turn^{116} (7) 79–1	——	——	——
		$Q2^{2}$	Special Tex^{111} (7) 32–1	65.60	24.80	14.40
Feb. 1: Fri.	1^{3}	$Q1^{1}$§§	Gold Collector^{116} (4) 41–1	——	29.40	15.20
		$Q2^{3}$	Hot Apple Pie^{106} (5) 28–1	——	——	——
	4^{12}_{M3}	$Q1^{3}$	Indian Magic^{117} (7) 44–1	——	——	——
		$Q2^{4}$	Thirty Love^{117} (A) 40–1	——	——	13.80
		$Q3^{5}$	Briar Jumper^{117} (A) 35–1	——	——	——
	5^{10}_{M3}	$Q1^{2}$	Cirrus^{120} (A) 28–1	——	——	——
		$Q2^{4}$	Flags Awhirl^{112} (4) 16–1	——	——	6.40
		$Q3^{5}$	Positive Ruler^{117} (4) 13–1	——	8.80	6.00
	6^{8}_{3}	$Q1^{1}$	Euphoric^{109} (7) 36–1	——	——	——
		$Q2^{2}$	Stanley the Great^{114} (4) 13–1	——	10.20	5.40
	7^{11}	$Q1^{1}$	Sparrow^{116} (5) 66–1	——	——	——
		$Q2^{4}$	Soaked^{114} (6) 24–1	49.60	15.80	12.20
	8^{9}	$Q1^{2}$	Dancer's Verde^{112} (10) 23–1	——	——	——
		$Q2^{3}$	Dr. P. F. Fox^{112} (6) 22–1	——	14.60	6.80
	9^{10}	$Q1^{1}$	Select Performance^{112} (6) 18–1	——	——	11.60
		$Q2^{3}$	Calabash^{113} (9) 17–1	——	——	——
Feb. 2: Sat.	2^{11}	$Q1_{Po}$	Nettie's Knave^{107} 20–1Po	——	——	——
		$Q2_{Po}$	Antix Again^{117} (6) 15–1Po	——	——	——
		$(Q3_{Po}$‖‖	Love and Peace^{116} (5) 12–1Po	22.20	10.00	6.40)

‡‡Q4 is the winner, and one good reason for taking a close look at Q4 in a filly/mare race is that of the distribution of the odds. When two of the qualifiers have odds ABOVE 75-1, it is often likely that you will have to go down at least four from the top to find a horse in the money. In this race, you will notice, Q1 at 101-1 came in third and paid $23.60. But the winner was in the group below 25-1, as many times happens.

§§Although this is a three-year-old race, we did not go to Q3 because the horse did not look too outstanding on form. Note that Gold Collector is apparently dropping in class. That is, the horse had three former races at a class higher than today's class. The move down, therefore, is not from the last race but from these three former races. Thus, one point is awarded for a drop in class.

‖‖Not a hit since this is Q3 in a regular race. Love and Peace actually went off at about 10-1, whereas there are eleven horses in the race. The 12-1 Po prediction didn't quite hold up. Results not included in calculations.

CHART XIII (continued)

	4^{12}	Q1^3	Va Flight^{112} (6) 44–1	— —	
		Q2^4	Tudor Song II^{115} (5) 34–1	— —	14.60
		Q3^5##	Watch Harvey^{116} (5) 23–1	— 23.20	14.80
	6^{11}	Q1^3	Miss Andyline^{107} (7) 17–1	— —	
		Q2^4	Happy Chant^{114} (6) 11–1	23.20 12.20	6.80
	8^9_3	Q1^1	Spirit Son^{112} (5) 36–1	— —	
		Q2^2	Tomholme^{113} (7) 16–1	— —	
		Q3^3	Buck's Bid^{112} (6) 12–1	26.60 9.80	5.20
Feb 4: Mon.	5^{10}_3	Q1^1	Quick Henry^{112} (4) 46–1	— —	
		Q2^2	Hitching Post^{116} (6) 24–1	— 15.80	8.20
	6^{10}_3	Q1^1	Empire Man^{122} (7) 45–1	— —	13.80
		Q2^2	Illiopolis^{116} (5) 20–1	— —	
		Q3^3	Bushongo^{113} (7) 17–1	— 12.00	8.40
	7^{12}	Q1^3	Uncopyable^{116} (5) 36–1	— 19.60	15.80
		Q2^5	But^{116} (5) 18–1	— —	
Feb. 5: Tues.	1^{12}_{MSW}	Q1^2	Queen Em^{119} (A) 34–1	— —	15.60
		Q2^3	Wacahoota^{109} (5) 29–1	— —	
		Q3^4	Contessa^{119} (A) 19–1	— —	
	2^{11}	Q1$_{PO}$	Lila's Poppy^{101} (4) 118–1	— —	
		Q2$_{PO}$	Royal Powder^{109} (5) 47–1	— —	20.20
		Q3$_{PO}$	Pago Girl^{107} (7) 46–1	— 25.40	13.60
	3^{12}_{MSwf}	Q1^2	Onamission^{119} (5) 56–1	— 31.80	13.80
		Q2^3	Dear Editor^{119} (4) 44–1	— —	
		Q3^4	Katie L^{119} (A) 41–1	— —	
	$4^8_{f/m}$	Q1^2	Pondering Jon^{106} (6) 17–1	35.20 10.80	4.20
		Q2^3	Mary Pat^{105} (5) 10–1	— —	
	$6^{10}_{f/m}$	Q1^1	Ms. Bloomers^{109} (5) 71–1	— —	
		Q2^2	Charming Diane^{114} (5) 33–1	— —	
		Q3^3	Isthmia^{114} (5) 22–1	— —	
		Q4^4***	Aloha Miss^{114} (6) 16–1	34.80 19.40	9.00
Feb. 6: Wed.	4^{12}	22Q1^3†††	Forgive Divine^{114} (7) 22–1	— —	10.20
		11Q2^4†††	Salem Knight^{105} (7) 20–1	— —	
		21Q3^5†††	Te. V. Frolic^{116} (6) 16–1	— 13.00	7.00

##Since this is a Perfecta Race, we look closely at all next-higher qualifiers, such as Watch Harvey, who is dropping $2,500 in class and raced just eight days ago. His finish of eleventh in a field of twelve last race is a bit misleading, and it helped his odds build up to 23-1. Watch Harvey came in second and combined with Evening Flight (F4) for a payoff of $359.00 in the Perfecta. Watch Harvey is five-down from the top in odds and is a bet in the SAM System described later in the book. Also, #5-down is combined with F4 and F5 in the Perfecta combinations, so that you would get the $359 payoff if you were playing the SAM System.

***In this filly/mare race, the Q4 horse turned out to be the winner. You should have had this one, since Aloha Miss is dropping $1,000 in class, from an allowance race to a $14,000 claiming race. The mare raced just eleven days ago, and all except one of her races have been in a class higher than today's $14,000. Isthmia is moving up $4,000 in class. Carrying the same weight in today's race, the edge is clearly on the side of Aloha Miss. She is also #4-down from the top in odds and is a bet in the SAM system, described later.

†††While attending the Gulfstream Park meeting in January and February, 1974, Sam developed a quick method of discriminating among the three top qualifiers in a regular race, so that he could eliminate a loser who just happened to be a Qualifier. This fourth race on February 6 illustrates his method well. The numbers before the letter "Q" are five-race ratings. They are derived very simply and quickly by looking at the last five races of a particular horse, subtract-

CHART XIII (continued)

ing the finish position from the number of horses in the race. For example, in Forgive Divine's last race he finished eighth in a field of twelve. Give him "4" as a rating in that race. Do the same for the last five races, then add the ratings for a total of twenty-two for Q1. Salem Knight gets a total of eleven points in the five races. Te. V. Frolic gets twenty-one. See charts below. Whenever one of the three horses has a five-race rating that is about 50 percent lower than either of the other two, you are pretty safe in throwing that horse out. On that basis, Salem Knight goes OUT and Te. V. Frolick becomes Q2. Of course, being five-down, he is already a bet in the other SAM system!!!

Incidentally, before looking at the charts, we might mention that the "five-race ratings" of the four horses in the sixth race above are fourteen for Ms. Bloomers, thirteen for Charming Diane, twenty-five for Isthmia, and fifteen for the winner, Aloha Miss. Note that Charming Diane is almost 50 percent lower than Isthmia, and Sam would throw out Charming Diane, admitting Aloha Miss as Q3. In several of the future listings, we will include the "five-race ratings" to illustrate further the efficacy of this shorthand method of eliminating a qualifier who is a loser.

And now, let us take a look at the charts of the three horses in the fourth race on February 6, to see exactly how these five-race ratings are derived:

Forgive Divine **114** B. h (1969), by Wolfram—Pardon Me Please, by Your Host.
Breeder, Harbor View Farm (Fla.). 1974 2 0 0 0 $138
Owner, Irene Coulson. Trainer, N. St. Leon. $9,500 1973 27 1 6 0 $11,722

Jan18-74^{2}GP	6 f 1:10$^{2}/_{5}$ft	$7\frac{1}{4}$	114	5^{4}	$6^{5\frac{1}{4}}$	6^{11}	8^{14}	StLeonG^{11}	9500	73	BlueMoral 116	WiseOldOwl II.	D'x III.	12	4
Jan 7-74^{7}Crc	7 f 1:27 ft	14	116	$6^{4\frac{3}{4}}$	$6^{5\frac{3}{4}}$	$4^{5\frac{1}{4}}$	$5^{3\frac{3}{4}}$	StL'nG^{12}	10000	77	M'j'rAp'tm't119	R'pidR'y	G'yL'ngl'gs	12	7
Dec24-73^{6}Crc	6 f 1:13$^{1}/_{5}$ft	$9\frac{1}{2}$	116	$6^{4\frac{1}{4}}$	$5^{1\frac{3}{4}}$	4^{2}	$4^{1\frac{3}{4}}$†	StLeonG^{6}	10000	85	LadyFort113	Fash'nL'm	R'fK'gB'g'r'k	10	6
†Dead heat.															2
Dec 4-73^{6}Crc	7 f 1:25$^{2}/_{5}$ft	$7\frac{1}{4}$	116	$5^{6\frac{1}{2}}$	5^{8}	6^{14}	7^{12}	MapleS^{3}	10000	77	Dod'y'sSkyH'h116	Tupi	R'ffK'gB'g'r'k	9	
Nov23-73^{7}Crc	Ⓣ $1\frac{1}{16}$ 1:44$^{1}/_{5}$fm	4	114	$2^{\frac{1}{2}}$	$6^{4\frac{1}{4}}$	9^{12}	9^{14}	W'dh'eR^{6}	10500	78	BramblesBoy116	Hilar'sR'd	V't'sVerse	12	3
Nov17-73^{2}Crc	6 f 1:13$^{2}/_{5}$ft	30	116	9^{4}	$6^{3\frac{3}{4}}$	4^{4}	$2^{\frac{3}{4}}$	StL'nG^{10}	10000	85	Dax III. 116	Forgive Divine	Noble Duel	11	22
Nov 3-73^{4}Crc	6 f 1:13$^{2}/_{5}$ft	35	119	$6^{3\frac{1}{4}}$	6^{5}	$6^{4\frac{1}{4}}$	$6^{5\frac{3}{4}}$	VieraM^{6}	12500	80	Humb'g'boo116	N'v'rGoB'ck	L'slieL'ne	6	
Oct20-73^{8}Crc	7 f 1:26 ft	15	119	$5^{1\frac{1}{4}}$	4^{3}	4^{6}	6^{8}	StLeonG^{3}	12500	78	Abnegado116	GrandHolme	SandyBoy	8	

Feb 5 Crc 3f ft :37$^{3}/_{5}$b

Salem Knight **105** Ch. g (1969), by Speak John—Salem Miss, by High Bandit.
Breeder, Wilson & Foley (Ky.). 1974 4 0 0 0 $240
Owner, G. Buhrmaster & J. Wall. Trainer, W. F. Caple. $9,000 1973 13 1 0 1 $3,388

Jan31-74^{4}GP	6 f 1:10$^{3}/_{5}$ft	62	113	8^{10}	7^{13}	8^{11}	$8^{9\frac{1}{2}}$	BoveT^{8}	10500	76	Opinionation113	GuyLee	WiseOldOwl	9	1
Jan15-74^{7}Crc	7 f 1:26$^{3}/_{5}$sy	7	116	$7^{2\frac{1}{4}}$	$6^{4\frac{3}{4}}$	$5^{7\frac{1}{2}}$	5^{7}	WinantR^{4}	c6500	76	Called Red 114	Rotarian	Algar	9	4
Jan 8-74^{1}Crc	7 f 1:27 ft	28	116	$9^{5\frac{1}{4}}$	$7^{3\frac{3}{4}}$	$5^{4\frac{1}{2}}$	$5^{\frac{3}{4}}$	WinantR^{3}	5000	80	Z Ron 116	Rotarian	Tobarra	10	5
Jan 2-74^{5}Crc	6 f 1:12$^{2}/_{5}$ft	176	116	12^{12}	11^{14}	11^{14}	11^{14}	Fiesel'nJ^{11}	6500	77	BlueMoral 116	J'staMite	MiloLanding	12	1
Dec28-73^{7}Crc	6 f 13$^{3}/_{5}$ft	67	116	10^{12}	10^{15}	11^{11}	$12^{7\frac{1}{2}}$	WinantR^{9}	6500	77	Mr.Export119	JestaMite	MidDancer	12	0
Dec18-73^{6}Crc	7 f 1:26$^{1}/_{5}$ft	26	116	$8^{7\frac{1}{4}}$	8^{12}	9^{11}	9^{10}	F'selmanJ^{9}	7500	75	Foolish Lad 116	Relator	Wildside	9	11
Jun23-73^{8}Cka	1 1:38$^{3}/_{5}$ft	$4\frac{1}{4}$	118	$6^{9\frac{3}{4}}$	$6^{8\frac{3}{4}}$	$6^{6\frac{1}{2}}$	$6^{5\frac{3}{4}}$	WellsJ^{8}	HcpO	86	Sailawayin123	Whisp'rS'ftly	Till'sJeff	9	
Jun12-73^{8}Cka	7 f 1:25$^{4}/_{5}$ft	2-5▲	118	1^{2}	1^{5}	1^{6}	$1^{5\frac{1}{2}}$	WellsJ^{4}	Alw	88	SalemKnight118	P'kCount	Pr'tyP'ble	9	

Feb 5 Crc 3f ft :37b Jan 23 Crc 4f ft :51b Dec 13 Crc 7f ft 1:30b

Te. V. Frolic* **116** Dk. b. or br. g (1967), by T.V. Lark—Twice Over, by Ponder.
Breeder, Mr. & Mrs. D. Sucher (Ky.). 1974 2 0 0 0 $350
Owner, T. Canonie. Trainer, M. Giardelli. $10,000 1973 27 1 3 4 $10,013 8

Jan28-74^{5}GP	7 f 1:23 ft	32	116	8^{11}	7^{8}	$4^{6\frac{1}{2}}$	$4^{5\frac{3}{4}}$	MapleS^{8}	1000	83	Dawn'sVisc't114	ChiefTamao	CozyOr	12	1
Jan 8-74^{6}Crc	7 f 1:25$^{4}/_{5}$ft	15	112	$4^{3\frac{1}{2}}$	$4^{6\frac{1}{2}}$	7^{13}	$7^{7\frac{1}{2}}$	CedenoM^{8}	10500	79	Gr'dH'me116	Nev'rGoB'k	W't'rH'lid'y	8	3
Dec22-73^{5}Crc	1 1:40$^{2}/_{5}$ft	$4\frac{1}{2}$	116	$6^{5\frac{1}{2}}$	7^{5}	7^{10}	7^{11}	CedenoM^{1}	10000	82	Trapalon 119	Gambier	Brambles Boy	10	5
Dec17-73^{7}Crc	7 f 1:27 ft	$7\frac{1}{2}$	116	$6^{8\frac{1}{2}}$	7^{11}	$6^{8\frac{1}{2}}$	5^{2}	CedenoM^{1}	10000	79	Prime Action 116	Andalien	Roji	10	4
Dec 8-73^{4}Crc	6 f 1:13$^{2}/_{5}$sy	12	116	$6^{8\frac{1}{4}}$	6^{5}	4^{6}	$3^{6\frac{1}{4}}$	MapleS^{2}	10000	80	S'n O F'n119	TheGr'tEt'lC.	Te.V.Fr'lic	7	21
Dec 1-73^{4}Crc	7 f 1:27 ft	$9\frac{1}{2}$	116	7^{8}	$8^{6\frac{1}{2}}$	8^{10}	$7^{7\frac{1}{4}}$	MapleS^{2}	12500	74	NobleDuel 115	CentralMissile	LastS'nt	9	
Nov 2-73^{8}Crc	1 1:41$^{2}/_{5}$ft	15	116	$5^{6\frac{1}{2}}$	6^{4}	$6^{4\frac{1}{2}}$	$6^{2\frac{1}{2}}$	Gonz'zG^{6}	12500	85	Outsville116	BlinkPrince	Vertiginoso	8	

Jan 16 Crc 4f ft 49h

Each chart is handled in the same manner, to get the ratings. We will not do them all but will go through the chart on Te. V. Frolic, which is the last in the group. In his last race, the gelding finished fourth in a field of twelve, for a rating of eight, as we have noted in the right-hand margin. In his next-to-last race, Te. V. Frolic finished seventh in a field of eight, for a rating of one. Moving down another race, he finished seventh again, this time in a field of ten, for a rating of three. Next race, he finished fifth in a field of ten, for a rating of five, and in the fifth race down, he finished third in a field of seven, for a rating of four. Total: twenty-one.

Salem Knight, as indicated, has a five-race rating of eleven, whereas Forgive Divine racked up the highest total for these three, of twenty-two. Eleven, of course, is exactly 50 percent of twenty-two, and we throw out Salem Knight. This method is not infallible, but it is a rough guide which works at least 90 percent of the time. In short, by using it we save more than we lose, and that is really what counts. Look at the eighth race on the same day, February 6, and we see that Out In the Cold has a five-race rating of seventeen, whereas the highest rating in the top three is garnered by Zippy Do, who has thirty-three. We can get rid of Out In the Cold, if we wish, and we should. Zippy Do went nowhere, but Shearwater (20) was the winner.

CHART XIII (continued)

Feb. 6:	8$^8_{f/m}$	33 Q1²	Zippy Do¹²² (9) 9–1	——	—— ——
		17 Q2³	Out In the Cold¹¹² (6) 9–1	——	—— ——
		20 Q3⁴	Shearwater¹¹³ (11) 9–1	19.20	7.40 4.20
	9$^{13}_3$	35 Q1¹	Neapolitan Way¹¹³ (6) 50–1	——	—— ——
		32 Q2²	Green Gambados¹¹² (8) 35–1	——	—— ——
		26 Q3³	Frankie Adams¹¹⁴ (8) 27–1	57.00	20.00 10.80
		(35 Q4⁴‡‡‡	Training Table¹¹⁶ (6) 27–1	——	10.20 12.20)
Feb. 7:	1^{12}	8 Q1¹§§§	Fair Hooker¹¹³ (6) 44–1	——	—— ——
Thurs.		16 Q2²	Added Splendor¹⁰⁹ (5) 38–1	——	33.80 17.40
		27 Q3³	Flying Albert¹¹⁴ (6) 18–1	——	—— ——
	8$^8_{f/m}$	23 Q1¹	Fair Skies¹¹² (12) 25–1	——	18.40 8.40
		21 Q2²	Petty Thievery¹¹² (5) 14–1	——	—— ——
		10 Q3³	Divine Pleasure¹¹² (6) 12–1	——	—— ——
Feb. 8:	1^{12}	Q1⁶‖‖‖	Always Near¹⁰⁶ (10) 17–1	36.20	11.60 7.80
Fri.		Q2⁸	Bay Voyage¹¹⁶ (6) 12–1	——	—— ——
	3$^{10}_{Msw(f)}$	Q1⁴	Elegant Nell¹¹⁰ (5)	——	—— ——
		Q2⁵	Noble Georgia¹¹⁶ (A) 12–1	25.40	11.60 4.60
	8$^{10}_f$	Q1²	Third Chance¹¹¹ (6) 47–1	——	34.20 12.40
		Q2³	One Blossom¹¹⁶ (7) 16–1	——	—— 6.80
		Q3⁴	Nurse's Purse¹¹⁶ (7) 15–1	——	—— ——
	10$^9_3$	20 Q1¹	Squire Henry¹¹⁶ (6) 25–1	——	—— 9.60
		32 Q2²	Mr. Faedo¹¹⁶ (8) 12–1	——	9.60 6.00
		30 Q3³###	Onaduel¹¹⁶ (4) 10–1	——	—— ——
Feb. 9:	2^{12}	14 Q1ₚₒ	Nettie's Knave¹⁰⁴ (8) 30–1Po	——	—— ——
Sat.		21 Q2ₚₒ	Grey Fighter¹¹⁴ (6) 30–1Po	——	—— 11.00
		29 Q3ₚₒ	Tombros¹¹² (10) 20–1Po	76.00	26.20 15.20
	4^{12}	Q1¹	Atorrante II¹⁰⁹ (10) 59–1	——	—— ——
		Q2²	Power Line¹⁰⁷ (8) 54–1	——	—— 13.60
	6$^8_3$	Q1¹	R. Tom Can¹¹³ (5) 26–1	——	—— 7.80

‡‡‡Since this is a race for three-year-olds, we look at three qualifiers, and also the fourth, for information, if not for play. The five-race ratings are too close to throw out any particular horse. In fact, it was the low-rater, Frankie Adams, with twenty-six, who proved to be the winner. Both Q3 and Q4 were 27-1 on the board, which is another reason for playing them both. Training Table, incidentally, is 4-Down from the top and with these odds is an automatic bet in the SAM system. This race, incidentally, was a pretty high-class stakes race, and yet it was won by a 27-1 shot. This is another proof of the efficacy of Sam's method of handicapping a race.

§§§Fair Hooker, with a five-race rating of eight is just 50 percent of the next higher horse, Added Splendor, with sixteen. Throw out Fair Hooker. Flying Albert, with twenty-seven, was out of the money, but Added Splendor did get in second and paid a remarkably handsome price of $33.80, with a respectable $17.40 to show. As you know, we play horses with odds of 30-1 or higher all the way: that is, across-the-board, and we get a good return on our show bet here, as in many other instances. And we only had to bet two horses in this three-year-old race.

In the eighth race on this same day, February 7, we can throw out Divine Pleasure (10), who has a five-race rating of less than half that of Petty Thievery (21).

‖‖‖As you see, we had to disqualify five horses before we got to Always Near. The point is, of course, that the top five horses did not have the points to qualify, and we still had high enough odds to find both a Q1 and a Q2. Incidentally, the Q1 qualifier, Always Near, was also an automatic bet in the SAM system. More about that system later. See Q2⁵:

###The five-race ratings are shown here. There is not enough difference to throw out any one horse. Thus, all must be kept in. If you insist on using just two high-odds horses in the Perfecta races, then you could throw out the low-rating of twenty, Squire Henry. Risky, but possible. In the second race on Feb. 9, see below, you can legitimately throw out Nettie's Knave, with a five-race rating of fourteen, since Tombros has twenty-nine, and fourteen is less than half of twenty-nine. Also, Nettie's Knave is a filly racing against males.

CHART XIII (continued)

				Win	Place	Show
	Q2²	The Grok^{112} (5) 15–1		———	10.60	6.00
Feb. 11:1^{12}	Q1²	Joyous Judge^{111} (6) 52–1		———	———	12.80
Mon.	Q2³	Boyd County^{109} (5) 52–1		———	———	———
2_3^{12}	26 Q1$_{10}^{1}$	Elfin Water^{108} (7) 47–1		———	———	———
	15 Q2$_{10}^{2}$	Liketurf^{114} (7) 40–1		———	28.60	15.20
	27 Q3$_{10}^{3}$*	Royal Powder^{107} (6) 25–1		———	———	———
$3_{MSW_3}^{12}$	Q1¹	Tu Gallant^{120} (4) 141–1		———	———	———
	Q2²	No Baubles^{120} (4) 124–1		———	———	———
	Q3⁴†	Majestic King^{120} (A) 28–1	59.00	21.80	10.60
6_3^{10}	Q1¹	Gallant Exchange^{105} (8) 48–1		———	25.00	9.60
	Q2³	More Hopeful^{116} (6) 23–1		———	———	———
	Q3⁴	New Needle^{116} (5) 13–1		———	———	———
7_{r3}^{9}	Q1¹	Dandy Lisa^{107} (9) 24–1		———	———	———
	Q2²	Mystery Markings^{112} (4) 21–1		———	———	7.60
	Q3⁴	Projectional^{114} (4) 12–1		———	———	———
10_3^{8}	7 Q1¹‡	Loyal Showman^{116} (4) 29–1		———	———	———
	19 Q2²	Thrust of Courage^{102} (7) 19–1		———	15.80	6.80
	16 Q3³	Soft Spot^{112} (5) 14–1		———	———	———
Feb. 12:1$_{MSWf}^{10}$	Q1¹	Right Fancy^{119} (4) 56–1		———	———	12.20
Tues.	Q2³	Timely Affair^{119} (7) 16–1		———	———	———
2_3^{12}	Q1$_{Po}$	Speedy Dunn^{106} (6) 20–1Po	49.60	16.80	8.60
	Q2$_{Po}$	Breezy Guy^{116} (5) 20–1Po		———	———	———
3_3^{8}	40 Q1¹	Desperate Action^{107} (8) 31–1		———	———	———
	22 Q2²	Pennamite^{112} (6) 22–1		———	21.00	7.80
NO BET—	20 Q3³	Wannigan^{111} (6) 11–1		———	———	———
7_{r3}^{12}	31 Q1²	Bolinas Jet^{112} (4) 43–1		———	———	———
	6 Q2³	Lotta Royal^{109} (6) 32–1		———	———	———
	14 Q3⁴	Mary's Little Pet^{105} (6) 31–1		———	———	7.60
Feb. 13:1^{12}	Q1⁴	Nettie's Knave^{104} (7) 35–1		———	———	———
Wed.	Q2⁵	Manchuria^{116} (5) 31–1		———	———	17.60
3^{8}	Q1³	Brass and Sass^{114} (7) 23–1	48.60	12.20	5.80
	Q2	(None for lack of odds.)				
7_{r3}^{12}	12 Q1¹§	Far More Knoble^{116} (7) 114–1		———	———	———
	22 Q2²	Rule of Success^{116} (7) 47–1		———	———	———
	23 Q3³	Moon Orbitor^{116} (5) 42–1		———	———	———
	25 Q4⁴	Flash Act^{116} (4⅝) 34–1		———	16.00	10.60

*The five-race ratings are shown here to illustrate the point that the lowest rating must be about 50 percent lower than any of the other two. If Royal Powder had been thirty, we would have thrown out Liketurf, the winner.

†A much-needed winner, since we have not had a winner recently. The last one was in the second race on Saturday, February 9. What you can't see here is that we won all three Perfectas on this date. See Chart XV.

‡The five-race rating of Loyal Showman is more than 50 percent lower than that of either of the other two. Throw him out, even though this is a Perfecta race. Q2 was the key horse in the race and completed the Perfecta, for a payoff of $162.80, the race being won by the favorite, Mr. Art.

§Since twelve is about half of twenty-three, and is less than half of twenty-five, Far More Knoble is no bet. Flash Act becomes Q3 in the series: this is a race for three-year-olds. Also, Jockey Ron Turcotte was riding Flash Act, and this was a Perfecta Race. The race was won by the favorite, Unanimous Verdict, and the Perfecta payoff was $149.40.

CHART XIII (continued)

10¹²	31 Q1¹	Watch Harvey¹¹⁶ (5) 38–1	——	——	——
	20 Q2²	Up Man Up¹¹² (6) 24–1	——	——	——
	(27 Q3³‖	T. Attack¹¹² (8) 22–1	——	26.00	10.00)
Feb. 14: 1⅕²	Q1²	Tom Nash¹¹⁷ (A) 95–1	——	——	
Thurs.	Q2³	Cirrus¹²⁰ (4) 23–1	48.00	14.40	8.00
2¹²	Q1ₐₒ⁵	Flashy Me¹¹³ (6) 25–1	——	——	8.40
		(No others)			
4¹²	Q1¹	Manchi¹¹² (6) 33–1	——	——	——
	Q2²	Country Editor¹¹⁶ (5) 31–1	——	31.60	16.40
8⅝/m	26 Q1¹	Peggy's Fling¹¹² (5) 42–1	——	——	——
	19 Q2²	Sandy Painter¹¹² (5) 14–1	——	——	——
	31 Q3³	Irish Donnybrook¹¹⁴ (6) 13–1	28.60	12.40	5.60
10¹²/m 24 Q1¹		Pondering Jon¹⁰⁶ (6) 83–1	——	——	——
NO BET—	15 Q2³	Vital Ray¹¹⁶ (6) 53–1	——	——	——
	31 Q3⁴	Mlle. Charlotte¹¹³ (8) 35–1	——	——	12.80
Feb. 15: 1¹¹ₘₛwₜ₃ 26Q1¹#		Solo Serenade¹¹⁴ (4) 62–1	——	——	——
Fri.					
NO BET—	11 Q2³	Tansor¹¹⁹ (4) 49–1	——	——	12.60
	31 Q3⁴	Halfway Up¹¹⁹ (5) 40–1	——	——	——
5¹¹/m	15 Q1¹	Pleine d'Amour¹¹² (8) 72–1	——	——	——
	18 Q2²	Let Em Boil¹¹⁶ (5) 35–1	——	——	——
	37 Q3³	Spanish Gypsy¹¹⁶ (4) 31–1	——	——	——
	10 Q4⁴**	Gloriosky¹¹⁶ (6) 30–1	61.40	19.80	10.00
9⁷	33 Q1¹	El Tordillo¹¹² (6) 18–1	——	——	——
	19 Q2³	Bob H.¹¹² (6) 11–1	——	——	——
	26 Q3⁴††	Barclay Jet¹¹² (6) 9–1	19.80	7.40	4.20
10⅝	33 Q1²	Gummo's Pride¹¹⁴ (6) 11–1	——	——	——

‖Since this is a regular race, we don't go to the third qualifier, except to check out the horse for an outstanding record. However, this is also a Perfecta Race, and it is wise to include Q3, if we cannot eliminate one of the other two. T. Attack has the higher five-race rating, if we look at him in contrast to Up Man Up (20). He also has two more points under the regular system. Both horses are carrying 112 pounds, and both are dropping in class. T. Attack has finished in-the-money five times in his past performance; Up Man Up has three seconds. T. Attack has two wins. The scales are tipped in favor of T. Attack quite clearly, and Sam would probably substitute him for Up Man Up.

#This is an example of the other ten percent, when the shorthand system throws out the wrong horse. But no system so mechanical as this five-race rating one is 100 percent. For instance, this shorthand method of rating does not take into consideration the class at which or in which the races are run. Sam recognized this actuely in the fifth race on February 15, when Spanish Gypsy ran up a five-race rating of thirty-seven to Gloriosky's ten. This would throw Gloriosky out of contention, but Sam had to disallow Spanish Gypsy's high rating since the Gypsy was winning and running second in $6,500 and $7,500 races, and today's competition was at $16,000. Hereafter, whenever a horse has a spectacularly high five-race rating, consider the class and disallow those races at a much lower class.

**As indicated above, Gloriosky was the next-in-line horse, at 30-1, with a five-race rating of ten. Contrasting the latter two horses, both are in that ticklish category of having been claimed last race and are moving up in class for this race. But it is a filly/mare race and some freedom must be allowed. Spanish Gypsy has never before run at $16,000, and seems to be getting way out of her class. Gloriosky has several races at a higher class than today's race and should get the nod. Being fourth down from the top in odds, Gloriosky is also an automatic bet in the SAM system.

††This is a regular race and Q3 is not in the series of bets, unless you substitute Barclay Jet for the low-rater Bob H. If Bob H. were seventeen instead of nineteen, we would have thrown him out. However, when we compare the form of the two horses, we find that both are experienced turf-course runners, both have numerous lengthy races, both are getting in at 112, and both are pretty well in their class. Barclay Jet has a considerably better finish-record, with six in-the-money races this year, to Bob H.'s four. A difficult choice, but Barclay Jet does appear to have the edge. For that reason, we keep him in the series and in the final calculations at the end of this chart.

CHART XIII (continued)

	21 Q2³	Squire Henry¹¹⁸ (5) 11–1	——	——	——
	16 Q3⁴‡‡	More America¹¹² (5) 9–1	20.80	8.00	4.40
Feb. 16: 2¹²	Q1ₚₒ	Rey Claro¹⁰⁵ (9) 20–1Po	51.60	26.40	11.40
Sat.	Q2ₚₒ	Fellow Diplomat¹⁰⁶ 20–1Po	——	63.80	23.40
		71–1Ao			
5⁸	Q1²	Down Among¹¹³ (10) 67–1	——	——	——
	Q2³	Trigger Happy¹¹² (5) 55–1	——	——	6.60
6⅜	Q1¹	Bronze Express¹¹⁶ (5) 89–1	——	——	——
	Q2³	Glazing¹¹⁶ (8) 20–1	——	——	——
	Q3⁴	Bottom Line¹¹⁶ (7) 17–1	——	13.40	6.20
8⁸	Q1¹	Amberbee¹⁰⁷ (8) 87–1	——	——	——
	Q2⁴	Strictly Business¹¹² (7) 17–1	——	10.80	4.60
Feb. 18: 4¹²ₘₛᵥ₃	Q1¹	Academician¹²⁰ (4) 44–1	——	——	——
Mon.	Q2²	Poker Hound¹²⁰ (5) 43–1	——	——	——
	Q3⁵	Count Dad¹²⁰ (5) 20–1	——	——	——
	(Q4⁶§§	First Standing¹²⁰ (4) 16–1	34.20	12.00	9.80)
7¹²	Q1¹	Flying Wedge¹¹³ (5) 45–1	——	40.20	12.80
	Q2³	Odd Z.¹¹⁶ (5) 41–1	——	——	——
10¹²	Q1¹	Amquillo¹¹² (6) 99–1	——	——	——
	Q2²	Upsurge¹¹⁶ (5) 60–1	——	22.20	15.20
Feb. 19: 1⅓¹¹	Q1¹‖‖‖	Lila's Poppy¹⁰⁴ (5) 126–1	——	——	——
Tues.	Q2²	Double Jackie¹¹³ (5) 72–1	——	——	——
	Q3³	Gunner's Hope¹⁰³ (7) 25–1	——	19.80	8.80

‡‡Another example of a misleading high-rating, on the part of Gummo's Pride, which had run all but one of his past races at a *Lower* class than today's class. Sam decided at this point to cut the rating exactly in half, when this occurs in future. That is, Gummo's Pride should really have a five-race rating of sixteen or seventeen. Thus, More America would stay in, and we would collect on another winner. This is merely an "adjustment" to the short-hand system of five-race ratings, which will be applied to all circumstances where appropriate in future. If as many as three of the last five races have been run at a *Lower* class than today's class, chop the five-race rating in half.

§§The winner, again, was the fourth qualifier in this Maiden Race for three-year-olds. We missed it in the regular series of three. First Standing had only one previous race, and it was difficult to say that the colt should replace any of those higher than him in odds. But he was an automatic winner in the #6-Down position of the SAM System. This win is not counted in the calculations at the end of this chart.

‖‖‖The race was seven furlongs in length, and the entire field of eleven horses crossed under the finish-wire in a body. It looked to Sam very much like a dead heat for the first four horses, but when the photo was displayed there was a nose between each two. Martini Time (#5-Down from the top) was the barest winner, by a nose, over Gunner's Hope, who was a nose in front of Elfin Water. Elfin Water was just a neck ahead of Fancy Diplomacy. There came a slight gap between Fancy Diplomacy and African Stone (half a length), and then there was another slight gap (one length) between African Stone and Not My Bid. The last five horses were separated by ¾ length, ½ length, a neck, and a neck. There were only 2¾ lengths between the winner and the last horse, Double Jackie. For his $20 on Martini Time, Sam picked up $262. See the chart below for the full picture:

FIRST RACE	7 FURLONGS (chute). (1:20⁴/₅). MAIDENS. CLAIMING. Purse $4,200. 3-year-olds. Weight, 122 lbs.
GP	Non-winners of two races in 1974 allowed 2 lbs.; two races since Nov. 25, 4 lbs.; maidens, 6 lbs. Claiming
February 19, 1974	price, $5,000. (Races where entered for $4,000 or less not considered.) (Winners preferred.)

Value to winner $2,520; second, $840; third, $420; fourth, $294; fifth, $126. Mutuel Pool, $43,625.

Last Raced		Horse	EqtAWt	PP	St	¼	½	Str	Fin	Jockeys	Owners	Odds to $1
2-14-74²	GP⁶	Martini Time	b3 114	5	11	10²	10½	8³	1ⁿᵒ	RGaffglione	F E Eckart	12.10
1-29-74²	GP⁹	Gunner's Hope	3 103	3	6	4½	4ʰ	3½	2ⁿᵒ	WCrews¹⁰	S G Babbitz	25.20

CHART XIII (continued)

1-31-74[1]	GP[9]	Baggie Sal	b3 113	9	2	1[h]	1[h]	1½	3[no]	JBLeBlanc	Jay N' Jay Stable			18.20
2-11-74[2]	GP[5]	Elfin Water	b3 113	7	10	9½	9[1]	6[h]	4[nk]	KSkinner	J L Levesque			9.60
1-15-74[6]	Crc[6]	Fancy Diplomacy	b3 113	1	5	3½	3[3]	4[2]	5½	MCastaneda	C E Pickering			2.90
1-31-74[1]	GP[6]	African Stone	b3 118	2	8	8[2]	7½	7½	6[1]	DBrumfield	Clements-Madden			7.50
2-12-74[2]	GP[3]	Not My Bid	b3 118	8	4	2[2]	2[2]	2½	7¾	MCedeno	Shakarian-Bucciero Jr.			2.50
2-11-74[2]	GP[9]	Royal Powder	b3 113	4	9	7[h]	8[2]	9½	8½	ESarmiento	F G Rivera			11.20
2- 5-74[2]	GP[8]	Lila's Poppy	b3 104	10	1	5[2]	5[2]	5[1]	9[nk]	RHudson[7]	Biljim Farm			125.60
1-29-74[2]	GP[5]	Dethroner	b3 116	11	3	6½	6½	10½	10[nk]	JVelasquez	Burke-Keefe			4.30
1-10-74[4]	Crc[7]	Double Jackie	b3 113	6	7	11	11	11	11	SGomez	J-B Gaudio Farm			72.10

OFF AT 1:15 EDT. Start good. Won driving. Time, :22⁴/s, :45³/s, 1:11⁴/s, 1:26. Track fast.

$2 Mutuel Prices:

Official Program Numbers

5-MARTINI TIME	26.20	13.20	7.20
3-GUNNER'S HOPE		19.80	8.80
10-BAGGIE SAL...........................			6.40

Ro. f, by Third Martini—Dusty Nancy, by Penaction. Trainer, S.E. Branham. Bred by J. Spencer (Fla.).

MARTINI TIME, slow to begin, came to the extreme outside in a late bid and, responding to pressure, was up in the final stride. GUNNER'S HOPE gained a forward position at once, rallied when roused in the stretch and narrowly missed. BAGGIE SAL held on stubbornly after making the pace throughout. ELFIN WATER found her best stride too late. FANCY DIPLOMACY also finished belatedly. AFRICAN STONE closed boldly following a sluggish beginning. NOT MY BID tired a bit from her early efforts. DETHRONER raced wide.

Overweight—Martini Time, 1 pound.
Corrected weight—Baggie Sal, 113.
Claiming Prices—All $5000.
Scratched—Marvelous Mix, Well Deserved, Mr. Pete G., Davlin, Midnight Laughter, Splash Lightly, Highland Maid.

Martini Time, in combination with High Tide Jack, the winner of the second race, resulted in a daily double payoff of $230.40. This is not a regular system winner and does not appear in the next chart. However, Sam had it in his special SAM system, to be explained later. But he was hardly prepared for what happened that same day, in the fourth race:

4¹²ᶠ₃##	Q1[4]	Hy Breeze[119] (6) 44–1	91.00	36.20	11.40
	Q2[5]	Misfesto[119] (A) 20–1	———	———	———
	Q3[6]	In the Boat[119] (A) 16–1			
8⁸ᶠ ₘ	Q1[2]	Homespun[113] (6) 15–1	———	11.40	5.20
	Q2[3]	Protesting Bid[112] (5) 10–1	———	———	———
	Q3[4]	Stolen Date[112] (6) 9–1			
10[9]	Q1[2]	Swift Dog[111] (7) (?)	———	———	———
	Q2[3]	Antix Again[116] (5) 34–1	70.60	24.40	5.80

##Q1, Q2 and Q3 were, of course, the qualifiers in the regular system. By coincidence, the same three horses were automatic bets in the SAM System, which you may know by now is involved with top-odds horses, the third fourth, fifth, and sixth-down from the top odds. At any rate, by the time Sam got over his amusement and amazement at this, he had just two minutes left before post time. He simply doubled his bets, putting $40 across-the-board on each of the three horses, for a total investment of $360. Then he watched the race with some palpitations of the heart. There were exactly nine horses which could mess him up completely, but his odds on collecting something were just 3–1. He wasn't too unhappy when he saw Misfesto leading at the quarter-pole by a length-and-a-half. Indeed, Misfesto ran a very good race and was knocked out of show money by a mere nose. It was a photo-finish for the second, third, fourth *and* fifth horses! Whoops A Daisy was second, just a neck in front of Backlash, who was a nose in front of Misfesto, who was another nose ahead of Jeffo. Jeffo was fifth in the race, just a nose ahead of the sixth horse, In the Boat. That accounts for two of Sam's selections. It was Hy Breeze, who went off at better than 44–1, who came into the stretch turn in sixth position, went wide on the outside and came down the stretch driving and won the race by a length and ¾. As the man said, Hy Breeze was "up with a rush in the closing sixteenth." And Sam collected $2,772 for his two $20 across-the-board tickets, for a net profit on the race of exactly $2,412. But what a day for close finishes!

Gulfstream Park, Jan. 21–Feb. 20 1974—Straight

SUMMARY:
Number of racing days: 26

CHART XIII (continued)

Number of races: 260
Unit of investment: $2
Number of Races requiring Q3 and Q4 investment: 100

	Q1		Q2		Q3/4	
	Win	*Place*	*Win*	*Place*	*Win*	*Place*
Return	472.60	604.80	554.00	587.20	680.00	422.60
Invested	520.00	520.00	520.00	520.00	200.00	200.00
Net Profit	−47.40	84.80	34.00	67.20	480.00	222.60
Percentage	———	16%	6%	13%	240%	111%
TOTALS:	*Q1, Q2, Q3 Win*		*Q1, Q2, Q3 Place*		*Combined Totals*	
Return	1,706.60		1,614.60		3,321.20	
Invested	1,240.00		1,240.00		2,480.00	
Net Profit	466.60		374.60		841.20	
Percentage	37%		30%		33%	

			Total return	*Average*
Number of Q1 Win hits:		10	$ 472.60	$47.25
Number of Q2 Win hits:		9	554.00	61.50
Number of Q3/4 Win hits:		16	680.00	42.50
Number of Q1 Place hits:		26	604.80	23.25
Number of Q2 Place hits:		28	587.20	21.00
Number of Q3/4 Place hits:		28	422.60	15.00
Number of Q1, Q2, Q3 Wins:		35	1706.60	48.75
Number of Q1, Q2, Q3 Pl.:		82	1614.60	20.00

NOTE: This is the first time we have done anything with the Q3 or Q4 investments. But during these twenty-six days, it was apparent that Q3 or Q4 was winning or running in-the-money more consistently than either Q1 or Q2. Thus, we calculated the total possible number of Q3/4 investments and found them to be 100. The amount won by Q3 or Q4 over the period was $680, with a total of $422.60 to Place. Since this came to better than a thousand dollars in the twenty-six days, it was significant enough to be included in the overall totals, shown in the preceding table. In the straight wagering, therefore, the percentage of profit on all investments came to nearly 34 percent.

The chief value of the Q3/4 selections is still in their use in the Perfectas. As you will see later, the net profit on Perfectas during this same twenty-six day period was $7,316.20. Adding that to the $1,614.80 from daily doubles and to the modest $841.20 in straight investments, we have a grand total of $10,782.20 in net profits at Gulfstream Park between January 21 and February 20, 1974. A review of all the summary tables on pages 137-38 will show that this is a return of 127 percent on your investment. It is exceeded only by the return of 133 percent at Gulfstream in April 1973. Of the five sample meetings shown, the month of May 1972 at Pimlico brought a return of 75 percent, and this was the lowest in the group. Even so, the net profits during May of 1972 at Pimlico were better than $6,500. With the use of a moderate progression, as explained in the section on money management, the profits could have been very much better. Still, if you stick to flat investments (no progression at all) and remain at the minimum $2 investment unit, you can take home between six and eleven thousand a month. And that's using only one of the two systems outlined in this volume.

CHART XIV   Gulfstream Park, Daily Doubles: Jan. 21–Feb. 20, 1974

Jan. 22:   F3 (Full Smile) with Q1po (Desoto Belle) $294.80

CHART XIV (continued)

Jan. 23:	#1 (Michelle's Story) with #4 (Harper)	98.80
Jan. 24:	#4q (Banana) with #4 (National Ad)	105.20
Jan. 25:	Q3 (Pari A. Docs) with #4 (Le Moqueur)	197.60
Jan. 29:	#3 (Ann's Valentine) with #4q (Angemar)	165.80
Jan. 30:	#3 (Seek Our Fortune) with #4 (Only Sunny)	146.40
(Jan. 31:	#5-Down from top-odds: with All horses listed in Top-5 Probable Odds who are Dropping in Class: (Saxs Chance) with (Iron and Steel)	713.40)*
Feb. 1:	#1$^{3\text{-}1}$ (Rio Lass) with #2 (Game Alibhai)	21.60
Feb. 5:	#4q (Shell Dancer) with #4 (Skykomish)	284.20
Feb. 6:	F2 (Blue Wonder)† with #3 (Landing Gear)	147.80
Feb. 7:	#1$^{3\text{-}1}$ (Butter Bean) with #3 (California Girl)	51.00
Feb. 8:	Q1 (Always Near) with #3 (Klondyke Champ)	146.40
Feb. 9:	F3 (School Year) with Q1$_{Po}$ (Tombros)	347.00
Feb. 11:	#3 (Licorice King) with #4 (Dandy Carl)	57.80
Feb. 14:	Q2 (Cirrus) with #3 (Falling Cub)	272.00
Feb. 16:	F4 (Just Like Doc) with Q1$_{Po}$ (Rey Claro)	531.00
Feb. 18:	#2 (Joan R. H.) with #3 (Hasam's Honey)	47.40

Gross Return: $2,914.80

*This double was a result of the SAM System described later herein. It is not included in the tabulations at the end of this chart.

†Blue Wonder was listed at 2-1 in the probable odds for the first race, but in reality it became F2 in the betting. We reject F1 (Raise the Axe) and take Blue Wonder in his place.

SUMMARY:
Number of racing days: 26
Number of investments: 26
Total investment, at $50 per day: $1300.00
Gross return: $2,914.80
Total invested: 1,300.00

Net profit: $1,614.80

Percentage of net profit: 124%

CHART XV Gulfstream Park, Perfectas: Jan. 21–Feb. 20, 1974

Jan. 21:	4^{12}	F2	(Unanimous Verdict) with F4 (Fencer)	$ 73.60
	7^{11}	F2	(Queen's Measure) with F3 (Quiet Suzanne)	20.80
	10^{12}	Q1	(Arms and Armor) with F3$_q$ (Nyasa)	1196.40
Jan. 22:	4^{12}	F1	(Lost Control) with Q1 (Speedy Lois)	290.40
	7^{12}	Q3	(Never Never Stop) with F1 (Lakeville)	158.00
Jan. 23:	10^{12}	Q2	(The General) with F4$_q$ (Victors Verse)	1407.80
Jan. 24:	4^{8}	F1	(Royal Poet)* with Q1 (Waist Band)	96.60
	7^{12}	F2	(Search the Farm) with Q1 (Fall Rush)	253.00

*The question is still unanswered: Was this race fixed? Was it set up by the Smart Money Boys? For a full discussion of the race, see the section entitled A Touch of Scandal.

CHART XV (continued)

	10^{12}	F4$_q$	(Roman Scout) with F2 (Brambles Boy)	102.20
Jan. 25:	7^{11}	F3	(Gavel to Gavel) with Q3 (Roman Decade)	258.80
Jan. 26:	$(4^{12}$		#5-Down from top-odds (Viel)	
			with F5 (Piper Cub)	530.80)†
	$(7^{12}$	F5	(Roji) with #-5 Down (Concorde)	287.60)†
	10^9	Q3	(Shark Boat) with F4 (Big Red L)	349.60
Jan. 28:	4^{12}	F4	(Plagiarize) with F2 (Emperor Rex)	74.40
	10^{12}	F2	(Firing Gun) with F3 (Harry's Runner)	68.20
Jan. 29:	4^{12}	F2	(Prime Mistress) with F3 (Cyn Cl Maid)	52.80
	7^{10}	F4	(Irish Brandy) with F5 (Beach Picnic)	133.80
	10^{10}	Q3	(Clear Echo) with F4$_q$ (Abe's Mood)	231.20
Jan. 30:	4^{12}	Q2	(Maharajo) with F1 (Blue Wonder)	477.60
Jan. 31:	4^9	F2	(Opinionation) with Q2 (Guy Lee)	130.40
	7^{12}	Q2	(Special Tex) with F3 (Dodeys Sky High)	519.00
	10^9	F2	(Dear Annie) with F4 (Countess V)	71.60
Feb. 1:	4^{12}	F2	(More Hopeful) with F3 (Tudor Scandal)	44.80
	$(7^{11}$	Q2	(Soaked) with F5‡ (Good For A Laugh)	375.80)
	10^{10}	F6	(Conflict) with F4 (Just Like Doc)	116.00
Feb. 2:	4^{12}	F4	(Evening Flight) with F6$_q$ (Watch Harvey)	359.00
	10^{12}	F3	(First Shout) with F4$_q$ (Never Explain)	111.80
Feb. 4:	7^{12}	F1	(Busher's Rule) with Q1 (Uncopyable)	211.00
Feb. 5:	4^8	Q1	(Pondering Jon) with F3 (Berth of Marwal)	256.20
	7^{12}	F2	(Dusty Collar) with F3 (Double Lightning)	81.20
Feb. 6:	4^{12}§	F3$_q$	(Vertiginoso) with Q2$_q$ (Te. V. Frolic)	174.00
Feb. 7:	10^8	F3	(General Beau) with F4 (Wishing Star)	58.20
Feb. 8:	10^9	F4	(Pass Muster) with Q2 (Mr. Faedo)	256.00
Feb. 9:	7^{10}‖	F6	(Sweet Manhattan) with F4 (Big Hobo)	146.80
Feb. 11:	4^{12}	F2	(Strong and Able) with F4 (Smyrna Road)	67.20
	7^9	F4$_q$	(Noble Memory) with F3 (Call Me Jackey)	92.60
	10^{10}	F1	(Mr. Art) with Q2 (Thrust of Courage)	162.80
Feb. 12:	10^{11}	F5	(Minstrel Jon) with F4 (Hitching Post)	133.20
Feb. 13:	7^{12}	F1	(Unanimous Verdict) with Q3$_q$ (Flash Act)	149.40
	10^{12}	F4$_q$	(Stairway to Stars) with Q3 (T. Attack)	397.60
Feb. 14:	4^{12}	F4$_q$	(Apple Eater) with Q2 (Country Editor)	803.80
Feb. 15:	4^{12}	F2	(Sun O Fun) with F3 (Vie)	64.40
	10^8	Q3	(More America) with F1 (Stanley the Great)	64.20
Feb. 16:	7^{12}	F4	(Busher Rule) with F2 (Brass Cannon)	52.20

†These two are not hits in the general system but are hits in the automatic SAM System, described later. Payoffs are not included in the calculations at the end of this chart.

‡Not a hit under the general system, since Good For A Laugh is the actual F5. F4 (Scorpius) would have been the selection. However, this race is included here as another example of the winning combination under the SAM System. Soaked was #4-Down and combined with F5 for the payoff of $375.80.

§Another Double hit. It was also F4 and #-6 Down in the SAM System.

‖Another Double. This was also #5-Down with F4 in the SAM System.

CHART XV (continued)

Feb. 18:	$(4^{12}$#	#6-Down (First Standing) with	
		F5 (Bold and Fancy)	562.20)
7^{12}	F4	(Full of Fight) with Q1 (Flying Wedge)	598.40
10^{12}	F1	(Tradesman) with Q2 (Upsurge)	298.40
Feb. 19: 4^{12}	Q1	(Hy Breeze) with $F4_q$ (Whoops A Daisy)	601.20
10^9	Q2	(Antix Again) with F4 (Scorpius)	353.80

#This is not a hit in the regular system but is in the SAM System.

SUMMARY:

Number of racing days: 26

Number of Perfecta races: 78

Average investment: $60 per race, for a total investment of: $4,680.00

Gross return: $11,996.20

Investment: 4,680.00

Net profit: $ 7,316.20

Return on investment: 156%

Breakdown of F4, F5, and F6:	Return:	$ 888.80
	Invested:	936.00
	Net loss:	−47.20
Breakdown of F1 with Q1 and Q2:	Return:	$1908.40
	Invested:	624.00
	Net profit:	$1284.40

SUMMARY   Hialeah Park, April 1972

	Straight	Doubles	Perfectas	Totals
Return	2,715.00	3,329.60	9,945.50	15,999.10
Invested	1,920.00	1,200.00	5,760.00	8,880.00
Net Profit	795.00	2,129.60	4,185.50	7,110.10
Percentage	41%	177%	72%	81%

Pimlico, May 1972

	Straight	Doubles	Exactas	Totals
Return	1,822.00	2,676.40	10,726.40	15,224.80
Invested	1,728.00	1,200.00	5,760.00	8,688.00
Net Profit	94.00	1,476.40	4,966.40	6,536.80
Percentage	5%	123%	86%	75%

Gulfstream Park, April 1973

	Straight	Doubles	Perfectas	Totals
Return	3,346.00	4,938.60	11,575.60	19,860.20
Invested	1,840.00	1,150.00	5,520.00	8,510.00
Net Profit	1,506.00	3,788.60	6,055.60	11,350.20
Percentage	81%	328%	109%	133%

Aqueduct, April 1972

	Straight	Doubles	Exactas	Totals
Return	2,048.40	5,682.80	7,325.80	15,059.00
Invested	1,728.00	1,200.00	4,320.00	7,248.00
Net Profit	320.40	4,482.80	3,005.80	7,811.00
Percentage	18%	373%	70%	107%

Gulfstream Park, Jan.–Feb. 1974

	Straight	Doubles	Perfectas	Totals
Return	3,321.20	2,914.80	11,996.20	19,242.20
Invested	2,480.00	1,300.00	4,680.00	8,460.00
Net Profit	841.20	1,614.80	7,316.20	10,782.20
Percentage	34%	124%	156%-	127%

6

Sam's Automatic Method (SAM)

Before getting into the details and mechanics of Sam's Automatic Method, we have time for two vignettes. Each in its own way has to do with the economics of horse racing, a subject which Sam himself found endlessly fascinating. It was a subject so full of mystery, and so full of challenge, that he was never very far away from it.

First, there is the story of Secretariat, the Super Horse of the 1970's.

Secretariat was born in "the lap of equine luxury" at The Meadow, a 2600-acre farm in Doswell, Virginia, once the property of Christopher Chenery, which passed at his death to his daughter Penny. Penny grew up in Pelham Manor, New York, where she was a rider of show horses from an early age. She attended Smith College, went to Europe during World War II as a member of the Red Cross, returning to enter Columbia's Graduate School of Business in New York City. She married John Tweedy, executive vice president of The Oil Shale Corporation, while she herself, maintaining her lifelong interest in thoroughbred horses, became president of Meadow Stud, Inc. In this tale of riches to riches, it was Penny Tweedy who arranged the mating of a mare called Somethingroyal, a daugher of Prince-quillo, to that breaker of records, Bold Ruler, winner of twenty-three races which included the Preakness of 1957. Called "one of the greatest sires of all time," Bold Ruler was the father of Secretariat in March of 1970. Mrs. Tweedy took one look at the new colt and wrote in her notebook:

"WOW!"

From the beginning, Secretariat was a picture of beauty, a colt which all colts would like to *be* like.

As a two-year-old, Secretariat ran his first race at Aqueduct on July 4, 1972. When they left the starting gate, another horse wheeled sideways into Secretariat. Had he not been so strong and powerful, the colt would have gone down. But he recovered as best he could, and from that fateful start he ran a remarkable race, making up nearly eight lengths in the last quarter-mile, finishing fourth. Never again out of the money, he won the next eight of his races in 1972. In fact, as a two-year-old, he was named Horse of the Year.

But 1973 was the year for Secretariat. By June, he had won four of his five races, including the Kentucky Derby and the Preakness. For reasons unknown, in late April he ran third behind Angle Light and Sham in the Wood Memorial at Aqueduct. No matter. He set a record by winning the Kentucky Derby in 1:59 3/5. That's one and a quarter miles in less than two minutes. As the 3-2 favorite, Secretariat paid $5 for every $2 wagered to win. Ron Turcotte, the Canadian jockey, was up as usual, and the trainer was another Canadian, Lucien Laurin, who had become the chief trainer at Meadow Stable in 1971, succeeding his son, Roger Laurin, who had moved over to the Ogden Phipps stable.

With Secretariat, following the Derby and the Preakness, owner Tweedy, Trainer Laurin, and Jockey Turcotte went for the Triple Crown, setting their sights on the Belmont Stakes, a marathon race of one-and-a-half miles, which is once around the Belmont Track. Belmont was Secretariat's home between races, and Secretariat was quietly happy to be home. But even before the Belmont Stakes and the Triple Crown, Secretariat's future was firmly established. He was to give up racing on November

15, 1973, and in the spring of 1974 he would begin life as a stud.

As a stud horse, Secretariat was syndicated at just over six million dollars. A total of thirty-two people paid $190,000 each for the privilege of being allowed to breed one mare to Secretariat per year for the remainder of his life. Super Horse was slated to become Super Stud. Do not forget that by June of 1973, Secretariat had won eleven of his fourteen races and had earned a total of $804,202. His earnings were short of a million; but his value as a sire was set at a round six million, and it might well have been higher if the syndicate had been formed after the Triple Crown.

Winners of the Triple Crown these days collect $25,000 better than half a million. And that's just the purse money. Syndication is a must because there are few indeed who can afford to own and operate a six-million-dollar-asset. The colts and fillies who come from the breeding of mares with Secretariat are themselves worth a fortune apiece. These are the economics of thoroughbred horse racing, when viewed from the heavenly seats occupied by a Penny Tweedy and a Lucien Laurin and a Ron Turcotte. Don't forget Ron Turcotte. The third member of the triumvirate who took the Triple Crown, with the aid of Secretariat. An apprentice jockey in Canada in 1961, Ron Turcotte rode 180 winners in 1962 and became the Top Jockey in the country. In 1964 he moved to the United States, with results which are familiar to almost anyone who follows horse racing. Diminutive of frame and hard of muscle, Ron Turcotte has a Profile to watch:

RON TURCOTTE

HOME: Belmont, New York, and Motels North, South, and West.

AGE: 31. (When he rode Secretariat in the Kentucky Derby. Now 32.)

PROFESSION: Specialist in Riding Winners.

INCOME: In 1972, his 10 percent of the Purse Money came to $278,000.

HOBBIES: Camping in the Canadian wilderness.

LAST BOOK READ: *The Guinness Book of World Records.*

LAST ACCOMPLISHMENT: Rode two succeeding Winners in the Kentucky Derby: Riva Ridge and Secretariat, 1972, 1973.

QUOTE: "The horse does the running. The biggest mistake a rider can make is to feel that he's more important than his horse and not give him credit for intelligence."

PROFILE: Dynamic, slim, shrewd, and unprepossessing.

FAVORITE DRINK: Mint Julep.

If you are like Sam Hirsch, the One Who Never Varies, you will back Ron Turcotte all the way. Provided, of course, he's riding a qualifier!

The point, of course, is that the Sport of Kings is a rich man's game, when you indulge in it from the angle viewed by Secretariat. But you'll never make a fortune backing Super Horse, collecting $2.20 for every $2 you put through the window. It's time now for our second vignette, which lies far to the south, in the State of Florida. We go by the fastest possible means to Gulfstream Park, in the late winter of 1973–1974.

The stables at Gulfstream Park are perhaps not up to those at Belmont Park, at least, not up to those occupied by horses who are trained by Lucien Laurin. But the activity around the stables is very much the same, beginning early in the morning, around six o'clock, when the stable hands and the exercise boys get to work. It was a bit after seven A.M. when Trainer J. H. Pierce, Jr. looked in on his compact little empire. This particular day was important to Pierce. It was Monday, February 18, and he had entered the four-year-old colt Flying Wedge in the seventh race, which was a mile and a sixteenth on the turf. Flying Wedge was one of a small group of horses owned by W. P. Burke, and Pierce knew that Burke would be around shortly to see how things were going.

Flying Wedge was a nice-looking colt but not extraordinary. He was just one of around 25,000 colts and fillies born into the world of thoroughbred racing in 1970. Of that number, approximately 20,000 are put into training every year, and each of those 20,000 costs its owner approximately $10,000 to stable and train and race. From somewhere, owners have to ante up two-hundred-million each year just to break even. Flying Wedge was out three times in 1973, and he brought in exactly $525. On

June 8, he ran fourth at Monmouth in a race that was at a mile and a sixteenth, but not on the turf. His first run on the turf came on May 14 when he finished eleventh in a field of twelve at Garden State. That had been an allowance race, and Flying Wedge was a bit out of his class. Still, he had picked up four lengths in the stretch run, and he was certainly a healthy colt, ready for action. Pierce had dropped him into a maiden race at Monmouth on June 8, and that fourth was an indicator to him. He began seriously to look for a "spot" for Flying Wedge. It had to be a mile and a sixteenth, and it had to be on the turf. Unfortunately, it was a $14,000 claiming race he found, on January 17 at Gulfstream Park, where he had moved for the winter season. He had told Maple, the jockey, that Flying Wedge needed a good workout on the turf. Flying Wedge couldn't be expected to handle $14,000 claimers, but he could use the experience. Burke had agreed. Neither the owner nor the trainer were surprised when he went off at 78-to-1 and ran last in a field of twelve. At the head of the stretch Maple had him trailing the leader by thirty lengths, and he crossed the finish line thirty-four lengths off. Maple weighed in at 112 pounds for that race, and he was pleased with the workout. Sir Omni took the race with not too great difficulty, and nobody, but nobody paid the slightest attention to Flying Wedge.

Pierce was not at all unhappy with Flying Wedge's performance. The odds would certainly be good the next time out. The next time out would probably be sometime after the middle of February. And meanwhile, over at Hialeah, a track which Flying Wedge preferred, there were two or three good workouts, one on February 5, when he breezed five furlongs in 1:03. On February 14, Maple took him out for six furlongs, which he did in 1:15 without raising much of a sweat. The track record for six furlongs at Gulfstream Park was 1:07 4/5, which meant that in his workout Flying Wedge was some thirty-five lengths off. But no matter. The race which they were looking for would be at a mile and a sixteenth, and it would be on the turf again. At Garden State last May, Flying Wedge had gone the mile and a sixteenth in 1:46 1/5. Pierce felt that he could do it today in 1:45, perhaps a little better.

The weight for today's race was 122 pounds, but Flying Wedge would get six pounds off for being non-winner of a race since January 17. This, of course, was highly significant, since January 17 had been the very day Flying Wedge had run the same distance at Gulfstream Park. A suspicious soul would say that the racing secretary had written the race to fit Flying Wedge. But that was nonsense. The January 17 date was a coincidence. Burke and Pierce were pleased, however, with this six-pound advantage, and they agreed to drop the claiming price on Flying Wedge from the $10,000 it should be down to $9,000, since they would gain a two-pound allowance for each $500 dropped, down to $9,000. This they did, which meant that Flying Wedge could get in at 112 pounds today, provided jockey Maple was at his usual slim and slender 112.

"We need that 112 weight," Pierce said.

Maple knew they needed that 112 weight, and he was on his best behavior where food was concerned. He had steak and just half a baked potato on Sunday, around noon, but after that he had practically starved himself. Both Pierce and Burke insisted on that 112 weight. At a mile and a sixteenth, every pound was worth a length.

At their eleven o'clock conference, Burke and Pierce laid their final plans. The *Racing Form* was out, of course, and the public selectors had picked Idol Hand (twelve points) and Landing Gear (seven points). The probable odds on Flying Wedge were listed at 20-1, which were the highest in the race. Everything was looking good. Remember that the seventh race at Gulfstream Park was one of the three races each day which were Perfecta Races. Flying Wedge wouldn't go off again at 78-to-1. But no doubt the odds would be pretty good. That last race jumped out at you in the *Form*. Dead last, thirty-four lengths off the winner. And other good things had been happening, almost too good to be true. Idol Hand was scratched. Landing Gear was scratched. Social Ladder was scratched. Three of the best in the field. Certainly, there were twelve horses in the field for the seventh race. That was a part of the plan. Part of the "set up," as the boys around the stable began to think of it. Confidence ran high. Everybody who had any connection with Flying Wedge was going to put his last dollar on the race.

Of course, there was still some stiff competition. Idealic was no slouch at this distance and on the turf. He'd run fourth last time out, which was right here at Gulfstream on February 9. Only two-and-a-half lengths off the winner. In June of last year, Idealic had won a race of this distance, on the turf, at Monmouth. He'd run then at $10,000, and he was in again today at $10,000. Fleet to Market was dropping $3,000 to get in today's race. But the horse that Pierce and Burke, and Maple, too, for that matter, were really afraid of was Full of Fight, a gelding who had made a profession of running a mile and a sixteenth on the turf. With Walter Blum up, Full of Fight was the horse to beat.

"And we *can* beat him" said Pierce.

"We damn well *better* beat him," said Burke. "I've got everything I own on Flying Wedge." He had him to win. He had him to place. He even broke a rule and put a few dollars on him to show. But mostly, of course, he had him in the Perfecta. That was the plan. If Burke and Company were to stay in business, he had to cash a goodly number of tickets after the seventh race. And not only Burke. There was Pierce. And there was——

But never mind! No use letting the whole world in on this thing. They had kept it to a minimum. An absolute minimum. The fewer people in the know, the better.

The first hint of disaster came when Maple weighed in at 113. Maple couldn't believe his eyes, or his ears. The scales must be wrong. But there was no arguing the fact: he was a pound overweight. Flying Wedge would carry 113 on this trip. He should have laid off the potato yesterday. But it had only been *half* a potato. He'd had no water all morning, and his mouth was dry as dust. But they had to live with 113 pounds. It was on the program. You can suck in your gut, but you can't lose a pound while you're standing on the official scales.

No great change of plans, however. Everybody who knew about that one pound overweight shrugged their shoulders and put another ten-spot to place. The Perfecta was still good. First or second, Flying Wedge would share in the Perfecta. At least, that was the plan. In the jockey's room, before the race, there was an unusual silence. None of the customary banter that precedes almost any race. Maple had things on his mind, and ordinarily he would have said them. But not today. His mouth was dry, and he felt just the hint of a knot in the muscles of his stomach. More than once he looked in the direction of Walter Blum. But Blum was perhaps the most casual man in the room. His face was lined, but the lines were not the lines of worry, or even concern. Blum was getting along in years.

Walter Blum was one of the professionals. A steady jockey. He'd been in the game much longer than most of the fellows in the room today. He'd grown up at tracks in the east and the north, as well as the south. He'd raced against Howard Grant and Nick Shuk and Willie Hartack at Pimlico and Laurel and Bowie in Maryland, back in the middle fifties and later. He'd watched Hartack go from a raw apprentice to the top, while the career of Walter Blum had rocked along without distinction. Blum was a reliable old propeller job, while Hartack was a jet. Not that Blum ever complained. He'd had a good life, for a jockey. He'd made money in his time. He was still making money. He had four mounts today, and he'd just picked up a few hundred by winning the fourth race on the maiden, First Standing. He'd beaten out Rivera by a neck, which had taken some doing, since Rivera was on Bold and Fancy, one of Vogell's horses. First Standing was an unknown quantity, but Blum had him out front at the quarter and was never headed. The stretch drive had been a dilly, and the finish was a photo. Rivera thought he had had it. But Blum was in front by a neck on First Standing, and the colt had paid $34.20 to win. The Perfecta had been nice: $562.20. Walter had done well on both counts.

In this seventh race, also a Perfecta race, Blum was riding a Fabry horse called Blue Moral, who would be favored by the fans. Not *the* favorite, perhaps, but he would be up there in the first three. Value to the winner was $3,300, and he wouldn't mind pocketing $330 for the ride. He knew his competition. There were two to beat: Idealic and Full of Fight. He was aware, too, of Flying Wedge, and rumor had it that Flying Wedge was *the* horse in the race. Blum didn't think so. The race would be over before Flying Wedge got started. The stretch duel would probably be between Blue Moral and Full of Fight, a horse being ridden today by Cordero. Full of Fight was one of Berrie's horses and on his last two outings Blum had been aboard. He'd finished third and sixth, and when it came to today's race, Monteiro had given the mount to Cordero. Blum really didn't mind. He would just as soon be aboard Full of Fight, but he was sure that Blue Moral was the better horse. Hernandez had ridden the gelding on his last out, but Hernandez was on Idealic today. Idealic was a Jan Hirsch horse and would undoubtedly go to the post the favorite. Idealic had earned better than $9000 last year, and he had only once run in a class as low as today's $10,000. Blum walked out of the jockey's room into the Florida sunshine. This was Monday, blue Monday, and the hunch bettors would be all over him.

"Blum on Blue Moral," the hunch bettors would say.

Up in the clubhouse stands, Sam Hirsch was almost ready. He'd already had a pretty good day, but he had been looking forward with particular interest to this seventh race. He'd picked up $400 on Brush Man in the second race, not under his regular system but using the Automatic Method, which is the subject of this chapter. Brush Man was the fourth-down from the top odds and paid $20 to place. Sam had two $20 win tickets and two of the same to place on Brush Man, for a net of $360 on the race. He also had $20 to show, which brought back $92, so that his actual net on the race was $430.

He'd also won the fourth race, both ways (that is, including the Perfecta), and had done that on his automatic system, too. He'd done that on the basis of the Rule which states—but we'll get into that in a moment.

The point is, he'd made $1,122 on his straight bets and $2,811 on the Perfecta. He was well ahead of the banker, and he was prepared for some heavy investing in the seventh. It was another Perfecta, and he had two qualifiers, Odd Z and Flying Wedge, the Number-one horse and the Number-three horse, both of whom were 45-1 on the board. Odd Z dropped to 40-1 and eventually went off at 41-1. Lord Godolphin was now at 45-1, along with Flying Wedge. Lord Godolphin was essentially dropping in class, but his last race had been at $10,000 and he'd finished eighth, about twenty lengths off the winner. Lord Godolphin could muster only three points and was out of contention. Here is the chart for Flying Wedge, and you can see how Sam got five points to Qualify the colt. The last race, at $14,000 was so bad that Sam didn't regard it as a race at all. It was a workout, with Maple trailing the field after getting out of the gate first.

Flying Wedge 112 Br. c (1970), by The Axe II.—Jetaway, by Polly's Jet.
Breeder, W.P. Burke & J. Atkins (Ky.). 1974 1 0 0 0 (—)

Owner, W.P. Burke.	Trainer, J.H. Pierce, Jr.					$9,000		1973 3 0 0 0			$525
Jan17-74^{10}GP	①a1$\frac{1}{16}$	1:54³/ssf 78	112	1½ 10^{18}	12^{30}	12^{34}	MapleE^5 14000	Sir Omni 114	Olmedo		Big Hobo 12
Jun 8-73⁴Mth	1$\frac{1}{16}$	1:44¹/sft 11	115	2¹ 2⁴	4$\frac{7}{2}$	4^{11}	Marq'zCH^5 Mdn 73	Ap's'ceV'nd'r115	P'ceGlad		St'gAtEve 7
May14-73⁷GS	①1$\frac{1}{16}$	1:43 fm 3$\frac{3}{4}$e	113	2² 7^{12}	11^{20}	11^{16}	Tich'norW^7 Alw 74	Trist'sPl'ge114	T'yH'ml't		ViveLaFr'ce 12
Apr30-73⁴GP	6 f	1:11²/sft 3½	120	5$\frac{3}{4}$ 4⁴	5⁵	5⁷	PerretC¹ Mdn 80	Mod Art 120	Algory Jeff		Prince Glad 9
May17-72⁴GS	5 f	:59²/sft170	120	8$\frac{7}{4}$ 5⁸	4$\frac{6}{2}$	5$\frac{7}{4}$	PerretC⁴ Mdn 81	See theU.S.A. 120	N't'lR's'lve		D'keT'm 12
Apr14-72³Hia	5 f	:59³/sft 56	120	10^{17} 10^{18}	10^{16}	8^{18}	Thorn'gB^5 Mdn	Decimator120	Mr.Debonair		Cheriepe 10
	Feb 14 Hia 6f ft 1:15b				Feb 5 Hia 5f ft 1:03b				Jan 29 Hia 5f ft 1:01h		

Flying Wedge last raced on January 17, just over a month ago, but he had had two good workouts recently, one on February 5 and the last on the fourteenth, which gave him two points.

He was running today at $9,000 (really at $10,000), and Sam went back to his June 8 race to finish his qualification. Flying Wedge also had one point for a $4,000 drop in class.

When a horse is dropping in class, you go back to the race, or to one of the races, prior to the last race. Flying Wedge finished fourth on June 8, and that finish was worth one point. His race-rating of four plus eleven, or fifteen, was worth another point, for a total of five. Flying Wedge was Q1, and since the odds were 45-1, Sam bet him across the board twice, at $20 each time, for a total investment in straight bets of $120. Odd Z got a similar bet.

The Perfecta was a little more difficult to figure. He lined up Q1 and Q2 and F1, F2, F3, and F4, putting the latter three in a box with Q1 and Q2. As always, he bet F1 ONLY with Q1 and Q2. There was no percentage in crisscrossing F1 and F2, since the payoffs were abominably low. After all, everybody else was doing that.

Sam then made several bets under the automatic system, and he returned to the stands to watch the race. It was just at that point, six minutes before the race was to go off, that he noticed something. He read again the conditions of the race, which was for four-year-olds and upward, a mile and a sixteenth on the turf, weight 122 pounds. He wondered idly how it was that Flying Wedge was getting in at 113, and he checked the chart. Just then, he noted the coincidence: the fact that Flying Wedge had last raced on January 17 and the fact that January 17 was the cut-off date in the race conditions for a six-pound allowance. He saw, too, that Flying Wedge was one pound over. His chart said 112. The Program had him at 113. The loudspeaker voice said: "The Number-three horse, Flying Wedge, is one pound over."

Sam stared at that date, January 17, in the conditions, and he stared at the chart on Flying Wedge, which also said January 17, the date of Flying Wedge's last race. Sam stood up automatically. It was now four minutes to post time and the horses were making their way to the gate.

"It doesn't mean a thing!" Sam told himself as he walked to the windows. He had his wallet in his hand. Racing secretaries don't write conditions just to fit one horse in a race. The whole thing was an accident of chance. Still....

Sam doubled each of his investments and was returning to his seat when the bell rang, locking the machines at the windows. The horses were off. He never made it back to his seat. He watched the race standing up, standing next to one of the uniformed attendants who monitored traffic in and out of the boxes in the clubhouse stands. At the quarter, Blum had Blue Moral out in front. At the half, Blue Moral was leading by two lengths, with Barbsfirstbid second, and Ringsend third. Odd Z had dropped from second to fourth at the half, and Flying Wedge was staggering along in ninth place. At the three-quarters, it was Blue Moral by a head, with Barbsfirstbid second, and two lengths back came Ringsend. Sam licked his lips, but he wasn't really worried yet. He was waiting to see the line-up at the head of the stretch. He didn't have long to wait. As they came into the stretch it was still Blue Moral in the lead. Blum had won the fourth, and he was going for another in the seventh. Sam had Blue Moral in the Perfecta with Flying Wedge and Odd Z, but that was all. He would just as soon Blue Moral would wear himself out and quit. Oddly enough, that is precisely what happened. Blue Moral had nothing left for the stretch drive.

Flying Wedge came round the stretch turn in seventh place, but only three lengths separated him from Blue Moral. Watching Maple, Sam could see that Flying Wedge was on his way. Ringsend was still third by a head over Full of Fight, who showed up in fourth place and was driving for the wire. Blum had had too much confidence in Blue Moral's powers of endurance. The gelding quit and coasted in to finish eighth.

The stretch duel, as Pierce and Maple had guessed, was between Flying Wedge and Full of Fight. This was fine with Sam, too. He wanted Flying Wedge under the wire first, and when the two horses crosssed the line they were driving hard. But it was Full of Fight by a length, with Flying Wedge second. One length too late. One pound too much. At 112, Maple would have had a photo-finish, perhaps a win, if only by a nose. One pound! One half a potato! Flying Wedge paid $40.20 to place (which was nice) but think of the money to win: in round numbers, $90 for every $2 to win. It didn't happen. The plan failed by a pound, by a length. But the stable was not badly off. Place was well covered, and of course the big money was in the Perfecta, which paid $598.40 for every $2 on the correct combination of 11-and-3.

Sam grossed $1930 on his straight bets and $5984 on the Perfecta, for a total gross on the race of $7914. He didn't stop to figure the net. He felt drained. It was as though he himself had run the race. He decided against the remainder of the program, and he walked out to the parking lot. For ten minutes he couldn't find his car. But it was there somewhere, and eventually he stumbled onto it. He was happy but a little dazed. Driving home, he kept thinking about that January 17 date. He could really make nothing of it.

"Forget it!" Sam told himself.

No use worrying over a simple date. The point was Sam had a system that worked. The odds were his guiding light. If the horse had some capabilities to meet the odds, then Sam had a bet. After all, it was a simple system, and the rules were logical rules. The seventh race at Gulfstream Park might have been set up, or it might not have been. It really didn't matter a great deal. Sam had the odds covered. When the big payoffs came, Sam was there. And that went double for the automatic system. It hadn't worked in the seventh race, but it had saved him in the fourth race. That was the beauty of the two systems: they dovetailed to cover the big ones.

It's time, now, to take a look at Sam's absolutely automatic system of winner selecting. There is no qualifying to do. All you need to play the automatic system is the odds board itself. You could do everything in your head, if you remembered a couple of simple rules. Sam used it faithfully during January and February at Gulfstream, and it paid off in flat-bet profits. Using simple escalation, after a series of hits, it would pay a fortune. He was working on that, too. That was a part of money management.

SAM'S AUTOMATIC METHOD (SAM)

Make your selections from the odds board about five or six minutes before post time. Select no horse whose odds are 50-1 or higher.

Rule Number One

In a field of nine or more horses, select the following:

a) The horse whose odds are 3-Down from the top, *if* those odds are between 09-1 and 49-1. If the #3-Down horse is dropping in class, or has a last-rating of less than ten, he may qualify with odds of 26-1 to 49-1. Calculate the last-race rating by adding the finish position to the number of lengths off the winner.

b) The horse whose odds are 4-Down from the top, *if* those odds are 22-1 to 49-1. If the #4-Down horse is dropping in class or had a last-race rating of ten or less, he may qualify with odds of 15-1 to 49-1.

c) The horse whose odds are 5-Down from the top, *if* those odds are equal to or higher than the number of horses in the race. Take no five-down horse whose odds are 50-1 or higher.

d) In the first race (or first half of the daily double), in Perfecta-Exacta races, and in maiden races, take the horse whose odds are six-down from the top, if those odds are equal to or higher than the number of horses in the race, but not to exceed 49-1.

e) In a few scattered races, particularly in fields of eleven or twelve horses, you may find a horse whose odds are 7-Down from the top and are at or above 15-1. If this occurs, select the #7-Down horse, the #5-Down horse and the #3-Down horse, provided their odds do not exceed 49-1.

f)   In even rarer races, the #8-Down horse will have odds of 13-1 or higher. Should this occur, take this horse, the #5-Down horse and the #3-Down horse as your selections, provided the latter two are not above 49-1.

Rule Number Two

In fields of eight horses or less, select *only* the #3-Down horse for investment. The odds, of course, should be equal to or higher than the number of horses in the race.

Daily Doubles

Examine all the horses in the first half of the daily double, and select those that qualify under any part of the two rules above. You will generally have from two to four qualifiers in the first race. Combine these with the following in the second half of the daily double:

a)   All horses who have probable odds listed at 5-1 or higher, provided:

b)   They are dropping in class. This drop may be from the last race to today's race, or the drop may be from the second or third race back *if* those races have been run within 30 days. *and:*

c)   The race-rating from the race used to calculate the drop should be less than twenty-five. *and:*

d)   If you have more than two horses that qualify on all three counts above, select the two which have the lowest last-race ratings, *plus* (if any) all those that have qualified on the three counts above *and* have gained four or more lengths in the stretch run of that last race. You will end up with from two to four selections in the second half of the double, which should be combined with the qualifiers in the first half, for your daily double selections. The total should be around six to eight tickets, but rarely if ever will exceed sixteen tickets. Average investment: $16.

The only possible qualifiers for the first-race selections must come from one of the following three groups:

1)   One or more of these four: #3-down, #4-down, #5-down

and #6-down. Or:

2)   #3-down, #5-down and #7-down. Or:

3)   #3-down, #5-down and #8-down.

In the second half of the double, you consider only those horses which have probable odds listed at 5-1 or more in the morning line. Of these horses, take only those which are dropping in class, as defined above. Of these, take only those which have a last-race rating of less than twenty-five. Of these, take the two with the lowest last-race ratings. These ratings must come, of course, from the last race at a higher class than today's class. Add to these two any horse still in contention who also gained four or more lengths in the stretch run of his last race at a higher class. If the horse gained two or three lengths in the stretch run (but not as many as four), and still has a recent race or workout, or some other good qualification, take him along. You'll never get more than four horses.

Perfecta—Exacta Selections

Take those horses which qualify under any part of the two rules given above and combine with the following:

a)   If you have only one qualifier, which will be called 1Q:

1Q with F4, F5 and F6 (in fields of 10 or more): 12 tickets*
1Q and F1, F1 and 1Q; 1Q with F2, F2 with 1Q: 4
1Q with F3, and F3 with 1Q: 2
                                            ―――――
                                            18 tickets

*1Q with F3, F4, and F5 in fields of nine or less, which will eliminate the need for a separate 1Q-F3 purchase, making sixteen tickets in all.

b)   If you have two qualifiers, 1Q and 2Q, combine with the following:

1Q with F4, F5, and F6, in fields of ten or more horses: 12 tickets†
1Q—F1 and F1—1Q: and 1Q—F2, F2—1Q: 4
2Q—F4 and F4—2Q: 2
2Q—F5 and F5—2Q: 2
2Q—F1 and F1—2Q: 2
2Q—F2 and F2—2Q: 2
                                         ―――――
                                         24 tickets

†1Q with F3, F4 and F5 in fields of nine or less horses.

c) If you have three qualifiers, 1Q, 2Q and 3Q, combine with following:

In fields of ten or more, 1Q with F4, F5 and F6:   12 tickets
(In fields of nine or less: 1Q with F3, F4, and F5)

1Q—F1, and F1—1Q; and 1Q—F2, and F2—1Q:	4
2Q—F4 and F4—2Q; and 2Q—F5 and F5—2Q:	4
2Q—F1 and F1—2Q; and 2Q—F2, F2—Q2:	4
3Q—F4 and F4—3Q; and 3Q—F5 and F5—3Q:	4
3Q—F1 and F1—3Q; and 3Q—F2, and F2—3Q:	4
	32 tickets

d) If you have four qualifiers, 1Q, 2Q, 3Q and 4Q, combine as follows:

1Q with F4, F5, and F6 (in fields of ten or more): 12 tickets
(1Q with F3, F4, and F5 in fields of nine or less.)

1Q—F1, F1—1Q; 1Q—F2, and F2—1Q:	4
2Q—F4, F4—2Q; 2Q—F5, F5—2Q:	4
2Q—F1, F1—2Q; 2Q—F2, and F2—2Q:	4
3Q—F4, F4—3Q; 3Q—F5, and F5—3Q:	4
3Q—F1, F1—3Q; 3Q—F2, and F2—3Q:	4
4Q—F4, F4—4Q; 4Q—F5, and F5—4Q:	4
4Q—F1, F1—4Q; 4Q—F2 and F2—4Q:	4
	40 tickets

The Perfecta-Exacta selections are really not as complicated as they appear in the above chart, but a few basic rules are in order.

1Q is generally the #5-Down qualifier, when there is only one qualifier.

Where there are two or more qualifiers, take #5-Down (if it is in the group) as the 1Q for purposes of making up the box of four horses. That is, use #5-Down with F4, F5, and F6, for crisscrossing, at a cost of twelve tickets, when the field is 10 or more horses. If the field is nine or less, use #5-Down with F3, F4 and F5.

Where there are several qualifiers, 2Q may arbitrarily be designated as #3-Down, 3Q as #4-Down, and 4Q as #6-Down. Use your own judgment. If you have any past results to go on, use these to help select the appropriate Q-number for a specific number-down. At Gulfstream, for example, Sam used #3-Down for 2Q, whereas at Santa Anita he would use #6-Down as 2Q, since experience showed that #6-Down recurred more frequently than any other except #5-Down, which is still 1Q.

There are no other boxes used except the first one with 1Q as noted above. The remainder of the combinations are between two horses. 1Q—F1 and F1—1Q simply means that you are playing the #5-Down horse to win and the Favorite to place, whereas you are also playing the Favorite to win and the #5-Down to place. And so on, with any two horses.

The more qualifiers you have in a Perfecta race, the higher the investment. You may wish to reduce the number by comparing any two and eliminating one. A simple method is to take a dropping horse over a horse going up in class, unless the horse going up is a real standout. Take a male horse over a filly or mare. If you get the five-race ratings of two horses, and one is about half the total of the other, take the higher and throw out the lower.

Or you may look at F3 in a race and discover that he is much better, on the matter of form, than the F6. F3, for example, is dropping three or four thousand in class and F6 was claimed last race and is moving up in class. F3 is a colt, whereas F6 is a mare. In such instances, substitute F3 for F6 in your box with 1Q. Statistics show that F3 is involved in Perfecta payoffs about three times for every one by F6. Of course, the F6 payoffs are higher. But sometimes we are more interested in frequency than in individual payoffs. This is especially true when we are going progressively upward in our investment program.

In the race where #7-Down is a qualifier, combine him with F1, F2, and F3 in a ten-horse field, but only with F1 and F2 in a nine-horse field.

Similarly, if #8-Down is a qualifier, combine him with F1, F2, and F3 in an eleven-horse field, but only with F1 and F2 in a ten-horse field. The reason is obvious. After all, in a ten-horse field, #8-Down and F3 are the same horse. At Santa Anita, as you will see from the accompanying charts, in the seventh race on February 9, #8-Down combined with F3 in an eleven-horse field, for a payoff of $513.50. The #8-Down had odds of 13-1 and was actually the same as F4. But our system calls for counting down from the top, which is the reason for designating the horse #8-Down. The rule that emerges from all this is simple: you never combine #7-Down or #8-Down with any horse carrying higher

odds than #7 or #8, but with favorites carrying odds lower than
his. You have many fewer combinations, of course. The cost is
light and the frequency of occurrence is rare. To catch that #8—
F3 payoff, the investment was six tickets (#8 with F1, F2 and
F3), costing $12.

SAM'S AUTOMATIC METHOD

CHART I   Gulfstream Park, January 19–February 20, 1974

Date	Race	#3-Down 33-1 Up		#4-Down 22-1 Up	#5-Down Nr. in race		#6-Down 16-1 Up
Jan. 19:	1			27-1	20-1		16-1
Sat.	2				13-1		
	4			22-1	21-1		20-1
	6(8)	11-1					
		24.20	11.60				
	7				14-1		
	8				13-1		
	9(8)	13-1					
Perfecta:	10(8)	15-1					
#3 & F4		32.40	11.80				
$327.40							
Jan. 21:	1	39-1		23-1	17-1		16-1
Mon.	2			22-1	17-1		
	3				12-1		
	4	35-1		31-1	19-1		19-1
	5	37-1		29-1	16-1		
	7			26-1	25-1		
	8				20-1		
	9				16-1		
Perfecta:	10	44-1	90.80	28-1	25-1		19-1
#3 & F5		36.40	21.60				
$1196.40							
Jan. 22:	1	36-1		24-1	17-1(P)	15.00	
Tues.	2				17-1		
	3	48-1		23-1	20-1		
	4	36-1		28-1	28-1		
	6	36-1			15-1		
	7				17-1	36.00	
#5 & F1:					9.20	6.20	
$158.00	10				15-1		

The preceeding chart covers but three of the twenty-seven days between January 19 and February 19, 1974, at Gulfstream Park. It illustrates how Sam kept his records and gives a fair idea of the frequency of hits. For example, during the three days shown in the chart, #3-Down was a qualifier in eleven races, and there were three occasions when it was a winner, the last one of the series coming on January 21, in the tenth race, when it was at 44-1 and paid $90.80 to win. In the Perfecta, the payoff was $1,196.40, and the other horse was F5. There were four qualifiers in this Perfecta race: #3 at 44-1, #4 at 28-1, #5 at 25-1, and #6 at 19-1. Before the race, when making up the combinations, #3 was 2Q and combined with F5.

Rather than take up space in presenting the entire twenty-seven days in this detailed manner, we have chosen to include a summary of the results in Chart II on pages 157-58. All investments are based on the $2 unit. It was estimated that, on an average, each Perfecta race cost $48, or twenty-four tickets. Some were a bit lower, others a bit higher. The total investment in Perfecta for the twenty-seven racing days was $3888, and the net profit was $2,833.60, for a 75 percent return on your money. In the grand totals, you will note that the overall investment, for all wagers, was $5,760, with a net profit of $5,380, or a return of 90 percent on your money in a period covering about thirty days. All of this comes from flat-bet wagers and does not take into consideration any of the methods of money management which are discussed later. Progressive "action", as you may imagine, would increase the net profit and the percentage of return manyfold.

CHART II   Gulfstream Park, Hallandale, Florida
(January 19–February 19, 1974)

	#3-Down		#4-Down		#5-Down		#6-Down		Totals	
	Win	*Place*	*Win*	*Place*	*Win*	*Place*	*Win*	*Place*	*Win*	*Place*
STRAIGHT Return	518.00	259.20	406.60	249.20	592.20	391.60	138.00	89.00	1654.80	989.60
Invested	184.00	184.00	194.00	194.00	350.00	350.00	74.00	74.00	802.00	802.00
Net Profit	334.00	75.20	212.60	55.20	242.20	41.60	64.00	15.60	852.80	187.60
Percentage	183%	42%	110%	29%	71%	13%	86%	21%	106%	22%

CHART II (continued)

DOUBLES					
Return	00	272.00	1355.60	146.40	1774.00
Invested	56.00	72.00	104.00	36.00	268.00
Net Profit	−56.00	200.00	1251.60	110.40	1506.00
Percentage	0%	277%	1203%	334%	561%
PERFECTAS					
Return	3620.20	1126.60	1412.60	562.20	6721.60
Invested	27 Days	81 Races	$48 Per	Total:	3888.00
Net Profit					2833.60
Percentage					75%

Data Base:
Total Number of Racing Days: 27
Total Number of Races: 270
Total Number of Perfectas   81
Nr. of #3-Down Qualifiers: 92
Nr. of #4-Down Qualifiers: 97
Nr. of #5-Down Qualifiers: 175
Nr. of #6-Down Qualifiers: 37

GRAND TOTALS	
Return	11140.00
Invested	5760.00
Net Profit	5380.00
Percentage	90%

CHART III   Santa Anita Park, Arcadia, California
(January 18–February 18, 1974)

	#3-Down		#4-Down		#5-Down		#6-Down		Totals	
	Win	Place	Win	Place	Win	Place	Win	Place	Win	Place
STRAIGHT										
Return	241.40	134.60	161.40	95.40	324.60	151.00	354.40	298.60	1081.80	679.60
Invested	146.00	146.00	148.00	148.00	218.00	218.00	144.00	144.00	656.00	656.00
Net Profit	95.40	−11.40	13.40	−52.60	106.60	−67.00	210.40	154.60	425.80	23.60
Percentage									65%	4%
DOUBLES										
Return	Avg: 8 tickets, or $16 per day								2089.80	
Invested									432.00	
Net Profit									657.80	
Percentage									152%	
EXACTAS										
Return	Avg: 24 tickets, or $120 per race at $5 per ticket								9482.00	
Invested									8280.00	

CHART III (continued)

Net Profit		1602.00
Percentage		19%

		GRAND TOTALS	
Number of racing days:	23	Return	13333.20
Number of races:	197	Invested	10024.00
Number of Exactas:	69	Net Profit	3309.20
Nr. of #3 Qualifiers:	73	Percentage	33%
Nr. of #4 Qualifiers:	74		
Nr. of #5 Qualifiers:	109		
Nr. of #6 Qualifiers:	72		

CHART IV   Winning Exactas, SAM Selections (Santa Anita Park, January 18–February 18, 1974)

Jan. 19:	5^{12}	F4 and #6-Down	$ 712.00
	9^8	#3-Down and F1	161.00
Jan. 24:	5^{12}	#5-Down and F2	524.50
Jan. 26:	7^{14}	#6-Down and F2	524.50
	9^{10}	#5-Down and F3	509.50
Jan. 27:	5^{10}	#4-Down and F6	545.50
	7^{10}	#5-Down and F1	157.50
Jan. 30:	5^{12}	#5-Down and F1	269.50
Jan. 31:	9^{11}	#5-Down and F1	383.50
Feb. 1:	7^9	#6-Down and F3	348.50
Feb. 2:	7^{10}	F1 and #5-Down	112.00
Feb. 7:	5^{12}	F5 and #6-Down	1,663.50
Feb. 8:	5^9	#3-Down and F1	217.00
Feb. 9:	7^{11}	#8-Down and F3	513.50
	9^{12}	F4 and #6-Down	1,027.50
Feb. 10:	5^{11}	#5-Down and F2	904.50
	9^{12}	F4 and #6-Down	567.50
Feb. 15:	5^{10}	#6-Down and F2	341.00

Total Invested: $8,280.00   Gross Return: $9,482.00
Net Profit: $1,602.00

7

Money Management

Among those who know, the controversy still rages as to which is more important: the system or technique of winner selection or the method of money management. Certainly both are important. Both are part of what Sam Lewin calls *The Education of a Horseplayer*.[1] Sam Toperoff, the scholar, poet and teacher, said it best in his fascinating little book, *Crazy Over Horses:*[2] "Handicapping is a skill, an art maybe; but betting is purely business."

Sam Hirsch would say it just a little differently perhaps. Handicapping is both a skill and an art It has the makings of becoming also a science. But the investment of money is strictly a business proposition. Money is capital, and capital is some thing without which you cannot operate your business. Being a very practical and hardheaded person, Sam knows that money is at the root of everything. But handicapping or winner selec tion is also essential. Without a reasonably good system of win ner (or in-the-money) selection, there would soon be no capital

1. Sam Lewin, *The Education of a Horseplayer* (New York: Hawthorn Books).
2. Sam Toperoff, *Crazy Over Horses* (Boston: Little, Brown), p. 54

to manage. It would be foolhardy, for instance, to attempt *both* of Sam's systems simultaneously without five or six thousand dollars in hand—or part of it in hand while the remainder lies in the bank, ready for emergency use. One big trouble faces you in the beginning: making investments at the track seems like gambling. The floor is covered with useless tickets. Appearances are deceptive, however. Nothing contained herein is a plea or an argument or an inducement to gamble. Never. If Sam has one very strong conviction about the horseracing business, it is this: do NOT gamble. In the name of all that is holy, do NOT venture money that cannot be reasonably lost. Spend only from your entertainment fund or from your investment capital. If you're out to kill a pleasant afternoon, the entertainment fund is your source of supply. It will be gone by the end of the day, but worry not one moment. You have had your fun. Only one man (or woman) in a thousand goes home a winner. And remember that the phrase "only one in a thousand" is more than a figure of speech: it is a fact of life.

So, the first rule is to go prepared for the worst. Take along enough capital (from the capital investment fund) to cover the entire day's work. Do not count on a single favorable return during the entire program. If you're using both systems, you can be sure there will be some return during the day. But never count on it. Those returns could very well be deferred until the following day. And furthermore, when you come back the second day, regardless of what happened the day before, come rejoicing but come prepared for a long and discouraging day. And keep coming with all necessary assets.

If you are of an extremely conservative nature, you will naturally wish to conduct your business on what is known as a flat-bet basis. That is, you will make your investments the same each time on each horse in each race. And $2 is the minimum unit you may use, except, as noted earlier, that Exacta tickets in California cost $5 each. But we will assume here that you are at Hialeah in Florida, or at Aqueduct in New York. Your basic unit of capital is $2. This is true for straight wagers, for Daily Doubles, and for Perfecta or Exacta combinations. All the calculations made in the tables or charts presented in this volume are on a flat-bet basis. There is no "progression," either after losses or after winnees. Using both of Sam's systems of play, you will earn considerable profit, following the flat-bet method of investing. You will be especially successful if you play *only to win*. Much of the time, place wagering shows only a slight profit, or even a slight loss during a period of time, such as a week or a month. There are times, too, when place wagering shows a very good profit, but this cannot be counted on. Place wagering should actually be used only with "progressive" action.

The wisdom of this can best be illustrated by a concrete example. If you will refer to the Summary at the end of Chart X, which records the results at Aqueduct during April, 1972, you will find that the gross return on place investments on Q1 and Q2 for the 24-day period came to $872.60, on an investment of $864. Not an encouraging figure. Now look at what happens when we use a simple form of "progression" based on an advancement of one unit on every fourth hit. For simplicity of presentation, we will start with $10 units and will advance $10 every fourth hit, until we reach $100. After four hits at $100, we will drop back to $20 and proceed by advancing $10 every fourth hit. The Table that follows shows exactly how this is accomplished and what results it brings.

Beginning with the first race on April 1, we lost $20 (that is, two $10 place investments on Q1 and Q2). Thus, the entry for the second race that day shows that we are "in" for a total of $40, representing the two tickets we lost on the first race and the two we have invested in the second race. Our first hit comes in the second race, when Q2Po Morrosen comes in at 10–1 and pays $12.60 to place.

TABLE I

Date	Race	Hit Number	Number of Tickets	Unit Cost	Total Cost	Return	Net/Race
Ap. 1	2	1	4	$10	$ 40	$ 63	23
	4	2	4	10	40	70	30
	6	3	4	10	40	31	−9
Ap. 3	5	4	16	10	160	40	−120
	6	1	2	20	40	128	88

TABLE I   (continued)

Ap. 4	5	2	16	20	320	60	−260
Ap. 5	3	3	14	20	280	112	−178
Ap. 6	8	4	28	20	560	50	−510
Ap. 7	2	1	6	30	180	1299	1119
	5	2	6	30	180	402	222
	6	3	2	30	60	180	120
Ap. 8	2 Q1	4	10	30	300	270	
	2 Q2	4				192	162
	7	1	10	40	400	528	128
	9	2	4	40	160	428	268
Ap. 10	2	3	4	40	160	448	288
	7	4	10	40	400	184	−216
	8	1	2	50	100	525	425
Ap. 11	4	2	10	50	500	450	−50
	7	3	6	50	300	435	135
	8	4	2	50	100	465	365
Ap. 12	2	1	6	60	360	786	426
	5	2	6	60	360	282	−78
	8	3	6	60	360	330	−30
Ap. 13	1	4	4	60	240	342	102
	3	1	4	70	280	583	303
	4	2	2	70	140	462	322
	6	3	4	70	280	987	707
Ap. 14	1	4	8	70	560	854	294
	6	1	10	80	800	208	−592
	8	2	4	80	320	320	0
Ap. 15	8	3	18	80	1440	232	−1208
Ap. 18	2	4	24	80	1920	704	−1216
	3 Q1	1	2	90	180	1008	
	3 Q2	1				864	1692
Ap. 19	8	2	14	90	1260	594	−666
Ap. 20	4	3	10	90	900	758	−142
	6	4	4	90	360	378	18
	8	1	4	100	400	520	120
	9	2	2	100	200	660	460
Ap. 21	4	3	8	100	800	630	−170
	5	4	2	100	200	500	300
	7	1	4	20	80	82	2

TABLE I   (continued)

	8	2	2	20	40	128	88
Ap. 22	2	3	6	20	120	86	−46
	6	4	8	20	160	88	−72
Ap. 24	1	1	8	30	240	372	132
	6	2	10	30	300	117	−183
Ap. 25	5	3	16	30	480	213	−267
	8	4	6	30	180	456	276
Ap. 26	6	1	14	40	560	160	−400
	7	2	2	40	80	104	24
Ap. 27	1	3	6	40	240	432	192
	2	4	2	40	80	292	212
	4	1	4	50	200	200	0
	5	2	2	50	100	130	30
Ap. 28	9	3	13	50	650	380	−270

TOTALS: Plus Returns: $ 9,173.00
         Minus Returns: −6,683.00
           Net Profit: $ 2,490.00

(See the first page of Chart X, for the complete record.) Our $10 place ticket on Morrosen brings in $63. Less our $40 investment, we have a net profit of $23. In the third race, we have no return, but in the fourth Folsom Blues (Q2⁴) at 17-1 comes in to place, paying $14 for $2. Again, our total investment in two races comes to $40, and the return is $70, for a net profit of $30 on the race. Note that the net profit shown in the final right-hand column is for each race and is not a cumulative total. That cumulative total comes at the end of the Table.

We will not detail each day's activity, but note that our first large investment comes at the beginning of the fifth race on April 3, when we have bought a total of sixteen tickets at $10 each, including the two on the fifth race itself. Our total investment to that point is $160, and our return is an unfortunate $8.00 to place on Messmate, or $40 in all, leaving us minus $120 on the race. As it happens during this April, 1972, we will have nineteen such negative results; that is, we will get back *less* than we have invested in the series between the last hit and this particular hit. On April 15, for example, we will be up to $80 units, and we will buy a total of eighteen tickets before our hit in the eighth race. Once again, the hit is an unfortunately low one: $5.80 to place on Odie Bob at 14-1. But we recoup $232 and note a loss of $1208 on the series. This is the fourth hit in the $80 series, and our next unit is $90. We need only two tickets, or $180, to bring back a double hit in the third race on April 18. Vain Beauty (Q1[1]) places at $22.40 and Huge Joke wins, paying a place price of $19.20. Our several tickets bring back $1,872, and we have a net profit on that race of $1,692.

When we come to the end of the series on April 28, finishing with the ninth race, we tally up our plus side of the ledger, which comes to $9,173. We deduct our minus side, a total of $6,683, and we arrive at a final net profit on the series of twenty-four-days of $2,490. This compares with a flat-bet profit of $8.60 for the same series, using $2 units. By advancing $10 on every fourth hit, we were, in effect, advancing $2.50 on or after each hit. Advances in the progression are made only after a hit, or a series of hits, never after a loss or a series of losses.

In this form of money management, Sam advocates a cut-off feature to prevent a prolonged series of losses. If your investment in one of the short internal series reaches $2,000, then drop back in $10 steps; that is, drop back $10 in the unit cost for every fourth loss. We regress at the same rate as we progressed, until we reach a hit. You will note that on April 18, the total investment in a series reached $1920. That was the exact moment when we made a double hit, and we did not have to regress. We proceeded to the $100-unit level, and after four hits on that level (the fifth race on April 21) we dropped back to $20-units, advancing by $10 steps every fourth hit from then until the April 28, which ended the series.

As stated above, this is a very simple form of progressive action, and it is based on the principle that you should advance only after a hit, or a succession of hits. The $2000-cut-off feature is there to prevent an unusually long series of no-hits, which sometimes occur, that is, to prevent such a series from exhausting your supply of capital. Clearly, if you are using this same progression in win betting, you will need a minimum capital supply of from $2,000 to $3,000, the same being required for place investments. Capital supply for the daily doubles and for Perfectas must be above and beyond these requirements. If you are also using Sam's Automatic Method, capital supply for *that* series requires from $2,000 up, according to your basic units. Perhaps the best way to get started, if you wish to do so on a minimum investment, is to follow one system until your profit allows you to participate in both systems. Begin with the Q1, Q2 system and play to win only, on a progressive basis, starting with $5 or $10 units and moving up $5 or $10 every fourth or fifth hit. At the same time, you will be investing in Doubles and Perfectas, using $2 units. It may be quite a period of time before you can indulge yourself in $10 Doubles and in multiple-Perfecta tickets. By that time, you should be managing not your own money but track money.

On the other hand, "perhaps" is not the way to launch yourself on the journey, the adventure, and the serious business of making a million at the races, and that, after all, is the point of the whole thing. Also, it may appear from statements made earlier that a large capital investment is necessary. That is true only if you wish to accelerate the process, and always the idea is in the back of our minds: do it now and make it fast. A large capital investment is necessary *if* you want to have some back-up money ready in case of emergencies. And, *if* you want to run three or four branches of the business simultaneously. Sam would say that two or three heads are better than one at the track. The atmosphere is not conducive to the strict conduct of business. Emotion gets hold of one. However, if the head of the corporation is accompanied by his expert handicapper and possibly by his top accountant-bookkeeper-secretary, there will certainly be more stability in the handling of company business. Naturally, if the secretary has a cousin named Leslie, and Cuzin Leslie is running in the fifth, there is no good reason why you shouldn't let her put a couple on the nose, regardless of the odds. It's *her* money. And it's not coming out of the investment fund.

It is quite possible to get started along the million-dollar road with less than $1,000. Using the Q1, Q2 system, you can operate the Daily Double end of the business on $50 a day. But with such limited capital, it will be necessary to limit your main-line operation to straight win investments, under a very rigid and profitable system of money management which will be called The Specific Amount Method, in honor of SAM. In this approach, you set the goal for each hit or win in advance, and you tailor your investments to reach that goal, using the odds as your lever. Table II carries all the calculations and records for a three-day application of this method.

In order to be absolutely realistic, we will assume that you are at Gulfstream Park on January 21, which is a Monday, in the year 1974, and that you are going to start your investment program on that Monday and continue throughout the thirty-day period. Your goal is to make $100 on each and every win or hit. This will require some strict bookkeeping, and you set up your notebook in columnar form, as shown in Table II. There is a column for date and race number, for the goal, a column for average odds, a column for investment, one for lose and one for win, and the final column for net. The last two columns will only be needed when a hit occurs.

TABLE II   Gulfstream Park—January 1974

Date	Race	$ Goal	Avg. Odds	Investment Q1	Q2	Q3	Loss	Win	Net
1-21	1	108.00	27	4.00	4.00		8.00		
	2	118.00	22	5.00	5.00		18.00		
	3	128.00	25	5.00	5.00		28.00		
	4	136.00	30	4.00	4.00		36.00		
	5	144.00	40	4.00	4.00		44.00		
	6	154.00	23	5.00	5.00		54.00		
	7	164.00	24	5.00	5.00		64.00		
	8	174.00	28	5.00	5.00		74.00		
	9	189.00	40	5.00	5.00	5.00		187.00	98.00
	10	108:00	30	4.00	4.00			181.60	173.60
1-22	1	110.00	20	5.00	5.00		10.00		
	2	124.00	15	7.00	7.00			130.20	106.20
	3	112.00	40	4.00	4.00	4.00	12.00		
	4	124.00	35	4.00	4.00	4.00	24.00		
	5	139.00	28	5.00	5.00	5.00	39.00		
	6	154.00	40	5.00	5.00	5.00	54.00		

TABLE II   (continued)

	7	174.00	37	10.00	10.00			180.00	106.00
	8	108.00	30	4.00	4.00		8.00		
	9	120.00	25	6.00	6.00		20.00		
	10	128.00	40	4.00	4.00		28.00		
1-23	1	138.00	28	5.00	5.00		38.00		
	2	146.00	41	4.00	4.00		46.00		
	3	170.00	36	8.00	8.00	8.00	70.00		
	4	180.00	44	5.00	5.00		80.00		
	5	210.00	30	10.00	10.00	10.00	110.00		
	6	230.00	25	10.00	10.00		130.00		
	7	250.00	28	10.00	10.00		150.00		
	8	271.00	40	7.00	7.00	7.00	171.00		
	9	301.00	35	10.00	10.00	10.00		341.20	141.20
	10	108.00	37	4.00	4.00			154.00	146.00
Total:						404.00		1174.00	770.00

Beginning with the first race on Monday, we enter under the goal heading the amount of $100 plus the investment needed in this race to gain our $100-goal—in this case a total of $108, since we have two qualifiers in the race, at average odds of 27-1, and we will need two $2 tickets to win on each. If either Q1 or Q2 wins, we will of course meet our goal on the first try. No such luck, however, We lose the first race. Our goal in the second race becomes $118, which equals our desired profit of $100, plus the $8 we just "lost" (see the entry in the loss column), plus the $10 required as our investment in Q1 and Q2 of the second race: $5 to win on each since the odds average only 22-1. We lose again, entering the figure $18 in the loss column, which gives us a cumulative total at the end of each losing race. Note that we lose eight straight races on Monday and are "in" for a total of $89 by the time the horses enter the starting gate. That includes $74 we have already lost and the $15 needed to finance our investments in the ninth race: three horses at $5 each, the odds being around 40-1. Fortune is with us and we win $187, recouping our investment to date and giving us a profit on the series of $98.

We begin the tenth race with a new goal of $100, plus the amount of our investment in that race: or $8 once more, $4 to win on each of Q1 and Q2, at odds around 30-1. We win again, the payoff being a goodly $181.60, for a net profit on that short series of one of $173.60, considerably higher than we aimed for since we hit the high-odds qualifier. We return to our $100 goal in the first race on Tuesday and proceed on our way, losing the first, winning the second, losing a few more, then winning again in the seventh. We have six hits in three days, invest a total of $404, get back $1174, for a net profit of $770. A return of 190 percent.

A few years back, in June of 1971, *Look* Magazine carried an article by James Morgan, entitled: "Can A Computer Beat the Horses?" The subtitle was even more intriguing: "Or how would you like to make $200 million a year?" The article was about a young man known then only as "The Wizard," who was reputed to be making thousands of dollars a month betting on horse races. At the time, this young man, who was under thirty, stated that he *could* be making $200 million a year, which amounted to 5 percent of the money being wagered on horse races annually in America.

"The Wizard" had devised a system to beat the horses. One afternoon at Aqueduct he was impressed by the amount of money being bet on each race and even more by the total amount of money which passed through the mutuel machines in the course of a single day. He said: "Everyone I knew who went to the track always lost, and I didn't think there was really any way to win." But after reading in the *New York Times* about an automatic calculator which was supposed to help one handicap the races, "The Wizard's" imagination was stirred. He bought everything in sight on handicapping and he tried out every gadget he could find at the track. Finally, he came to the conclusion that he would have to go to the computer to process the data needed to discover a system to win. He purchased five years' worth of *Racing Forms*, and he started with Hialeah, analyzing favorites. He dug out enough information on each horse, each favorite, to fill three IBM cards. Every possible pertinent detail was included: the horse and his record, the jockey, the trainer. He looked at 2,000 favorites and filled 6,000 IBM cards, then went to work with a computer expert and devised a program. Each factor, such as weight and class and speed and post position, was evaluated singly and then in conjunction with other factors. One hundred and twenty handicapping "factors" were developed and analyzed and evaluated. When he read about it, Sam was astonished at the time and effort wasted. Of the 120 handicapping factors analyzed, only three or four seemed to have any great influence on the outcome of the race. By the end of April, 1972, Sam had made much the same discovery without the aid of a computer.

But "The Wizard" continued his efforts, and with some degree of success. The computer revealed an average of seven "plays" every ten days. And the profit percentage, based on an investment of $1,500, worked out to "a staggering fifty-five percent." If you will glance again at the tables, you will note that the lowest return Sam achieved was a 75 percent return at Pimlico.

The young man became known as The Wizard of Odds, and he teamed up with Random Research, Incorporated, to produce something called "The Harvard Logarithmic Selector." This "selector" was designed for the new breed of horseplayer, the computer racing fan. The going price for one of these Selectors in 1974 was $100. The Wizard of Odds (call him Joe) now and then walked away from Hialeah with winnings of as high as $4,500 in a single month. (Sam picked up $4,500 on one good Perfecta race at the same track, and he did even better at Gulfstream.)

The moral of the story, of course, is that Joe was approaching the problem from the low end of the odds scale, from the point of view of the favorite. Sam had long ago learned that the opposite end of the scale was not only more dramatic and more interesting: it was vastly more profitable, when correctly interpreted. But the story of Joe, the Wizard of Odds, is interesting to us because it reveals the fact that many people are seriously convinced that it is possible to make at least a million at the races. Since 1972, Sam has never doubted this. By using only one of his systems, and on a minimum investment unit of $2, he has demonstrated that he could walk away from any track in the east or the south with from $6,500 to $11,000 a month. Of course, Sam, being who he is, would never operate on a minimum unit of $2. His units were closer to $20. And he was beginning to learn that it was profitable to double up on the double; that is, to buy two tickets of each combination, for an investment on the double of $104 a day, rather than the $52 recommended herein. In one of the earlier chapters, we were using a method of selection which required only twenty tickets or $40 per day in the double program. But later, when completely refined and expanded, the double investment became twenty-six tickets, or $52 a day.

Flat-bet investments were never Sam's style either. As long as he kept ahead of the game, he was willing and eager to go into progressive action, and after trying a number of methods of progression, he came to favor the one which established a goal of so-much per hit or win. At first he went for $200 a hit, until his confidence in the system increased, after which he also increased his goal. When last heard from, Sam was using a goal of $500 a hit and was doing quite well. He kept open three avenues of investment at the same time: Q1, Q2 to Win, Q1, Q2 to Place, and the automatic plays on #3-Down, #4-Down and #5-Down. The latter three were considered a "unit" and investments were made on all three (when appropriate) in such a manner that if either of the three produced a winner, he was $500 ahead on that particular series. (The #6-Down was also played in first races, Perfecta races and in maiden races.) If you glance at Chart II under Sam's Automatic Method, you will note that the percentage of return on win investments alone, in the combined #3 thru #6-Down, was 106 percent, and that was achieved on flat wagers, with no progression being used. Add to these three avenues the Doubles and the Perfectas, and you will get some small idea of the profit potential which Sam faced each day. While Joe, the Wizard of Odds, is staggering along at 55 percent, with only about seven plays in ten days, Sam is investing in four or five horses in each race, but doing it in such a way that every avenue leads directly to pay dirt.

Admittedly, Sam is an expert, who can juggle with the best of them, keeping four balls in the air while he catches one in his hand, and every time he catches one in the hand, he puts another $500 in the till. It takes very little arithmetic to show that a profit of a thousand dollars a day, over a period of just 100 racing days, will gross one-tenth of a million dollars. The fly in the ointment is clear: as Sam says, it doesn't pay to make too much too quickly. Lower the gross and extend the period, and you're actually better off. No man is an island. We are all a part of the whole. Both church and state are grateful for your success. The point is that your success is assured if you become a follower of Sam, the bombardier from Florida, whose hit-record at Hialeah is better than it was over Hamburg in the fiery days of World War II.

8

The Best Method

It is Sam Hirsch's considered opinion that the best method of managing your money while at the track is to use the Total Deficit Goal method. The central idea is to go for a definite goal, which will be achieved whenever a hit comes. The goal, of course, should be such that it recoups all previous losses and includes the investment in the current race. To see how this works, let us look at Table III, on page 186. The goal here is to take in a minimum of $50 (over and above previous losses and current investments) whenever a hit occurs. We are also assuming a minimum investment on the current race of $4, since in all probability we will be investing in two horses in that first race. To complete our assumptions, for the purposes of this example, let's assume that we do no handicapping. We are going to make our selections by simply playing the two or three horses whose odds are below 50-to-1, and we are going to do this in every race that comes our way *until* we make a hit. In order to conduct a realistic test, we are going to be at Gulfstream Park on Saturday, January 19, 1974.

The first race on the program this Saturday is for three-year-olds who will be going a mile and a sixteenth. It's a claiming race and the claiming price is $12,500, which means that we have some pretty fair thoroughbreds in our view. Five minutes before post time, which is 1:15 p.m., we see that the three horses whose odds are under 50-1 are: Butter Bean at 30-1, Joy Quibu at 27-1, and Lt. Ted at 20-1. Being conservative in the beginning of our endeavor, we will invest in all three to win. (If we were ultraconservative, we would also invest in the same three horses to place, but we shall leave that matter until later. Experience has also shown us that the best returns always come from investments to win.) We go into the first race this Saturday with three investments. Look at line number 2 of Table III. Our goal is $58, or very close to that amount. Our first investment is at 30-1, so we look under Column E: 30. The second line shows a "2", and we invest $2 on Butter Bean to win. Similarly, we invest $4 on Joy Quibu (line 2, column H: 27), and we invest $4 on Lt. Ted (line 2, column 0:20). The columns show the odds, of course, and they are listed from 50-1 downward, just as the odds boards will carry them: 50, 45, 40, 35, 30 and then one at a time, down to 9-1, which is about as low as we expect to go. We have a total of $10 invested in the first race, and we lose it all when First of the Fare (at 9.60-to-1) wins the race.

Add the loss of $10 to our goal of $50, and we have a new goal of $60. We will have to use line 3, which is as close as we can get to $60. In the second race, our three investments are on horses at 40-1 ($2), at 14-1 ($5) and at 13-1 ($5), for a total of $12. We lose everything in the second race, although our third choice, the 13-1 horse comes in to place and pays $16.20 for $2. More on that a little later. We are now down $22, as we go into the third race. Our horses in that race are at 45-1, 21-1, and 12-1, and we use line 4 on the Table, which is closest to the $72 we need to get back. Our investments are $2 on the 45-1 horse, $4 on the 21-1 horse, and $6 on the 12-1 horse, for a total of $12. We lose again, when the favorite loses by a neck to Replate, at 6.50-to-1. Our new goal, entering the fourth race, is $85, and we use line 7 to find our wagers. Our investments are $4 on each horse, the two at 30-1 and one at 22-1. Another $12 goes down the drain when the favorite wins and pays $4.80 for $2. We look at the fifth race with just a bit of apprehension. But remember that we are using a method of selection which hits only about once a day, so we cannot become discouraged this early. We press on with the fifth race, and our investments are only two: on the 25-1 horse and the 17-1 horse, for $4 on the former, and $7 on the latter. We lose $11, and our new goal is approximately $110, in round numbers. This is midway between lines 10 and 11. We go to line 11, to be on the upper side, the safe side if we should win the sixth race.

In the sixth, our investments are: $8 on the 16-1 horse, $8 on the 14-1, and $10 on the 11-1 horse. Eureka! The 11-to-1 horse wins the race and pays $24.40 for $2, or $122 for our $10. We have just "earned" $62 on the series of six investments, with a bonus of $12 over the goal of $50. We are on our way. In the seventh race, our three investments are: $2 on the 40-1 horse, The General; $2 on the 30-1 horse, Luck Ahead; and $4 on the 27-1 horse, Sigh. Lightning strikes twice in one day. Luck Ahead wins the race at 30.10-to-1 and pays a nice $62.20 for our $2. Our investment was $8, and our net win is $54.20. (If our goal had been $100 per hit, we would have had $4 to win on the 30-1 shot and $8 on the 27-1 shot.) But we are now about $116 ahead of the game, as we go into the eighth race. Here our investments are: $2 on the 29-1 horse, $4 on the 27-1 horse, and $4 on the 24-1 horse. We lose. We are $10 down on the new series, and we are on line 4 for our investments in the ninth race.

These are: $2 on the 45-1; the sum of $4 on the 30-1; and $4 on the 20-1. Again we lose, but don't be surprised. We *must* lose most of the time. We are investing in high-odds horses, and our hits are going to be infrequent. So we press on. In the last race of the day, our investments are: $4 on the 28-1, $4 at 18-1, and $5 at 15-1. There is a slight problem in this last race: there are two horses at 15-1, and for our third investment we must choose between these two, which are Spot T.V. and Adaptive Ace. How to choose? Neither horse has raced within the past fourteen days. Both are carrying 116 pounds this race. But we are not handicapping. We can add the place pool to the win pool and divide by the show pool, to find which stable is backing their horse most heavily. This little trick comes out in favor of Adaptive Ace, with E. Maple aboard, and so we go for that one

We are right. Adaptive Ace wins the race at 15.20 to 1, and pays $32.40. We have $5 to win, for a return of $81. We were shooting for $70, and so we get a bonus of $11. But our net profit on the series is $61, and for the day we are ahead by about $177. This is more than we really expected; but we had three hits in one day. (We might have missed that third hit had we gone for Spot T.V.)

If we return on Monday, January 21, 1974 (and why not? since we are ahead of the game), we would find ourselves doing rather well. On that Monday there were two solid hits, coming in the ninth and the tenth races: Bend An Ear won the race at nearly 37-1 and paid $75.60 for $2. By this race we are on line 14 in our investment scale, and we have $5 to win, which brings back a total of $189, for a net on the series of approximately $55. In the tenth race, lightning strikes again. Arms and Armor wins at 45-1 and pays $90.80 for our $2 investment. We also had $2 on a 28-1 horse and $4 on a 25-1 horse. Net on the race is $82.80, for a net profit on the day of about $138. (Incidentally, in that tenth race, which was a Perfecta race, Arms and Armor combined with an 8-1 horse, Nyassa, to pay $1196.40.)

Let us consider place investments for a moment. Looking back across these two days at Gulfstream Park, if we had invested just $2 straight on each horse to place, we would have had a total of $118 invested. The return on those two days came to $171.60. In short, there were eight Place hits in two days. Had we been edging our investments upward as we went along (in much the same fashion as we were doing on the win side), we would have come out considerably better. But these two days are not sufficient to make any generalizations about place wagers. Place wagering can be looked upon as insurance. For every five win hits, we will have about eight or nine place hits. (Naturally, every win hit means a place hit too. The others come from actual place-hits, where the horse comes in second.)

What we are doing here is investing in three-down-from-50-to-1. In those two days we were looking at, these three-down were involved in three very nice Perfectas. On Saturday, in the seventh race, Luck Ahead won at 30-1 and the place horse was Applesauce Vender at 14-1. The Perfecta paid $980.40. In the final race that day, Adaptive Ace won at 15-1, and O So Big was second at 10-1, the Perfecta paying $327.40. And in the tenth race on Monday, as we noted, a 44-1 horse won, with an 8-1 second, and the Perfecta paid $1,196.40 . If we follow the rule that says: combine the three-down-from-50 with everything in the race from 8-1 thru 15-1, what would it have cost?

In the fourth race on Saturday, a Perfecta race, our three combined with 8-1, 9-1, and 13-1 would have cost two tickets (or $4) for each combination, for a total investment of $36. No return. In the seventh race, we would have had to combine our three with 11-1, 13-1, 14-1, and 14-1, for a total investment of $16. x 3, or $48. Return: $980.40. In the tenth race on Saturday, our three were combined with 10-1 and 15-1, for a total investment of $24. Return: $327.40. In the fourth race on Monday: investment equals $24; return: zero. Seventh race: investment, $24, return: zero. In the tenth race: investment: three with only one: 8-1, for an investment of $12. Return: $1196.40.

Total investment, for the two days, in Perfecta races: $168.00. Total return: $2504.20. Net Profit: $2336.20. A remarkable return, indeed, and surely not typical. But we did take a look at the following five days at Gulfstream Park. We found two win hits on Tuesday, the first coming in the second race, when a 17-1 shot paid $37.20 to win and $13.60 to place. It happened again in the seventh race, when a 17-1 horse took it all and paid $36.00 and $9.20. (The Perfecta was with the favorite and paid $158.00.) On Wednesday, there were two even bigger hits: in the ninth race, a 34-1 horse won and paid $70.20, $29.40 and $9.40. In the final race of the day, a 37-1 shot paid $77 to win, $32 to place, and $14.60 to show. The Perfecta, with an 11-1 horse, paid an astonishing $1407.80 for the correct combination of win-and-place. On Thursday, there was one win hit (for $32.40) and four heavy place hits, three of them for better than $22.20. Friday was a no-hitter. But Saturday was bargain day at the races, for the three-under-50 players.

In the first race, the number 3 down, at 15-1, paid $31.60 and

$13.00. (Forget the show price of $7.20.) In the fourth race, number-3 down again hit, at 21-1, paying $44.80 and $19.00. This was also a Perfecta race, and the number-3 down combined with a 10-1 horse for a payoff of $530.80. Those two Perfecta payoffs, the first on Wednesday and the second on Saturday, add up to nearly $2000.00. The tenth race brought another winner at 16-1, the win price being $35, the place price $10.60. This, too, was a Perfecta race, with a smaller than usual field of nine horses. The number-three down with a 7-1 horse paid $349.60. (In smaller fields, of nine horses down to six horses, we play our three down with everything from 7-1 through 16-1, or as high as 18-1, if we have to go that far to get two or three good plays.) That puts the three Perfecta payoffs in five days at more than $2250.00. As Sam says, Perfectas are the best ways to keep Florida green.

There is one final note, which brings you into the fringes of handicapping. If you have an aversion to playing three horses in one race, use some simple method of discrimination and play the best two out of the three down. If one of the horses was claimed last race, throw him out. If one is moving up in class and the other two are not, eliminate the one moving up. If one of the three has not raced within a month or so, throw him out. If two of the three have very recent workouts and the third does not, throw out the third.

And: always take a quick look at the number-4 horse down from 50. This is especially helpful when you are dealing with the first two races and Perfecta or Exacta races. Whenever that number-4 horse down has worked within three days of today, take him or her over the number-3 horse, provided that horse has *not* worked within three days. This rule holds true, even though the number-3 down has raced more recently than the number-4 down. (Whenever the number-4 down is dropping sharply in class, either from the last race or from the next-to-last race, take him or her over the number-3 down, if the latter is not dropping in class. Select a male number-4 over a female number-3, of course.)

To complete this short section, let us take a look at a week's racing at some other track. Quite arbitrarily, let's select Bowie, and let's look at the first six racing days in February 1974. How frequently will we hit if we play the three-down-from-50 method? And what are the payoffs? We will look at both win and place hits, and of course we will note any Perfecta payoffs in which one of our selections is involved. Here's six days of racing at Bowie, from February 1 through February 7:

Friday:	3rd, #2-D,	17-1, won:	$35.60 and $14.40. With a 5-1 horse, the Exacta paid $153.40.
	9th, #4-D,*	13-1, won:	$28.80 and $10.00. (Show prices not shown.)
Saturday:	7th, #2-Down,	22-1, placed:	——— $22.40
	9th, #2-Down,	17-1, won:	$36.80 and $9.40 (Exacta with F1 paid $110.20.)
Monday:	1st, #1-Down,	24-1, won:	$51.00 and $22.40, and $11.40 show
	5th, #1-Down,	34-1, placed:	——— $21.00 $8.00
	7th, #3-Down,	17-1,	won the race but was disqualified.
	9th, #2-Down,	24-1, placed:	——— $22.20 and $12.60
		(With a 6-1 horse, the Exacta paid $304.60.)	
Tuesday:	1st, #4-Down,†	15-1, won:	$32.80 and $14.80
	2nd, #1-Down,	27-1, placed	——— $17.80 $8.20
	3rd, #1-Down,	23-1, placed:	——— $13.40 $5.80
	6th, #2-Down,	18-1, placed:	——— $13.20 $5.60
	8th, #3-Down,	18-1, placed:	——— $10.60 $ 5.60
Wednesday:	1st, #2-Down,	15-1, placed:	——— $16.80 $10.20
	3rd, #2-Down,	18-1, won:	$39.20 $10.00 $ 6.00
		(Exacta, with 5-1, paid $182.00.)	
	7th, #2-Down,	placed:	——— $13.80 $ 7.00
		(Exacta, with F1, paid $59.00.)	
	8th, #2-Down,	27-1, placed:	——— $17.20 $ 8.80
Thursday:	1st, #4-Down‡,	21-1, placed:	——— $ 9.20 $ 6.20

*This number-4 down had worked within three days; number-3 down had not. Also, we skip races with six or less horses. The odds are usually too low. However, if we find one or more horses with two-digit odds, we may choose to play one or both
†Number-4 Down was dropping $2,000 in class from the next-to-last race. Whereas, the Number-3 down was running in same class.
‡This Number-4 down was a male, whereas the number-3 down was a filly. Also, this was not a good day at Bowie, since the fields were generally small. There were four races with eight or less horses, and no good high odds were generated therein.

During these six days, which were chosen at random, we find seven winners among our selections, although one was disqualified. These six winners paid from $28 to $51 to the fortunate holders of the proper tickets, and the average price was about $38. There were seventeen place-hits during the same period, and the average payoff on these was $15.00.

To summarize quickly, this automatic method of selection is an easy and sometimes profitable way of spending an afternoon or two at the races. We have observed that it brings a little better than one win-hit per day and an average of two to three place-hits per day. Using the debit-goal money management system, it is possible to come out well ahead of the game. Perfectas or Exactas are never sure things, but for the long-shot player, there is a nice challenge and an occasional spectacular payoff.

Essentially, we are concerned with larger fields of horses, preferably nine or more in a race. We are looking at four down from odds of 50-1, and selecting the three we like best, using the simplest rules:

1.   Choose a male over a female, all other factors being equal.

2.   Choose a horse dropping in class over one running in the same or higher class.

3.   Choose a horse who has worked out within three days, over one which has not. This is particularly true if neither horse has raced very recently. Of course, when you find a horse who has raced within *seven* or eight days, that horse takes precedence over anyone with a recent work. Unless your recent work is also dropping in class.

4.   Any horse dropping five or more pounds from his last race should be looked at closely. Given one or two other positive factors, this horse would become your choice over those carrying higher weight. But weight alone should not be a deciding factor.

Of course, if you wish to play only two out of the first three-down, use these same rules for eliminating those not desired. You are becoming a modest handicapper when you do this, and you will undoubtedly need a copy of the *Racing Form* or the *Telegraph*. If you don't have one of these papers and you ask your neighbor for help, he may give it to you, but the chances are he will regard you as some sort of nut for looking at horses whose odds are above 15-to-1. Nobody, but nobody plays dogs like that!

Spend a buck and get a copy of the *Form* for yourself. In a few days, after you learn how to read those past performances, you will be able to sit up there in the clubhouse stands with Sam Hirsch. And you may discover that you've found a way to beat inflation. Beating inflation is harder than beating the races any day. Keep that special account of yours green, and let Florida take care of itself.

THE USE OF TABLE IV AND TABLE V

Table IV shows you how much to wager to win when your goal is to make $100 per hit. As noted earlier, perhaps this is quite a modest goal since we know in advance that we are going to hit about once in ten tries. And that averages out to about $10 per race, or a profit of $100 per day at a track with a ten-race program, such as Gulfstream Park or Hialeah. In addition to having Table IV at hand, you need a notebook in which to keep a strict record of your wins and losses. Let's assume that you are down $30 or so, and you have two selections in the next race at good odds. The first is going off at 35-1 and the second at 24-1. Glancing along Line 3, you note under Columns D and K that you are going to spend about $10 to recover your losses. Actually, therefore, you're going to be "in" for a total of $40. So, use Line 4, your debit goal being $140. Your win-investment on the 35-1 horse will be $4, and on the 24-1 horse $6. If you win either of those investments, your return will recover all your losses and give you a minimum profit on the series of $100. After each hit, you return to Line 1 on the Chart for your next investment.

If a profit per hit of $100 is indeed too modest for you, it is always possible to move up in $100-steps. Let's assume that you are interested in $200 per hit. You can still use Table IV if your investments are all to win. Start your series on Line 7 of the Chart. If your horse in the first race has high odds and you're betting only one horse, Line 7 will do the trick. If the odds are 40-1, you will need only $5 on your horse. If the odds are much lower (below 18-1, for example) and especially if you're wagering on two horses, you can see that your investment in the race will be fifteen or twenty dollars, and you had best go to Line 8. Run along Line 8 until you come to the proper column (according to the odds of your selections), and if you win either of your bets, you will get a return of at least $225. The point is that you need to know your actual losses to date, then add your goal ($100 or $200 or $300) and find the line on the Chart which gives you that total. If your investment in the current race is going to be considerable, drop to the next line, so that your return will exceed your losses plus your goal. After each hit, start your series over again, using the line which comes closest to your goal. The Chart stops at Line 22, with a debit goal of $1,000. Using your electronic calculator, you can extend if as far as you wish.

Table V is for place Investments. Over a period of time, it can be shown that the dollar-return on most place Investments will be approximately 60 percent of the odds of the horse. If your selection is going off at 50-1, for instance, the place payoff will be around $30. Of course it will vary with each race, but we are dealing in averages. Thus, the odds line on the Chart will show two figures. The top figure is the actual odds of the horse. The figure under the slant mark is the estimated place-return odds. If you're down $50 and you have one selection in the next race, your debit goal being $150 since you wish to make $100 if the horse places, you are on Line 5 of the Chart. The odds are 50-1, and you need to wager $5 to place. Your probable place-return will be about $150. (If you were putting $5 to win on the same horse, and he did win, your return would, of course, be $250 plus your investment, or $255.)

Using one of Sam's methods of selection, you can expect a place-hit about once every five races. That's twice a day at Hialeah or Gulfstream. It is always possible to run the two series (one to win and one to place) simultaneously. Your bookkeeping has to be fairly strict, and you will probably need an extra head and certainly an extra hand to help you at the track. If you run into a losing streak, your place investments can become rather heavy, especially if your debit goal is $500 per hit, as Sam used on several occasions in Florida. But over the long haul, your frequency of hit will generally come out at one in five, which should keep you in business (and in profits) for quite a spell.

One final word: you can operate profitably to win by using flat-bets, which you can escalate as your success increases. This is true even if you are winning only once in ten attempts. As your capital goes up, you increase the level of your flat-bets. However, if you are wagering to place, the only road to profit is through Table V. You simply must use this form of money management to come out ahead in the long run. Even when you use Sam's method of winner-selection (in-the-money selection), you cannot hope to do much better than break even on flat-bet place wagers. And you certainly aren't at the track to break even. If you're running a strong win series on limited capital, you may wish to use flat-bet place wagers for insurance. But your *profits* will come only from your win wagers.

TABLE III

TOTAL DEBIT GOAL ($50)	Win Loss	A	B	C	D	E	F	G	H	I	J
		50	45	40	35	30	29	28	27	26	25
1. $54		2	2	2	2	2	2	2	2	2	4
2. 58		2	2	2	2	2	2	2	4	4	4
3. 64		2	2	2	2	4	4	4	4	4	4
4. 70		2	2	2	2	4	4	4	4	4	4
5. 75		2	2	2	4	4	4	4	4	4	4
6. 80		2	2	2	4	4	4	4	4	4	4
7. 85		2	2	4	4	4	4	4	4	4	4
8. 90		2	2	4	4	4	4	4	4	4	4
9. 95		2	4	4	4	4	4	4	4	4	4
10. 100		2	4	4	4	4	4	4	4	4	4
11. 120		4	4	4	4	4	4	5	5	5	5
12. 140		4	4	4	4	5	5	5	5	6	6
13. 160		4	4	4	5	6	6	6	6	6	7
14. 180		4	4	5	5	6	6	6	7	7	7
15. 200		4	5	5	6	7	7	7	8	8	8
16. 250		5	6	6	7	8	9	9	10	10	10
17. 300		6	8	8	9	10	10	12	12	12	12

K	L	M	N	O	P	Q	R	S	T	U	V	W	X	Y	Z
24	*23*	*22*	*21*	*20*	*19*	*18*	*17*	*16*	*15*	*14*	*13*	*12*	*11*	*10*	*9*
4	4	4	4	4	4	4	4	4	4	4	4	5	5	5	6
4	4	4	4	4	4	4	4	4	4	4	5	5	5	6	7
4	4	4	4	4	4	4	4	4	4	5	5	5	6	6	7
4	4	4	4	4	4	4	4	5	5	5	6	6	6	7	8
4	4	4	4	4	4	4	5	5	5	5	6	6	7	7	8
4	4	4	4	4	4	5	5	5	5	6	6	7	7	8	9
4	4	4	4	5	5	5	5	5	6	6	7	7	8	8	9
4	4	4	5	5	5	5	5	6	6	6	7	7	8	9	10
4	4	5	5	5	5	5	6	7	7	7	8	8	8	9	10
5	5	5	5	5	5	6	7	8	8	8	8	8	9	10	10
5	6	6	6	6	6	7	8	8	8	8	9	10	10	10	10
6	6	7	7	7	7	8	8	9	10	10	10	12	12	14	14
7	7	7	8	8	8	9	9	10	12	12	12	14	14	15	15
8	8	8	9	9	9	10	10	12	14	14	14	15	15	17	18
8	9	9	10	10	10	12	12	14	15	16	16	17	17	18	20
10	12	12	12	14	14	14	15	16	18	18	20	20	22	24	25
14	14	14	15	15	16	17	18	18	20	20	22	22	25	28	30

TABLE IV Win

TOTAL DEBIT GOAL ($100)		A	B	C	D	E	F	G	H	I	J	K	L
		50	*45*	*40*	*35*	*30*	*29*	*28*	*27*	*26*	*25*	*24*	*23*
1	$ 110	2	4	4	4	4	4	4	5	5	5	5	5
2	$ 120	4	4	4	4	4	5	5	5	5	5	5	6
3	$ 130	4	4	4	4	5	5	5	5	5	6	6	6
4	$ 140	4	4	4	4	5	5	5	6	6	6	6	7
5	$ 150	4	4	4	5	5	6	6	6	6	6	7	7
6	$ 175	4	4	5	5	6	6	7	7	7	7	7	8
7	$ 200	4	5	5	6	7	7	8	8	8	8	9	9
8	$ 225	5	5	6	7	8	8	8	9	9	9	10	10
9	$ 250	6	6	7	8	9	9	9	10	10	10	11	11
10	$ 275	6	6	7	8	10	10	10	11	11	11	12	12
11	$ 300	6	7	8	9	10	11	11	12	12	12	14	14
12	$ 350	7	8	9	10	12	12	14	15	15	15	15	15
13	$ 375	8	9	10	12	14	14	15	15	15	15	16	16
14	$ 400	8	9	10	14	14	14	15	15	16	16	18	18
15	$ 450	9	10	12	14	15	16	16	18	18	18	20	20
16	$ 500	10	12	14	15	18	18	18	20	20	20	22	22
17	$ 550	12	14	14	16	20	20	20	22	22	22	24	24
18	$ 600	12	14	18	20	20	22	22	24	24	24	25	25
19	$ 700	14	16	18	20	22	22	24	25	27	28	30	30
20	$ 800	16	18	20	24	28	28	28	30	30	32	32	34
21	$ 900	18	20	24	28	30	32	32	34	34	36	38	38
22	$1000	20	24	25	30	34	35	35	36	38	40	42	42

M	N	O	P	Q	R	S	T	U	V	W	X	Y	Z
22	*21*	*20*	*19*	*18*	*17*	*16*	*15*	*14*	*13*	*12*	*11*	*10*	*9*
5	6	6	6	7	7	7	8	8	9	9	10	12	12
6	6	6	7	7	8	8	8	9	10	10	12	12	14
6	7	7	7	8	8	9	9	10	10	12	12	14	15
7	7	7	8	8	9	9	10	10	12	12	14	14	16
7	8	8	8	9	9	10	10	12	12	14	14	15	16
8	9	9	10	10	12	12	12	14	14	15	16	18	20
10	10	10	12	12	12	14	14	15	16	18	20	20	22
10	12	12	12	14	14	14	15	16	18	20	22	24	25
12	12	14	14	14	15	16	18	18	20	22	24	25	28
14	14	14	15	16	18	18	20	20	22	24	25	28	32
14	15	15	16	18	18	20	20	22	24	25	28	28	34
16	18	18	20	20	22	22	24	25	28	30	32	35	40
18	18	20	20	22	22	24	25	28	30	32	34	38	42
20	20	20	22	22	24	25	28	30	32	34	38	40	45
22	22	24	24	25	28	28	30	32	35	38	42	45	50
24	24	25	28	28	30	32	35	36	38	42	45	50	55
25	28	28	30	32	34	35	38	40	42	46	50	55	65
30	30	30	32	34	36	38	40	44	46	50	55	60	70
34	34	35	38	40	42	45	48	50	55	60	65	70	80
38	38	40	42	45	48	50	55	60	65	70	75	80	90
42	45	45	48	50	55	60	60	65	70	75	85	90	100
46	48	50	55	60	60	65	70	75	80	85	95	100	110

TABLE V Place

TOTAL DEBIT GOAL ($100)	A $80/48$	B $70/42$	C $60/36$	D $55/33$	E $50/30$	F $45/27$	G $40/24$	H $35/21$	I $30/18$
1 $ 110	5	5	6	6	7	8	9	10	12
2 $ 120	5	6	7	7	8	9	10	12	14
3 $ 140	6	7	8	8	10	10	12	14	15
4 $ 160	7	8	9	10	10	12	14	15	18
5 $ 180	8	9	10	12	12	14	15	18	20
6 $ 200	8	10	12	12	14	15	16	20	22
7 $ 230	10	12	14	14	15	18	20	22	25
8 $ 260	12	12	15	16	18	20	22	25	28
9 $ 290	12	14	16	18	20	22	24	28	32
10 $ 325	14	16	18	20	22	24	28	32	36
11 $ 350	15	18	20	22	24	26	30	34	38
12 $ 375	16	18	22	24	25	28	32	36	42
13 $ 400	18	20	22	25	26	30	34	38	45
14 $ 450	20	22	25	28	30	34	38	44	50
15 $ 500	22	24	28	30	34	38	42	48	55
16 $ 550	24	26	30	34	36	40	45	52	60
17 $ 600	25	28	34	36	40	45	50	58	66
18 $ 650	28	32	36	40	44	48	54	62	72
19 $ 700	30	34	40	42	46	52	58	66	78
20 $ 750	32	36	42	45	50	55	62	72	84
21 $ 800	35	38	45	48	54	60	66	76	88
22 $ 850	37	42	48	52	56	64	70	80	95
23 $ 900	38	44	50	55	60	66	75	85	100
24 $ 950	40	46	54	58	64	70	80	90	105
25 $1000	42	48	55	60	65	75	85	95	110

J	K	L	M	N	O	P	Q	R	S	T
29-26/16	25/15	24-23/14	22-21/13	20/12	19-18/11	17-16/10	15/9	14-13/8	12-11/7	10/6
14	15	16	18	18	20	22	25	28	32	36
15	16	18	20	20	22	24	26	30	34	40
18	20	20	22	24	25	28	32	35	40	46
20	22	24	25	26	30	32	35	40	45	55
22	24	26	28	30	32	36	40	45	52	60
25	26	28	30	34	36	40	45	50	58	66
28	30	34	35	38	42	46	52	58	65	78
32	35	38	40	44	48	52	58	65	75	86
36	38	42	45	48	52	58	65	72	82	96
40	44	46	50	55	60	65	72	82	95	108
44	46	50	55	58	65	70	78	88	100	115
46	50	54	58	62	68	75	85	95	108	125
50	54	58	62	66	74	80	90	100	115	135
56	60	65	70	75	82	90	100	112	128	150
62	66	72	78	84	90	100	112	125	145	165
68	74	78	85	92	100	110	122	138	158	185
75	80	86	92	100	110	120	135	150	172	200
82	86	94	100	108	118	130	145	162	185	215
88	94	100	108	116	128	140	155	175	200	235
94	100	108	115	125	135	150	165	188	215	250
100	106	115	125	135	145	160	178	200	228	265
106	114	122	130	140	155	170	190	212	245	285
112	120	128	138	150	165	180	200	225	258	300
118	125	135	145	160	175	190	210	238	270	315
125	135	145	155	165	180	200	225	250	285	335

9

Summary of Rules

In the pages that follow, you will find a complete summary of the rules for selecting high-odds winners, or horses which have a good probability of running in-the-money. We are particularly concerned with the place money, but in the case of horses whose odds are 30-to-1 or higher, we are also interested in show money. These rules are for Sam Hirsch's general system for winner selection, as opposed to his Automatic Method of play, which is covered elsewhere.

What Sam wanted to put together was a system which would cover, if at all possible, every race on the card. Rarely do you have to skip a race when using this system. Indeed, it is best not to skip a race. That long-odds winner or place horse can come at anytime, in any type of race. Many systems of play eliminate maiden races and races for two-yr-olds, etcetera, etcetera, and they give you but two or so plays per day. The professional investor can't live with this sort of limitation. His time, for one thing, is too important.

Thus, Sam took great pains to develop a universal system, which could be used at any track, in any season, and which would apply to all types of races. He did, in fact, come up with two systems, which he claims can be used profitably at the same time. It is possible, of course, to use one and not the other. But for maximum profits, use them both. Bookkeeping and money management must be kept separate, however. Using both systems at the same time often requires that you invest in three or four or even five horses in the same race. Most veteran horseplayers would be appalled at this approach, but let us point out in Sam's defense that if you play five horses in a ten horse race, your actual chances of catching a winner are one in two, and the odds you are playing are invariably better than 10-to-1, which means that you can't help but break at least even over a period of time, even so short a time as one day at the track. And most of the prices are well above 10-1, when the accounts are all in. Remember, too, that when you play both systems simultaneously, you will be using two different units of investment, and that these units will vary according to your success or failure in the recent past. This "progressive action" on two scales will insure you a satisfactory, perhaps even an amazing profit on each scale.

There will be many very experienced horseplayers, also, who will scoff at the multitude of "if's" and "and's" and "exceptions" shown in these rules. The entire system, they will say, is too complicated for the average horseplayer. But Sam, really, is not concerned with the average horseplayer. He is concerned with the serious investor, with the man who wishes to establish and run a small but lucrative business, which happens to be set at a racetrack. He needs no office except his seat in the stands. He needs no tools except his knowledge of the system and the odds board itself. He does need something called capital. But every business requires capital. Any businessman knows that it often requires a capital outlay of $40,000 to bring back an income of $20,000 in a single year. At the track, using Sam's methods, on a capital of $10,000 (or somewhat less), you can reasonably expect to walk away with a net profit of $10,000 every thirty days.

Perhaps, too, this is the place to make a few comments on the percentages shown in the charts that are given in Chapter VII. The percentage of profit is figured on the basis of the amount of money invested over the entire period of the play, that is, between two definite dates which are not more than thirty days apart. This investment total is divided into the net profit for the period to give the percentage of profit. This assumes that every dollar invested is from your pocket or your account. In actuality, such is not the case. If you begin with a thousand dollars on the first day at Hialeah, and you use $2 units throughout the day, you finish that Saturday (April 1, 1972) with four winners in the straight wagers or investments, the odds on those winners being 14-1, 59-1, 11-1, and 19-1. On that same day, you had a daily double win of $202.20, and you had three Perfecta wins out of a possible four, although the payoffs were not spectacular, being in the $50 to $55 range. However, you left the track on Saturday, April 1 with considerably more than a thousand dollars. Much of your next day's investing will now be done with track money, that is, with the profits from your original investments. Since there is a race every 30 minutes or so, you will be investing and re-investing much of the same money, either your own or that from profits. After a couple of days, your original thousand dollars can safely stay in the bank, accumulating some interest, while you continue on the previous profits. Thus the actual percentage of return on your original investment is difficult to compute and would be vastly different at every track during each thirty-day period. However, for bookkeeping purposes, and to satisfy the requirements of the logical mind, the percentages are given as shown.

We mentioned earlier that there is nothing in this system, or method of investment, which cannot be mastered by anyone possessing a slightly better-than-average mentality and education. You do not have to be a Phi Beta Kappa, or even a member of the National Honor Society, to take up this track investment program. Sam himself was a member of the National Honor Society in his high school, and, if the truth be known, he does have a Phi Beta Kappa key hidden away somewhere in one of his jewelery boxes. But that doesn't mean that each of his followers had to pass through the same doorways in order to win success. Sam has already accomplished the hard thinking, and he has done the basic research and bookkeeping which resulted in the formulation of the two systems. All that is now required is for you to become thoroughly familiar with the rules, and very possibly to do some practice work, using old *Racing Forms*, to be sure that your investment company has sufficient expertise to go into actual business. One step you should always take is to look at the results of the week just past, to allow yourself the satisfaction of knowing that all systems are go.

Let's just take one "for example." The handicapping expert in your company must know that Section e) under Rule 2 is important. This Section deals with a minor but significant situation. A three-yr-old maiden is running against winners, which ordinarily means that he must be very sharp to qualify. He would need seven points, as a matter of fact, under Rule 3, were it not for another fact: the maiden is running in a claiming race *for the first time*, or he is running at the lowest claiming price ever in his career. Obviously, this maiden must have at least one previous race, or else he would be a first-time starter, and then he would fall under a different rule. The veteran horseplayer will ask: Why make an issue of this maiden running against winners, who is also running in a claiming race for the first time? The answer is: First, we do not take all candidates. We eliminate those who did not show a position of five or less lengths off the winner at the first call, or who did not gain some ground between any two calls. This maiden must display some early speed or some evidence of a winning effort. The key here is that we don't ever know what a maiden can do in a race against winners. But the trainer does know. The trainer has carefully selected the "spot" to place his horse. It would be more logical for the Trainer to enter his maiden in a race with other maidens. But the trainer knows the capabilities of his horse better than anyone else. If the horse showed signs of winning effort (as defined in the conditions of the section of the Rule), then the Trainer will drop him into a lower level claiming race (the lowest at which the horse has ever run, for instance) or into a claimer for the first time. The general public will never spot this move, especially since the odds on the horse are flashing away at 60-1, or 70-1 or 80-1. The average fan doesn't so much as look at the past performance on a dog like this. High odds are reserved for "dogs," are they not? Here again, the average racegoer is making his first big mistake. He starts by looking at the favorites and then moves up, perhaps to horses with odds as high as 10-1 or even 12-1. Forget the "others" because they rarely win. The fact is that those "others," up there on the high-odds scale, do win occasionally, and the point is to catch them when they do.

And, as Sam often says, these occurrences take place in key races, in the first or second half of the daily double, or in Perfecta-Exacta Races, where the payoffs are such that they will pay for the horse's keep for a year or two. That is, if the trainer (owner, stable boys, etc.) had a few dollars in the right place. Look at what happened to a maiden colt named Turn to Riches, in the second race at Santa Anita on February 9, 1973. The chart on Turn to Riches is given below.

Turn to Riches   114   Dk. b. or br. c (1970), by Riches and Honor—Faila Bell, by Faila.
Breeder, D. Yoakum (Texas).

											1973	1	M	0	0		—
Owner, R.S. Braugh.	Trainer, R.D. Kaufman.							$8,000			1972	5	M	0	1		$1,014
Jan13 73²SA	6 f	1:10³/sft	80	118	7⁴²	9⁶¼	12¹²	12¹⁶	SellersJ⁸	Mdn	72	GumFourMe118		HopAshore		Hillmoss 12
Sep 7-72²Dmr	6 f	1:10⁴/sft	19	118	8⁵	7⁵	6⁶²	5⁸³	CampasR⁴	Mdn	76	Chios113		ColdRuler		Hunter'sTreasure 11
Aug26-72²Dmr	6 f	1:09⁴/sft	43	118	6⁴½	4⁸	0⁹	9¹⁰	CampasR²	Mdn	80	Autry118		Out of theEast		Turn toRiches 11
Aug 9-72²Dmr	6 f	1:10¹/sft	112	118	11¹⁴	11¹⁶	10¹⁸	9¹⁷	R'rig'zL¹	AlwM	71	Naud110		OcalaBoy		FreeSpace 11
Jly 7-72³Hol	5½ f	1:04	ft	82	118	11¹¹	11¹⁴	12¹³	11¹⁹	RosalesR⁵	Mdn	74	AncientTitle118	SpinLightning	Nuba 19
May 5-72¹³Sun	5 f	:59³/sft	4²	120	7⁶½	7⁵½	7⁹½	5⁶¼	Nicod'sJ³	SplW	81	T'rnHimOn120	H'stleY'rB'stle	TwoDov's 8
Jan. 31 SA 5f gd 1:02²/sh				Jan. 26 SA 5f ft 1:01h					Jan. 10 SA (trt) 5f gd 1:03⁴/sh							

Turn to Riches's last race was on January 13, less than twenty-eight days ago, for one point, and his last workout was on January 31, just ten days ago. Under Category A, the colt has a race within twenty-eight days and a work within ten days, for two points. One more point for dropping four pounds off the last race. (Incidentally, whole systems have been based on horses dropping four or more pounds off their last race.) One other point for finishing third in his past performance, and that's a total of four points for Turn to Riches, who is running in an $8000 claiming race, the first claiming race of his career. At the first call in his last race, Turn to Riches was 4 3/4 lengths off the leader. If the average fan even looked at that last race and saw the finish of twelfth in a field of 12, the immediate reaction was: "Forget him!" Not so, Average Fan. Trainer Kaufman knows on what side his bread is buttered. He's got $200 to win and $200 to place. Also, Trainer Kaufman has already bought a wheel of $10 tickets with everything running in the first race. He knows better than to waste money like this, but he also knows that anything can happen in a horse race. His confidence in his horse Turns to Riches indeed. As you see in the results chart below, the colt was four lengths off the leader at the quarter, and moved up to one length off at the half, and by the head of the stretch was himself leading by a length, when he suddenly turned on the steam and drew away for a six-lengths-win, paying $174 to the fortunate few who held the right tickets and $48.80 to place.

SECOND RACE
SA
February 9, 1973

6½ FURLONGS. (1:14³/₅). CLAIMING. Purse $4,000. 3-year-olds. Weight 122 lbs. Non-winners of two races since December 25 allowed 2 lbs.; of a race since then or three races at any time, 5 lbs.; of two races at any time, 8 lbs. Claiming price $8,000. (Races when entered for $5,000 or less not considered.) (Winners preferred.)

Value to winner, $2,200; second, $800; third, $600; fourth, $300; fifth, $100. Mutuel Pool, $165,669.

Last Raced		Horses	EqtAWt	PP	St	¼	½	Str	Fin	Jockeys	Owners	Odds to $1
1-13-73	³SA¹²	Turn to Riches	b3 114	10	7	8⁴	3¹	1¹	1⁶	R Campas	R Braugh	86.00
1-11-73	²SA⁷	Gamut	b3 115	8	6	5½	6⁴	4½	2¹	LPincayJr	Marion R Frankel	2.50
2- 2-73	²SA⁴	Cal Cartage	b3 115	6	5	1ʰ	1ʰ	2½	3¹	APineda	Ridgeley Farm	1.10
1-17-73	²SA¹¹	Viking Witch	b3 110	9	2	2¹	2½	3½	4ʰ	JRamirez⁵	D C Short	45.70
1-26-73	²SA⁹	Foxie Greine	b3 105	7	11	11⁵	9½	7½	5½	SValdez⁵	Mr-Mrs I Koulax	16.60
1-23-73	³SA⁶	Nationality	3 115	12	1	7¹	5ʰ	5½	6½	DPierce	Buckley-Hoon	33.30
1-24-73	²SA⁶	Bernwood Quest	b3 114	1	12	10½	10²½	9ʰ	7½	RRamirez	Mr-Mrs J Sulli	41.90
1-30-73	²SA⁹	Promising Maid	3 109	4	9	9ʰ	8½	8²½	8³	RCSmith	Palmsy Adams	118.10
1-10-73	²SA⁶	Hello Good Times	b3 114	2	4	3½	4½	6¹	9⁴	JTejeira	Cossack Farm	5.50
2- 2-73	³SA⁸	Calgary Kid	3 114	11	10	12	11¹½	11¹⁰	10²½	DVelasquez	Hartstone Hartstone	49.00
1-25-73	²SA⁷	Candlelight Capers	3 109	3	8	4½	7	10ʰ	11¹²	RBianco	Dr-Mrs G J Shima	42.90
1-24-73	³SA¹¹	Zap	b3 115	5	3	6¹	12	12	12	JSellers	P L Grissom-Son Inc	10.80

Time, :22³/₅, :46³/₅, 1:12³/₅, 1:19¹/₅. Track slow.

$2 Mutuel Prices:
10-TURN TO RICHES	174.00	48.80	13.40
8-GAMUT		4.70	2.80
6-CAL CARTAGE			2.60

Dk. b. or br. c, by Riches and Honor—Faila Belle, by Faila. Trainer, R. Kaufman. Bred by D. Yoakum (Tex.).

IN GATE—1:31. OFF AT 1:31½ PACIFIC STANDARD TIME. START GOOD. WON DRIVING.

TURN TO RICHES rallied along the outside to catch the leaders in the upper stretch, responded to steady urging and drew out. GAMUT raced unhurried early when behind horses, got clear in the final furlong but could not threaten the winner. CAL CARTAGE saved ground while volleying for the lead on the final turn and tired in the last sixteenth. VIKING WITCH forced the pace around the turn from between horses then tired. FOXIE GREINE raced wide. HELLO GOOD TIMES was an early factor along the inside then faltered. ZAP showed nothing.

Overweight—Cal Cartage, 1 pound, Zap, 1; Foxie Greine 1; Gamut, 1; Nationality,1.

Cal Cartage claimed by W. Kaufman Jr., trainer W. Greenman.

Claiming Prices—All $8000.

Scratched—Rapid Dumpty, Early Merly, Convalescent, Sugar Belle.

Daily Double (1-10) Paid $1,139.20. Double Pool, $146,034

Kaufman's two straight $200 tickets brought him back $17,400 to win and $4,480 to place, while the $10 double ticket converted to $5,696. For a gross on the race of $27,976. Of course, if you ask Kaufman about this, he will deny it, as well he should. What Kaufman makes in a year is between him and the IRS.

The trainer, of course, is not always right. In that same race, Calgary Kid, who was running at the lowest claiming price ever, qualified otherwise but finished tenth, seventeen lengths off the winner. Sam would have played them both!! He would also have played Silver Salute in the fifth race that same day. Silver Salute raced last on January 27, after a work on January 26. He finished ninth last race, in a field of ten, twenty-five lengths off the winner. In his next-to-last race, he finished fifth, also twenty-five lengths off the winner. Ordinarily this double-twenty-five figure would have disqualified Silver Salute, but he was dropping into a claiming race at $12,000 for the first time. And in his last race, he moved up from twenty-nine lengths off the leader to twenty-five lengths off. A four-length gain, which indicated something to Trainer Ensey. Back in mid-December of the previous year, Silver Salute had run third in a maiden allowance race, which, along with that weight drop of nine pounds and the recent race and workout, gave him five clear points. Silver Salute was the only qualifier (under Section e, Rule 1), and he went off at 62-1, winning the race by nearly a length over the Favorite, Fleet Trader, who was even money on the board. Silver Salute paid $127 to win and $26.60 to place, which was fine for all the stable supporters, but take a look at the Exacta pay-off. Even with the favorite running second, the Exacta paid $1855 for a $5 ticket. Silver Salute was Q1 in Sam's book and he had him combined with F1 a couple of times, while the average fan groaned in his seat. The Exacta Pool on his fifth race came to $195,975, which means that only 105 tickets were sold on the winning combination of 7-4, Silver Salute and Fleet Trader. Oddly enough, only 128 daily double tickets were sold on the 1-10 combination earlier in the program. In all probability, fewer than fifty people owned those tickets in both the double and the fifth-race Exacta. That's fifty out of some 18,000 who were at the track. Which is another reason they say that fewer than .1 percent of all race goers emerge as winners. That percentage of winners may increase slightly after Sam's Systems become public knowledge, which will occur for the first time with the publication of this book.

But there will be many who read but few who believe. Only the believers will make any serious attempt to put these systems into operation. And not all of them will succeed. Only those will succeed who have something more than faith. Hard cash, of course, is a prerequisite, but more than that is the self-discipline required to follow any system of investment through to its logical conclusion—self-discipline and knowledge of what it is all about. You have to know the system, but you must also have a feel for the particular situation, and that comes only with a great deal of experience, only part of which can be gained from paperwork. Most of it must come at the track itself.

After that brief dissertation, here are the rules in summary form, all together in a single section of the book, for handy reference and use. They are the same as carried earlier in the text, which means that if they are removed from the book physically, the volume will still be complete.

RULES FOR SELECTING Q1, Q2, Q3

1. To Qualify for Q1, Q2, or Q3, a horse generally needs five points. In general, pass any race with less than eight starters.
2. However, a horse may qualify with only four points if:
    a) He has only one race in his past performance chart and two points come from Category A.
    b) Horse shows both a race and a workout within ten days. (Add four days to this for fillies or mares and maidens.)
    c) Horse is a two-yr-old or a three-yr-old maiden, or is a filly. In filly/mare races, the filly needs four points, the mare five.
    d) Horse is carrying less than 109 pounds today and has two points from Category A.
    e) Horse is a three-yr-old maiden running in a claiming race for the first time. However, to qualify here, horse must also have been running within five lengths of the winner at the first or second call of his last race, *or* must have gained ground between any two calls in his last race. If the three-yr-old maiden is running at his lowest claiming price ever, he also qualifies with four points with the same provision as for maidens above.
3. Horse needs seven points to qualify *if*:
    a) His last-race odds were 102 or higher. Exceptions: maiden races and races for three-yr-olds.
    b) Fillies/mares running against males this race. Except in maiden races and races for three-year-olds.
    c) Any horse (except a maiden) who finished twenty

lengths or more off the winner in both of his last two races.

A horse is an automatic bet (needs no points) if:

a)   He is dropping $10,000 or more in class, or moving down two steps in class. However, his odds must be in the top four today, or in the top five if the field is ten or more horses.

b)   If his odds today are in the top four (or five in large fields), and he finished fourth or better in 60 percent of his past races, provided a minimum of eight races are shown in the past performance chart.

c)   Horse is a first-time starter in a Maiden Race, a two-yr-old race, or a race for three-yr-old fillies, *and* has at least one recent workout shown.

d)   A two-yr-old with one race shown, and that within fourteen days, *or* one recent race *and* a workout within ten days, i.e., the workout within ten days.

5.   A horse claimed last race is disqualified, unless:

a)   he is running again within fourteen days; and

b)   he is carrying less than 118 pounds today; and

c)   he has a last-race rating of less than 16 points; *or*

d)   he can produce at least eight clear points.

6.   A horse claimed last race *and* moving up in class for today's race is disqualified, unless he can produce ten clear points.

7.   In maiden races with special weights, if there are two distinct age and weight groups, take the lower-weight group first and examine the contenders with the top odds and go down the odds scale to find your qualifiers. If you do not find three qualifiers in the lower-weight group, go to the top odds of the higher-weight group.

8.   In pursuing qualifiers, go down the odds scale from the top, but do not go below those odds which equal the number of horses in the race, e.g. in a twelve-horse race, do not go below 12-1.

9.   Disqualify any horse who ran dead last in his last race if he was fifteen or more lengths off the winner, unless:

a)   the horse is dropping in class, *and*

b)   he has two points from Category A.

CATEGORY A: RACE RECENCY

For a race within twenty eight days: ONE POINT

For maidens, fillies, and mares, for a race within thirty days: ONE POINT

For a race within fourteen days: TWO POINTS

For Maidens, fillies and mares, for a race within fifteen days: TWO POINTS

For a workout within fourteen days: ONE POINT

For maidens, fillies, and mares, for a workout within fifteen days: ONE POINT

For a workout within four days: TWO POINTS

For maidens, fillies, and mares, for a workout within five days: TWO POINTS

For two races within twenty-eight days: TWO POINTS

Maidens, fillies, and mares, two races within thirty days: TWO POINTS

For two workouts within fourteen days: TWO POINTS

Maidens, fillies, and mares, two workouts within fifteen days: TWO POINTS

For a race within twenty-eight days *and* a workout within ten days: TWO POINTS

NOTE: If any horse has received one or two points in Category A, *and* if his or her last race was at the same distance and on the same surface as today's race, award: ONE-HALF POINT

CATEGORY B: LAST RACE FINISH

1.   Check the last race at today's class or at today's distance, whichever is the better race.

2.   If the horse has two races within twenty-eight days at today's class, check them both and choose the better race. Use last two races for maidens, fillies, and mares.

3.   If a horse is moving up in class, check the race at today's distance, or as close to today's distance as possible.

Point Awards

For a finish of fifth or better in a field of eight horses in his last race: ONE POINT

For a finish of sixth or better (or six lengths or less off the winner) in a field of nine or more horses: ONE POINT

For maidens, fillies, and mares, add ONE to above figures, e.g., for a finish of seventh or better (or seven lengths or less off the winner) in a field of nine or more horses: ONE POINT

Compute last-race rating by adding the finish position to the number of lengths off the winner. For a rating of ten or less: TWO POINTS

For a last-race rating of twenty or better (except when horse finished last in the race), award: ONE POINT

For maidens, fillies, and mares, allow a last-race rating of twenty-five or less: ONE POINT

If a horse received a point for finishing sixth or better (fifth or better in small fields, or seventh or better for fillies, mares, and maidens), *and* if the horse gained in the stretch run of that last race checked, award for every length gained in that stretch run: ONE POINT

If horse finished worse than sixth (or worse than fifth in small fields, or worse than seventh for maidens, fillies, or mares) *but* gained in the stretch run of the last race checked, for every *two* lengths gained, award: ONE POINT

If a horse won his last race, is in top-five odds (in large fields) or in top-four odds in smaller fields, and is not moving up more than $1000 in class, award: ONE POINT

If a horse has run in four or more races at a class higher than today's class, and has gained in the stretch run in more than half of those races: ONE POINT

If a horse improves his position in the field as he goes from the head of the stretch to the finish wire (e.g., fifth at head of stretch, fourth at wire) in 75 percent of the races listed in his past performance (minimum: four races):   ONE POINT

For every three races in his listed past performance, when a horse finishes 6½ lengths or less off the winner: ONE POINT

In maiden races and races for three-yr-olds and for fillies, if a horse has gained a point from Category A, and if he gained just one length in the stretch run of his last race (regardless of finish position):   ONE POINT

CATEGORY C: IN-THE-MONEY

For finishing once in the money in past performance: ONE POINT

For one win in last three races: ONE POINT

For two wins in last five races: TWO POINTS

For five or more firsts or seconds in past performance: ONE POINT

For finishing in-the-money in half or more of all races in the past performance (minimum: four races):   ONE POINT

For two fourths in a field of ten or more:*   ONE POINT

For maidens, fillies, and mares, for one fourth in a field of ten or up: ONE POINT

Or, for one fifth, *if* less than six lengths off the winner: ONE POINT

NOTE: These last two awards are for horses who have not finished in-the-money in any of their races listed. Horses who have finished in-the-money in any of their listed races are not eligible for these awards.

*If a horse has two points from Category A, race recency, but has not finished in-the-money in his listed past performance, but has one fourth in a field of ten or more: ONE POINT

CATEGORY D: WEIGHT

For carrying 105 pounds or less today: TWO POINTS

For carrying 106–110 pounds today: ONE POINT

For dropping 3–6 pounds from last race: ONE POINT

For dropping 7 or more pounds: TWO POINTS

Horse dropping in class, maidens, 2-yr-olds, fillies & mares dropping two pounds from last race: ONE POINT

If horse is carrying 5 or more pounds LESS than the top-weighted horse in the race: ONE POINT

Penalties

For carrying 118–122 pounds today: Minus ONE POINT

For carrying 123 pounds or more today: Minus TWO POINTS

For picking up 3 to 6 pounds over last race: Minus ONE POINT

For picking up 7 or more pounds today: Minus TWO POINTS

NOTE 1: Do not exact penalty if all the horses in a race are carrying the same high weight; e.g. 122 pounds. *Or*: All horses but one.

NOTE 2: Do not exact penalty if horse carried exceptionally low weight last race due to apprentice jockey allowance, shown by two or three asterisks: ** ***

NOTE 3: If horse is dropping in class, he or she may pick up as much as four pounds without penalty.

NOTE 4: Any horse may pick up as much as four pounds without penalty *if* he is carrying a total weight of no more than 114 today.

NOTE 5: Before exacting penalty for carrying 118 or more today, examine last few races and see whether or not horse has carried this high weight successfully before today. If so, no penalty today, e.g., if horse was in-the-money at 122 last race and is carrying 122 pounds today, no penalty.

CATEGORY E: CLASS

For a drop in class, either from last race or from next-to-last race: ONE POINT   (Class drop must be $1,000 to $5,000.)

For a drop in class of $6,000 or more: TWO POINTS

For a one-step drop in class: ONE POINT

For a two-step drop in class: TWO POINTS

Penalties

For moving up in class $1,000 to $5,000:   Minus ONE POINT

For moving up in class $6,000 or more: Minus TWO POINTS

For a one-step move up in class: Minus ONE POINT

For a two-step move up in class: Minus TWO POINTS

CLASS RANKINGS

Class One: Stakes races and named handicaps (often with money added).

Class Two: Claiming races for $16,000 and up.

Class Three: Allowance races and overnight handicaps; claiming races at $15,000 and up to $16,000.

Class Four: Claiming races for $14,500 and less.

Class Five: Starter handicap and starter allowance races.*

Class Six: Maiden races and maiden special weight races.

Class Seven: Maiden claiming races.

Class Eight: Two-year-old races and races for first-time starters.

*A Starter Handicap with a number following, e.g., H5000, is the equivalent of a $5000 claiming race. Similarly, a Starter Allowance Race with a number following e.g., A10000, is the same as a $10,000 claiming race.

NOTE 1: If today's race is the second step up in a row, i.e., two step ups in three races (including today's), then double the penalties.

NOTE 2: If all of a horse's races (except the last race) have been run at a higher class than today's class, consider the horse to be dropping in class and award the appropriate points.

NOTE 3: If a horse shows four or more at a class higher than today's class, consider that horse to be dropping in class.

RULES FOR SELECTING F2–F4

A. **Race Recency.**   Horse must have raced within twenty days, or worked out within ten days.

   Exceptions: 1)   Horse is dropping $3,000 or more in class, or is dropping two full steps in class.

   2)   Horse is dropping $1,000 to $2,500 in class and gained in the stretch run of his last race.

   3)   Horse has a last-race rating of twelve or less.

   4)   Horse finished in-the-money in two of his last three races.

B. **Finish Position.**   Disqualify any horse who was beaten by more than fifteen lengths in both of his last two races.

C. **In-The-Money.**   Disqualify any horse who was not in-the-money at least once in the last four of his races.

   Exceptions: 1) and 2)   Same as #1 and #2 above.

   3)   Horse shows one fourth in the last four races and in that race had a rating of twelve or less. (That is, he was eight lengths or less off the winner, if he finished fourth.)

   4)   Horse finished three lengths or less off the winner in one of his last four races.

D. Weight Factor.   Disqualify any horse who is picking up four or more pounds today.

    Exceptions: 1)–4)   Same as #1 thru #4 in "A" above.

5) Horse won his last race carrying 119 pounds or more.

6) Horse is getting in today at 117 or less.

E. Class Factors.   a. Horses running today in the same general class or dropping generally in class must have a last-race finish of three or more places below the number of runners in the race.

    Exceptions:

1) Horse finished his last race eight lengths or less off the winner.

2) His next-to-last race was very impressive and was run in a class considerably higher than today's class.

3) Horse is dropping five or more pounds off his last race *and* is getting in today's race at 112 pounds or less.

b. Horses moving up in class, generally speaking, must have a last-race finish position of four or more places lower than the number of runners in the race, *and* should show most or all of the following:

1) Won his last race.

2) Or was in-the-money in both of his last two races.

3) Gained two or more lengths in the stretch run of his last race.

c. Horses moving up in class by $3000 or more must:

1) Be running again within fourteen days, *or*

2) Have had a workout within the past two days.

F. Odds Factor.   Disqualify any horse whose last-race odds were 90-1 or higher.

Exceptions: 1)–4) Same as #1 thru #4 in "A" above.

G. Male-Female.   a. When fillies or mares are running against male horses (or when maidens are running against winners),disqualify any horse moving up in class.

Exceptions: 1) Horse won his last race very impressively, *or*, she meets three out of the following:

      a) Is running again within ten days, or worked out within two.

      b) Finished five or more places lower than the number of horses running in that last race.

      c) Gained two or more lengths in the stretch run of the last race.

      d) Is dropping more than six pounds off his last race.

    b. Disqualify fillies or mares running against males (or maidens when running against winners), even when running in the same class.

Exceptions: 1) Horse is running again within ten days *and* finished in-the-money in two of the last three races.

H. Claimed.   Disqualify any horse who was claimed in his last race *and* is generally moving up in class.

Exceptions: 1) Same as #1 in "G" above.

After you have made your selections for F2 through F4, look at F1, provided his odds are 4-1 or higher, and include him if he looks outstanding. Also, look at F5 (the fifth favorite) and check him against the following criteria:

1)   Is racing again within fourteen days, or had a workout within past two or three days.

2)   Is definitely dropping in class.

3)   Gained two or more lengths in the stretch run of his last race.

4)   Finished his last race five or more places lower than the number of runners in that race.

5)   If dropping six or more pounds off his last race, or is getting in today at 112 or less.

6)   Has been in-the-money in two or three of his last five races.

IF the F5 horse meets several of these qualifications, add him to your list, or use him in place of one of your ho-hum qualifiers already selected (F2 thru F4). It is often valuable to contrast F5 with F4 (or with F3), and take the better of the two. If both look very impressive, keep them both in.

THE PASTOR'S WIFE

(an easy method of play,
using only money from the entertainment fund)

Inevitably, Sam received a dozen or more requests from people living in and around Miami Shores for what they called "the pastor's wife system," and he was forced to sit down one evening and codify the thing, then type it up for Xeroxing, so that he could hand it out to any and all comers. He charged nothing for this little service since most of the requesters were members of the pastor's congregation. But he did mention the fact, when he gave out the pastor's wife system, that he expected a contribution, amounting to ten percent of the net, to go to the general fund of the church. In every instance, he was assured that this would be done.

At this writing, it is not known to what extent the general fund has benefited from Sam's thoughtfulness, but when he mailed these pages to me late in the year he stated that there was a very good likelihood that the pastor's wife had done more for the church in these modern days than the widow's mite had done in ancient times. The method of play which he codified and passed out differed somewhat from the original plan which he gave to the pastor's wife. But the differences are of no great consequence, except that they may account for a higher return in actual practice, especially if the users of the plan are sophisticated enough to take the optional or second method of selection. At any rate, here are the simple rules of the pastor's wife method of play, designed for casual race goers who are drawing on the entertainment fund.

Rules of Play

1.   Do not play a race in which there are less than six horses.
2.   When there are six horses in a race, start with the horse whose odds are 6-1, or as close to that as possible, moving upward. Select the *two* horses with odds from 6-1 upward.
3.   When there are seven horses in a race, start with the horse whose odds are 7-1, or as close above that as possible, and select the *two* horses from 7-1 upward.
4.   When there are eight horses in a race, start with the horse whose odds are 8-1, or as close above that as possible, and select the *two* horses with odds of 8-1 upward.
5.   When there are nine or more horses in a race, start with the horse whose odds are 9-1, or as close above that as possible, and select the *two* horses whose odds are 9-1 upward.
6.   If you wish to play the daily double, make your *two* selections in the first race as outlined above, then combine each of them with those horses in the second race whose morning-line odds are 12-1 and 10-1. This will give you from two to four combinations with each. If you wish to expand your investment (and your winning possibilities), combine each of your two selections from the first race with the 8-1 horses, the 6-1 horses, and then upward with the 15-1 horses. Or any part of this schedule, according to your desires. (If you don't want to waste capital, find someone who can read the *Form*, and combine your two selections in the first race *only* with those in the second race, with morning-line odds between 5-1 and 15-1, who are dropping in class, either from the last race or the race-before-last, *or* with those whose last-race rating is fifteen or less. If a horse finished his last race sixth, just nine lengths off the winner, his last-race rating is 15, and he qualifies. Use both criteria to get the best of

those horses between 5-1 and 15-1. Don't use more than five horses in the second race, giving yourself not greater than a $20 investment in the double.) Using this method of selecting double combinations, over a three or four week period, you will hit two or three doubles paying $200 and upward.

Finally, if you wish to limit your doubles investment to two or four tickets, take your *two* selections in the first race and combine them only with the 10-1 horses in the second race, if those two horses are dropping in class from one or two races back, *or* if they have last-race ratings of 15 or less. If not, go to the 12-1 horses. If nothing here, go to 15-1. If nothing here, go to 8-1 or to 6-1 if necessary.

7.   If you are dealing with an Exacta or Perfecta race and wish to play the Perfecta, take your two selections, combine them with each other, and then combine them with any of the other horses in the race whose odds are between 7-1 and 15-1, beginning at the lower odds and going upward. Each time you take your *two* selections and combine them with *one* other horse, you will need *four* tickets to cover the win-place combination possibilities. You already have *two* tickets, so you can judge how far you want to go by the amount you have to spend. If you have a 9-1 horse and an 11-1 horse and a 14-1 horse, you have five horses to "box", which costs you 5 x 4 (20) tickets, or $40. This seems expensive, but when you hit, you will get from $400 to $1,400 back. However, for a one-day racegoer, this is not recommended. Actually, you can expect to hit one of these only once or twice in a month's time, playing three Perfecta races a day for twenty or thirty days. There's a much better combination which is outlined a little later in this chapter. Remember that the Pastor's Wife only spent $4 on the Perfecta, combining two 10-1 horses (whose numbers happened to be ten and one). This, as you can imagine, was a lucky happenstance, or a holy accident, as Sam said.

Alternate Method of Play

After the incident with the Pastor's Wife, Sam devised an alternate method of selecting two out of four possible horses in each race:

In a field of eight horses, start with the 8-1 and go upward

four horses. In a field of nine or more, start with the 9-1 horse
(or as close above that as possible) and go upward four horses.

Take each of these horses, and about five minutes before post
time, do the following:

Add the place pool to the win pool and divide by the show
pool, to get the index number of the horse. Example: If the place
pool is $12,340, round it off at $12,000 and add that to the win
pool, which could be $16,120. Total in round figures is $28,000.
Divide by show pool, which is, say, $4,400. Four into 28 give you
an index number for this horse of "7". Get the index number for
each of the four (or five or six, if you wish, going one below the
8-1 or 9-1 and one above the 12-1 or 14-1 you originally chose),
and then play the *two* with the highest index numbers.

The reason for doing this is simple. Since the public plays to
show quite heavily, and the inside money boys almost *never* play
to show but do play heavily to win and somewhat less heavily to
place, you can discover by the above method which stable or
stables are backing their horse to the hilt. The horse with the
highest index number is getting the most inside or smart money.
If possible, the index numbers of your selections should be at
least *two* points higher than the next higher number. Should you
find one horse with an index number three points higher than
the closest neighbor, or perhaps four points higher, you are in a
very dynamic situation indeed. At a major track, this means
that a great deal of inside money has been wagered on the high
index horse. The stable is very confident. If the horse also has
good odds, from 7-1 upwards, the best thing to do is to come up
out of your seat and climb aboard with a good healthy wager, to
see how it all turns out. Follow this sort of smart money. Heavy
to win and a bit of insurance to place.

But one word of caution is in order. Don't expect Mr. High
Index Number to win every time, or even to place every time.
Things don't happen that way. Now and then, Mr. High Index
will run out. But each time you find a high index number three
or four higher than the nearest neighbor, get aboard, increasing
your wagers as time progresses, until you hit, and hit you will
within a day or two at most. If you *do* lose six or seven in a row,

cut off your series and drop back. After all, there *is* a limit to that entertainment fund.

The Pastor's Wife is not a system but a method of play, and it was designed for people who do not want to handicap a race, or who cannot. Sam can tell you that at Gulfstream Park, for a thirty day period in January and February, 1974, a strict playing of the Pastor's Wife method showed a slight flat-bet profit to win. For a period of twenty-seven racing days at Gulfstream, there were forty-one win hits, for a return of $1094.20 on an investment of just over a $1000. That's one and a half hits per day, averaging $26.60 per hit. Not a fortune by any means, but a good long-term average. If you use a simple form of money management, you can turn such a series into real money-profit. But, of course, the Pastor's Wife is not a money-making system. It is simply a way of keeping up with, and getting a little ahead of, the Joneses. Some days you get one good hit. On other days you get two or three or even four.

Valentine's Day, February 14, 1974, was a good day at Gulfstream Park, if you were following the Pastor's Wife. In the fourth race, there was a 10-1 win hit, paying $23.60. This was a Perfecta race, and it so happens that the place horse went off at 31-1, and the Perfecta paid $803.80. In a few moments, if Sam is willing, we will show you how you could catch this payoff, and others like it, without handicapping a race. (Before we get into that, let me remind you of an interesting and valuable fact: when you buy a Perfecta ticket, or double ticket, and the payoff is better than 299-1 [or the ticket pays $600 or more], in order to cash the ticket, you must furnish the track your name and social security number. The track then reports all such payoffs to the IRS, and the IRS will expect to see this $600 or more listed on your tax return as income.) But to continue: in the eighth race, there was a 13-1 winner paying $28.60. If you are following the Pastor's Wife, play to win only. During the same twenty-seven racing days of 1974, at Gulfstream, there were ninety-four place hits, but the average return was only $10.40. In dollars, the total return was $977, on an investment approximating $1,000. The place hits came at a rate of about four per day. To make money on them, it would be necessary to use a strict money-management system.

But you are really not at the races to do a lot of work. You're there for the pleasure of the chase. This being so, Sam has another suggestion for you. It's for those who don't wish to do a great deal of handicapping. The Social Security Set will love it, and it's also for those who are thirty-nine and holding. For identification purposes, it's called Two-Under-Sixty Automatic.

TWO-UNDER-SIXTY AUTOMATIC

1.   Ignore everything on the board showing odds of 60 and up.

2.   If there are three or less horses with odds of two digits, take the first and the second ones under 60. Example: the odds on the board are 70, 30, 5, 7, 9, 22, 5-2, 3, 7-2, and 2. The field has ten horses. You take the ones whose odds are 30 and 22. In Harness Races, bet #2 and #3 down from 50, to win.

3.   If there are four horses with odds in two digits, and the highest odds are under 40, take the number one and two down from 40. Example: the odds are 35, 28, 15, 11, 6, 4, 3, 5, 5-2, 2. Again, there are ten horses in the line up. Your selections are the 35 and the 28.

4.   If there are four or more horses with odds in two digits, and the highest odds under 60 are 40 or over, take the second and the third down from 60. Example: the odds are 50, 35, 10, 19, 8, 7, 5, 4, 3, 7-2, 2. There are eleven horses in the field. Your selections are the 35 and the 19.

5.   In a small field, if there is only one horse with two-digit odds, take that horse and the next highest beneath him. Example: the odds are 11, 9, 7, 5, 3, and 2. Take the 11 and the 9. But never select a horse whose odds are *lower* than the number of horses in the field.

6.   Bet to win and to place. When the odds are 25 or higher, you may also bet to show, but this is optional.

7.   In the daily double, take your *two* selections in the first race and combine them with everything in the second race listed in the morning line at 5-1 thru 15-1. If you wish more bets, lower the limit to 3-1 and raise to 20-1.

If you have a copy of the *Form* and can do a little elementary handicapping, also look at the fourth and fifth horses down from 60-1 and *if* one of these two is outstanding, take him too, giving you three bets in the race. In the second race (of the daily double) select those horses between 5-1 and 15-1 who are dropping in class either from the last race or the next-to-the-last, or even the third back if it was run within 30 days. Use also any horse from 3-1 thru 20-1 who gained four or more lengths in the stretch run of his last race.

Add also those horses in the higher odds bracket who were first or second in their last race at today's distance.

8.   In a Perfecta-Exacta race, take the *two* horses selected by use of the rules above and combine them with three horses whose odds range between 7-1 and 15-1. If you have more than three in this range, limit them to three by narrowing the range to 8-1 and 14-1 or even 9-1 and 13-1. In fields of eight horses or less, you should drop to 6-1 on the lower end. You end up with five horses in the Perfecta box, or crisscross, and that requires twenty tickets, or an investment of $40. This should be your minimum investment in a Perfecta-Exacta race. Further, it is also wise to take the two major selections and combine them with the favorite, requiring four additional tickets, and a total investment of $48.

9.   Note that in certain cases, there will occur a potential investment or bet among horses whose odds range between 45 and 55 on the board. (See Rule 4 above, where the 50-1 horse was eliminated.) Include these horses between 45 and 55 in maiden races and races for fillies or for fillies and mares. Also, include them when they occur in Perfecta-Exacta races. To limit your investment in the straight betting, go for win and place only, eliminating the show bet. In the Perfecta races of this sort, you now have three major selections, and of course you combine these with two selections whose odds range between 7-1 and 15-1, or between 8-1 and 14-1. Let us say there are more than two in that group: there are odds of 8-1, 10-1 12-1, and 14-1. Use the two lower odds for your box or crisscross of twenty tickets. Then combine the remaining two with your *three* major selections individually, for a total of six more tickets. This will mean twenty tickets for the box, six more for the added two, and six more

for the three major selections with the favorite, for a grand total of $64. If you must limit your investment, omit the last step, or the last two steps, in which case you are back to your $40 investment. Since there are generally three Perfecta races per day, you will need at least $120 to cover, but more than likely, you will need $150 to $160 to cover. Naturally, you will not hit every Perfecta or Exacta race. You will probably hit one out of five or six. But when you do hit, you will be in at least three figures and possibly in four figures: that is, the pay-off may be over a thousand dollars.

Examples: February 14, 1974, at Gulfstream Park (GP). In the fourth race, your two selections were each listed on the board at thirty. Combine with 10-1, 11-1, and 14-1. The 11-1 horse won; the 31-1 was second. The pay-off was $803.80. The odds were above 300-1, so your name and social security number are listed with the IRS.

Race seven, January 19, 1974, GP: Your choices are at 30-1 and 27-1. Combine with three horses between 8-1 and 14-1. There are four in the race, two of them at 14-1. Choose the 14-1 horse whose win pool is higher. That one has the lower odds of the two.

Race ten, January 23, 1974, GP: 35-1 on the board (actually 37-1) combined with 11-1 for a pay-off of $1,407.80 The General won the race and paid $77, $32, and $14.60, and you should have been on him across-the-board several times.

Ideas born in Florida are good in other states as well. Sam was sure of this fact, but out of curiosity he took a fairly close look at the charts from Fairgrounds in New Orleans, from Latonia in Kentucky, from Bowie in Maryland, and finally he went to California and looked at Santa Anita. He could see at a glance that the Pastor's Wife method of play was averaging two hits every three days or so and these win hits were paying from $21 to $28 for every $2 invested. At Bowie, on January 25, 1974, in the third race was an 11-1 winner, paying $23.80. In the fourth race, with only seven horses, the 12-1 horse won, paying $26.40. In the fifth race, the 10-1 horse was the winner, paying $21.80. This was an Exacta race, in which a 7-1 horse ran second, the

Exacta paying $128.20. Then lightning really struck in the seventh race: the two Pastor's Wife selections came in one-two: the 13-1 horse won, paying $28.20; the 9-1 placed, paying $12.20, and the Exacta paid $333.40. Investing $4 on the two to win and $4 on the Exacta, the gross return was $361.60. Here's the chart·

SEVENTH RACE **Bow** January 25, 1974	6 FURLONGS (chute). (1:08³/₅). CLAIMING. Purse $4,700. Fillies and mares. 4-year-olds and upward. Weight 122 lbs. Non-winners of two races since Dec. 14 allowed 3 lbs.; a race since Dec. 7, 8 lbs. Claiming price, $6,500; 1 lb. for each $250 to $6,000. (Races where entered for $5,000 or less ·ot considered.)

Value to winner $2,820; second, $1,034; third, $564; fourth, $282. Mutuel Pool, $48,746. Exacta Pool, $82,202.

Last Raced		Horse	EqtAWt PP	St	¼	½	Str	Fin	Jockeys	Owners	Odds to $1
1-15-74⁷	Bow⁴	Curru Miss	b7 114	5	2	2ʰ	2²	2²½	1ⁿᵒ	GCusimano	A V Kelley	13.10
1-17-74⁶	Bow⁸	Salty Rose	b6 115	1	4	1ʰ	1¹	1ʰ	2²½	RBarnes	R N Lombardo	9.20
1-17-74⁶	Bow⁷	Facilimyd	b4 114	6	3	4³	3²	3²	3½	EWalsh	S Karasic	4.70
1-17-74⁶	Bow⁶	Tutu	b4 114	3	8	7ʰ	7ʰ	6²	4²½	EMBelville	H Schifrin	7.60
1- 8-74⁶	Bow⁷	Rombon	b4 114	7	11	11	10½	7²½	5¹	GMcCarron	Balmak Stable	24.60
1-15-74⁷	Bow³	Billie Gen	4 112	11	5	6³	5²	4½	6¹	JKurtz	E J Ramsey	6.20
1- 8-74⁶	Bow⁶	Lets Bid	6 115	2	7	9³	9ʰ	10½	7ⁿᵏ	GLerma	W R Harris	17.80
1- 8-74⁶	Bow⁴	Virtu	b4 119	9	6	5ʰ	6ʰ	8½	8ⁿᵒ	VBraccialeJr	D R Lasater	2.10
1- 9-74⁷	Bow	Fancy Face	6 114	10	1	3ʰ	4½	5½	9¹²³	WJPassmore	J M Leverton	13.80
1-15-74⁷	Bow¹⁰	Hong Kong Lady	b6 112	8	9	8½	8³	9½	10⁴	RHoward	J C Burke	14.10
11-27-73⁴	Lrl⁷	Piave's Sting	b4 114	4	10	10⁴	11	11	11	BMFeliciano	Mrs C O Isclim Jr	27.90

OFF AT 3:52 EDT. Start good. Won driving. Time, :23¹/₅, :46⁴/₅, 1:13¹/₅. Track muddy.

6-CURRU MISS	28.20	14.40	8.60
1-SALTY ROSE ,,,,,,,,,,,,,,,,,,,,,,,,,,		12.20	7.00
7-FACILIMYD			5.00

Φ2 Mutuel Prices:

$2 EXACTA (6-1) PAID $333.40.

Dk. b. or br. m, by Duke's Lea—King's Gamble, by Kingsway II. Trainer, A. V. Kelley. Bred by R. N. Miller and R. W. Everitt (Ind.).

CURRU MISS forced the pace from the outset challenged outside SALTY ROSE throughout the drive and prevailed narrowly. SALTY ROSE rushed up to get the lead before a quarter, drew clear on the turn, resisted gamely but just missed. FACILIMYD, never far back, lacked the needed closing response. TUTU lacked early speed, rallied in the middle of the track when roused for the drive swerved inward and impeded FANCY FACE leaving the eighth pole and failed to menace. ROMBON found best stride too late. BILLIE GEN went evenly. VIRTU was never a factor. FANCY FACE, prominent outside horses to the stretch, was tiring when impeded.

Overweight—Salty Rose, 1 pound; Lets Bid, 1.

Tutu claimed by W. Gustafsen, trainer T. Hills. Virtu claimed by Deborah A. Lamparter, trainer H. Steward Mitchell. Claiming Prices (in order of finish)—$6500, 6500, 6500, 6500, 6500, 6000, 6500, 6500, 6500, 6000, 6500.

Scratched—Fifty Coins, Wiletta, Crafty Ways, Frappe, Only Jezzy, Five Stitches, Horizontal.

Salty Rose, at 9-1 on the board, was your first choice, followed by Curru Miss at 13-1. Fancy Face was showing odds of 13-1 on the board also, but Curru Miss had more money in the win pool than did Fancy Face, which means that Curru Miss was the lower in odds and was therefore the choice between these two. Hong Kong Lady was next at 14-1. Had you been at the track in reality, you could get the high index numbers of these four horses. Note that Curru Miss won the race by a mere nose, which was fortunate for followers of the Pastor's Wife, since 13-1 pays better than 9-1.

Incidentally, on that same day at Bowie, if you had been following the Two-Down-From-50 method of play, as Sam recommended should be played in conjunction with the Pastor's Wife, you would have the following results from the first race of the day:

FIRST   RACE   7 FURLONGS (chute). (1:21). MAIDENS. CLAIMING. Purse $4,000. 3-year-olds. Weight, 120 lbs.
Bow   Claiming price, $5,000.
January   25,   1974   Value to winner $2,400; second, $880; third, $480; fourth, $240. Mutuel Pool, $34,953.

Last Raced		Horse	EqtAWt	PP	St	¼	½	Str	Fin	Jockeys	Owners	Odds to $1
1-17-74[1]	Pen[5]	Bengie Man	3 120	1	10	5h	4½	3[1]	1nk	RHoward	G C Brothers	49.90
12-19-73[4]	Lrl	Cross The Rubicon	b3 120	2	9	6[1]	6[3]	4½	2[1]	GCusimano	J W Crossman	2.20
1-10-74[1]	Bow[7]	Summer Morning	3 110	5	4	1½	2[2]	1h	3h	TMaguire[5]	M Church III	37.20
1- 4-74[1]	Bow[5]	Nikiriki	b3 120	4	12	10½	10[2]	6½	4nk	VBraccialeJr	W EDempsey	2.70
1-10-74[1]	Bow[5]	New France	b3 120	3	7	2h	1[1]	2[2]	5nk	JKurtz	Windfields Farm	8.90
12-19-73[4]	Lrl[3]	Vibration	3 115	9	8	7h	7½	5h	6[3]	PFeliciano	M F Wettach	9.90
		Nell Nell	3 115	8	11	11[5]	9[2]	7[3]	7½	ELGreen	E E Green	24.40
1-10-74[1]	Bow[4]	Dottie Andrews	b3 108	10	6	9[2]	8½	8½	8[2]	AVillon[7]	Checca Farm	15.30
12-29-73[2]	Lrl[12]	Sonic Girl	3 115	6	5	4h	3h	9[3]	9[5]	BMFeliciano	C Lee	25.30
1-15-74[1]	Bow[8]	High Living	b3 120	11	3	8h	11½	10[2]	10[2]	HHinojosa	Foxhill Farm	6.20
1- 4-74[3]	Dov[2]	Last Sandal	b3 120	12	10	12	12	11h	11[2]	LLGino	Mom's Delight Stable	14.70
1- 4-74[3]	Dov[7]	Impulsive Fox	b3 120	7	2	3[1]	5½	12	12	TLee	T J Albert Jr	37.10

OFF AT 1:00½ EDT. Start good. Won driving. Time, :24, :48²/s, 1:15⁴/s, 1:30. Track muddy.
Official Program Numbers

$2 Mutuel Prices:
1-BENGIE MAN	101.80	36.00	17.20
2-CROSS THE RUBICON		4.80	4.00
5-SUMMER MORNING			15.20

B. c, by Rough Justice—Melissa's Folly, by Panacean. Trainer, A. H. Eberly II. Bred by G. C. Brothers Jr. (W. Va.).
BENGIE MAN, forwardly placed early, swung wide to rally entering the stretch, gradually wore down the leaders and was up in the closing yards. CROSS THE RUBICON, forwardly placed near the rail early, eased outside on the turn, rallied far wide in the stretch and was getting to the winner at the end. SUMMER MORNING got the lead coming onto the main track, could not keep pace with NEW FRANCE after the quarter, regained the advantage in the middle of the track near the eighth pole, but hung near the end. NIKIRIKI lacked early speed, rallied near the rail through the stretch but was too late. NEW FRANCE took a clear lead leaving the backstretch, resisted when challenged but gradually weakened in the final furlong. VIBRATION found best stride too late. SONIC GIRL, wide while prominent to the stretch, tired in the drive. HIGH LIVING showed nothing. IMPULSIVE FOX darted to the lead soon after the start, could not hold the lead and tired in the stretch.
Cross The Rubicon claimed by Margaret Hyde, trainer G. G. Delp.
Claiming Prices—All $5,000.
Scratched—Stiff Lip, Strauss, In Your Favour, Bring On Spring, Rulei, Waza Keel.

Bengie Man was number-one down from 50-1. If the computer were working properly at Bowie on January 25 (the weather was cloudy and the temperature was a chilly thirty-four degrees), Bengie Man was flashing odds at 40-1. When the odds reach 50-1, the number "50" appears on the board. Since this is a maiden race, it would be well to accept those 50-1 horses, if there are any. (In maiden races and races for fillies or for fillies and mares, as well as for two-year-old races and even three-yr-old races, we should look at those horses whose odds are at 50-1. But disregard all horses with odds of 60-1 or higher.)

Lightning struck in the first race at Bowie on January 25, 1974. Looking back a few days, Sam noted that in the seventh race on January 21, the number-one down was a horse with odds at 25-1. This turned out to be the winner and paid $52.40, $11.60 and $7.40. Under the rules (since the odds were 25-1) we would be playing the horse across-the-board. Since, too, it was an Exacta, and we have the 25-1 horse combined with the favorite, F1, we would win the payoff of $246.20. The very next day, in the second race at Bowie, the number-two down, at odds of 29-1, placed and paid $18.20 and $8.60. Again, on January 23:

Second race: the winner went off at 34-1, and paid $69.20, $20.20, and $10.60. This was the number-two down from 50-1. In the third race, same day, the number-one down, at 17-1, was the winner and paid $36.80, $11.20, and $4.40. (You see here why it doesn't generally pay to show when the odds are below 25-1.)

January 24: sixth race, number-two down, at 22-1, won and paid: $46.00, $20.40, $13.40.

ninth race, number-one down, at 28-1, won and paid: $57.60, $22.80, and $11.40.

The Exacta was with F2, second favorite, and paid $509.40. Add that second favorite!

Incidentally, let's go back for a moment to January 25 and look at the first two races, the Daily Double. Bengie Man came in to win the first race, and if we were playing him with all the horses with morning-line odds between 3-1 and 15-1, we would have caught the double, which was completed by Hello Kim (with 4-1 probable odds) in the second race. The Double paid $1066.60. Quite naturally, the broader your play, the better are your chances of catching the big ones like this. (If you were handicapping the second race, according to Sam's instructions, you would have discovered that Hello Kim was dropping $5,000 in class, from $8,000 in her last race to $3,000 on the January 25 and had a last-race rating of 22. True, she was listed at 4-1 instead of the 5-1 which Sam required, but with fillies and maidens you give more leeway than usual, and you would have taken her in your combinations.)

Meanwhile, over at little Latonia, in Florence, Kentucky, January 21, 1974 was another cloudy Monday, and the temperature was 34 degrees. But 4,356 brave souls were out that afternoon and pushed $458,769 through the mutuel machines. Following the one-or-two down-from-50 method of play, here's the results for the day:

4^{11} #1-Down, at 44-1, came in to show and paid $25.80.

#2-Down, at 28-1, won and paid $57.20, $27.40, and $19.00

6^{10} #1-Down, at 19-1, won and paid $39.20 and $13.00.

7^8 #2-Down, at 22-1, placed and paid $12.60.

8^{11} #1-Down, at 16-1, won and paid $34.40 and $8.60.

9^8 #2-Down, at 12-1, won and paid $25.40 and $10.00.

That's four win hits and six place hits in a single day. Admittedly, an unusual day, but those are the kind that keep your average up. If you're using a good money management method (and you should be with this kind of play), you went home happy on that cloudy Monday in wintry Kentucky. But let's take a quick look at what was happening out in sunny California. Here's January 23 at Santa Anita:

1^{10} #2-Down, at 18-1, won the race and paid $37.60, $18.40.

3^{12} #1-Down, at 28-1, won and paid $57.80, $19.00 and $9.20.

The next day, January 24:

1^{12} #1-Down at 23-1, won and paid $48.20 and $21.60.

Daily Double, with the 15-1 Probable Odds horse: $996.20.

(Buck the Tiger was the 15-1 Po horse in the second race. He was dropping in class from his third race back, which was run on December 29, less than thirty days ago. His last-race rating was a low, low 7: he finished third, just 3¾ lengths off the winner.)

2^{11} #2-Down, at 18-1, won and paid $37.80, $18.40 and 13.80. This is Buck the Tiger again, and he's a system winner two ways.

3^{12} #1-Down, at 48-1, won and paid $97.60, $25.60, and $16.00.

8^9 #2-Down, at 17-1, placed and paid $11.20.

The next day, January 25:

3^{12}_M #1-Down, at 42-1, won and paid $86.40, $19.20 and $8.80.

On January 30:

3_M^{12} #2-Down, at 34-1, won and paid $70.20, $22.60 and $11.40.

Back across the country, to New Orleans. At Fairgrounds on a cloudy Thursday, January 24:

1^{12} #1-Down, at 45-1, won and paid: $91.40, $21.60 and $12.60.
Daily Double, with a 12-1 Probable Odds horse, Slippery Bill: $432.40.

(Slippery Bill was dropping in class, was 12-1 in the morning line, and had a last-race rating of 15.)

9^{10} #1-Down, at 19-1, placed and paid $19.40 and $13.40.
Exacta, with the Favorite, F1, paid $135.40.

January 30:

1_M^{12} #1-Down, at 48-1, won and paid: $97.80, $28.00, and $14.80.

The Daily Double, with Pose for Me, a filly, at 20-1 in the morning line, paid $715.60. Pose for Me was higher than the regular cut-off point of 15-1, but remember that she is a filly and we give fillies a bit of leeway. Checking her record, we find that Pose for Me was dropping in class, from the second race back on January 16, and she had a last-race rating of 24, just under the 25 limit.

2^{12} #1Down, at 21-1, won and paid: $45.00, $16.20 and $10.60. This is Pose for Me again. Two Win Hits in one day, and of course they are the daily double.

During early and middle February of 1974, there were numerous "hits", both to win and to place, over the country. But let us go for one or two more examples, also at Fairgrounds, on Wednesday, February 13. The result charts of these two examples, both Exacta races, are shown on the following page. In the seventh race, Harlenquinade, at 45-1 was number one down, won the race and paid: $93.60, $28.00, and $11.80. The co-second-favorite, at 4.40 to 1, was the place horse, completing an Exacta payoff of $810.60. This and others of its kind may induce you to add the second favorite to your list of plays in the Exacta-type races. In the ninth race, Gallamiss, at 23-1, was number two down, won the race and paid: $47.60, $21.21, and $15.60.

SEVENTH RACE
FG
February 13, 1974

6 FURLONGS. (1:09³/₅). CLAIMING. Purse $8,700. 3- and 4-year-olds, non-winners of two races. 3-year-olds, 112 lbs.; 4-year-olds, 120 lbs. Maidens allowed 4 lbs. (Winners preferred.) Claiming price, $7,500.
Value to winner $2,220; second, $740; third, $407; fourth, $222; fifth, $111.
Mutuel Pool, $31,752. Exacta Pool, $45,910.

Last Raced		Horse	EqtAWt	PP	St	¼	½	Str	Fin	Jockeys	Owners	Odds to $1
1-18-74⁷	FG⁶	Harlequinade	b3 113	1	2	2½	3³	3³	1½	RBreen	Scott-Stiegel	45.80
3-29-73⁹	FG⁸	Plenty Red	b4 120	6	4	4³	2ʰ	2ʰ	2²	JFYoung	J W Almond	4.40
2- 1-74⁶	FG⁴	Perfect Reason	b3 112	5	8	7½	7⁴	7²	3½	KLeBlanc	Steg's Stable Inc	4.40
2- 2-74⁷	FG⁹	Sammy Sam	b3 112	3	3	3ʰ	4ʰ	4ʰ	4ⁿᵏ	LDupuy	Hibiscus Stable	11.80
1-24-74⁶	FG³	Bella G.	3 116	4	5	8³	8²	8²	5½	DCopling	R Giardina	23.10
2- 8-74⁴	FG⁴	Royal Attraction	3 110	9	6	6¹	6ʰ	6ʰ	6½	JDomingue	Susan Stable	17.60
2- 6-74⁷	FG⁸	Highwiden'handsome	b4 120	10	9	9²	9⁸	9³	7²½	OSanchez	N Sitzman	30.30
1- 2-74⁶	FG⁶	Spirits	b3 107	2	10	5¹	5²	5²	8⁵	PWorley	Mrs T S Montagnet	6.20
1-23-74⁷	FG⁴	Miss Mickey A.	3 107	8	7	10	10	10	9¹³	MBacon	Shinrone Farm Inc	7.00
1-28-74⁷	FG¹	County Line Boy	b3 112	7	1	1⁷	1⁷	1ʰ	10	NMenard	Audley Farm Stable	1.80

OFF AT 3:46 CDT. Start good. Won driving. Time, :21²/₅, :46²/₅, 1:13¹/₅. Track fast.

1-HARLEQUINADE	93.60	28.00	11.80
6-PLENTY RED		5.80	7.00
5-PERFECT REASON			5.40

$2 Mutuel Prices:

$2 EXACTA (1-6) PAID $810.60.

Ch. g, by Nevada Battler—Leisurely Kin, by Kingly. Trainer, C. Scott. Bred by Mr. and Mrs. H. Harcourt (Cal.).

HARLEQUINADE raced forwardly, reached even terms in midstretch and drew clear in the late stages. PLENTY RED reached even terms in midstretch from between horses but could not keep pace with the winner in the late stages. PERFECT REASON had a mild stretch response. SAMMY SAM was gaining slowly at the finish. SPIRITS had nothing left for the stretch run. MISS MICKEY A. bore out on the turn. COUNTY LINE BOY was sent off to a commanding lead along the backstretch but flattened out in the final eighth.
Overweight—Harlequinade, 1 pound; Bella G., 7; Royal Attraction, 3.
Claiming Prices—All $7500.
Scratched—Ft. Mill, Deed of Daring.

NINTH RACE
FG
February 13, 1974

1¹⁄₁₆ MILES. (1:43). CLAIMING. Purse $3,300. 4-year-olds and upward. 4-year-olds, 120 lbs.; older, 121 lbs. Non-winners of three races since Dec. 13 allowed 3 lbs.; two races, since then, 5 lbs.; a race, 8 lbs. Claiming price, $3,200.
Value to winner $1,980; second, $660; third, $363; fourth, $198; fifth, $99.
Mutuel Pool, $34,691. Exacta Pool, $52,368.

Last Raced		Horse	EqtAWt	PP	St	¼	½	¾	Str	Fin	Jockeys	Owners	Odds to $1
2- 4-74⁹	FG⁹	Gallamiss	b7 107	11	3	2¹	3²	3½	4²	1²	ALeBlanc⁵	Funny Farm Inc	22.80
2- 4-74⁹	FG⁷	Sabang	6 115	8	7	4½	2ʰ	2ʰ	3ʰ	2ⁿᵏ	TBarrow	Perry-Moran	13.00
2- 4-74⁹	FG¹	El Pibe	4 115	9	5	8²	9¹½	4²	1½	3¹½	PRubbicco	V-H Stable	10.90
1-27-74⁴	FG⁶	Vazuero	b6 118	10	2	1½	1²	1¹½	2¹½	4¹	MBacon	Shinrone Farm Inc	2.30
2- 4-74⁹	FG⁵	May Issue	b7 113	4	6	5½	4ʰ	5½	5¹	5ⁿᵏ	RBreen	A L Zuppardo	6.90
1-24-74⁹	FG⁹	David the Great	5 113	2	1	3ʰ	5½	7²	6²	6²½	HCopling	Ducoing-Kowall	3.20
2- 4-74⁶	FG⁵	Chocolate Boy	7 116	3	8	9ʰ	10⁶	9ʰ	7½	7ⁿᵏ	LTauzin	Jean J Laffargue	12.40
2- 2-74¹⁰	FG²	Sun Special	7 115	6	9	10⁶	8ʰ	8ʰ	10⁴	8⁴	HLaviolette	H New	10.20
2- 4-74⁶	FG⁸	Mat's Anything	5 115	1	4	6ʰ	6¹	6ʰ	8ʰ	9¹	CJAlleman	Cooper Stable	17.00
2- 3-74⁸	FG⁸	Kagatiri	b5 115	7	11	11	11	11	11	10½	LAdams	W H Bishop Sta Inc	25.50
2- 9-74²	FG⁸	Suvaro	b5 113	5	10	7½	7ʰ	10⁵	9ʰ	11	JSibille	H Hefnier	9.70

OFF AT 4:37 CDT. Start good. Won driving. Time, :24²/₅, :49¹/₅, 1:14²/₅, 1:40²/₅, 1:46⁴/₅. Track fast.

11-GALLAMISS	47.60	21.20	15.60
8-SABANG		12.40	8.00
9-EL PIBE			11.20

$2 Mutuel Prices:

$2 EXACTA (11-8) PAID $905.40.

Dk. b. or br. m, by Condiment—Diesel Oil, by Shadows Start. Trainer, J. E. Broussard. Bred by Mrs. J. M. Branham (Tenn.).

GALLAMISS raced forwardly, responded to pressure in the final eighth, gained command in the late stages and slowly increased the margin. SABANG, never far back, could not stay with the winner late, but outfinished the others. EL PIBE rallied after a half, gained command in midstretch, but could not stay.

The second horse, or place finish, was Sabang, who went off at 13-1. The rule states that you combine your number-one-down and number-two-down horses with all those whose odds range between 8-1 and 14-1. But you will note that there are *six* horses in this race who fit the rule. Obviously, you cannot play all six with your two selections. Therefore, you must select about three. The simplest way to select is to start with the higher odds and count down three. You would then have the 13-1 horse, Sabang, the 12-1 horse, Chocolate Boy, and the 11-1 horse, El Pibe. Your selections would then be:

Kagatiri (the number-one-down) with Sabang, Chocolate Boy and El Pibe: 6 tickets.

Gallamiss (the number-two-down) with the same three: six tickets.

That's a $24 investment already. If you wish to expand that somewhat, then take your number-one-down with F1, and your number-two-down with F1. You may, of course, go also to F2 with these two. With F1, you have an $8 investment; with F2 you have an additional $8 investment.

In the seventh race, you recall, there were TWO F2's, for another $8 investment. Of course, you have to draw the line somewhere, and that is the subject of the next couple of pages.

HANDICAPPING FOR BEGINNERS

When you are playing with the Pastor's Wife, you need to follow the rules, certainly, but you also need a little flexibility. You should operate within a definite range. For example, in a race with ten horses, the rule states that you choose the two horses whose odds start at 9-1 and move upward. This means that you may end up playing a 10-1 horse and a 19-1 horse. To achieve more flexibility, you need to consider at least *three* horses up from the base of 9-1 or of 8-1 in a field of eight horses. That means, you must select two out of three, and to do this requires some mild form of handicapping.

Look always, then, at three of the horses from the base-odds up, and in fields of eleven and twelve, look at four horses from the base-odds upward. Select the best two out of the three or four. To do this:

1.   Select the horse or horses that are dropping in class, either from the last race, or from any of the last three races if they have been run within thirty or so days. If the third race back was run thirty-two days ago, or even thirty-five days ago, don't fret. Let that count, *if* the drop in class is from that third race.

2.   Select the horse that raced or worked out most recently. In any case, the race should have been within fourteen or fifteen days and the workout within eight or nine days. A race within seven days or a work within four days is good.

3.   A last-race rating of ten or less, or even twelve or less. You get this rating by adding the finish position to the number of lengths off the winner. For example: $3^9 \ 2^7 \ 2^6 \ 2^2$.

The right-hand figure states that the horse finished the race second, just two lengths off the winner. His last-race rating is four. Incidentally, to clear up any possible misunderstanding, if a horse *wins* the race, the figure 1^8 indicates that he won by eight lengths. His last-race rating is one, not nine. When a horse wins, his last-race rating is always 1. Ignore the small upper-script number.

The three rules above are sufficient, in ninety-nine cases out of one hundred, to narrow your three or four contenders to the two you want. You may get your two by use of Rule One alone. If not, go to Rule Two, and so on until you reach a definite two. Inevitably, you will run into some sticky situations. Let's say that all four of your contenders are dropping in class. This is unlikely, but it could happen. Go to Rule Two. Suppose that one of the four had raced within ten days and the others have raced within from fourteen to twenty-eight days. Take the ten-day horse and look at the others again. Suppose one of them has worked within six days, another within eight, and the third within twenty. Take the eight-day horse and the six-day horse and throw out the twenty-day horse. Compare the six-and eight-day horses by means of Rule Three. Select the better of the two in terms of his or her finish position in the last race, or the last two races if run recently. The one you select goes along with the horse that has raced within ten days to become your team for the race.

If the race is the first race of the Daily Double or is a Perfecta-type race, always look at four contenders. Select the best two out of the four. This rule applies to both the Pastor's Wife method of play and the two-down-from-50 play. However, in the latter case, we need a little more Handicapping expertise. Let us advance to another stage. You are no longer a beginner, and you have learned to read the *Form*. We are going to look at those four horses from 50-1 down, say the 45-1 horse, the 35-1 horse, the 28-1 horse and the 23-1 horse. Which two are we to play?

TEN CONDITIONS

We set up ten basic criteria. Select the two horses which meet the most criteria out of the ten. In order to qualify for an investment at all, however, the horse should meet at least five of the ten. In the case of maidens, fillies, or two- and three-year olds, make that a minimum of four out of the ten.

1. Raced within fifteen days or worked within eight days.
2. Worked within four days.
3. Dropping in class from last race, or from two or three races back *if* those races have been run within thirty-five days.
4. Carrying 114 pounds today, *or*, carrying eight pounds less than the horse with the top weight today, *or*, dropping three or more pounds from the last race.
5. Running at same distance and on same surface as last race.
6. Finished fourth or better, *or* within four lengths of the winner in two of last six races. Allow 6½ lengths for maidens, fillies, two- and three-year-olds.
7. Gained three or more lengths in stretch run of last race.
8. Winner of one of last three races, *or*, finished within four lengths of winner in fifty percent or more of listed races. (Minimum, five races in past performance.) *Or*, in-the-money three times in listed past performance.
9. Improved position from head of stretch to finish of race in three of last four races.
10. Rating of twelve or less in any race within thirty-five or so days. If dropping in class, rating of twelve or less in any of last four races. Allow fourteen for maidens, fillies, two- and three-year-olds.

NOTE: First-time starters, within the odds-range, are automatic plays. Must meet no conditions except that they must have one workout shown on their chart. A horse may acquire a maximum of two points from any one Condition. For example, under Condition Four, he may be getting in today at 112, for one point, and he may be dropping three pounds off his last race, for a second point. He still needs five points to qualify, unless he is a maiden or a two- or three-year-old (or a filly) and needs four.

To illustrate the best method of checking the past performance of a horse against the Ten Conditions, look at the three charts on the following page. The first chart is that of Speedy Dun, winner of the second race at Gulfstream Park on Tuesday, February 12, 1974. Before the race, the odds board was showing Curious Byrd at 50-1, Adda Win at 26-1, and Speedy Dun at 23-1 or 24-1. Neither Curious Byrd nor Adda Win could generate four points from the Ten Conditions, and we had to go to Speedy Dun. He worked out six days ago, too long for a point under Condition Two. Getting in at 106 pounds gave him two points, one for being 114 or under, and one for dropping three or more pounds off the last race. His race today is at the same distance and on the same surface as his last race, Condition Five, and he finished less than 6½ lengths off the winner in his third and fourth races back, Condition Six. The numerals 4, 4, 5 and 6 are set alongside his chart. He is a three-year-old and qualifies.

In the seventh race at Fairgrounds on the following day, February 13, 1974, Harlequinade was showing odds of 45-1. He was the number-one-Down from 50-1, and was, in fact, the highest odds on the board. He worked on February 11 and gets one point under Condition Two. He's carrying 113 pounds today (overweight by one pound), Condition Four. He's running the same distance on the same surface today, Condition Five, and he has a rating of fourteen in his last race. Since he is a three-year-old, he gets credit for a point under Condition Ten. The result chart on page 227 shows that he went off at 45.80 to 1, won the race and paid $93.60, $28.00, and $11.80. Plenty Red was the co-second-favorite who placed and completed the Exacta payoff of $810.60.

2nd Gulfstream Park—February 12, 1974

6 FURLONGS
GULFSTREAM

6 FURLONGS (chute). (1:07⅘s). CLAIMING. Purse $4,200. 3-year-olds. Weight, 122 lbs. Non-winners of three races since Nov. 26 allowed 2 lbs.; two races, 4 lbs.; maidens, 6 lbs. Claiming price, $5,000. (Races where entered for $4,000 or less not considered.) (Florida-breds preferred.) (Winners preferred.)

Speedy Dun **106** B. c (1971), by Dunfee—Hurry On Gal, by Picafort.
Breeder, Wood Creek Farm (Fla.). 1973 11 M 0 2 $794
Owner, S. G. Babbitz. Trainer, R. E. Jacobs. $5,000
Dec. 27-73^{3}Crc 6 f 1:14 ft 21 120 $5^{2\frac12}$ $4^{1\frac12}$ $5^{9\frac12}$ 8^{14} MiceliM^{8}M5000 69 BeautyClove120 H.R.Boy RockCanDo 9
Dec21-73^{2}Crc 6 f 1:15^2/₅sy 10 120 1^3 1^3 $5^{2\frac34}$ $11^{8\frac14}$ Mic'iM^{11}M5000 68 Banana 117 Snake Hips Turbinette 12
Dec10-73^{4}Crc 6 f 1:14^2/₅ft 42 109* $4^{2\frac12}$ $3^{4\frac12}$ $7^{8\frac12}$ $9^{6\frac12}$ OuztsP^6 5000 74 RichLaugh117 NationalAd BaggieSal 12 4
Dec 4-73^{2}Crc 6 f 1:15^1/₅ft $2\frac34$▲ 120 7^7 6^5 $6^{7\frac12}$ $6^{5\frac12}$ MapleS^8 M5000 71 MarvelousMix120 H.R.Boy Swoon'sJoy 12 4
Nov10-73^{4}Crc 6 f 1:14^1/₅ft 53 116 $2\frac12$ 2^2 10^{10} 11^{14} MapleS^9 7500 68 GardenMusic111 TheOrchan Onaduel 11 5
Nov 2-73^{2}Crc 7 f 1:29^2/₅ft 5 118 $7^{3\frac14}$ 4^3 $6^{6\frac12}$ $10^{9\frac34}$ RogersC^6 Mdn 59 Alleviate 117 Not My Bid Li'l Bo Bo 12 6
Oct15-73^{2}Crc 6 f 1:15^2/₅ft 9-5▲ 118 $6^{5\frac14}$ 3^5 3^1 2^4† Her'zR^{11} c5000 72 GunnersHope108 Sp'dyDun R'ckCanDo 12
†Purse taken away.
Oct 4-73^{5}Crc 6 f 1:15 sy $3\frac14$ 109* 2^h 1^2 1^1 $3^{4\frac14}$ ClarkWC^4 5000 73 J'ry'sPainter118 AllDusty SpeedyDun 9
Feb 6 Crc 5f ft 1:03b Jan 30 Crc 6f ft 1:18b Jan 24 Crc 5f ft 1:03b

7th Fairgrounds—February 13, 1974

Harlequinade **112** Ch. g (1971), by Nevada Battler—Leisurely Kin, by Kingly.
Breeder, Mr. & Mrs. H. Harcourt (Cal.). 1974 2 0 0 0 (—)
Owner, Scott & Stiegel. Trainer, C. Scott. $7,500 1973 16 1 0 5 $6,854
Jan18-74^{7}FG 6 f 1:14^2/₅sy 87 112 $4^{2\frac12}$ $4^{3\frac12}$ 5^5 $6^{8\frac14}$ RamosA^6 6500 68 B'dSim'n116 OneL'tleK's Ch'oCh'oL'u 9
Jan11-74^{5}FG 6 f 1:13^4/₅ft 42 115 $6^{1\frac34}$ $5^{2\frac34}$ 8^{10} 8^{23} NicholsJ^7 6500 56 Gr'np'rtRed115 ChooChooL'u B'ttPil't 8 2
Dec24-73^{7}FG 6 f 1:14^2/₅ft 46 116 $9^{6\frac14}$ 10^{12} 7^{10} 10^8 R'bbiccoP^{3}6200 68 F'r in aRow120 C'st aP'nt'g R'kyCr's't 12 4
Dec17-73^{5}FG 6 f 1:14^2/₅ft 33 116 5^5 $5^{9\frac12}$ $8^{9\frac14}$ 11^{18} NicholsJ^6 7500 58 Mr.Church115 JulieCoy NewObstacle 12 5
Dec 7-73^{1}FG 6 f 1:13^9/₅ft $4\frac12$ 120 $3^{1\frac12}$ $6^{5\frac12}$ $6^{9\frac12}$ 6^{11} Rubb'coP^9 7500 69 ComeUp117 NewObstac'e Ch'oCh'oLou 12 10
Nov19-73^{7}Spt $6\frac12$ f 1:19^4/₅ft $8\frac12$ 116 $7^{4\frac34}$ $5^{6\frac12}$ $5^{3\frac12}$ 3^6 MoraG^3 7500 72 HaiTiara118 RockyCr'ss't Harleq'n'de 9
Nov15-73^{6}Spt $6\frac12$ f 1:20^4/₅sy $6\frac34$ 115 8^7 $8^{5\frac04}$ 7^{13} 7^{18} AhrensL^4 7500 54 HaiTiara115 Mr.Tickertape Tr'yC'm'l't 9
Feb 11 FG 3f ft :38^2/₅b Feb 8 FG 4f gd :50b Feb 4 FG 4f ft :51^4/₅b

1st Race, Santa Anita Park—January 24, 1974

Cassie Grey **114** Dk. b. or br. f (1970) by Grey Eagle—Limit Cycle, by Seaneen.
Breeder, F. Lamazor (Cal.). 1973 1 0 0 0 (—)
Owner, Daverick Stable. Trainer, J. Fanning. $8,000 1972 2 1 0 0 $2,200 2
Jan 5-73^{2}SA 6 f 1:12^2/₅ft 16 118 $10^{9\frac12}$ 9^7 9^{12} 9^{10} Mah'yW^3 16000 69 ⒻO.K.Pal 118 MostPrec's D'dy'sDat'n 11 3
Dec28-72^{6}SA 6 f 1:11 ft 16 118 $10^{9\frac12}$ 9^7 9^{12} 9^{10}Mah'eyW^{3}16000 69 ⒻO.K.Pal 118 M'stPrec'us D'dy'sD'n 11 4
Nov21-72^{4}BM 6 f 1:10^3/₅ft 12 118 $6^{4\frac34}$ $9^{6\frac12}$ $6^{4\frac34}$ 12^{16} OlivaresF^3 Alw 70 ⒻGoddessRoman115 Sphere Yofit 12 4
Jan 22 SA 5f hy 1:05^2/₅h Jan 16 SA 4f ft :48^1/₅h Jan 8 Hol 4f m :56h 5

The third, or bottom chart, is that of Cassie Grey, a four-yr-old filly who appeared in the 1st race at Santa Anita on January 24, 1974. Having worked on January 22, two days ago, she gets a point under Condition Two. This automatically gives her another point under Condition One. She's dropping $8,000 in class, for a point under Condition Three, and she is carrying exactly 114 pounds, for a point under Condition Four. She's also dropping four pounds off the last race, for another point under Condition Four. Today's race is at 6½ furlongs, and since her last race was at 6 furlongs, she gets a point under Condition Five. In a race for fillies and mares only, she needs but four points. She has six and qualifies well. As you see from the results charts on the next page, she won the first race, paying $48.20,

$21.60 and $11.60. She also started off the big daily double which paid $996.20. Buck the Tiger was listed in the probable-odds chart (morning line) at 15-1. A check of his past performance shows that he was dropping in class from $10,000 to today's $6,250. The drop was from the third race back, on December 29, which falls within the required number of days. His last-race rating was a good, low seven, since he finished in-the-money in his last race: third, 3¾ lengths off the winner. Round that off at four, add it to three, for the rating of seven.

Incidentally, when you came to the second race, and the odds began to develop, you found that Alabama Dude was 50-1, Patient Won was 22-1, and Buck the Tiger was 18-1. Since this is not a maiden race, or a race for fillies and mares, nor a two- or three-year-old race, we ignore the 50-1 and up. Both Patient Won and Buck the Tiger can garner five points, and these are your investments for straight wagering. You know the results.

Santa Anita Park—January 24, 1974

FIRST   RACE
SA
January 24, 1974

6½ FURLONGS (chute). (1:14³/s). CLAIMING. Purse $5,500. Fillies and mares. 4-year-olds and upward. 4-year-olds, 120 lbs.; older, 121 lbs. Non-winners since Dec. 26 allowed 3 lbs.; of a race since Nov. 3, 6 lbs. Claiming price, $8,000. (Races when entered for $6,250 or less not considered.)

Value to winner $3,025; second, $1,100; third, $825; fourth, $410; fifth, $140. Mutuel Pool, $105,710.

Last Raced		Horse	EqtAWt PP	St	¼	½	Str	Fin	Jockeys	Owners	Odds to $1
1- 5-73²	SA⁹	Cassie Grey	4 114 12	2	3^{1}½	1^{h}	1²	1^{1}½	FOlivares	Daverick Stable	23.10
1-10-74¹	SA³	Gaelic Coffee	5 110 3	10	8½	5½	2^{1}½	2⁵	GBaze⁵	Heinrich-LeValley	5.80
1-11-74⁹	SA⁶	Scottina B.	6 116 10	5	5½	4²½	4^{1}½	3½	JLambert	Aaronson-Falk-Odell	12.90
1-10-74¹	SA⁷	Lolla Lee Lau	4 114 8	7	9^{h}	10½	10²	4^{nk}	FToro	Gold Dust Stable	86.50
1-10-74¹	SA²	Last of the Rulers	4 117 6	3	4^{h}	8½	7½	5½	LPincayJr	Banken-Banken	1.90
1- 1-74⁴	SA⁶	Lacey Lil	5 115 11	8	10^{1}½	6¹	8^{1}½	6½	ALDiaz	J A H Cooper	116.60
1-10-74¹	SA¹¹	Mizzy Fancy	b4 114 5	11	11⁵	9³	5¹	7no	ASantiago	Mary Wilkins	70.70
1-28-73¹	SA⁴	Carousel Song	5 115 7	1	2¹	2½	3¹	8⁴	LRodriguez	Gerry Day	9.70
1-10-74¹	SA⁹	Drucilla Duke	b4 112 1	4	1¹	3²½	6¹	9³	JFelton⁵	Dohgel Stable	166.20
1-11-74⁴	SA¹⁰	Elko Chan	4 114 9	6	7¹	11¹	11^{1}½	10½	FMena	Sledge Stable	211.80
1-13-74⁹	SA⁶	Salty Orphan	4 115 2	12	12	12	12	11no	DPierce	D J Agnew	8.00
1-10-74¹	SA¹	Lucky Account	b4 114 4	9	6¹	7^{h}	9²	12	ALFern'dez	B B B Barn	1.90

OFF AT 1:03 PDT. Start good. Won driving. Time, :22²/s, :46¹/s, 1:12¹/s, 1:19. Track good.
Official Program Numbers

$2 Mutuel Prices:

12-CASSIE GREY	48.20	21.60	11.60
3-GAELIC COFFEE		7.20	3.80
10-SCOTTINA B.			8.40

Gr. f, by Grey Eagle—Limit Cycle, by Seaneen. Trainer, J. Fanning. Bred by F. Lamazor (Cal.).

CASSIE GREY attended the early pace on the outside, responded into the stretch to draw clear and held GAELIC COFFEE safe late. The latter, without early speed, rallied into the stretch from the middle of the track to loom a bold threat but hung late. SCOTTINA B. raced close up, but hung. LOLLA LEE LAU was outrun. LAST OF THE RULERS flipped over in the gate while waiting for the start, unseated her rider and showed little in the running. LACEY LIL rallied wide around the turn, then tired. CAROUSEL SONG forced the pace and faltered. SALTY ORPHAN had no speed. LUCKY ACCOUNT raced poorly.

Overweight—Salty Orphan, 1 pound; Scottina B., 1.

Lucky Account claimed by Dr. and Mrs. G. J. Shima, trainer G. J. Shima. Salty Orphan claimed by M. Ritt, trainer R. Frankel. Claiming Prices—All $8000.

Scratched—Kins Berseen, Vanmyra, Happy to Go, Pageant Beauty.

SECOND RACE
SA
January 24, 1974

1¹⁄₁₆ MILES. (1:40²/₅). CLAIMING. Purse $6,000. 4-year-olds and upward. 4-year-olds, 120 lbs.; older, 121 lbs. Non-winners at one mile or over since Dec. 26 allowed 3 lbs.; of such a race since Nov. 3, 6 lbs. Claiming price, $6,250. (Races when entered for $5,000 or less not considered.)

Value to winner $3,300; second, $1,200; third, $900; fourth, $450; fifth, $150. Mutuel Pool, $174,737.

Last Raced $1		Horse	EqtAWt PP	St	¼	½	¾	Str	Fin	Jockeys	Owners	Odds to $1
1-18-74¹	SA³	Buck the Tiger	b4 115	5	2	2³½	1½	1½	3ʰ	1ⁿᵒ	DTierney	Garcia-Suri	17.90
1- 6-74⁹	SA⁹	Lemon Cooler	5 115	2	1	3½	4¹	2½	2ʰ	2ⁿᵏ	WHarris	Icic St-Dollar-Stillw'l	9.40
1- 9-74¹	SA⁷	Patient Won	5 115	6	6	9½	9²½	5ʰ	4½	3²½	APineda	J N Economou Inc	22.00
1-18-74¹	SA⁵	African Flyer	4 114	10	7	7½	6¹	6ʰ	5³½	4ʰ	JRamirez	G Anderson	55.00
1-17-74⁹	SA³	Chickaboom Charlie	4 114	9	5	4½	5³½	3½	1½	5ⁿᵏ	RRosales	Sandringham Stable	13.00
12-28-73⁹	SA²	Alabama Dude	5 116	11	11	11	11	11	8½	6³½	LPincayJr	Jenkins-Schimmick	2.20
1-16-74⁹	SA¹⁰	Pelican Pete	b4 112	4	9	6½	7½	8½	10⁵	7½	ORamirez⁵	Mrs F A Spencer	50.10
1-11-74¹	SA³	Getting Lucky	7 116	8	8	10⁵	10⁵	9¹	7ʰ	8²½	WHartack	Phillips-Worley	2.90
1-10-74⁵	SA⁹	Sir Francis S.	b6 121	1	4	1ʰ	2ʰ	7⁴	9½	9ʰ	SValdez	Jaff Stable	3.80
1-20-74¹	SA⁸	Linilo	5 110	3	3	5⁴	3½	4²	6½	10¹⁰	JFelton⁵	Hale-Ross-Wall	82.30
1-17-74⁹	SA²	Born Again	b4 117	7	10	8²	8²	10½	11	11	WMahorney	Mr-Mrs H McElroy	8.50

OFF AT 1:33 PDT. Start good. Won driving. Time, :23³/₅, :48¹/₅, 1:14¹/₅, 1:41, 1:47³/₅. Track good.

$2 Mutuel Prices:

5-BUCK THE TIGER	37.80	18.40	13.80
2-LEMON COOLER		8.60	9.00
6-PATIENT WON			12.80

Dk. b. or br. g, by Game—Money Bush; by Mr. Busher. Trainer, M. C. Goodsell Jr. Bred by J. F. McHugh (Wyo.).

BUCK THE TIGER broke alertly to get the early lead from SIR FRANCIS S., drew clear, then briefly propped from the gate into the stretch, responded to get the lead again inside the furlong pole and held gamely over LEMON COOLER. The latter raced close up from the outset, hesitated in the stretch when intimidated by the winner, rallied but hung late. PATIENT WON lagged early, closed ground into the upper stretch and finished willingly along the outside. AFRICAN FLYER rallied wide on the far turn, found an opening inside horses nearing the upper stretch for his best bid and lost his punch. CHICKABOOM CHARLIE raced within easy striking distance, rallied to hold a slim edge briefly in midstretch and slackened. ALABAMA DUDE had no early speed, then raced in traffic near the quarter pole. GETTING LUCKY was outrun. SIR FRANCIS S. broke through the gate and faltered early. CHEROKEE CHARLIE WAS ORDERED SCRATCHED BY THE VET. ALL REFUNDS INCLUDING A CONSOLATION DAILY DOUBLE. THE RIDER ON LEMON COOLER CLAIMED FOUL AGAINST THE WINNER BUT THE INCIDENT HAD NO BEARING ON THE OUTCOME AND IT WAS NOT ALLOWED.

Overweight—Buck the Tiger, 1 pound; Getting Lucky, 1; Alabama Dude, 2.

Sir Francis S. claimed by P. Fairchild, trainer J. L. Mosbacher. Lemon Cooler claimed by Laura Hug, trainer F. W. Jones. Born Again claimed by Mr. and Mrs. N. Kelin, trainer J. Manzi. Alabama Dude claimed by Mr. or Mrs. J. Wilson, trainer J. Sharp.

Claiming Prices—All $6250.

Scratched—Renescure, Buck B., Wall, Cherokee Charlie.

Daily Double (12-5) Paid $996.20; Double Pool, $132,554.
Consolation Double (12-9) (Cherokee Charlie, late scratch) Paid $130.60.

SELECTING WINNERS ELECTRONICALLY

A thousand different methods have been devised to determine the relative class of horses in a particular race, but perhaps the newest and most precise method involves the use of the pocket-sized electronic calculator. In a January, 1975 article in *The Star*, Ray Kerrison describes the method. He starts with New York, where the prize money is divided four ways: sixty percent to the winner, twenty-two percent for second, twelve percent for third, and six percent for fourth. The principle of the method is simple: divide these percentages into the amount of money earned by a horse, and you can find instantly the kind of competition the horse can handle.

On December 28, 1974, at Aqueduct, the seventh race had a

purse of $25,000. It was a one mile allowance race for fillies. One of the entries was Shy Dawn whose 1974 earnings totalled $99,603, with four wins, three seconds, six thirds and a few fourths. In her four wins, Shy Dawn took down sixty percent of the purse, so we multiply four by .6 and get the result 2.4. She also had three seconds, which means that we multiply .22 by 3, for .66. Six thirds means .12 multiplied by six, or .72. Now add them together: and the total is 3.78. Divide 3.78 into $99,603, and you get $26,350. All of this means that Shy Dawn has won her money, on an average, in races with a purse of $26,350, and in today's race at Aqueduct (for $25,000) she seems very well placed. If you calculate, in a similar fashion, the other horses in the race, you discover that Shy Dawn is the only filly in the race with an average above $25,000. Flo's Pleasure has an average of $23,540, while Lady Barbizon is rated at $20,530. The figures, then, show that Shy Dawn has a definite class edge in the race. Suprisingly enough, she went off at about 7-1. To anyone who carried an electronic calculator in his pocket, she looked an outstanding bet. Shy Dawn won the race and paid $15.80.

Later that same day, in the Display Handicap, a $50,000 added event, the horse called Outdoors had a rating of $74,480, while all the other horses in the race were below $50,000. You guessed it. Outdoors won the Display Handicap and paid $7.20. In the ninth race, again, which was an $11,000 claiming race, the horse named Tropiquillo was the only contestant with a class rating ($13,040) that was above the purse. He won and paid $20.60, and in so doing he set up a triple or trifecta payoff of $1,569. This was a rather unusual day, admittedly. (It must be pointed out that in the fifth race that day, Mr. Sad had a $41,350 rating in a $20,000 allowance race, but he lost. No great surprise, however, since this race was on the clay, and his two earlier wins were on the grass.)

On the following Monday at Aqueduct, only one horse met the conditions. Delta's Moneytree was the name, and he won and paid $5.60. There may be days, too, when no single horse meets the conditions. But patience is a rewarding virtue. The process of establishing a horse's class rating by use of the electronic calculator can be accomplished in seconds. The frustrating thing is that in some races you cannot find just *one* horse whose rating is higher than the value of the purse. In some races, for example, it would appear that almost all the horses are dropping in class, while no single one is outstanding. Or, conversely, there are races when almost all of them seem to be moving up in class. The calculator can't point to any specific one as the best bet, and then your work is in vain. But the electronic calculator may well become a handy tool to carry with you to the races. Once in a while it will point you toward a particular horse which has a money-average higher than the purse today, whereas the others fall below. And as often as not, you will be able to get some pretty fair odds. Not all fans are carrying electronic calculators!

Of course, it is assumed that you have mastered the use of the calculator before you go to the track. If so, then you can handicap an entire race in roughly five minutes. A calculator won't do for you what Sam's system will do, but it certainly could be a valuable back-up tool. It could, for example, be used to split a tie, that is, determine the better of any two horses, so far as dollar-winnings are concerned. Every little bit helps. You can bet your computer on that!

10

Summary

It is now time to summarize. We must find out just what it is we have learned and precisely how to apply that knowledge in action. And we mean Track Action. Back in 1748, Ben Franklin said: "Money can beget money, and its offspring can beget more." Translation: "Money makes money, and the money that money makes makes money." But we are really talking about having fun at the races and *not losing money*. Breaking even can be a victory, you know, and there's always the chance that we will hit a good day and make a bundle. Gravy for the Pastor's Wife.

First of all, Straight Investments: There are two or three ways of selecting your straight wagers, under the Pastor's Wife method of play. Don't play races with less than six horses. Select horses whose odds are no lower than the number of horses in the race: e.g., in a six-horse race, your lowest odds are 6-1, or as close above that as possible. Now, you can take the two horses from 6-1 upward and bet them to win. This may mean, in a particular race, according to the distribution of the odds, that you have an 8-1 horse (as close as you can get above 6-1) and a 12-1 horse. Very well. Those are your two investments for the race, to win. Or, you may look at the three or four horses from 6-1 upward. Choose your two, after adding the win pool and the place pool of each horse, and divide by the show pool, to get your index numbers. Take the two highest index numbers of the three or four in contention.

In an eight-horse field, bet to win only. In fields of nine or more, bet to win and to place. In fields of eight or more, when you find the index numbers, and if you discover one horse with an index that is two higher than the nearest neighbor, you have a good investment. If it is three or four higher, you have a remarkable situation, and you should take advantage of it by investing more heavily. As you proceed from race one through race nine or ten, set a goal for the particular race. Let us assume that you wish to make $50 when you do hit. And remember that you will hit, on an average, once or twice in a day.

Therefore, if you have a field of twelve in the first race, you begin with the odds of 9-1. Let us assume that there is a 9-1 horse in the race and the next higher is 11-1. Invest $8 to win on each, for a total investment to win of $16. If the 9-1 horse wins, you receive $80, and your net profit is $64. Of course, if the 11-1 horse wins, you receive $96. If both lose, you proceed to the next race, placing the $16 in the debit column. Your goal for this race is a minimum return of $50 plus $16, or $66. It's an eleven-horse race, and the lowest odds available are 10-1 and the next 12-1. Another $8 investment on each is in order. If the 10-1 horse wins, you receive $88. You're down $16 and your investment in this second race is $16, for a total of $32. Deduct the $32 from $88, and you have a net profit on the two races of $56. You are right on target. If the 12-1 horse wins the second race, you are even further ahead. If both lose, put the $32 in your debit column, shoot for $82 (plus your investment) in the third race. The third race will probably be a maiden race with from ten to twelve horses, and your odds will be good. Your investment will be about $10 to win on each of two horses, in order to get back $100 or so, which would wipe out your investment and give you $50 profit. If both horses lose again, you have an investment of $52. In the fourth race, you will need to make at least $120 to attain your goal. Your investment on each horse to win the fourth race will be about $10 to $12. If you don't hit by the fourth race, you have two choices: either accept your losses and start over again, or continue with the progression until you hit. The chances are good that you will hit once during the day. This is particularly true if you check the results of yesterday and the day before and find that there were no more than two hits in those two days. On an average, you will get three hits in two days, or one and one-half hits per day, to win. If you are also playing to place, there will be an average of four hits per day. Average return: $10.40 each. For $10 to place, that's $52. If you invest to place in six races during the day, averaging $20 per race, your four hits ($208) will more than pay their way, since the cost was $120. This, of course, is on a flat-investment of $10 to place on each horse in each of six races. If the place hits were heavy during the last two or three days, don't expect more than two today. If they were light, expect from four to six today. Like all statistics, the average is over the long run

If making $50 when you hit is too rich for your blood, then cool it a little. Go back to $20 for a hit-goal. Or go the whole day on flat bets (say a minimum of $5 each) and come back tomorrow, if you can, and if you lose, for a day of flat-bets of $8 or $10. It's all a part of the entertainment fund, and you don't want to spend a lot of time figuring how much to invest and when.

The Daily Double. The simplest play here is to take your two selections in the first race, derived from a base of 9-1 undoubtedly since there will be from ten to twelve horses in the first race—take the two horses from 9-1 upward and combine them with two horses in the second race whose probable or morningline odds are 10-1 upward. That means four tickets at a cost of $8. As we said earlier, if you wish to expand your double investments and go for a higher probability of hit, you can combine your two in the first race with anything in the second race which has probable odds of 5-1 upward. If you can read the *Form*, or have a friend who knows a bit of handicapping, use only those at 5-1 upward which are dropping in class and which gained four or more lengths in the stretch run of their last race, regardless of what class it was run.

Perfecta or Exacta Races. Take your two selections, usually

at 9-1 upward, add the favorite, and get a box of the three horses, so that any combination of these three will bring a payoff. The cost is $12. Or, take your two selections and combine them with anything in the race at 8-1 thru 14-1. This usually means a total of five horses will be involved. That would cost twenty tickets, or $40. Add F1 to your two selections, for another $8. Add F2 to your two selections, for another $8. For a very minimum investment, take your two selections and cross them 1-2, and 2-1, for a cost of $4, as did the Pastor's Wife. This will hit once in a blue moon for a payoff of from $300 to $800.

If you are a lover of the long shots, you will want to choose the two-down-from-50 method of play. As noted above, ignore everything from 50-1 upward. (Except in a maiden race or a race for fillies or fillies and mares only, where you look at the 50-1 horses and ignore everything from 60-1 upward.) In an ordinary race, then, you will play the two horses *below* 50-1. The first two you come to on your trip down the odds scale. Better still, look at the first four down the scale, and play the two with the highest index numbers. Or the two that are dropping in class and have the lowest last-race rating, providing they have run within the past twenty-eight days or have worked out within about eight days. A race within ten days or a workout within four days is good. If that horse has a high index number, relatively speaking, you are onto something hot.

In Daily Doubles, take the first four down the scale (or the two which are showing the highest index numbers) and combine with anything in the second race between 5-1 and 15-1, or even 20-1, in probable odds, that is dropping in class, has a last-race rating below 25, and/or gained four or more lengths in the stretch run of its last race.

In Perfecta Races, take your two best down from four, by whatever method of selection, and combine with anything from 7-1 or 8-1 up through 14-1 or 15-1, according to what you wish to invest. You can discriminate among these 7-1 thru 15-1 horses by getting two with the highest index numbers, or two which are dropping in class or have very low last-race ratings and have raced recently or have worked within a few days. Combine your two best down-from-50 with F1 and F2, if you can, for more complete coverage and a possible good payoff. You won't hit often, but when you do, you will be in the higher brackets.

Good luck! And don't forget: ten percent of the net goes to the General Fund. . . .

After making his final corrections on a typescript of *How To Make A Million At The Track*, Sam mailed the thing back to me, and he sent along with it a letter which contained an account of a small but probably insignificant incident which happened at Hialeah, just a week after the season opened. As sometimes occurs at the beginning of a season, the horses were not running strictly to form, and a goodly number of long shots were getting their nose under the wire first.

Sam was playing it strictly according to the rules, and as a result he had some nice winners with high odds. One afternoon he was backing away from the $100-cashier's window when he came very close to stepping on the toes of a lady approaching the same window.

"I beg your pardon," said Sam, and he retreated a few feet to the rear. Of course, he didn't retreat too far, since his curiosity was distinctly aroused by the sight of so attractive a lady cashing a ticket or two (he couldn't see how many) on a horse who had just paid $120 to win. And if, or rather, *since* she was patronizing the $100 window, clearly she had just made a bundle, even as he had. The lady turned away from the window, slipping the crisp $100 bills into her pocketbook, and she glanced at Sam, who was still in the immediate area.

"It," she said, "most unexpected!"

Sam blinked and the lady smiled. He had no doubt of her meaning, and yet "It, most unexpected!" was not exactly the combination of words he had been anticipating. She may have been a little flustered at the moment, either by his presence or by the fact that she had just placed in her purse a sum of money which ran into the thousands. Sam was aware, from considerable experience, that women at the races tend to fall into one of two classes: they play it very conservatively and generally have a surplus of show tickets, which they occasionally cash; or they give in to the most outlandish hunches and play anything on the program if it has even the faintest resemblance to a name or a place with which they are now or have been familiar. In short, there's no accounting for their selections, and once in a while they cash a ticket or two on a long shot paying $120 to win.

Sam was curious as to which class this attractive lady fell into, and he was not averse to a minute or two of conversation if he could find out what he wanted to know. To smooth the way, Sam introduced himself, adding:

"I'm an investment consultant by profession, which probably doesn't really explain the reason for my being here on an afternoon when I should be in the office working."

The lady had her purse very securely under her arm. Perhaps she felt that an explanation of her own presence here was in order. But first she put out her hand and said:

"My name's Penny, and I'm very happy to meet you, Mr. Hirsch."

For the merest fraction of an instant, Sam toyed with the impression that she was another "Penny", whose picture he had seen in the *Form* on more occasions than once, but he rejected the idea on two grounds. The "Penny" he was thinking about would never be at Hialeah at this time of year, and if she were, she certainly wouldn't be cashing tickets at the $100 window. Any winnings due her would undoubtedly be paid by check by the management and sent to the proper address. Secondly, the Penny he had seen in the *Form* did not resemble this Penny. At any rate, when she told him with a smile that she was very happy to meet him, Sam lost no time in replying:

"The pleasure is mutuel, I'm sure."

A reply like that is better appreciated when seen rather than heard, but Sam didn't have to wait very long for her laughter.

"Very good," the lady said; "but, Mr. Hirsch, since you *are* an investment consultant, our meeting is a fortunate circumstance. I may just be in the market for some professional advice——"

On the personal side, there is no telling what developments could develop. We can only hope that she will turn out to be a very rare and precious Penny.